Elton John

Other Books by Author

A History of Women in Astronomy and Space Exploration
A History of Women in Mathematics
A History of Women in Medicine and Medical Research
A History of Women in Psychology and Neuroscience

Coming Soon

A History of Romance Novels
A History of Women in Music From Antiquity to Present Day

Elton John

Album by Album

Dale DeBakcsy

WHITE OWL

AN IMPRINT OF PEN & SWORD BOOKS LTD.
YORKSHIRE – PHILADELPHIA

First published in Great Britain in 2025 by
White Owl
An imprint of Pen & Sword Books Limited
Yorkshire – Philadelphia

ISBN 978 1 03610 428 3

A CIP catalogue record for this book is
available from the British Library.

Typeset by Mac Style
Printed in the UK by CPI Group (UK) Ltd, Croydon, CR0 4YY.

The Publisher's authorised representative in the EU for product
safety is Authorised Rep Compliance Ltd., Ground Floor,
71 Lower Baggot Street, Dublin D02 P593, Ireland.
www.arccompliance.com

For a complete list of Pen & Sword titles please contact

PEN & SWORD BOOKS LIMITED
47 Church Street, Barnsley, South Yorkshire, S70 2AS, England
E-mail: enquiries@pen-and-sword.co.uk
Website: www.pen-and-sword.co.uk
or
PEN AND SWORD BOOKS
1950 Lawrence Road, Havertown, PA 19083, USA
E-mail: uspen-and-sword@casematepublishers.com
Website: www.penandswordbooks.com

For my Dad,
And those long afternoons
driving around San Diego,
listening to the radio.

Contents

Chapter 1

Regimental Sgt Zippo

Recorded: February 1967 to April 1968
Released: 2021
Producer: Caleb Quaye

The Story

In June 1967, Reginald 'Reggie' Dwight (*b*.1947) and Bernard 'Bernie' Taupin (*b*.1950) both responded to an advertisement in the *New Musical Express* placed by Ray Williams (*b*.1947) seeking new musical talent. Reggie was invited to play some of his material for Williams and launched into an idiosyncratic set of past their prime standards, including Al Jolson's (1886–1950) 'My Mammy'. Everything about Reggie seemed wrong: he didn't look like a pop star, the songs he'd chosen to play were all slow tempo laments and he was a piano player in a rock guitar scene. But there was 'something' about him, and when he admitted to his one great weakness: an inability to write decent lyrics, a connection was formed in Williams's brain, and he reached for an envelope of curious lyrics sent to him by a young man from Lincolnshire who had confessed that he could write lyrics, but not music.

Shortly thereafter, Reggie (who we'll refer to as Elton from here on in as he'd soon adopt the name – borrowed from his Bluesology bandmate) and Bernie met, and instantly connected over a shared encyclopaedic love of pop music. They signed a songwriting contract for Dick James (1920–1986) – the publisher who had risen to international prominence on his decision to sign an up-and-coming band by the curious name of The Beatles – in November 1967, and thereupon followed a year and a half of struggling to determine what their way forward ought to be. In one ear, they had the advice of James himself, telling them to write standard commercial songs that could then be sold to other recording artists. In the other, they had the swirl of new and boundary expanding music being released all around them – albums like The Beatles' *Sgt Pepper's Lonely Hearts Club Band* (1967) and *Magical Mystery Tour* (1967), Procol Harum's self-titled album (1967) and hit single 'A Pale Shade of White', The Moody Blues' *Days of Future Passed* (1967) with its genre-breaking tracks 'The Afternoon' and 'Nights in White Satin', the poetic tour de force of Leonard Cohen's (1934–2016) debut *The Songs of Leonard Cohen* (1967), the piano-based storytelling of David Ackles's (1937–1999) self-titled debut (1968), The Doors' first album (1967), the psychedelic explorations of Jefferson Airplane's *Surrealistic Pillow* (1967), and the eye-opening Americana and grounded musicianship of The Band's *Music from Big Pink* (1968).

Added to the advice in their ears was a growing desire to write music of an entirely new sort, one that would allow Bernie to compose poetic tales untethered by commercial viability and Elton *carte blanche* to fuse together the myriads of musical traditions he carried within him. In January 1968, based on the promise shown in their demos (as well as out of an impending sense that The Beatles may incinerate at any moment and that having a new talent ready to fill the void wouldn't be a bad idea), Elton and Bernie were given a five album recording contract, and they set about assembling an album using the material they had been amassing. Each time a new album dropped at Musicland record shop on Berwick Street – their regular haunt – aspects of its lyrical and musical structures would influence the next batch of songs, resulting in substantial differences in output from one week to the next, a diversity of creative instincts and musical appetite that is fully displayed on *Regimental Sgt Zippo*, recorded here and there from November 1967 to April 1968.

Steve Brown (1955–2000), who had been assigned by Dick James to develop Elton and Bernie's talents, didn't see *Regimental Sgt Zippo* as a full representation of their potential as songwriters and the album was shelved, clearing the way for *Empty Sky* to become their true debut album the following year. Songs from the album were finally released as part of *Jewel Box* (2020) – a compilation album (the full album was first released as a limited vinyl edition in 2021).

The Songs

'When I Was Tealby Abbey' – the first song on what Elton and Bernie believed was going to be their first ever full album – is a perfect example of what their unique working arrangement could produce. Read on its own, Bernie's lyrics treat of a somewhat sombre theme: the gradual crumbling of an old abbey into a state of picturesque ruination. It could well have gone the way of future Elton-Bernie pieces meditating sorrowfully on the erosion of local history in the face of time and technology like 'Indian Sunset' but that is decidedly not the direction that Elton's music goes, and instead we are treated to a catchy pop tune full of tooting recorders, which recasts the passing of time as some sort of great cosmic joke on us humans, not to be taken too seriously.

'When I Was Tealby Abbey' gives us a glimpse at what can happen when the lyricist and songwriter are two separate individuals. 'And the Clock Goes Round' evinces a desire to play with song structures, which will eventually result in some of the most fascinating pop musical productions of the early 1970s, but which in this song haven't quite gelled. The transition from rhythm and blues verses to the spaced-out chorus is so sudden that it might well have been meant as a parody of hippie paeans to listlessness, a type of mockery through exaggerated structures, which Elton certainly employed on later songs, but that didn't quite come off here.

'Sitting Doing Nothing' is the first of two tracks on the album written by Elton and Caleb Quaye (*b*.1948), the other being 'You'll Be Sorry to See Me Go'. The absence of Bernie's verbal magic is palpable, with Elton seemingly matching the level of his compositional complexity to the level of the lyrics, with the latter song sounding like a Beatles' track from three years prior, and the former being lifted from the realm of a genre exercise by Elton's Leon Russell (1942–2016) style beats-akimbo piano wizardry. The album's fourth track, 'Turn to Me', meanwhile, does have Bernie lyrics, but it, and Elton's music, are both evidence of the lingering need to create a simple commercial standard, resulting in a ballad that wouldn't have been out of place as the B side of a Bluesology single.

Bernie returns to form in the next track, 'Angel Tree'. For most Elton fans, the phrase 'Angel Tree' conjures up the opening line of 'Burn Down the Mission' – 'They tell me there's an angel in your tree' – a recurrence, which suggests to some that, in Bernie's rich world of mental images, rural life experiences and literary references, there's a powerful link between those two terms. In this song, however, 'Angel Tree' seems to simply be the name of a locally famous willow tree with a particularly rich lore surrounding it detailing what happens to people who spend too much time under its branches. Like 'When I Was Tealby Abbey', this lyric seems tailor made for the sort of neo-Gothic trappings that were growing increasingly popular, but Elton surprises us again, producing a jaunty strut that suggests more a piece performed by an American jug band at a county fair than a cautionary tale whispered by a town elder. The juxtaposition between lyrical and musical tone makes the piece memorable in a way that a straight-out spectral rendering would likely not have been.

The second side of the album leads off with 'A Dandelion Dies in the Wind', which, like 'And the Clock Goes Round', is trying to stretch the confines of the traditional pop song. The song has, in deference to Bernie's lyrics, a much pared down chorus, over almost as soon as it has begun, leaving the bulk of the song to the more exploratory verse sections, an innovation, but more noticeable still is the section that begins with 'But a dandelion sighs', which is undergirded by an almost military strut from the piano, organ and percussion that isn't only a totally different atmosphere from what we had been experiencing thus far but also represents a violent attack on the imaginative world represented by the dandelion, which with the arrival of the chorus proceeds to its fate of dying in the wind.

'Nina' brings an interesting glimpse of a mode we have yet to see emerge on an Elton record. Dominated by the atmospheric wah guitar and rock organ, the instrumental carpet of 'Nina' is overlain by Elton's stylised Jim Morrison (1943–1971) adjacent vocal intonations, which compensate for the uncharacteristic blandness of Bernie's lyrics. Incidentally, my best guess who 'Nina' might be is Nina Myskow (*b*.1946), a writer for *Jackie* magazine and the first journalist to take an interest in the pair's work, and whom Elton once asked to write some lyrics for him during those early months.

'Tartan Coloured Lady' takes up the slack left behind by 'Nina'. The song is a neo-Baroque harpsichord and flute infused framing of the mystical woman potentially doubling as drug metaphor trope seen in the pair's first single of note, 'Lady Samantha'. While the 1950s and early 1960s specialised in songs about women whose primary characteristic was being physically desirable, distinguished only by the differences in their names – 'Sherry' (1957), 'Peggy Sue' (1957) and 'Help Me Rhonda' (1965) or for being unfaithful harpies – 'Runaround Sue' (1961) and 'Jezebel' (1952) – by the late 1960s songwriters were slowly coming around to the idea that women had other personality traits that might be interesting to explore. 'Lemmon Princess' (1966) by The Leaves and 'Witchcraft' (1969) by Coven, detail in their own way women as forces of nature beyond easy comprehension, and 'Tartan Coloured Lady' seems to lie in this tradition, with the lady in question being an individual whose connection with nature allows her to revive the dying landscape.

Of course, another tradition of this time was songs that used women's names as code for experiencing hallucinogenic drugs, which purportedly allow an individual access to unearthly sensations that have long since ceased to exist in the regular world, a claim that resonates well with lines in 'Tartan Coloured Lady' like, 'Take yourself the tartan coloured lady/And smell the grass in Ashfield Park once more'.

Neither Bernie nor Elton at this time were interested in the drug scene, but the imagery and music emerging from that world had a profound influence on them, and so it's thoroughly possible that, 'Tartan Coloured Lady' represents an innocent attempt to play act as psychedelic troubadours.

The tendency on many albums of the 1960s was to bury the least promising (or least commercially viable) tracks of an album towards the end of the second side. With the case of 'Hourglass' the placement is due more to its unconventional structure, its willingness to break its forward momentum with new tempos and rhythmic ideas in the third verse, where each line is essentially doing its own thing, which is a big ask of educated pop audiences even today.

The album concludes with 'Watching the Planes Go By', notable for the unusually straightforward arrival of the chorus, which hits us straight with a powerful tonic to dominant leap, rendered all the more powerful by having been held in reserve until the last song of the record, an impression that is solidified by the subsequent rock-solid transition to the dominant's parallel minor, and thence to the dominant of that parallel minor, producing a sense of flight and openness tinged by a touch of melancholy, and buoyed by a small sense of impossible hope that a relationship which existed once, might again.

The Stats

Album/Single	US	UK	Australia	Canada
Regimental Sgt Zippo	197			

The Players

Elton John: piano, vocals, organ and harpsichord
Caleb Quaye: guitar, flute, cymbals, percussion and backing vocals
Dee Murray: bass and backing vocals
David Hynes: drums and backing vocals (all but 5 and 8)
Roger Pope: drums (5 and 8)
Paul Fenoulhet Orchestra: (1, 4, 5, 9, 10 and 12)

The Tracks

Side one:
  1. 'When I was Tealby Abbey' (John, Taupin) (2.35)
  2. 'And the Clock Goes Round' (John, Taupin) (3.06)
  3. 'Sitting Doing Nothing' (John, Quaye) (2.30)
  4. 'Turn to Me' (John, Taupin) (3.16)
  5. 'Angel Tree' (John, Taupin) (2.04)
  6. 'Regimental Sgt Zippo' (John, Taupin) (4.44)

Side two:
  7. 'A Dandelion Dies in the Wind' (John, Taupin) (3.14)
  8. 'You'll Be Sorry to See Me Go' (John, Quaye) (2.34)
  9. 'Nina' (John, Taupin) (3.50)
  10. 'Tartan' Coloured Lady (John, Taupin) (4.09)
  11. 'Hourglass' (John, Taupin) (2.44)
  12. 'Watching the Planes Go By' (John, Taupin) (4.07)

Musician's Corner: 'Regimental Sgt Zippo'

This song lies at the crossroads of several traditions and trends, certainly, but shows, at its heart, the musical sensibilities that will drive Elton's work in the decades to come. The introductory material is full of references to the era's most influential music, from the oscillating vocal note reminiscent of the conclusion to The Beatles' song 'A Day In the Life' (1967) to the Brian Wilson (b.1942) like harmonies to the twangs of the sitar that George Harrison (1943–2001) introduced to Western pop on 'Norwegian Wood' (1965).

That mix of sounds is over in an instant, however, and we move onto the core of the song, where Elton is presented by Bernie with a puzzle. Bernie's lyric centres on a boy obsessed with the pageantry of war, daily inspired by the picture on the wall of his military father, and who dreams of standing one day amid combat himself.

It's about war but it's also about childhood. It's about a kid with dreams of killing but it's also about the psychological impact of an overbearing father whom you must live up to. The central character is a villain and victim, and the boy will grow up to order the deaths of others from afar but we also know he got to be that way, by growing up seemingly alone in a military household.

The year 1968 was full of musical models for military commentary. Bob Dylan's (*b*.1941) 'Masters of War' (1963) and The Doors' 'Unknown Soldier' (March 1968) are pieces of unmitigated anger directed at the anonymous government figures who relentlessly shove the innocent into the maw of death. The Byrds' 'Draft Morning' (1967) and Simon & Garfunkel's '7 O'clock News/Silent Night' (1967) highlight the reality of war by contrast with the serenity of life, while Country Joe and the Fish's 'I Feel Like I'm Fixin' to Die' (1967) employs a rag-time musical genre to dig fully into the macabre absurdity of the war.

Elton, given lyrics that don't quite fit any of these traditions, deftly threads the needle between them. The verses, which are primarily depictions of childhood fancy, are woven by Elton with more whimsical chord choices, shifting to new chords that aren't part of the root key signature but take us on new journeys, reflecting a child's imagination. For the chorus, however, that whimsy disappears and Elton shifts to chunky familiar chords of the rock tradition, so solid against the previous material experienced that they strike with a force of satire.

Regimental Sgt Zippo has several moments where you see flashes of the mature Elton that haven't quite cooked yet, but the title track isn't one of them. Take away the introductory seconds and you have a piece that artfully engages with difficult lyrics that combines apt instrumentation decisions with a rich sense of the potential of mirroring a story through chord choice. Here, Elton has all but arrived.

Chapter 2

Empty Sky

Recorded: November 1968 to January 1969
Released: 6 June 1969 (UK) and 1975 (US)
Producer: Steve Brown

The Story

Halfway through the process of recording *Regimental Sgt Zippo*, Elton proposed to his girlfriend Linda Woodrow, moving into her flat, and taking Bernie along with him. The arrangement didn't work out and within a few months Elton and Bernie were back living in Elton's old bedroom at his mother's house. For the next eighteen months, the pair developed a method that would launch them into international stardom. Bernie worked in the bedroom, taking on average an hour to produce new lyrics, which he'd then hand to Elton at the piano, who'd produce the music, usually in the space of a half an hour. This was musical productivity of an astounding level, made even more jaw-dropping by the consistent quality of what was being produced.

In October 1968, Elton, with the help of a band assembled by Caleb Quaye, recorded the single 'Lady Samantha'/'All Across the Havens', which was released in January 1969. It was hailed for its intriguing Elizabethan and gothic sensibilities, gaining good reviews and radio play but it ultimately only sold a few thousand copies. Still, the buzz was promising and betokened interest in the new idiosyncratic direction that Elton and Bernie were forging with their combined art. All signs pointed to good results for their next attempt at a studio album, primarily recorded in late January 1969. ('Lady What's Tomorrow' was laid down in November 1968.) The album that would become *Empty Sky* was, as Elton would later describe, an example of an 'everything and the kitchen sink' approach to producing a record, with too much creativity going in too many directions.

Certainly, Elton and Bernie are trying a variety of things but it's all held together by Bernie's eclectic lyricism and Elton's distinct musical sensibilities in a way that is consistent from track to track. It's never mistakable as anything but the result of the Elton-Bernie creativity nexus.

Somewhere in the movement from 1968 to 1969, and the pressure to create something distinctly different to avoid *Empty Sky* ending up next to *Regimental Sgt*

Zippo on an anonymous basement shelf at Dick James Music, Elton and Bernie's songs made the significant leap from exercises paralleling their favourite bands, with elements of Elton and Bernie in them, to Elton and Bernie songs, injected with elements of other favourite artists as appropriate. The overwhelming impression one gets from *Empty Sky* is that of young musicians working on a shoestring budget (the whole effort cost a mere £2,000), doing everything they can think of to make a fresh impression with their artistry.

In sessions lasting until 3.00 am, Elton's team worked to build up his piano versions of each new song into sprawling new sonic worlds that incorporated every novelty that Elton could think of to make the new album stand out. 'Empty Sky' features reversed guitar tracks, an extended jam session at its core and a deceptive ending. The vocals for 'Skyline Pigeon' were recorded on the fire escape to give a sense of isolation. Meanwhile, limitations on the number of tracks available in the lower-scale recording studio meant that, on tracks like 'Western Ford Gateway', Elton had to sing harmonies over the original tracks. The poignant ode to the memory of Bernie's childhood dog, 'Gulliver', is succeeded by a lengthy sax, piano and guitar jam that couldn't be further removed from the spirit of Bernie's lyrics.

Beneath all the production novelties, however, is the formula that, when backed by directed production support, would prove irresistible in the decades to come – thoughtful chord progression grounded in lyrics that pulled their inspiration from personal history, the myths of distant lands and uncommon perspectives on the everyday.

Eclectic and full of more inventiveness than any freshman album had a right to possess, upon its 6 June release *Empty Sky* nonetheless failed to grab the attention of the public, who faced a true embarrassment of riches to select from in May and June 1969, including Joni Mitchell's (*b*.1943) *Clouds* (1 May), the debut album of Crosby, Stills and Nash (29 May), *The Age of Aquarius* by The 5th Dimension (29 May), Johnny Cash's (1932–2003) *Johnny Cash at San Quentin* (4 June) and Alice Cooper's (*b*.1948) debut album *Pretties for You* (25 June). Despite Dick James's attempts to push Elton as the next big thing, *Empty Sky* only sold approximately 4,000 copies, and the pressure was on. Elton's next album had to be a smash.

The Songs

'Empty Sky' and 'Skyline Pigeon' present two different facets of the instinct for freedom, the former a cry of defiance against physical incarceration, while the latter represents a yearning for freedom from a soul entrapped by poor life decisions. The structure of 'Empty Sky' is a unique one, lulling us into the belief that it's going to have a traditional verse-chorus structure through two repetitions of that pattern before giving us two further verses that seem to be winding down with the instruments and vocals fading out, when suddenly, at the front of the mix we have Elton's voice again, whispering at us to all be quiet and get down with him, calming down the instruments as well in the process, until everything is brought back again in a grand crescendo that brings us to the actual ending. This structural play is accompanied by instrumental shenanigans from the introductory conga drums to the reversed guitars during the first instrumental, to the interjection of jazz flute blasts, all expressing the torment of the incarcerated.

'Val-Hala' dives into a realm of ancient myths beloved by Bernie but largely untouched in *Regimental Sgt Zippo*. What confuses people about this song is the calm echo-swathed setting that Elton gives the piece. Elton could easily have gone in the direction of a Led Zeppelin style rock brawler, but he read the lyrics more closely and understood that it isn't about the clash of metal in combat but about the tranquillity and peace when the battle is over. Keep in mind, this song is from the heart of the Vietnam War era, which seeped into every aspect of creative culture. Bernie's tale not only richly evoked the Norse afterlife but also spoke to a fervent wish that the kids sent off to die in a foreign land might, at the end of their short lives, find rest.

'Western Ford Gateway' is an exploration of myths more recently established and is the first of a long tradition of Bernie evolving his conception of America as a land of myth and heroic tragicomedy, in this case one where drunkenness is the rule. This piece is a fine example of Elton's practice of using descending notes in the bassline to create one sense of movement, while the chords on top have a different motion entirely.

And now we come to the small issue of 'Hymn 2000'. Nobody has anything nice to say about it – Elton summarised it as, 'Bernie and I at our worst'. Bernie called it 'the cryptic abomination'. Romuald Ollivier and Olivier Roubin, in their study of most of Elton's songs, call it 'the most obvious misstep on Elton John's freshman album'.

But I love it. It does many daring things, some of which will work their way into Elton's standard arsenal in the years to come, while others will get curbed as Gus Dudgeon (1942–2002) and Paul Buckmaster (1946–2017) arrive on the scene. The first chord has nothing to do with the key we're in throughout the song and the intro is a dance between it and a nearby chord but we're not given any clues as to which is the real chord and which the imposter, which is a perfect place to be for a song highlighting some of Bernie's most striking imagery. The whole song is rife with sudden cuts into surprising progressions (the big examples being the C major chords we end each verse section on, which sounds totally foreign here).

Meanwhile, Bernie's lyrics, which deal largely with themes of disillusionment, hypocrisy and the inability to find comfort in the world, return in the chorus to the theme of escape, in this case to a fanciful underwater society (though from time to time Bernie's lyrics strike me less as an imaginative fantasy flight, and more as release through suicide – the body of the subject lying ultimately at the bottom of the sea, dead eyes reflecting the submarines passing overhead).

The next two songs on the album deal with a theme virtually untouched by rock until this time, that of childhood relations between siblings, the most famous expression of which will come on the *Elton John* album in the form of 'The Greatest

Discovery' but is represented in two equally beautiful pieces here, 'Sails' and 'Lady What's Tomorrow'. 'Sails' is a perfect encapsulation of childhood play, centred on a brother and sister out on the docks, playing swashbuckling pretend games and watching the boats, with Elton instinctively honing in on the different pacing each section of play ought to have. The siblings' adventures are further portrayed, in a more natural setting, in 'Lady What's Tomorrow?' with a wistful overtone of rural England's uncertain ecological future. These charming, bittersweet songs will be less evident in Bernie's output as he experiences the larger world and turns his mind towards encapsulating those experiences, so treasure them while they're here.

Bernie is usually more interested in using the form of poetry to encapsulate narratives than creating a succession of striking images that conjure an atmosphere. This isn't the case with 'The Scaffold', which is a parade of his most evocative image clusters. Elton has said that it is an homage to his favourite narrative titans of the era – figures like Leonard Cohen and David Ackles, but though Bernie's lyrics possess the same capacity for the accumulation of striking images that Cohen exhibited on his first album, Elton's music here is much more nuanced. Meanwhile, the phrasing and chord structures do have a feel of Ackles to them but the lyrics venture far more afield than Ackles's intricate tales of human drama. It's a song meant to be savoured and Elton has the good sense to resist the urge to over-produce this track, using restrained vocals, interesting but not outlandish chord progressions and pared down instrumentation.

'Skyline Pigeon' (which we analyse in more detail at chapter's end) was the standout song from *Empty Sky* and had, in fact, been previously covered by Guy Darrell (1944–2013) and Roger James Cooke (*b*.1948) in August 1968, and Elton would himself rerecord it in 1972, swapping out the distinctive harpsichord of the original for a more mellow piano accompaniment.

The strangest track of the album is its closer, 'Gulliver/Hay Chewed/Reprise'. We've already mentioned the odd structure of the piece, from poignant ode about the passing of a beloved childhood pet to farcical jazz jam session to a mechanical highlights reel of material we just heard. This experimentation was done perhaps from a desire to live up to the notes they had received on *Regimental Sgt Zippo* and push themselves to create songs that were wholly different from what the rest of the industry was producing, even if that meant the juxtapositioning of a dog funeral with groovy jazz improv.

The Stats

Album/Single	US	UK	Australia	Canada
Empty Sky	6			30

The Players

Elton John: vocals, piano, organ, Hohner Pianet and harpsichord
Caleb Quaye: electric guitar, acoustic guitar and congas
Tony Murray: bass guitar
Roger Pope: drums (all but 5) and percussion
Nigel Olsson: drums (5)
Don Fay: tenor saxophone (9) and flute (1 and 4)
Graham Vickery: harmonica (1)

The Tracks

Side one:
1. 'Empty Sky' (John, Taupin) (8.26)
2. 'Val-Hala' (John, Taupin) (4.09)
3. 'Western Ford Gateway' (John, Taupin) (3.12)
4. 'Hymn 2000' (John, Taupin) (4.27)

Side two:
5. 'Lady What's Tomorrow' (John, Taupin) (3.08)
6. 'Sails' (John, Taupin) (3.39)
7. 'The Scaffold' (John, Taupin) (3.13)
8. 'Skyline Pigeon' (John, Taupin) (3.32)
9. 'Gulliver/Hay Chewed/Reprise' (John, Taupin) (7.01)

Musician's Corner: 'Skyline Pigeon'

Let us speak of chords. The rhythm and blues and country music that fused to form early rock 'n roll traditionally featured three chords over the course of a given song: the tonic, the sub-dominant and the dominant (or the I, IV and V chords). For a song in E, for example, the I chord would be E major, the IV chord would be based on the fourth note in the E major scale, which is A, and the V chord would be based on the fifth note in that scale, which is B. E-A-B, in various successions, over and over for two and a half to three minutes, and that was pretty much your song. Here, for example, is the chord structure to 'Good Golly Miss Molly' by Little Richard (1932–2020):

I, I, IV, I
V, IV, I
I, I, I

The simplicity of the chord structure made for good dancing, and allowed for a pounding, driving sound that was the hallmark of late 1950s rockabilly, and that simplicity was maintained, for different reasons, by the folk music of the early 1960s that overtook rock 'n roll as the preferred vehicle for the young.

The arrival of The Beatles brought with it the popularisation of more complicated chord progressions in the halls of rock 'n roll. Just the first line of 'In My Life', for example, starts in A, then heads right to an E chord (the V) and then a more classically-inspired move to an F-sharp minor (the vi chord), and then returns to A again, but now it's an A7 (an A chord with an extra G thrown in), and not only that, but the G is in the bass, which provides this wonderful sense of having kind of returned home, and kind of not, which the song uses as a launchpad into the next line, which features a IV chord like we've come to expect, which shifts almost instantly into the minor version of that chord, again subverting our expectations, and providing our ears with more to munch on, allowing the musical structure to tell a story that you can feel without knowing a thing about how chords work.

Elton continues the trend of chord-based storytelling in 'Skyline Pigeon'. Look at the first seven chords he employs in this song:

See how we start on our old friend E major? Simple enough, but immediately Elton starts messing with us, giving us the V chord next, which is B major, but the bass note, isn't playing the B from the B major chord, it's playing the D sharp. He does it again a few chords later, with an arresting F sharp chord. Now, staying within the traditional motions in the key of E major, that chord should be F sharp minor, with an A natural sitting in the middle of it, but Elton goes for the major version, which has an A sharp in the middle, and not only that, but he puts that interloper A sharp right in the bass, where its alien nature will have the most psychological impact.

And Elton's not done yet. Technically, F sharp major is what we call a V/V chord – it is the V chord for B major, which is the V chord of the key we're in, E major, and should be followed by a B chord, but Elton doesn't do that, and instead lets that left hand A sharp slide down a half step to A, as the tune moves into A major, the IV chord! The result feels incredibly good to play and sounds dramatic without being distracting. This playing with the tension between what the bass note is and where it belongs in the chord Elton is featuring is a signature piece of Elton's classically trained sense of both musical fun and psychology to keep an ear out for in all his music to come.

Chapter 3

Elton John

Recorded: January 1970
Released: 10 April 1970
Producer: Gus Dudgeon

The Story

By 1970, Dick James was concerned about his Elton project. Despite tens of thousands of pounds invested, and two years of development, the young talent had yet to sell more than 5,000 copies of a single or album. Everyone at Dick James Music liked Elton, and the reviews of what had been released so far were good, so there was an inclination to give him another shot at recording a new album but the instinct to cut losses was strong. As Elton headed into production for his second record, it was with the knowledge that it was a do or die situation, failure would likely spell the end of his career.

Steve Brown, the producer of *Empty Sky*, realised that, for this album to be a success, Elton needed someone in the control booth who could impose a consistent vision in the studio and he couldn't be that person. Instead, George Martin (1926–2016), the legendary producer for The Beatles, was approached, but as he insisted on doing the music arranging as well as the production, the idea was rejected and Brown turned to Buckmaster to act as the arranger for Elton's new album and he in turn convinced Dudgeon to act as its producer.

Buckmaster and Dudgeon were the missing pieces of the puzzle, sharing a mission to discover what the essence of each song was. Buckmaster envisioned a new symphonic rock amalgam of sounds to underpin Elton's complicated progressions and Bernie's evocative thematic shadings. Dudgeon refined the new sounds such that each song was displayed to its best advantage and lay in the same sound space as the rest of the tracks.

Buckmaster and Dudgeon achieved their objective with *Elton John*, keeping the recording sessions focused, allowing the album to be recorded in the course of two weeks. Everyone involved in the process knew that this record was something special, potentially something to change the face of rock itself, a passing of the torch that became all too literal with the release of The Beatles' last studio album, *Let It Be*, almost one month to the day after *Elton John* hit store shelves. Disc jockeys in the US who ignored the A side of Elton's second single to play the B side, a little number called 'Your Song', and ecstatic word of mouth from those who attended Elton's first concerts, drove an American passion for Elton's music that fuelled his long-delayed success in the UK.

And with that, Elton John and Bernie Taupin were on their way.

The Songs

Elton John is a disciplined album leading off with one of the all-time side-one-track-ones in the history of popular music, 'Your Song'. Heralded by John Lennon (1940–1980) as the first truly new piece of music to come out of England since The Beatles, it is credited as essentially creating an entirely new direction in music, away from the control room experimentation, psychedelia and brute force rock of the late 1960s and towards introspective and nuanced work produced by singer-poet pianists including the first albums of Billy Joel (*b.*1949) and Gilbert O'Sullivan (*b.*1946) and Carole King's (*b.*1942) *Tapestry* album (all released in 1971).

The final version of the lyrics was written by Bernie over breakfast – famously the manuscript copy still bears an egg stain from that meal – and the music was produced by Elton in twenty minutes, employing a double verse structure that heightened the song's tension by delaying the traditional onset of the chorus. Buckmaster and Dudgeon replicate that instinct in their flawless production of the song, letting the song start simply with piano, bass and voice and then bringing in new elements one by one, beginning with strings at the second verse, nylon guitar in the chorus, and then finally, allowing the drums to come in with the third verse. For his part, Bernie has stated on numerous occasions that the power of the song comes from its honest naïvety, written as it was by a young man who had yet to have a real relationship, allowing him to capture the warm desire for companionship that more jaded songwriters spend their lives trying to replicate.

'I Need You To Turn To' at first seems like an odd choice to follow 'Your Song' as it is the closest in spirit to the first track, so you would think that it would be shunted to the other side of the disc. One's first instinct on hearing it is likely to compare it to 'Skyline Pigeon' due to its harpsichord introduction and pleading lyrics. In the song we get an Elton who is figuring out how to achieve the same effects with less radical means, with more borrowing from parallel modalities and less secondary dominant fireworks. Bernie's lyrics, meanwhile, are of the same cloth largely as 'Your Song' – a wide eyed view of love as a safe harbour.

Which brings us to 'Take Me to the Pilot'. Fan theories regarding what this song is all about include the idea that it is inspired by Bernie's reading of the Michael Moorcock (*b.*1939) novel *Behold the Man* (1969), in which a time traveller from 1970 ventures to AD 28 to meet the real Jesus, only to end up taking on the role himself when he discovers Jesus is a mentally challenged hunchback. By this theory, the song's 'stranger' is the traveller from another time and 'the pilot' is, in fact, Pontius Pilate.

That explanation is a possibility but the official explanation remains that it is about nothing at all. Elton, of course, picked up on the fact that there was something not quite right with the lyrics and created a musical structure to reflect that chaos, with jerky piano work and a relatively simple chord structure allowing Elton to rock out more explosively with the vocals.

'No Shoestrings on Louise' is the real odd man of *Elton John*, a song which should be on *Tumbleweed Connection*, perhaps in exchange for 'Come Down in Time'. It's about a Cadillac driving woman wreaking havoc on a hapless rural town 'milking the male population' in Bernie's visually suggestive lyrics. Elton's vocals are in full-on Western drawl mode to a degree that we won't see again until 'Country Comfort' and the backing vocals go far to create a sense of a grand country sing along event replete with Bernie's fantastical countrified lyrics.

Closing the album's first side, we come to its final love ballad, 'First Episode at Hienton', which, like many Bernie lyrics, is a tale of regretful retrospection, of an adolescent love who is now grown and lost to him. In terms of structure, it is one of the most complex pieces Elton composed for this album, postponing the chorus to the end of the song and instead opting for a bridge after the first verse that sends us to a different tonal centre and a new verse structure. Just as the song is about an early love slipping away from the narrator's grasp, Elton's music features a steady slippage away from the tonal world in which it began, moving from the world of G minor into a tonally destabilised world that has flavours of A minor and C major, neither of which live in the universe of G minor and finally coming to rest in the long delayed chorus in B flat major, the relative major of our original key, and which leads us at last, in our closing moments, back to where we began, albeit with a more tension filled inversion reflecting the fact that we are where we started, still alone, and now even a bit more miserable for having remembered what we lost. Keep an ear out for the haunting melody played during the instrumental – it was composed by Buckmaster's then girlfriend Diana Lewis (1919–1997) on a Moog synthesizer.

Side two begins with Buckmaster's legendary arrangement of 'Sixty Years On', kicked off by buzzing strings that resulted when he and the orchestra had to take a break while the recording equipment was repaired and he decided to try out something he'd heard on a Krzysztof Penderecki (1933–2020) recording. Unbeknown to him, that bit of unscripted horseplay was captured by the now functioning equipment and Dudgeon decided it would make a good intro to the dark world of the song, a call that originally infuriated Buckmaster but that he ultimately saw the beauty of.

'Border Song' famously features the return of Elton the lyricist in the track's closing section. By Bernie's reckoning, Elton's additional lyrics elevate his original material, about the drive to find one's way back home after years in the wilderness, backed by a full gospel choir, which is one of Elton's go to musical traditions for expressing themes of rebirth. The two halves of the song have never *quite* fit together, with the first promising an exploration of personal trials of alienation that are dropped to pursue a theme of universal brotherhood.

'The Greatest Discovery', led off by a soulful cello solo played by none other than Buckmaster, represents the most famous entry of the unofficial 'sibling trilogy', which started on *Empty Sky* with 'Sails' and 'Lady What's Tomorrow'. A song about a child's discovery that a new baby brother has entered his life, it is an utterly unique topic, set perfectly by Elton as a dreamy lullaby without a chorus. The story Bernie is telling is one of the great examples of Elton's musical instincts and willingness to explore new territory in order to actualise them.

Up next, 'The Cage' represents a plunge into profound ambiguity. One interpretation is the literal idea that it is a song about an animal in a cage, complete with awoo-hoo-ooo wolf calls. More mainstream are the ideas that it is either about being trapped in a relationship that is ruining you but you won't give the horde the satisfaction of renouncing, ('I walk while they talk about virtue') or that it is about self-built cages, cellars that we descend drunkenly into when we are out our lowest point of self-flagellation. For Bernie's part, he says in his memoir *Scattershot* (2023) that the song's general atmosphere reflects his reading of the Gormenghast series by Meryne Peake (1911–1968).

'The King Must Die' played a large role in the ultimate success of Elton and Bernie. On the strength of the demo recording, Buckmaster agreed to be their arranger, resulting in the subsequent and fateful drafting of Dudgeon as well. The song is an echo of Bernie's youth spent absorbing the great historical poems of the English tradition from his grandfather and reading about the history of Europe, where courtiers were anything but friends for a sitting monarch. The title was a reference to the Mary Renault (1905–1983) novel, *The King Must Die* (1958) – which was also a likely inspiration for *The Hunger Games* series of novels half a century later. The verses detail the shadowy world of dynastic courts, abounding in paranoia. From this stew of deceit, there emerges one certainty, repeated with all the instrumental power Elton can manage, and that is that the king must die, an act carried out after the repeat of the first verse, leading to the bloody declaration that the deed has been done, concluding on the chilling line, 'Long live the king', which is declared mournfully, full in the knowledge that the newcomer is a sacrifice to come.

The Stats

Album/Single	US	UK	Australia	Canada
Elton John	4	5	2	4
'Border Song'/'Bad Side of the Moon'	92			34
'Take Me to the Pilot'/'Your Song'	8		11	3
'Your Song'/'Into the Old Man's Shoes' (UK release 1971)		7		

The Players

Elton John: piano, vocals (all tracks) and harpsichord (2)
Barry Morgan: drums (1, 3, 4, 7 and 9)
Diana Lewis: Moog synthesizer (5 and 9)
Caleb Quaye: lead guitar (3, 4 and 5) and additional guitar (9)
Dave Richmond: bass guitar and double bass (1, 7 and 8)
Brian Dee: organ (6 and 7)
Skaila Kanga: harp (2 and 8)
Frank Clark: acoustic guitar (1) and double bass (10)
Colin Green: additional guitar (1, 7) and Spanish guitar (6)
Clive Hicks: twelve-string guitar (1), rhythm guitar (4), guitar (7, 8 and 10) and acoustic guitar (9)
Paul Buckmaster: cello (8), orchestral arrangements and conductor
Roland Harker: guitar (2)
Alan Parker: rhythm guitar (3)
Alan Weighall: bass guitar (3, 4 and 9)
Les Hurdle: bass guitar (10)
Terry Cox: drums (8 and 10)
Dennis Lopez: percussion (3 and 4)
Tex Navarra: percussion (9)

The Tracks

Side one:
1. 'Your Song' (John, Taupin) (4.04)
2. 'I Need You To Turn To' (John, Taupin) (2.32)
3. 'Take Me to the Pilot' (John, Taupin) (3.46)
4. 'No Shoestrings on Louise' (John, Taupin) (3.31)
5. 'First Episode at Hienton' (John, Taupin) (4.48)

Side two:
6. 'Sixty Years On' (John, Taupin) (4.35)
7. 'Border Song' (John, Taupin) (3.22)
8. 'The Greatest Discovery' (John, Taupin) (4.12)
9. 'The Cage' (John, Taupin) (3.28)
10. 'The King Must Die' (John, Taupin) (5.21)

Musician's Corner: 'Sixty Years On'

One of the things you learn as a classical pianist playing Frédéric Chopin (1810–1849) is the power of the pedal point – a note that repeats often with an insistent uniform rhythm, staying in place even as the chords around it are shifting. There's a lot of musical power in having one note stand unmovable in the foreground while all around it there's change. You can see it at work in one of Chopin's most narratively evocative preludes, the 'Raindrop' (#15):

Elton takes this to a powerful extreme later with 'Indian Sunset' on the *Madman* album, which features a persistent E flat in the bass that beautifully accents the theme of an ages old civilization facing radical change. Here, in a piece tinged with themes of a fragile mortal existence, Elton employs it to two different effects. In the introduction, the B underneath sets up a steady thrum to the arpeggiated harp runs above it, suggesting someone stuck in time (here the bassline of the original eight measures has been taken down to four):

Throughout the verses, the bass note generally takes on a descending motion, until the instrumental ending, when we get the return of the B pedal point, but instead of serene arpeggios on top, we now get big smashes of chords of irregular lengths that tell a tale of frustration aimed at the despair evoked in the verse. Where the harp was all fluidity, these chords start and stop, tying over bar lines, swooping in attack then lying still, each thrust of anger perfectly captured by Buckmaster's revolutionary orchestrations.

Chapter 4

Tumbleweed Connection

Recorded: March to August 1970
Released: October 1970 (UK) and January 1971 (US)
Producer: Gus Dudgeon

The Story

Elton and Bernie's bunkbed productivity was of such an astounding degree that, when it came time to record *Elton John*, the duo had a good three album's worth of material to choose from, an embarrassment of riches that allowed Dudgeon to group the songs into albums that had a more cohesive feel than *Empty Sky*. *Elton John* received most of the introspective pieces that would do best under the arrangement of Buckmaster. For the follow-up album, *Tumbleweed Connection*, he selected the harder driving pieces, and those centred on Elton and Bernie's sense of the American Old West, for which a stripped down rock aesthetic was more suitable.

Returning to the studio two months after recording had wrapped on *Elton John*, buoyed by the buzz that album had created among the Dick James employees and which translated into an immediate green light to proceed with a new record, Elton and the band slipped into an easy groove laying down the tracks for *Tumbleweed Connection*, songs which they had already performed live dozens of times together, the only limitation on the speed of the production being everyone's increasingly cramped schedules, which delayed completion until just before Elton left for his date with destiny in the US in late August 1970.

The Songs

With *Tumbleweed Connection*, Elton was sending a clear message of his musical versatility, aimed at those critics who might, after the release of *Elton John*, seek to relegate him to the category of a talented ballad craftsman perpetually hemmed in by symphonic embellishments. From the first track, 'Ballad of a Well-Known Gun', that gauntlet is thrown down in a guitar-led strut that gives way to a looser structure than anything heard on *Elton John*, allowing for more instrumental improvisation, giving a pure rock 'n roll foundation to Bernie's tale of a wanted man apprehended by Pinkerton agents and sent to the chain gang.

As if to reassure listeners that the Elton they loved hasn't gone entirely rogue, the second track, 'Come Down in Time', is a gorgeous and wistful Buckmaster arranged song featuring a character reflecting back, as he does often, upon a time long ago when he ventured forth late at night to have a romantic rendezvous with a woman who never came. It is one of two songs on the album that breaks from the overall Americana theme (the other being 'Love Song') to tell a simple and universal tale of love, loss and regret.

'Country Comfort' is something of an anomaly on this record. Whereas most of the strictly Western evocations centre around murder ('Son of Your Father' and 'My Father's Gun'), incarceration ('Ballad of a Well-Known Gun'), shame ('Into the Old Man's Shoes') and death ('Talking Old Soldiers'), 'Country Comfort' is a set of mini-portraits introducing us to a cast of rural characters that Bernie knew well from his Lincolnshire youth, each of which is facing in their own way the encroaching realities of modernity with an admirable stubbornness, as machines work the fields and old farmers look in vain for young people to take an interest in the old ways, and yet the country spirit thrives in them. Everything about the song production is over the top, with Elton's vocals mimicking an exaggerated country twang while instrumentally 'everything' is brought into the studio: a lap steel guitar, a harmonica, a fiddle and a twelve-string guitar.

One of the mysteries of the album is the placing of 'Son of Your Father' directly before 'My Father's Gun', with writers insisting that the placement of the two tracks next to each other must carry some profound significance, an idea lent credence by the fact that another song, which ultimately didn't make the cut, 'Into the Old Man's Shoes', about how a father's reputation can ruin the lives of those who can't measure up to it, also centres around paternal themes. The two songs that remain, however, while having 'father' in the title, aren't really about fathers. 'My Father's Gun' is primarily a proxy tale for the romanticised notion of the American South, in which Southern soldiers fought valiantly for their freedom, while the whole slavery issue was shuffled off into a picturesque background. Yes, a father dies at the start of 'My Father's Gun', but the story is really about the son's donning of the greys and fighting for 'The Cause' so that children might laugh again and women… sew again.

'Son of Your Father' is, likewise, not so much about fathers but the tension between the power of social conventions in the Old West and the often deadly cost of ignoring them. If this song is linked to 'My Father's Gun' it is less through the titular paternal figures and more as displays of larger social codes in which sons and fathers are both bound.

'Where to Now St Peter?' is an enigma not remotely clarified by the music and production choices. Clearly, it is a song about a wayward soul either literally confronting St Peter and waiting for his pronouncement about whether he is bound for heaven or hell, or a more metaphoric account of someone at a life's crossroads wondering what their life amounts to. Some theories fixate on the term 'blue canoe' maintaining that this references Confederate Army slang for a bullet, so the song is about an American Civil War soldier who has been shot, is strapped to a medic's stretcher ('They took the paddles, my arms they paralysed') and is confronting the afterlife while dying from the wound. A rival troupe, however, with more experience of the American drug scene in the late 1960s, points to the fact that, at Woodstock, mescaline doses were referred to as 'blue canoes' and that 'Where to Now?' should be interpreted more as drug-induced hallucination narration. The funky guitar of the song and Elton's trippy vocals, fit in with the latter interpretation, but I've always seen it in the context of a person who has led a disreputable or violent life, realising who they are and trying to figure out where they can go from there.

'Love Song', meanwhile, is a straight-out alien presence. There are just two chords that alternate back and forth over a repetitive set of melodic lines – everything seems off. The reason is that this is the only track on the album not written by Elton or Bernie. Rather, it as an intimately recorded cover of a beloved friend's music somewhat at odds with the theme of the material surrounding it, but representing a nice moment to catch our breath.

The story behind 'Amoreena' is a strange one. It represents Elton and Bernie's first exploration of the genre of musical portraits of women seen primarily from a sexual perspective. The song is essentially about how much the narrator misses having sex with a particular woman. Later, these tales would morph into more complicated narratives of women's sensuality, from the sex work lament of 'Sweet Painted Lady' to the lesbian tragedy of 'All the Girls Love Alice' to the domestic abuse of 'Angeline' as Bernie became progressively more aware of the darker aspects of men's fascination with, and treatment of, women. What's truly strange about this story is how Elton and Bernie approached Ray Williams and insisted that he name his soon to arrive daughter 'Amoreena' after the sex song that they were writing, which has always struck me as a very odd ask.

The two closing tracks of *Tumbleweed Connection* represent opposites of musical treatment, even as they are unified by some of Bernie's darkest lyrics on this album. 'Talking Old Soldiers' is a solo number by Elton, in which we find the influence of David Ackles, and particularly of his song 'Down River', which features a melancholic one-sided conversation about past times. Whereas 'Down River' is about catching up with a long lost love who has since moved on to a happy life, 'Talking Old Soldiers' is told from the perspective of an old soldier lamenting not only the loss of his friends but the fact that no one is able to understand why he can't move on from the things he has seen and the people he has lost. The chords Elton chose are intriguing but limited in number, driven by the contrast between the overall key of C minor and the repeated borrowing of the dominant chord from C major, creating a sense of sounds that are related but still alien, which unsettle us in subtle ways. It's one of the greatest creations of Elton and Bernie, made all the more effective by its contrast with the rock 'n roll grandeur and Old West accessories that permeate the rest of the album and makes this dark solo number stand out in all the grim truth of the humanity it portrays.

Every early Elton album had at least one experimental number in which Elton permitted himself to stretch the boundaries of what a rock 'n roll album can be. *Empty Sky* featured both 'Empty Sky' and 'Gulliver/Hay Chewed/Reprise' as experimental pieces that owed much to The Beatles. 'Sixty Years On' tackled the problem of convincingly melding symphonic forms onto rock 'n roll sub-structures that represented a qualitative leap beyond the idiosyncratic solutions offered by The Beatles and The Moody Blues. Arguably, 'Burn Down the Mission' is the first of these pieces to present an experimental structure uniquely showcasing Elton's approach to music that will inform all those that follow it. Elton has stated that his inspiration to push himself structurally was the work of singer-songwriter Laura Nyro (1947–1997) whose revolutionary album *Eli and the Thirteenth Confession* (1968) showed Elton a new way forward from the verse-chorus-verse-chorus-bridge-chorus structure that had dominated pop music for decades. Nyro pushed *avant-garde*, classical and jazz influences into her pop music, including her use of sudden key or rhythmic transitions, which put structure in the service of storytelling, instead of shoving the story into the confines of traditional structures.

The story here works on two levels. First, taking the title at face value, as a retelling of the explosion of Native American resentment against the ruination of their society at the hands of the Spanish mission system. Alternately, the song can be taken as an extended allegory, with the subjugation of the Native population by the Spanish as a clever way of talking about the subjugation of normal people by the magnates of capitalism, whose reign must be ended if we are all to stay alive. Elton uses this song, with its wide shifts between thoughts of desperation, rage, revenge and resignation, as a perfect template for musical experimentation.

The Stats

Album/Single	US	UK	Australia	Canada
Tumbleweed Connection	5	2	4	4
	P	G	G	
'Country Comfort'/'Love Song' (Australia, New Zealand and Brazil)				

The Players

Elton John: lead vocals, acoustic piano (1, 3 to 6 and 8 to 10), Hammond organ (8) and backing vocals (10)

Caleb Quaye: lead guitar (1, 4, 6 and 8), acoustic guitar (1, 3, 5 and 6) and electric guitar (5)

Roger Pope: drums (1 and 4 to 6) and percussion (1)

Les Thatcher: acoustic guitar (2 and 10) and twelve-string acoustic guitar (3)

Nigel Olsson: backing vocals (3 and 6) and drums (8)
Brian Dee: Hammond organ (10 and 13)
Gordon Huntley: steel guitar (3)
Lesley Duncan: backing vocals (1, 4, 5 and 7) and acoustic guitar (7)
Mike Egan: acoustic guitar (10)
Dave Glover: bass guitar (1 and 4 to 6)
Herbie Flowers: bass guitar (2, 3 and 10)
Chris Laurence: acoustic bass (2 and 10)
Dee Murray: backing vocals (3 and 6) and bass guitar (8)
Barry Morgan: drums (2, 3 and 10)
Robin Jones: congas (10) and tambourine (10)
Karl Jenkins: oboe (2)
Skaila Kanga: harp (2)
Ian Duck: harmonica (3 and 4)
Johnny Van Derek: violin (3)
Paul Buckmaster: orchestral arrangements and conductor

The Tracks

Side one:
  1. 'Ballad of a Well-known Gun' (John, Taupin) (4.59)
  2. 'Come Down in Time' (John, Taupin) (3.25)
  3. 'Country Comfort' (John, Taupin) (5.06)
  4. 'Son of Your Father' (John, Taupin) (3.48)
  5. 'My Father's Gun' (John, Taupin) (6.20)

Side two:
  6. 'Where to now St Peter?' (John, Taupin) (4.11)
  7. 'Love Song' (Lesley, Duncan) (3.41)
  8. 'Amoreena' (John, Taupin) (5.00)
  9. 'Talking Old Soldiers' (John, Taupin) (4.06)
  10. 'Burn Down the Mission' (John, Taupin) (6.21)

Musician's Corner: 'Amoreena'

What makes up the rhythm and gait of an Elton song? It's a complicated question, but 'Amoreena' is one of the best songs to study to see how songs propel themselves forward. In the opening bars there are a pair of double grace notes that bend through two half steps to land on the desired note, a technique associated with Floyd Cramer (1933–1997), which was employed by Leon Russell, and, through him, made its way into Elton's fingers. We hear this straightaway in the first three notes that Elton plays:

These bent structures provide a cheeky, slide-on-up-and-say-hi approach to playing a note that adds a little extra bit of down-home flavour.

What we can also see in 'Amoreena' is Elton's style for communication between the two hands. Let's single out one bar of music:

The vertical bars represent the four beats of the measure. In terms of notes, besides the A sharp that Elton uses to bend into the B, there's nothing here except what one would expect from the G major that this section is grounded in. What's interesting here is how the hands talk to each other, swapping responsibilities back and forth. The left-hand G at (1) hands off to a G in the right hand (2), which comes in on an offbeat. The next full note, B, would be on the beat, but because it is being bent into from the quick A sharp before it, it doesn't feel that way, and the two note G-D power chord that follows hops in before the strong third beat, but sustains across it while the left hand gives us that third beat pulse (3), which then throws the music back to the right hand and plays off the beat (4) and then back to the left hand, which has also managed to dodge the beat (5).

This back and forth between the hands, with the right doing everything it can to avoid playing squarely on a beat, and the left taking up the responsibility for telling us where that beat is, but only sometimes, has traditions going all the way back to the rag music of the late nineteenth and early twentieth centuries, which made their way to Elton through the exuberant renditions of Winifred Atwell (1914–1983) that Elton so loved as a child, among other sources.

Chapter 5

Friends

Recorded: September 1970
Released: 24 March 1971
Producer: Gus Dudgeon

The Story

I n December 1970, the film *Love Story* hit cinemas and over the next month proved a financial juggernaut of unanticipated proportions, staying at the #1 spot for four weeks, and bringing in $173 million. Three months later, *Friends* debuted, a controversial love story of underage lovers running away from society, with every hope of raising similarly massive international romantic enthusiasm, a hope buoyed by the fact that it boasted a soundtrack written by the world's most important emerging rock star: Elton John.

With his American tour of August 1970 a rousing success, and both *Elton John* and *Tumbleweed Connection* achieving gold record status, Elton seemed an unstoppable force, and upon hearing his work, director Lewis Gilbert (1920–2018), already famous for *Alfie* (1966) and the James Bond film *You Only Live Twice* (1967), decided that he needed Elton's skills for his upcoming film, to be titled *The Intimate Game*. There was a lot riding on this – Gilbert had walked away from *The Godfather* (1972) to direct it and, even with the international euphoria over *Love Story*, the idea of a film with underage sex as a prominent component raised eyebrows, and having not only a world famous musician but one not associated with sexual and narcotic excesses, tied to it could go far in giving it a wider commercial appeal.

Elton said yes on the condition that Gilbert change the title of the film, ultimately settling on the more wholesome *Friends*. With their characteristic speed, Elton and Bernie wrote three original songs for the film (four if you count the reprise of 'Friends'), 'Friends', 'Michelle's Song' and 'Seasons', while Buckmaster arranged instrumental variations of the songs. When plans for the release of a film soundtrack surfaced Elton, unwilling to put out a record with only three original songs on it, offered to add two rejected pieces from the upcoming *Madman Across the Water* album, 'Honey Roll' and 'Can I Put You On?'. Those songs, not having been composed for the film, had nothing really to do with it, and so had to then be shoe-horned in as background music.

There was a lot working against the success of the album – the less than cohesive nature of the music, the unattractive album packaging (which Elton ranks as among the worst album covers of his career), the increasing feeling that the market was oversaturated with Elton material (this would be the fourth Elton related album within the span of a year) and the ultimate critical failure of the film itself, which earned one star ratings. And yet, such was the power of Elton at this time, particularly in the US, that *Friends* hit #34 on the US charts, and the title track #36, with the album eventually joining *Elton* and *Tumbleweed Connection* in achieving gold certification. In the UK, meanwhile, the album was met with scepticism, and failed to chart, turning up the pressure to make the next studio album something special.

The Songs

Restricting ourselves to the five original Elton-Bernie compositions on the album, it would be clear to anyone listening without any other information, which two are the odd ones out. 'Friends', 'Michelle's Song' and 'Seasons' all have thematic similarities centring around the blossoming of friendships into something deeper. Musically, Elton does a few subtle and clever things with his storytelling. Whereas 'Friends' begins with a series of G minor chords that suggest the troubled position the heroes find themselves in and the loneliness of a world without someone to rely on, by the time we get to 'Seasons' and the next mention of the word friend, it hits in the key of G major, a musical suggestion that the longed for friendship has been found.

'Michelle's Song' is an underappreciated song in the Elton canon. Placed anywhere but on the *Friends* soundtrack, it would have become a standard. Bernie's lyrics combine complex tone painting in the verse, with a wide-open call to joint flight in the chorus, which Elton matches by his usual intricate chord shifts and inversions in the verses before switching to big and open I-IV-V transitions in the chorus that are made doubly effective by Elton's sustained top notes.

Instrumentally, the overall atmosphere of the soundtrack material as arranged by Buckmaster leans heavily into the ideal pastoral setting the characters find themselves in, with a lot of the woodwind colouring that has for so long in the Western classical tradition stood for nature.

The two tacked on tracks include another of my favourites, 'Can I Put You On?', which features priceless Bernie lyrics about a big city charlatan who comes to working class districts on weekends to sell the people there things they don't need for prices they can't afford. Elton reaches into his bag of gospel and soul tricks for the music here, deftly associating the hucksterism of the main character with the *Elmer Gantry* like showmanship of American revivalism, and the frenzied end, with its unchained choral repetition of 'People, can I put you on?' is straight from a rural tent meeting, where the donation plate is being passed feverishly while the choir, backing a sweat-drenched itinerant preacher, exhorts one and all to give and give.

'Honey Roll' hearkens back to the early years of rock 'n roll's evolution, when blues was picking up the tempo and lyricists delighted in getting as sexually explicit as they could get away with, both the terms 'rock' and 'roll' being code for straight-out sex. When rhythm and blues, and rock, were both effectively tamed by the late 1950s through commercialisation, the old terms remained in a sanitised form, and were directed into vapid dance craze numbers, like the dozens of songs attempting to capitalise on 'The Twist'. Elton and Bernie's song sounds like a return to the dance craze era, encouraging us to do the 'Honey Roll', but as record buying fiends steeped in the old rhythm and blues traditions, they must have known about the more salacious aspects of the word 'roll' and the references to riding other people's ponies. This whole thing is an homage to that early, less vanilla, era of rock, played as a wholesome number.

The Stats

Album/Single	US	UK	Australia	Canada
Friends	36		19	17
	G	G		
'Friends'	34		96	13

The Players

Elton John: piano, vocals
Caleb Quaye: guitar (2 and 6)
Barry Morgan: drums (1 and 7)
Dee Murray: bass guitar (2 and 6)
Nigel Olsson: drums (2 and 6)
Paul Buckmaster: orchestral arrangement
Rex Morris: saxophone (2)
Madeline Bell: backing vocals
Lesley Duncan: backing vocals
Liza Strike: backing vocals

The Tracks

Side one:
1. 'Friends' (John, Taupin) (2.20)
2. 'Honey Roll' (John, Taupin) (3.00)
3. Variations on 'Friends Theme' (The First Kiss) (John, Buckmaster) (1.45)
4. 'Seasons '(John, Taupin) (3.52)
5. Variations on 'Michelle's Song' (A Day in the Country) (John, Buckmaster) (2.44)
6. 'Can I Put You On?' (John, Taupin) (5.52)

Side two:
7. 'Michelle's Song' (John, Taupin) (4.16)
8. I Meant to Do My Work Today (A Day in the Country) (John, Buckmaster, Le Gallienne) (1.33)
9. Four Moods (Buckmaster) (10.56)
10. Seasons Reprise (John, Taupin) (1.33)

Musician's Corner: 'Friends'

'Friends' is something far more complicated than the simple ode to the beauty of friendship it appears. Elton lets us know this from the start with a martially regular succession of eight G minor 7 chords. That's the setup for a funeral dirge, and at first glance it seems like Elton's being perverse for the sake of it, but a little closer inspection shows that he is keying into an element of Bernie's lyrics that calls for exactly what Elton's doing. The basic fact of this song is that the friends aren't yet here. When they do get here, things will be great, but as of right now, they are not, and in that absence, life is hard. Elton, who understood something of loneliness himself, zeroed in on that fundamental fact and encased it in those opening chords.

What is more brilliant still is the call-back to this mood that we see in the song's most famous line, 'If your friends are there, then everything's all right'. By this point, the piece has moved itself effectively from G minor into B flat major but Elton, instead of giving into the fantasy that friends will show up and everything will be fine, flashes that G minor 7 one more time, reminding us that the line is 'If your friends are there' not 'Now that your friends are here', before giving us the big major chord, feel-good resolution. It's the same slash of minor chord unease amid a generally major setting that you'll find in ABBA's 'Dancing Queen' (1975) where it has the similar effect of making us feel that there's something darker going on here, that deserves thinking about.

Chapter 6

Madman Across the Water

Recorded: 27 February and 9, 11 and 14 August 1971
Released: 5 November 1971
Producer: Gus Dudgeon

The Story

B etween *Elton John*, *Tumbleweed Connection*, the live album *11-17-70* and *Friends*, all released within a year of each other, there was a growing consensus in some sectors of the musical criticism world that Elton was overextending himself, to capitalise on his American fame while it lasted. Fans of *Elton John* in particular, who lionised that album for its symphonic settings of intricate personal moments, felt that the following three albums were a betrayal and turned from some of Elton's biggest supporters to his biggest critics.

Dudgeon realised that a return to form was called for, an album that would show the *Elton John* fans that Elton and Bernie could still craft a complex ballad, while demonstrating to the *Tumbleweed Connection* fans that they weren't about to abandon their cataloguing of the fascinating contradictions of American culture. The album that was to accomplish this task had to be recorded in between the increasingly sprawling live performance schedule that Elton's handlers had committed him to, resulting in the whole record being laid down in four days, with one of them separated by months from the other three.

The need to get things down quickly had one important casualty: Buckmaster. While trying to handwrite all the orchestral scores in a night of frenetic activity, he happened to spill ink all over the master (and only) copy, compelling him to start from scratch, and delaying recording to a degree that Elton found unacceptable, and after the resulting argument we shall glimpse Buckmaster only sparingly on Elton's albums of the 1970s and 1980s.

The album represents a further parting of ways, as it was the last to feature guitarist Caleb Quaye and drummer Roger Pope (1947–2013) until 1975, while Elton's touring band of Dee Murray (1946–1992) and Nigel Olsson (*b*.1949) were only employed on one track: 'All the Nasties'. Meanwhile, two new stars in the Elton firmament arrived in the band, the acoustic guitarist Davey Johnstone (*b*.1951), whose grasp of multiple string instruments shone on records by his band Magna Carta and who'd soon become an electric guitar virtuoso, and Ray Cooper (*b*.1947), one of the greatest studio percussionists of all time.

While four days might sound an impossible span in which to record a modern album, it was well within the capacities of Elton and Bernie, the problem being that there was hardly any time to consider how all these songs went together. That dilution of theme was often remarked on by reviewers and was responsible for the album's relatively poor showing in the UK, where it topped out at #41. Unlike *Tumbleweed Connection*, two singles were released from *Madman Across the Water*, and neither performed as hoped. 'Tiny Dancer', now considered one of the greatest songs of that decade, only hit #41 in the US and wasn't even considered for release in the UK, while 'Levon', which was released in the UK, failed to chart there, and although it out-performed 'Tiny Dancer' in the US, it still didn't climb higher than #24.

Today, *Madman Across the Water* is generally considered as one of Elton's great albums of the 1970s, boasting an array of complex songs that defied pop traditions, and which boggle the mind when one considers the amount of quality that was squeezed out of four days of composing and recording. At the time, however, the relative lack of success was frustrating, and called for a new approach that involved moving from Trident Studios and experimenting with new environments.

The Songs

Today, 'Tiny Dancer' is one of a handful of songs that we have all agreed to loudly and publicly sing along with the chorus of, regardless of where you are or who you are with.

Of course, in 1971, the case was rather different. Leading off an album that was supposed to be a return to *Elton John*, meant that 'Tiny Dancer' had to fill the shoes of 'Your Song', and Elton's solution to that problem seems to have been to dial everything up. Bernie's lyrics had all the poignancy of a young man expressing his first real love for a woman – his soon to be wife, Maxine (*b*.1952) – on the composition side, the 'push the chorus back by another verse' innovation that Elton introduced in 'Your Song' is taken to extremes here, with the chorus not arriving until two minutes and thirty seconds into the song. Taking his time to build to this high point meant that 'Tiny Dancer' ended up at six minutes and seventeen seconds as opposed to the four minutes and four seconds of 'Your Song', but so perfect is the production that it is hard to think of anything that could be trimmed to create a radio-friendly track that wouldn't result in a far less satisfying experience.

'Tiny Dancer' builds its musical layers slowly, starting with Elton and his piano, then slowly adding in a slide guitar, then bass, guitar and drums followed by an atmospheric chorus as we head into the bridge, with its characteristic sigh motif in the steel guitar, and ultimately to the famous refrain backed by the deep bass of Buckmaster's strings. As perfect as we find it today, however, audiences of the time simply weren't ready for a six minute plus love ballad and it would have to wait for the film *Almost Famous* (2000) to see its resurrection in the hearts of the public.

Structurally, 'Levon' has a fair amount in common with 'Tiny Dancer' – the layering of the instruments, the central role of the strings, the narrative centred on giving a full picture of the personality of an uncommon individual, and the rise from where the fourth verse starts to where the chorus does, all speak to a drive to provide a solid punch to anyone who doubted that Elton and Bernie could produce material like on the *Elton John* album. What sets the song apart from 'Tiny Dancer' is the enigmatic nature of the titular character, the whimsical Levon (whom Bernie has denied naming after Levon Helm (1940–2012) of The Band) and his equally quirky son Jesus.

Although the chorus sounds like a celebration of an individual, the story is a sad one about two worthy individuals unable to connect. Levon, whose business involves selling balloons, who managed to hold onto a sense of individuality despite having scrambled up from the depths of poverty, ought to be a perfect companion for his son, who dreams of space travel and loves watching balloons ascend into the sky. And yet, he isn't. Levon hasn't done much wrong, except perhaps become fixated on his income, but Jesus wants out to go far away and leave his father to die, unsupported in his old age. It's an exploration of what happens when dreams exert a stronger pull on you than the people you love, a story without villains *per se*, but with plenty of tragedy.

On *Elton John*, the first two tracks were love ballads, followed by the inspired insanity of 'Take Me to the Pilot' for track three, a pattern which is re-established on *Madman Across the Water*, with the quirky 'Razor Face'. It can be read as the story of a destitute veteran *á la* 'Talking Old Soldiers', but some instrumental choices seem to speak against that idea. Rick Wakeman's (*b*.1949) organ, and Jack Emblow's (*b*.1930) accordion live in a wholly other sonic world. The former adds these almost church organ flourishes and the accordion is going nuts, both of which seem out of place for a song about a down on his luck soldier. I prefer David DeCouteau's (*b*.1962) interpretation, which is that the old figure in the song is an elderly jazz or blues musician who has sunk upon hard times.

Finishing the first side of the record we have 'Madman Across the Water', a song originally intended for the *Tumbleweed Connection* album but which Dudgeon couldn't stand. Yet, the composition was too interesting to let die and the song was given a second chance. Johnstone's acoustic guitar restraint (as compared to his sprawling *Tumbleweed* rendition) grounded the song's narrative of a psychiatric ward patient's life in a fragile context, with the electric guitar adding rhythmic accents that don't threaten to destroy the overall structure. In the absence of the extended electric guitar solo, there was now more room in the composition for Buckmaster to arrange string parts that lifted Elton's music elements to a perfect state of fragmentation that whip themselves into different ideas that wax and wane with the central character's grasp on reality.

'Holiday Inn' is the sort of thing that happens when the legal department starts getting involved in musical decisions. The original lyrics by Bernie were about the monotony of the series of Holiday Inns that he stayed in while being dragged back and forth across America for Elton's tours. It was laid down by Elton as the first song of the August 1971 recording sessions, just some eighteen hours after having returned to England after a tour in Portugal. This was the first track Elton recorded with Johnstone, who immediately felt comfortable suggesting to Elton that he ditch his usual piano introduction and launch straight into the vocals, backed by Johnstone's mandolin playing. Bernie's original lyrics featured lines calling the Holiday Inn a motel prison, complaining about the poor service and broken amenities. Lawyers for Dick James Music, however, advised him that such lyrics could constitute a lawsuit and so the most offending line was cut entirely and 'motel prison' was changed to 'motel, baby'. Lacking the bite of the original lyrics, however, meant that what was left was a peppy setting that seemed like an advertisement for how great Holiday Inns are, a welcome and familiar friend for the tired musician. I've often wondered why, with its meaning so changed, it was kept on the album, and if I ever get a chance to ask Elton about it, I'll let you know what he says.

In my head, 'Rotten Peaches' is the sequel to 'Ballad of a Well-Known Gun', which fills in the back story of the main character and tells us his fate after being arrested. To be clear, I have zero evidence to back this up, but this is how I came to that conclusion: first, the tonal similarities. Second, the fate of the main character in 'Ballad of a Well-Known Gun' is being placed on a chain gang, which is where the main character from 'Rotten Peaches' is as we start the song. Third, both songs are about someone who had to keep on the move because of their inability to keep to the laws of society.

What strikes me about this song is Elton's sheer power of musical craftsmanship. Given the line 'Rotten peaches rotting in the sun', he was able by raw force of charisma to change that into the catchiest intro to a chorus you're ever likely to experience, an entirely infectious little earworm about a symbol of the unending monotony of the prisoner's life of unpaid state labour.

And now we come to the gay liberation song that nobody realised was a gay liberation song, 'All the Nasties'. The official explanation for the song was that it was Bernie's response to Elton's request to write something about the critics who had turned from his greatest admirers when he was unknown into his biggest detractors now that there was money to be made in knocking him off the pedestal he'd worked so hard to mount. That explanation, however, makes absolutely no sense considering how Elton structures the song. Instead of a thrashing romper what we get is an intricately chorded lament sung in a fragile voice. And that's because this song isn't really about music criticism, it's about Elton's anxieties regarding publicly acknowledging his sexuality. This was 1971 and Elton had no way of knowing whether revealing this side of himself would be accepted. That anguish manifests here as a profound need for solace, which Elton expresses in the song's concluding gospel-infused section, with the simple cry of 'Oh my soul' repeated over and over, to an extent unusual in any Elton recording as if the sheer magnitude of the repetition is his way of getting us to pay real attention to the request for compassion that lies at its core.

At this point, Elton might have been expected to end his album on a sprawling historical epic on the order of 'The King Must Die' or 'Burn Down the Mission'. But in an album full of large-scale pieces clocking in at over five minutes, such a song would hardly have stood out, and so the only place to go was in the opposite direction, towards a piece of through writing eschewing any traditional structure, highlighting the evocative power of Bernie's image-crafting, a whimper of impermanence known as 'Goodbye' in which Elton sings from the point of view of both Bernie and himself as artists who produce creations that are always slightly out of sync with their time (which shine only when it starts to rain).

The Stats

Album/Single	US	UK	Australia	Canada
Madman Across the Water	8	41	8	9
	2P	G	G	P
'Levon'/'Goodbye'	24			6
'Tiny Dancer'/'Razor Face'	41		13	19

The Players

Elton John: acoustic piano and vocals
Davey Johnstone: acoustic guitar (1, 4 and 7), mandolin (6) and sitar (6)
Caleb Quaye: electric guitar (1, 2 and 3) and acoustic guitar (6)
Dee Murray: bass guitar (8) and backing vocals (1, 6 and 7)
Roger Pope: drums (1, 3 and 6)
Nigel Olsson: drums (8) and backing vocals (1, 6 and 7)
Ray Cooper: percussion (4), tambourine (7 and 8)
Rick Wakeman: Hammond organ (3 and 7)
Diana Lewis: ARP synthesizer (4 and 7)
B.J. Cole: steel guitar (1)
Chris Spedding: electric guitar (4) and slide guitar (7)
David Glover: bass guitar (1, 3 and 6)
Brian Odgers: bass guitar (2)
Brian Dee: harmonium (2)
Jack Emblow: accordion (3)
Herbie Flowers: bass guitar (4, 5 and 7)
Chris Laurence: double bass (5)

Barry Morgan: drums (2)
Terry Cox: drums (4, 5 and 7)
Paul Buckmaster: orchestral arrangements and conductor (1, 2, 4, 5, 6, 8 and 9)
David Katz: orchestra contractor (1, 2, 4, 5, 6, 8 and 9)

The Tracks

Side one:
1. 'Tiny Dancer' (John, Taupin) (6.17)
2. 'Levon' (John, Taupin) (5.22)
3. 'Razor Face' (John, Taupin) (4.42)
4. 'Madman Across the Water' (John, Taupin) (5.57)

Side two:
5. 'Indian Sunset' (John, Taupin) (6.47)
6. 'Holiday Inn' (John, Taupin) (4.17)
7. 'Rotten Peaches' (John, Taupin) (4.58)
8. 'All the Nasties' (John, Taupin) (5.09)
9. 'Goodbye' (John, Taupin) (1.49)

Musician's Corner: 'Indian Sunset'

There's an entire mountain of interesting musical techniques to talk about for 'Tiny Dancer', but since that has already been beautifully done by Kirk Hamilton in an episode of *Strong Songs*, I'll simply point you in that direction while talking myself about the hidden gem that is 'Indian Sunset'. In an album full of intriguing songs it is perhaps the most unique. Firstly, it is set in E flat minor, a key you almost never see in pop music thanks to the six flats of its key signature. Look on any chart of the circle of fifths, and you'll find E flat minor at the bottom, the most extreme key you can choose to write in while still staying within the boundaries of traditional Western music.

Further, once you move past an opening surge of an unworldly synthesizer pulse that I think must have been contributed by Diana Lewis what you get for the first ten bars of music is Elton singing without accompaniment of any sort, something that to my knowledge he never did again to open a song. And not only that, but in and amongst those ten bars there are two changes of metre, where he switches, for one bar only, from the 4/4 time most of the piece is in, to a 2/4 time. This switch reoccurs throughout the song and, while changing metres were a mainstay of classical and artsy rock music they were a rarity in the pop music of this era.

Once the accompaniment does come in, the bass note is stuck firmly on a low E flat, giving the song the declarative boldness suggested by the lyrics – here is one man standing against the fate of his tribe, rooted in his position as he watches his traditions fall apart all around him.

We are set stoutly in this defiant stance until, suddenly, everything melts away and the key turns to, of all things, G major, as the speaker moves from defiance as his central emotion to empathy, a transition more heart-breaking for the musical stridency of what preceded it. At this point, the young warrior knows what he must do, even as knows what his fate will be. Just as in 'Friends', where the G minor we started with is replaced by its relative major key of B flat to evoke a hopeful transformation to better times, here we have a similar shift, but with opposite meaning. The temporary tranquillity of G major shifts to its relative minor key, E minor, as our central figure makes reluctant peace with the fact that his tribe's way of life is over, and that the only satisfaction left is through reunion with his loved ones in death. The key, the pedal point, the chord transitions, the use of relative majors and minors, are all employed perfectly to tell a story, the contours of which we could feel even without the lyrics. I'm sure that there are those who will instinctively avoid this piece in the name of cultural appropriation and I understand where that argument is coming from but in terms of pure musical storytelling, it doesn't come much better than this.

Chapter 7

Honky Château

Recorded: 15 to 23 January 1972
Released: 19 May 1972
Producer: Gus Dudgeon

The Story

With the relatively lukewarm British reception of *Madman Across the Water*, a course correction seemed to be in order, which required a few acts of minor scapegoating. The phrase which emerged to encapsulate what happened with *Madman Across the Water* was 'pocket symphony'. All the Buckmaster arrangements, all the meticulously planned sessions, all the six minute plus narrative odysseys, all the elaborate double-sleeved album design art, all that had to go in favour of a more stripped down presentation that relied on the members of the band being trusted to find their own way to best support the song at hand.

Dudgeon remained at the helm, the magnitude of his task amplified by how much work he'd now have to do in post-production, but otherwise this was a fresh start. For tax reasons, Elton eschewed using Trident Studios, in favour of a converted (and supposedly haunted) château located at Hérouville, some 18 kilometres from Paris, that was a favourite of the Grateful Dead and would in time host the recording of David Bowie's (1947–2016) *Low* (1977) album. Rejecting the studio musicians that had been the backbone of his previous recordings, Elton elected to go with his touring band of Olsson and Murray, now with Johnstone, who had proven his mettle on *Madman Across the Water*, as a permanent member.

One of the benefits of the château was the ability to live on site, allowing the band to avoid the time-consuming procedure of setting up their equipment anew each day. Instead, they had the entire run of the premises and could structure their days so as best to support their creative processes, a luxury that allowed them to record songs at a legendary speed. Bernie would write lyrics at night, which Elton would work into songs in the morning, taking the rough products into the band at breakfast, who'd begin hashing out their own parts, with everything being settled by evening, when they'd lay down for all posterity the song that had not existed the day before. In one storied morning, Elton wrote 'Mona Lisas and Mad Hatters', 'Rocket Man (I Think It's Going to Be a Long, Long Time)' and 'Amy', all before breakfast, so ideally suited to his working style was the new arrangement.

The results of giving each musician more creative responsibility were predictably mixed, with some songs suffering from the lack of an overarching plan but most of the up-tempo numbers gained from the inventiveness spawned by the new working arrangement. Focus in on any instrument and something interesting will be happening there, something you don't always get from more planned-out tracks. Taken to an extreme that density of musical happenings can dissipate focus, making the listener unsure of what the main thread of the song is but Murray and Olsson had been working with Elton for so long, and Johnstone's instincts as a band musician so honed, that what you get on *Honky Château* is the perfect balance between the needs of the song and the expressive instincts of the musicians involved.

The public seemed to agree, with *Honky Château* shooting right to the top of the charts in the US (starting a string of seven chart-topping albums there) and to the #2 position in the UK. More significantly for Elton, the single 'Rocket Man (I Think It's Going to Be a Long, Long Time)' also penetrated to the #2 spot in the UK, thawing at last the frosty reception that his singles had generally received in his native country. Elton, who by the end of 1971 was throwing out heavy hints that he expected to be done with the music business by 1973 or 1974 at the latest, had weathered the storm of criticism and not only survived but emerged stronger than ever.

The Songs

Elton's first songs are usually tailored to send a message about what to expect in what follows. 'Empty Sky' faithfully let us know that *Empty Sky* was going to be an eclectic and experimental blend of ideas offered with the full force of youth. 'Your Song' taught us to listen for how each element supported the vision of the whole on *Elton John*. 'Ballad of a Well-Known Gun' let us know that *Tumbleweed Connection* was going to take us out West and rock. 'Tiny Dancer' assured us that all that rocking had not shaken the brains out of Elton's head, and that *Madman Across the Water* would deliver unconventionally structured perspective-driven stories.

Honky Château leads off with 'Honky Cat' (in French, 'cat' is 'chat', so the title represents a slightly hidden homage to the band's new recording haven), a blisteringly paced number expanding on Bernie's experience as a country mouse coming to the big city, where he is warned repeatedly to 'get back' to the safe and unchanging world he knew. Musically, the piece is a festival of frenetic syncopation, where so much is happening that the brain boggles before the chaos threatening to break out all around. A simplistic critique would be to say that this is what you get when the musicians are given free rein to do what they want. But that would be to ignore Elton's repeatedly demonstrated skill of subtly telling stories through structure. 'Honky Cat' is all about a country kid finding himself stunned before the imposing big city, a feeling perfectly conveyed here by Elton and the band through the multiplicity of instruments, playing as fast as they can, each a fully developed voice in its own right, competing to be heard in the bustle that is undeniably seductive and definitely more than a little dangerous to the uninitiated.

At the opposite end of the spectrum from the alluring pace of city life is that described in 'Mellow', a love song to the idyllic existence that Bernie and Maxine had found at their whimsically named cottage, Piglet-in-the-Wilds. Elton's languorous music echoes Bernie's lyrics, which speaks to the simple pleasures of long hours spent doing nothing in particular: trips to town to buy beer and lots of sex. The whole affair is enlivened by the presence of Jean-Luc Ponty's (*b.*1942) electric violin improvisations but at the same time weighed down by the dark clouds surrounding the lyrics. The Maxine of 'Tiny Dancer', who had interests and personality, has been reduced here to a succession of body features that Bernie finds captivating. It's one of those cases where knowing the subject of a song reduces rather than enhances one's pleasure in it, but if there's a silver lining, it's that the lyrics are still much better than most depictions of women in pop music from its time.

Leaving behind portentous domestic omens, we come to the topic of suicide. When Elton and Bernie took up the topic in 1972 for 'I Think I'm Going to Kill Myself', focusing on a shallow youth threatening suicide over having a 10.00 pm curfew and lack of sexual access to Brigitte Bardot (*b.*1934), they left no doubt about the satirical intent of their work. Set to a jaunty honky tonk piano stroll, with an extended section featuring the tap dancing skills of Bonzo Dog Doo-Dah Band drummer Larry 'Legs' Smith, concluding with Elton hooting 'Kill myself!' and 'Suicide!'. Half a century later, the song has taken on extra meaning in the age of social media, when performing oversized and melodramatic acts out of all proportion to their prompting stimuli to escape boredom and gain clout ('I'd like to see what the papers say') has become a normal and accepted way of spending one's short time on this planet.

'Susie (Dramas)' is a historically significant piece in the Elton canon, representing the first time that Johnstone switched from the world of mandolins, sitars and acoustic guitars that were his folksy comfort zone, and laid down a solo on the electric guitar at the urging of Elton. Beyond that, it's another song about a girl who drives the narrator crazy with her moonlight lovemaking, dancing and black eyes. The instrumental work is great, and the clarity of Olsson's drum here more than justifies the two days spent finding the perfect recording balance for every range of his kit, but spoiled by so many great Bernie lyrics centring around compelling characters, it's hard not be a bit let down by Susie as a protagonist.

Next on the album we have one of the greatest songs ever recorded, 'Rocket Man (I Think It's Going to Be a Long, Long Time)'. Bernie's reworking of the 1970 song 'Rocket Man' by Pearls Before Swine is both a return to the form of 'Your Song', 'Tiny Dancer' and 'Levon', and something entirely new. It's true that the overall form that had been perfected with Dudgeon and Buckmaster of a gradual layering of musical elements is at work here, with the vocal backgrounds provided by the golden trio of Murray, Olsson and Johnstone (which, once Dudgeon figured out how to record and mix their very different voices, would become a staple of Elton's music in the future) and the spacey synth crunches of David Hentschel (*b*.1952) being the elements that kick the mid-song development up into the stratosphere. At the same time, Elton seems to be pulling back on some of the elements that might have kept 'Tiny Dancer' from success, and in particular places the chorus right where we'd traditionally expect it, after the first verse. Though having a relatively traditional verse-chorus-verse-chorus structure, each run through features such different instrumentation that even when singing the same words, we get an entirely different sense from them each time.

There are two schools of thought about the starting track on the second side, 'Salvation'. One, which is backed by the band's assertions that everyone expected 'Salvation' to be the first single released from the album, is that the song was meant as a deep call to brotherhood through the defeat of the devil and a finding of one's salvation in the gospel. Before I knew those facts I always interpreted the song as a clever parody of the worst aspects of glum Sunday morning church music. As much, however, as I desire it to be the case that 'Salvation' represents a more subtle version of the dig at revivalist hucksterism we saw in 'Can I Put You On?', I have to admit it's probably not the case, and that it is what it seems to be: a straightforward, lyrically clunky Christian song.

'Slave' is the song on the album that most misses the genius of Buckmaster. Portraying the realities of nineteenth century American slavery is a weighty challenge requiring tact, particularly when the creators and performers of the song are not of African heritage. Looking ahead to Buckmaster's arrangement of 'Have Mercy on the Criminal', which successfully set the anguish of a hunted prisoner in a dramatic structure that conveyed both the fundamental dignity of the chased man and the terror of the situation he was in, we get a glimpse of what might have been. As it is, I can't fathom what they were thinking. The first run-through of the track, which was published in 1992 on *Rare Masters*, is a hyper-fast almost Jerry Lee Lewis (1935–2022) style rocker, which the band laughed out loud at upon hearing it for the first time, so incongruous was the delivery as against Bernie's dark lyrics. The solution to this problem wasn't to go back to first principles and fundamentally rework the song, but rather to do the same thing, but much slower, with Johnstone encouraged to play a variety of instruments to produce a swampy sound. The result was better but was still problematic. The stereotyped hokey Southern riffs, the presence of conga drums, the steel guitar solo, and the clunky goofiness of the chorus' culminating moment, when Elton drags the word 'Sla-a-a-a-a-ave' across a descending scale, all combine to make a particularly unapt setting for Bernie's lyrics, which I'm surprised Dudgeon's usually spot-on instincts allowed through to the final album.

With 'Amy' we see Elton doing a few very Elton things with his chord work, including a steady back and forth between the tonic and the IV chord from the song's parallel major key, and the use of chords separated by a third and which have two notes in common but totally opposed modalities. Jean-Luc Ponty is on the scene again, adding his characteristic high energy electric violin to the track, and in post-production Dudgeon brought in Ray Cooper to lay down some congas. Musically the rollicking track is firing on all cylinders, which brings us once again to the question of what all this is for. One theory holds that the song is a joke aimed at Dudgeon's wife, whose nickname was Amy, and who was reportedly often frustrated by Elton's behaviour. So, Bernie wrote these lyrics, about a young man sexually fascinated by a 'fab and insane' older lady named Amy, apparently as either a generally well meant if over the top way for Elton to thaw the ice between them, or as a joke meant to cause embarrassment. I can't imagine the latter being the case for someone as perpetually concerned about the comfort and feelings of other people as Elton, so I'm going with the former, in which case we can listen with clean consciences to this big and delightful campy romp in the name of breaking down barriers between individuals in the silliest way possible.

Thus far, *Honky Château*'s second side has leaned towards the uneven, with flashes of fun intermixed with fascinating misses but just when you're wondering if Elton and the lads have lost their way, along comes 'Mona Lisas and Mad Hatters', another absolute gem in the Elton pantheon. Unlike most of the songs on *Honky Château*, which Bernie composed on site, this song had its origins in 1970, when Elton and Bernie were on tour in New York and Bernie witnessed a man get gunned down by the police outside his window. The experience shook him and he wrote down the lyrics as a direct counterpoint to the romanticisation of New York that he'd imbibed in his youth through songs like Ben E. King's (1938–2015) 'Spanish Harlem' (1960), which speaks of a red rose growing up through the concrete of a Spanish Harlem street, a rose which is yet 'soft and sweet and dreaming' despite the difficulties it has known. That myth, of beauty and softness in the big city, was exploded for Bernie that night, causing him to write that 'Now I know that rose trees never grow in New York City'.

It would have been the easiest and most understandable thing for Bernie to dive deeper into that disillusionment, railing as so many have done against the despair rising up from the pavement of New York's streets, but Bernie's take is characteristically more complex than that, aided in that task through explorations of the city helmed by his friend Eric van Lustbader. While recognising that New York is a city of 100 small horrors he takes time to understand how the hardest of these people, the bankers and lawyers, became who they are, kept in their offices, blinded by the city lights, bent to their tasks so they can't look up and see that simplest of things, the sky. Even the successful are plodding along, living a deprived semi-life, but the solution is ultimately not despair, but the warmth of other people who can be found even in a place like New York City. Lyrics that started by rejecting the simplistic narrative of King's rose work their way around to a new space of semi reconciliation and Elton and the band instinctively give Bernie's lyrics space to breath, eschewing all percussion, setting the words in a soft web of piano, acoustic guitar, mandolin and bass, while Elton's voice radiates a warmth full of pity for the panorama before him and of gratitude for the light that others bring with them into these dark places.

It shouldn't be too surprising that the album that began as differently from *Madman Across the Water* as possible also ends that way. There can be few tracks in the Elton canon as different as the mournful, self-sacrificial 'Goodbye' and the jolly romp that is 'Hercules'. The song is solidly in the spirit of late 1950s rock 'n roll, where the focus is on everyone simply having a good time. While Johnstone, Murray and Olsson intone shoo bop do wops, Dudgeon gets in on the action both with loose backup vocals added in post and by playing a ludicrous whistle that's supposed to represent a rhinoceros for some reason, and Elton seems to be having the time of his life. After the weighty journeys through themes of slavery, damnation and murder that dot the second side of *Honky Château*, 'Hercules' comes in like a breath of fresh air, encouraging us to forget all that reality for a moment, get out of our chairs and dance.

The Stats

Album/Single	US	UK	Australia	Canada
Honky Château	1	2	4	3
	P	G	P	
'Rocket Man (I Think It's Going to Be a Long, Long Time)'/'Suzie (Dramas)'	6	2	13	8
'Honky Cat'/'Slave'	8	31	78	10

The Players

Elton John: vocals, acoustic piano (1 to 6 and 8 to 10), Fender Rhodes (1), Hammond organ (2 and 4) and harmonium (6)

David Hentschel: ARP synthesizer (5 and 10) (credited as 'David Henschel' on sleeve)

Davey Johnstone: banjo (1 and 7), electric, acoustic and slide guitars (2 to 10), backing vocals (3, 5, 6, 8 and 10), steel guitar (7) and mandolin (9)

Dee Murray: bass guitar and backing vocals (3, 5, 6, 8 and 10)

Nigel Olsson: drums (1 to 8 and 10), tambourine (2 and 4), backing vocals (3, 5, 6, 8 and 10) and congas (7)

Ray Cooper: congas (8)

Jean-Louis Chautemps: saxophone (1)

Alain Hatot: saxophone (1)

Jacques Bolognesi: trombone (1)

Ivan Jullien: trumpet (1)

Jean-Luc Ponty: electric violin (2 and 8)

'Legs' Larry Smith: tap dance (3)

Gus Dudgeon: brass arrangements (1), additional backing vocals (10) and rhinoceros whistle (10)

Madeline Bell: backing vocals (6)
Tony Hazzard: backing vocals (6) and additional backing vocals (10)
Liza Strike: backing vocals (6)
Larry Steel: backing vocals (6)

The Tracks

Side one:
1. 'Honky Cat' (John, Taupin) (5.12)
2. 'Mellow' (John, Taupin) (5.33)
3. 'I Think I'm Going to Kill Myself' (John, Taupin) (3.35)
4. 'Susie (Dramas)' (John, Taupin) (3.25)
5. 'Rocket Man (I Think It's Going to Be a Long, Long Time)' (John, Taupin) (4.40)

Side two:
6. 'Salvation' (John, Taupin) (3.59)
7. 'Slave' (John, Taupin) (4.22)
8. 'Amy' (John, Taupin) (4.03)
9. 'Mona Lisas and Mad Hatters' (John, Taupin) (5.01)
10. 'Hercules' (John, Taupin) (5.21)

Musician's Corner:

'Rocket Man (I Think It's Going to Be a Long, Long Time)'

There are so many things going on with this song musically. We begin with that same G minor 7 chord that formed the opening dirge of 'Friends'. What is really arresting is how quickly Elton knocks us out of that place, the second measure being anchored in a C9 chord.

Now, in G minor, the four chord should be a C minor thing. That is what hundreds of years of hearing songs in the Western tradition has primed us for, but here on the second bar, we're given this major shaped thing, but for only a fraction of a moment before we get slammed back into G minor, and this whiplash is going to be the defining characteristic of the verses, with sometimes C11 taking the place of C9. Psychologically, this bends our brain back and forth like a piece of cardboard, until we don't quite know what to think. It's so weird and I love it.

In between slapping us around with that Gm7-C9/11 transition, Elton does another bit of brain bending with the 'I'm gonna be high'-type portions of the verse. Everything is trending upwards, with words like 'high' and 'timeless' accompanying that vocal climb towards a high B flat. But look at what's happening with the chords:

Just as the vocal line is going up, the bass note is heading downwards, again adding this sense of ambivalence to the section. In the background, our brains are freaking out trying to decide what we should be feeling here, who we should trust, and that confusion is a large part of what makes this song so compelling.

The chorus is lodged firmly in B flat major, which is the relative major of G minor, so what we might expect is that we are heading into more straightforward triumphant waters, though with those tinges of ambiguity left over from the still fresh connections to the earlier relative minor key. And that's largely what we have here, except Elton's not quite done messing with us because, right at the moment of self-declaration, 'I'm a Rocket Man', Elton goes right back to that C chord that doesn't belong in the key of B flat any more than it did in the key of G minor. In short, listening to 'Rocket Man (I Think It's Going to Be a Long, Long Time)' is more than a journey through an astronaut's life, it's a journey through everything that a musician can do to confound our expectations for dramatic purposes.

Chapter 8

Don't Shoot Me I'm Only the Piano Player

Recorded: 10 to 19 June 1972
Released: 22 January 1973
Producer: Gus Dudgeon

The Story

The unambiguous global success of *Honky Château* meant that, for the first time, Elton and Bernie were entering a new album without any pressure to radically change direction in their methodology or sound. People seemed to like the more straightforward lyrics and rock drive of *Honky* so it made sense to keep the winning streak going by adhering to the formula. For *Don't Shoot Me I'm Only the Piano Player*, Elton used the same recording studio, the same producer, the same musicians and the same accelerated routine that had been employed on *Honky Château*, the only significant change was the return of Buckmaster but only as an over-dubber of strings onto already recorded tracks, not as an arranger.

The watchword on *Don't Shoot Me I'm Only the Piano Player* was spontaneity. Elton wrote twelve songs in a record-breaking two days, with everything rehearsed and recorded as quickly as possible under the guiding philosophy that overthinking a song dulled its edges and killed the freshness of the recording process. With anybody but Elton at the helm, that approach could have spelled disaster, but it was an even greater success than *Honky Château*, its occasional theme of nostalgia for the early days of rock 'n roll striking a chord in English speaking countries that stood in good need of a bit of escapism from the political realities of the time. Those who were teenagers during the heyday of Little Richard and Jerry Lee Lewis were now in their early thirties, a little bit worse for the journey, and ready to return with Elton to the sounds of a simpler time.

Critics noted with approval that Bernie seemed to be moving towards simpler stories with clearer characters, with but a few stalwart souls expressing dismay at the toning down of Bernie's challenging side. Meanwhile, Johnstone had distinctly grown into the electric guitar that Elton had thrust his way, producing moments of towering narrative poignancy, as in the triple layered guitarwork of 'Have Mercy on the Criminal' or the crunching sinister refrains of 'Midnight Creeper'. More importantly, the band had truly got the hang of how best to support Bernie's words with their instruments and background vocals.

Don't Shoot Me I'm Only the Piano Player perfected the formula originated in *Honky Château*, and the public wasn't long in responding, sending it to the top of the charts, with both of its singles breaking easily into the Top 10 on both sides of the Atlantic. The blend of unabashed retro rock and simple character tales effectively told, with occasional Buckmaster flourishes to keep the old school fans happy, and dark lyrics given up-tempo settings was on point, and would serve as the template for Elton's biggest recording project to date, a double LP that many still consider his finest work.

The Songs

'Daniel' represents a new direction for Elton on many levels. The new soundscape lacks the signature tones of an acoustic piano and instead delivers a binormal distribution of pitches, with the bass and drums ringing in the low register, and the synth – played by Ken Scott (*b*.1947) – and flute-approximating Mellotron – played by Elton – taking most of the attention in the higher register. That lack of a percussive piano in the middle space might have been a problem, but Dudgeon found a solution to the issue by waking Elton early one morning so that he could sing the song without any preparation, hoping that the natural roughness of his I just woke up voice would grit up his performance. It worked and provided the missing element linking together the two extremes of the song's sound profile and demonstrating that Elton and the band could successfully navigate new approaches to Bernie's material that didn't involve an obligation to have a traditional piano element.

The song is an example of a new drive for compression. Bernie's story of a Vietnam veteran no longer able to live with the contradiction between his hero status and his knowledge of what he and his fellow soldiers experienced, to the point that he feels compelled to leave the US to find some sense of peace is a complicated tale that could easily have been another six or seven minute character-driven epic, but by cutting out blocks of the original poem (at least according to Johnstone – Bernie says he can't remember one way or another if that happened), the end song clocked in at under four minutes, in fact the same length as 'Crocodile Rock' from later in the album. The new run time made it easier to cajole Dick James into releasing it as the album's second single and the missing material made Daniel more of a mystery that listeners are still trying to solve.

As if to reassure listeners who were worried that Elton had gone completely electric in an act of betrayal, the second track on *Don't Shoot Me*, 'Teacher I Need You', begins with the piano front and centre, with triplet arpeggios that herald the arrival of a quick paced rocker, that soon bounces forward with youthful exuberance on the back of Murray's perfectly judged back to basics bass groove. Bernie's lyrics focus on an aspect of growing up that hadn't really been touched by the pop universe before: the teacher crush. Some Elton fans have put themselves in an apoplectic state trying to decide whether these are innocent lyrics about a young boy appreciating a teacher who had brightened his life or a lusty fantasy rocker on par with Van Halen's

'Hot for Teacher' (1984). The brilliance of the lyrics is that the answer to both of those questions is, yes! Murray, Olsson and Johnstone add background harmonies that enhance the nostalgia of the song about a time when nothing made sense, and everything was brand new.

If you listen to 'Elderberry Wine' and don't understand English, you'd most likely think that it was an homage of some sort to the novelty dance craze of the early 1960s, with its groovy brass embellishments, rhythmic introductory honky tonk piano matched beat for beat by the drums, and playful vocalisations. If, conversely, you only read the text and had a little knowledge of Bernie's story following its composition, you would likely feel a shiver of prophecy and wonder how Elton and the band could ever match the pathos of the lyrics. The song is about a man whose life comes to a standstill after his wife leaves him. As the song progresses, we learn why she left, as he laments about how he can't get his life back together without having 'a wife in line' to 'pick the crop' of elderberries required to make his favourite drink. That image, of a woman taking the emotional brunt of her husband's addiction to alcohol, was prescient of the road ahead, as Bernie regularly passed out drunk with Rod Stewart (*b*.1945) and Ringo Starr (*b*.1940) while sinking further into alcoholism. In 1976, the first of Bernie's four marriages ended in divorce.

I can only think of two explanations for the massive but certainly compelling distance between the spirit of the words and that of the music: first, the status of wine as the beverage of choice for relaxation at the château. If you hone in on the line, 'Drunk all the time, feeling fine on elderberry wine' you might convince yourself that this song is mainly a paean to bacchanalia with intermittent elements of tragedy. Second, Elton's sense of humour and defiance simply turns this way sometimes. When presented with a downer lyric like 'Pain' or 'Billy Bones and the White Bird' sometimes he chooses to confront it with the most powerful weapon in his arsenal, rock 'n roll, sweeping the darkness away and showing us all how to dance even through our misery.

'Blues for My Baby and Me' is something of an enticing confoundment. While 'Daniel' had large chunks of its compelling hero's story shorn away, 'Blues for My Baby and Me', a relatively simple tale of a guy and a girl running away together under the disapproving eye of the girl's father, is given a luxurious five minutes and thirty-nine seconds to see itself through. Some see Buckmaster's name on the song and roll their eyes and say, 'Of course, if Buckmaster is on it, it can't be less than five minutes' but that's the thing, Buckmaster wasn't brought on board until after all the recording wrapped and Elton was safely in Paris. All he could do was layer in strings and winds over what was already in place. Don't get me wrong, I really like how this song is paced, it's just always confused me why Daniel's story wasn't given a similar lot of album real estate to tell his full tale.

Of course, the other thing that's always confused me about this track is Johnstone's sitar. You hear some explanations that Dudgeon wanted this brought on to bring something sonically different into the song, to break up the acreage of strings and piano a bit. I can see that, but as the song is about a journey from the American heartland, where sitars were few and far between in 1972, its presence always seemed strange to me until I started thinking of it not as a representation of where they had been, but where they're going, out to California where Eastern mysticism was formalising itself into new vogues, with the sitar acting as a beacon to experience new things, thoroughly justifying its presence on the track.

Okay, it's time for 'Midnight Creeper', everyone's favourite serial killer jam. One might wonder why it entered Bernie's mind to write about a man with victims locked in his cellar with not the faintest sense of conscience about his actions, and then why Elton set it as a danceable rock number replete with horn section. Clearly, one important reference for this dark turn is The Rolling Stones' 'Midnight Rambler' (1969) off their *Let It Bleed* (1969) album, which was a portrayal of the life of the Boston Strangler (1931–1973), a mass murderer of the early 1960s. A further clue to the mystery is perhaps located in a statement that Elton made about how easy it was to write *Don't Shoot Me I'm Only the Piano Player* because of the sheer density of new musical ideas in the air in the early 1970s, a time when, as he put it, 'every week brought a dozen or so new top-quality records to store shelves to be consumed and mined for ideas.' One of the figures looming during this time was Alice Cooper, who was bringing live performance to a spectacle that Elton strove to match in his own shows. In November 1971, Cooper released the album *Killer*, which explored the thrills of dark topics. With the Zodiac killings still an ongoing investigation, but before the world knew about killers like Ted Bundy (1946–1989, captured 1975), 'Midnight Creeper' lives in that time when the mass murderer was still rare enough to be titillating to ponder.

Beginning side two is 'Have Mercy on the Criminal', the most ambitious track on *Don't Shoot Me I'm Only the Piano Player* and which I of course, for no actual reason, see as the continuation of the story in 'Rotten Peaches'. Everything here is operating at the highest level, beginning with the frenzied call and response between Johnstone's electric guitar and Buckmaster's strings, with the bass notes of Elton's piano pounding underneath. That 'chase' motif is easy to appreciate, but I like even more the little call and responses in the verse between the piano and the electric guitar set way back in the mix, like the voices of a search party calling to each other in the distance as they close in on their target. The whole piece, in fact, is rife through with these twirling figures that turn back around on themselves, now in the strings, now on the piano, the whole acoustic space being combed back and forth. The rules for fusing strings with rock instruments that Buckmaster laid down on *Elton John* are perfected here, with the ascending, descending and twisting figures in the strings trading off with the sudden shrieks of the electric guitar, creating this sense of discovery that utilises the best features of both the classical and rock traditions. Special mention should also be made to Johnstone's electric solo, the second half of which features a layering of guitar tracks recorded separately, which produce a perfect atmosphere of dread and dire inevitability. Though never released as a single, 'Have

Mercy on the Criminal' has continued to be a favourite component of Elton's live show thanks to its cinematic storytelling and instrumental moments.

For years, it was assumed that 'I'm Gonna Be a Teenage Idol' was a song about T-Rex founder Marc Bolan (1947–1977), but in *Scattershot* Bernie denies this, stating that the would-be teenage idol of his lyrics is more of a composite figure. Since Bolan, however, is likely an important component, it's worth taking a little time to acknowledge him and the place he played in the early days of Elton's career. In 1967 Bolan, former guitarist with the band John's Children, struck out on his own and formed his own group, Tyrannosaurus Rex, fired by the ambition to become the next big thing in pop music. That band, and its eclectic folk music sensibilities marshalled in support of Bolan's gift for confounding imagery ('Oh Debora, always look like a zebra'), performed well, but it wasn't until 1970, when Bolan turned the band electric and shortened its name to T-Rex, that it truly took off, with the single 'Ride a White Swan' (1972) an omnipresent force on radio stations in 1970. Bolan and Elton, both having risen at about the same time, and both known for the extravagance of their style, became good friends in time (as a matter of fact, put this book down right now and go to YouTube and look for the clip of Elton, Bolan and Ringo Starr performing 'Tutti Frutti' together for Bolan's film *Born to Boogie* (1972), if for no other reason than to watch Elton murder the piano during the instrumental break). Elton wanted Bernie to write a song about Bolan, who had an endearing tendency to make grandiose claims about his own fame, including once stating that he'd sold 1 million records in a single morning but Bernie couldn't just write a song about Bolan and instead keyed into the general type of figure of which he was one significant instantiation. The result was 'I'm Going to Be a Teenage Idol', the story of a young man determined to make it in rock 'n roll, if only he can catch a break. Elton punctuates the song's sliding pulse with off-beat piano stabs and slurs.

There are small episodes of inventiveness throughout 'Teenage Idol' but maybe my favourite is at the line 'turn this guitar into a Tommy-gun' (Bolan wore his guitar low on his hip at roughly gun holster level, wielding it like a weapon during his solos while wandering the stage), which is followed by a series of blasts from the horns, as of a volley of machine gun bullets being hurled forth by the band. It's aggressively literal and ridiculous, and I love it so much.

By *Don't Shoot Me I'm Only the Piano Player*, Bernie had come a long way from the romanticisation from afar that characterised his conception of the South on *Tumbleweed Connection*. Whether through more direct contact as a result of Elton's touring, or through personal growth via a wider net of acquaintances, Bernie had come to see the real darkness of the Southern landscape, and poured it all into 'Texan Love Song', a piece which delves deep into the violent aversion to difference that manifested itself in the racism, anti-intellectualism and poverty of spirit that characterised the white Southern male at his worst. Elton, for his part, is locked into Bernie's message, singing in a stereotyped Southern drawl that makes his vocalisations on 'Country Comfort' seem restrained. Musically, the stage is cleared of instruments to focus all attention on the virulence of the character Elton's portraying.

Having moved through the dark valley of Southern intolerance, Elton rewards us with a bit of levity in the form of 'Crocodile Rock', an anything goes love song about the late 1950s (according to Bernie) and early 1960s (according to Elton) rock 'n roll that the pair grew up with, which we'll be talking about later, so we'll move to the album closer, 'High Flying Bird'. Looking back, it's telling how many of the songs on *Don't Shoot Me I'm Only the Piano Player* are about loss – 'Elderberry Wine' is about a man's brutishness costing him his wife, 'Midnight Creeper' is about flat out murder, 'Have Mercy on the Criminal' is about the loss of freedom, 'Texan Love Song' is about white fear of the loss of their traditional values, 'Crocodile Rock' is about the passing of a beloved musical era and capping it all off we have 'High Flying Bird', which is likely about suicide and forms a sombre pair with 'Elderberry Wine'. Whereas 'Elderberry Wine' features a woman leaving a churlish man, 'High Flying Bird' is about a decent man whose partner is deeply troubled and suffering from delusions that the one person who wants to help her the most is trying to persecute her. It's a song that resonates deeply with anyone who has ever had to care for someone with deep depression, only to be helpless in the final event when that person's inner demons take hold. The lyrics are heartbreaking and this time Elton gives himself over entirely to exploring the pathos of Bernie's words, with Murray, Olsson and Johnstone providing ethereal backing vocals. While *Honky Château* ended on a raucous celebration of life, *Don't Shoot Me I'm Only the Piano Player* closes with the sobering but true message that sometimes love isn't enough to keep those we care about bound to their own existence.

The Stats

Album/Single	US	UK	Australia	Canada
Don't Shoot Me I'm Only the Piano Player	1	1	1	1
	3P	G	3P	
'Crocodile Rock'/'Elderberry Wine'	1	5	2	1
'Daniel'/'Skyline Pigeon'	2	4		1

The Players

Elton John: vocals, Fender Rhodes (1 and 5), Mellotron (1 and 2) and acoustic piano (2 to 4, 6, 7, 9 and 10), Leslie piano (7) harmonium (8) and Farfisa organ (9)

Davey Johnstone: acoustic guitar, electric guitar, Leslie guitar and banjo (1), backing vocals (2, 7 and 10), sitar (4) and mandolin (8)

Dee Murray: bass (all tracks) and backing vocals (2, 7 and 10)

Nigel Olsson: drums (all tracks), maracas (1) and backing vocals (2, 7 and 10)
Gus Dudgeon: brass arrangements (3, 5 and 7)
Paul Buckmaster: orchestral arrangements (4 and 6)
Jean-Louis Chautemps: saxophone (3, 5 and 7)
Alain Hatot: saxophone (3, 5 and 7)
Jacques Bolognesi: trombone (3, 5 and 7)
Ivan Jullien: trumpet (3, 5 and 7)
Ken Scott: ARP synthesizer (1)

The Tracks

Side one:
1. 'Daniel' (John, Taupin) (3.55)
2. 'Teacher I Need You' (John, Taupin) (4.10)
3. 'Elderberry Wine' (John, Taupin) (3.34)
4. 'Blues for My Baby' and Me (John, Taupin) (5.39)
5. 'Midnight Creeper' (John, Taupin) (3.52)

Side two:
6. 'Have Mercy on the Criminal' (John, Taupin) (5.58)
7. 'I'm Going to be a Teenage Idol' (John, Taupin) (3.56)
8. 'Texan Love Song' (John, Taupin) (3.33)
9. 'Crocodile Rock' (John, Taupin) (3.55)
10. 'High Flying Bird' (John, Taupin) (4.12)

Musician's Corner: 'Crocodile Rock'

'We're going to do a song now which was, huh, is not one of my favourites, but we're going to do it all the same.' This was Elton's not particularly inspiring lead-in to his and Ray Cooper's performance of 'Crocodile Rock' during their legendary Moscow concert of 1979, and it is indicative of how many 'serious' Elton fans view the song. In a few years, we'll see Caleb Quaye only rejoining the band on the provision that they never play 'Crocodile Rock' and for many Elton fans, the image of Elton singing the song in a mirror-bedecked swimming cap and ostentatious feather shoulder piece while conducting a chorus of crocodiles on the *Muppet Show* is one they'd rather forget. But Elton's doing something worthwhile here, which also happens to be tremendous fun, namely paying homage to the music he grew up with, much as the inspiration for this song, Daddy Cool's track 'Eagle Rock' (1971), paid homage to the dance traditions of the 1920s African American community. This wasn't, however, a blindly nostalgic track but rather a tribute to the rock of the 1950s and 1960s in both its best and worst aspects, and to the latter end, Elton chose to perform the keyboard part on a Farfisa organ. The choice was aimed at reproducing the wonderfully obnoxious organ sound he heard growing up on records by Johnny and the Hurricanes.

The most distinct reference, however, can be heard in the chorus, where the 'laaaaa-la-la-la-la-laaaaa' is more or less a direct quote from the 'plaintive cry of a young Mexican girl' from Pat Boone's (*b*.1934) novelty recording of 'Speedy Gonzales' (1962), written by Buddy Kaye (1918–2002), and which during the verses also features the quick run up then slow walk down pulse that winds its way through 'Crocodile Rock'. While Elton and the band are doing everything they can to pull in references to the instrumentation and melodies of the past, Bernie is mirroring their efforts in the lyrics, dropping references to Bill Haley and His Comets' 'Rock Around the Clock' (1954), canonically considered the first explicitly rock 'n roll song, and 'hopping and bopping', which refer to the sock hops of the 1950s (events for teenage dancing usually held at high school gymnasiums) and The Bop (a teenage dance popular in 1957), which moved a young Jiles Richardson (1930–1959) to change his public persona to that of 'The Big Bopper'. The 'But the years went by and rock just died' line, meanwhile, is a reference to the sudden death of the golden age of rock 'n roll occasioned by Elvis Presley (1935–1977) being drafted into the army, Chuck Berry's (1926–2017) arrest on sexual assault charges, Jerry Lee Lewis's disgrace for marrying his underage cousin, Little Richard's sudden turn to gospel music, and the deaths of Buddy Holly (1936–1959), The Big Bopper and Eddie Cochran (1938–1960), all of which took place in a tight radius around the year 1959, and left a vacuum that the music industry was quick to fill with a less explosive roster of commercially produced singers who never resonated with the teenage crowd like that legendary first crop.

Chapter 9

Goodbye Yellow Brick Road

Recorded: May 1973
Released: 5 October 1973
Producer: Gus Dudgeon

The Story

Coming out of *Honky Château* and *Don't Shoot Me I'm Only the Piano Player*, Elton, Bernie, Dudgeon and the band were on a creative and commercial tear. It made sense to keep the momentum going by returning to Strawberry Studios at the Château d'Hérouville for the next album. The problem was that the château was in the middle of an ownership dispute and was unavailable. Asking around, they got a 'hot tip' from Charlie Watts (1941–2021) of The Rolling Stones that Dynamic Sound Studios in Kingston, Jamaica, where they had recorded *Goats Head Soup* (1973), was the place to be. Elton booked recording time there and headed to Jamaica in late January 1973, only to find Kingston in a state of violent agitation, the studios in the middle of a labour dispute and the studio facilities positively medieval by the château's standards.

Lacking a decent piano, the extensive web of microphones that Dudgeon used to balance the drum kit sound, and the elaborate 'inverted piano' setup that he used to eliminate the sound of the other instruments from the piano track and with Elton holed up nervously in the hotel composing on an ancient electric piano, emerging tentatively only to sample some of the legendary musical offerings of Kingston, the band nevertheless made a game attempt to record 'Saturday Night's Alright for Fighting', which emerged sounding, in Dudgeon's memorable phrase, 'Like thirteen million very small Japanese radios full crank'. The staff at Dynamic Sound Studios promised to bring in better equipment but it never materialised, and with the presence of protesters who thought nothing of blowing dangerous fiberglass dust at the band to punish them for crossing strike lines and the general unrest from the masses of the poor, the decision was made to pull up stakes, even in the face of threats by local officials to impound their equipment and rental cars to prevent them from leaving without paying the full amount for the reserved resources.

Elton and his crew made it out of the country and the decision was made to wait until the château was available again and record there. In early May 1973, the team reassembled in France, newly appreciative of the amenities offered at Strawberry Studios, and fell easily to work. Three to four songs were recorded a day. Within two weeks a solid sixteen quality songs, and also 'Jamaica Jerk-Off', were ready for mixing, enough to fill a double album in the tradition of *The White Album*. As it emerged, *Goodbye Yellow Brick Road* was everything Elton, representing the full scope of his musical interests, from towering instrumental dirges to comic novelties, and soulful hymns to barn-burning rockers. Johnstone ran wild overdubbing guitar tracks on the harder rocking tunes, while Del Newman (1930–2020), coming off his work on Cat Stevens's (*b*.1948) *Tea for the Tillerman* (1970), was brought in to fill the Buckmaster role, providing orchestral support for 'Goodbye Yellow Brick Road', 'Sweet Painted Lady' and 'I've Seen that Movie Too', while a young sax player by the name of Leroy Gómez (*b*.1950) who stumbled by the studios found himself asked to lay down tracks for 'Social Disease' and 'Screw You', and paid twice his asking rate for his efforts.

Magic was striking everywhere, even Dudgeon got in on the action, making some iconic additions to 'Bennie and the Jets' and 'Funeral for a Friend' during the mixing stages, which made their way onto the final record and thence into history. Featuring David Larkham's iconic cover art, the double album was given top-notch production and a clever advertising push that included a stunt press conference where Elton appeared over a television monitor, pretending to be halfway across the country, when, in fact, he was in a room a few feet away, answering questions from the press (even pretending to experience connection lag) before appearing suddenly in person at the post-conference party. At first, Elton worried that the cost of the album would inhibit sales but he needn't have. Almost universal critical praise and a string of solid singles sent the album not only to the top of the charts (giving Elton his third consecutive #1 in the US), but kept him there, with *Goodbye Yellow Brick Road* remaining in the American Top 200 for two full years. Some fifty years later, when Elton was putting together his farewell tour, it would be called the Farewell Yellow Brick Road tour, and featured heavily the iconography of the album, which represented for many fans the crowning moment of his recording career.

The Songs

For Elton's first double-album venture, Dudgeon believed that something of cinematic scope was required as a starter. He'd long wanted Elton to write a purely instrumental track, and in response Elton composed the sort of music that he'd like to have played at his own funeral, a mixture of pathos, triumph and rock, of almost superhero proportions. That would have been a musical event enough on its own, but Elton and Dudgeon kept adding to it. Elton felt that it was strange to have no vocals at all on the track, and so they melded onto it another song in the key of A, 'Love Lies Bleeding'. Meanwhile, in the mixing process, Dudgeon thought that the intro lacked the appropriate level of pomp and asked Twentieth Century Fox for the rights to use their famous film fanfare as the record opener but upon being turned down asked David Hentschel to compose an original synth fanfare. Hentschel listened to the album and composed a towering pipe organ intro, featuring thematic elements from the songs we hear on the album in a nod to the overtures of classic Hollywood musicals and the operatic tradition of Western Europe. With the overture dying away, we come to Elton's piano, playing mournfully in the middle of empty space before being joined by Johnstone's soaring guitar, blaring synth scales and the echoing gun-shot punctuation of Olsson's drum kit, steering us towards material that is more adventure serial soundtrack than funeral.

'Love Lies Bleeding' is another melancholic lament from a man unable to keep hold of the woman he loves in the tradition of 'Elderberry Wine' and which Elton has set in a relatively up-beat musical idiom, with the chorus refrain 'Love lies bleeding in my hands' producing this tantalising contradiction between the lyrics, which are dark, the chord, which is a cool minor version of the secondary dominant, and the exuberance with which the vocals are delivered. Between the addition of 'Love Lies Bleeding', Hentschel's fanfare, and the wind and bells, *Goodbye Yellow Brick Road*'s lead track ballooned out to just over eleven epic minutes, too long to release as a single but so sweeping in the musical territory it covers that disc jockeys used to play it anyway, and the merest hint of those wind noises over the speakers at an Elton concert has been enough to send crowds into paroxysms of joyful anticipation ever since.

After the grandeur of 'Funeral for a Friend' the album heads directly into killer's alley, representing perhaps the best three consecutive songs on any album in the rock canon: 'Candle in the Wind', 'Bennie and the Jets' and 'Goodbye Yellow Brick Road', all filing in one after another in a fireworks display of raw creativity. Lyrically, 'Candle in the Wind' is about the de-humanisation of Norma Jeane Mortenson (1926–1962) as the Hollywood machine commodified her into the persona of Marilyn Monroe. More broadly, it was an appeal to realise the humanity and pain that lurk behind the superstar facade of many who had to shoulder the burden of fame. For musicians particularly the song had an extra weight of tragedy due to the recent loss of two young talents: Janis Joplin (1943–1970) and Jim Morrison.

Elton's music stays within the traditional structure of a hymn, with the chord changes almost entirely laying within the realm of the expected, allowing us to focus on the human tragedy in the words instead of being distracted by the tonal progressions. Whereas Elton usually let the band construct their own parts without interference in this instance Elton had a guitar lick that he wanted Johnstone to add while he sang the words 'candle in the wind', which Johnstone thought was irredeemably hokey, nearly refusing to perform it until Elton insisted. That lick is now iconic and Johnstone realised that Elton's instinct was spot on and laid an extra harmony track for its recurrence towards the song's end. Besides Elton's poignant melody, the song is made by the vocal backings of Murray, Olsson and Johnstone laid down as was their habit when Elton was no longer in the studio so that they could have more time to perfect their approach. The result was a wall of lamentation in descending lines that meant more work for Dudgeon (how the human voice produces each of the sounds involved is significantly different) but that gives the sense of the larger world outside of Elton adding their own sorrow to the singer's.

A 180° turn in atmosphere and theme brings us to the futuristic android rock of 'Bennie and the Jets', a glorious study in barely controlled chaos, with everyone involved adding their own flashes of whimsy, beginning from the first chord. On the master recording, for some reason, several seconds before they began laying down the proper song, Elton hit a single chord on the piano. In production, that errant chord would usually have been muted out, but its randomness reminded Dudgeon of a live performance so he decided to do what he did with 'Rock and Roll Madonna' and patch in previously recorded live audience sounds and slap some reverb onto Elton's voice to make it sound more like the track was recorded in concert. What pushed this idea over the top was the recurrence of wonderfully canned applause after the mid-song piano solo.

The masterpiece, however, comes with the inserted audience clap-along segments, as worked out by Dudgeon and Hentschel post-production. The whole thing is a subtle satire at the tendency of British audiences to always clap along on the on-beat. So, the producers set to work not only laying down a clap track that was aggressively on the wrong beat but also delayed so that it fell just to the wrong side of that beat, producing perfectly the sense of a band playing to a slightly sloshed British audience doing their level best to participate.

Meanwhile, Elton's having a field day making the piano as percussive as possible in line with Bernie's vision of 'Bennie and the Jets' as a futuristic android band, while vocally stuttering on the B of Bennie in the chorus like a malfunctioning robot, and drawing out the s of Jets seemingly just for the oddball fun of it. Everyone is having the time of their lives figuring out how to make the song as strange as possible, and by the end the song was so out there that American promoters had to convince Elton to release it as a single as he thought that there was no way it could be a hit. However, it was released and hit not only #1 on the Billboard Hot 100, but #15 on the Hot Soul charts.

By the by, in case you were wondering about who the Bennie in 'Bennie and the Jets' is, the best theory seems to be that it is a reference to Sally Bennington, who went by the nickname 'Bennie' and was considered by a young Bernie to be the most beautiful woman he'd ever seen.

One could write an entire book about the interesting things going on in 'Goodbye Yellow Brick Road', which seems the summit of so many aspects of Elton and the band's craft, from vocal expansiveness and song architecture to arrangement and production, to backing vocals and lyrical impact. It is simply a perfect song. Bernie's lyrics about a young kept man trapped by a bored upper society woman, yearning for a return to his simpler rural life, is echoed brilliantly in Elton's chord choices. The verses are master classes in how you convey aimlessness in music. With the song's intro establishing the key of F major, we'd expect to start the verse there as well, but instead start on G minor, which is the same minor secondary dominant move we heard in 'Love Lies Bleeding' and which here sets up a downwards journey through the circle of fifths, as we move from G to C to F to B flat to E flat in a steady rootless progression further and further away from our tonic chord that highlights the anchorless existence the song's protagonist is trapped in, having his needs attended to but without any real purpose to his existence. Those verses then culminate in the high D-flat moment of 'singing the blues', a note of course nowhere in the key signature of F, and which sets up movement even further from the key we're in, as we explore foreign chords like A flat major and B flat minor, in a moment that feels, for all its expansive scope, like the chorus, until we get to the real chorus, which lands us at last firmly back in F, only to meet a whole new roster of borrowed chords that cycle right back into the sustained notes of the deceptive chorus, landing us only at the end back in F, and with it some sense that our hero has slipped the confines of his cage and made it back home. Perfection.

When I was a kid, I remember going to the record store and reading the song names on the back of all the Elton CD's and being instantly struck by the presence of a song called 'This Song Has No Title'. I wanted to know what that song was all about and made *Goodbye Yellow Brick Road* the third Elton album I ever bought, not to hear the title track or 'Candle in the Wind' but to get to the bottom of 'This Song Has No Title'. Suffice to say, the song wasn't what I was expecting, and after that initial disappointment of not getting a Tom Lehrer (*b.*1928) style send-up, what I found was that each time I listened to the record, I liked it more and soon identified with it more than any other song on the album. After all, it's about an enthusiastic young man who wants to learn everything he can, experience all he can and distil that into art as fast as he can, in the full rush of youthful impatience to devour and create in a breathless cycle that was all too familiar to me. 'If we're all going somewhere, let's get there soon', was the life motto I didn't know I had until Bernie threw it into my lap.

Musically, 'This Song Has No Title' stands as the only song on *Goodbye Yellow Brick Road* recorded entirely by Elton, providing his own harmonic vocal accompaniment and his own organ work. It's an interesting question why Elton picked this one as a pure solo, my thought being that it is the most personal song on the album, one about a young person starting out on their own before having chance to meet a group of like-minded individuals, and performing that song by one's self simply makes sense.

'Grey Seal' distinguishes itself from the rest of *Goodbye* in the boundless verbal imagery of the lyrics, which hearkens back to *Empty Sky* and *Elton John*, and for good reason. The track dates back to the old bunk-bed days, when Elton recorded it as the B side to the single 'Rock and Roll Madonna', and thus represents Bernie in the full flower of his youthful arresting and evocative phraseology. The love of sound, without being tied to an overall narrative, is fully in evidence, and while Elton kept the basic melody from the original 1970 recording, the approach is different, taken at a faster pace driven from the start by Elton's quick descending arpeggiated chords and the grace noted duplets of Murray's bass, taking the place of the more methodical original. The sound is also thicker, with the original relying on Elton's bare voice sitting disconcertingly far front in the mix, while the *Goodbye* version has Elton laying down secondary vocal harmony tracks. Meanwhile, the strings of the original have been entirely tossed to make room for Johnstone to quote Elton's piano figures in the electric guitar, and Olsson to go absolutely ape with the percussion. The new version definitely sounds like a more polished song, and rocks significantly harder than the original but I have to say I think the original captured the spirit of Bernie's lyrics better, the sense of wonder of sitting at the feet of somebody who has seen much with a clear eye.

And now we come to the part of every *Goodbye Yellow Brick Road* discussion that everyone dreads – what to make of 'Jamaica Jerk-Off'. To understand that reluctance, you must remember the state of Jamaica in the early 1970s. The nation had only gained full independence in 1962, which was followed by a period of economic growth for the wealthy but also an explosion of the Kingston shanty towns where the poor were compelled to reside. By 1970, economic growth had slowed down significantly, and, in 1972, a new government was brought into power to address the gross inequalities of the nation. Economic uncertainty brought with it violence, a rise in gang activity and a general misery that Michael Manley's (1924–1997) government sought to alleviate with more progressive policies that were still in their early stages when Elton and Bernie wrote 'Jamaica Jerk-Off'. At that moment, to release a reggae style song, with Englishmen imitating Jamaican exclamations in the background, with lines like, 'We're all happy in Jamaica do Jamaica Jerk-Off that way?' wasn't in the best of taste. Of course, the song might be a satire of the stereotypical view of Jamaica held by Western tourists but as I've not read about anyone concerned saying anything other than it was a joke song (Bernie doesn't even remember writing the lyrics) I'm going to guess that isn't the case.

The album finds its footing again with the closer for the first record, 'I've Seen That Movie Too', where Elton sets the tone with a blues-infused noir-style piano intro. The lyrics find our protagonist faced with their partner's feeble attempts to cover up a personal betrayal, not behaving as themself but rather slipping into a stereotypical silver screen role. Elton conveys the deception at the lyrics' heart through the steady descent of his bass notes, the F-Eb and Db-C progression that recurs throughout the song, while Johnstone employs striking alternations of inverted electric guitar work to create a swirling destabilised atmosphere in the instrumental section, backed by Del Newman's (1930–2020) solid arrangement of strings.

The first side of the second LP of *Goodbye* is basically the 'Three doomed girls and also Danny Bailey' section of the record. Bernie's work producing character studies of women in verse had been, to date, on the inconsistent side, with each deeply conceived 'Tiny Dancer' seeming to have its shallower 'Mellow'-like counterpart. Disc two, side one, continues this trend, with two poignant pictures of women doomed by the way society treats people of their persuasion and one that was misogynistic even for its time, and has seemingly only got worse since. Let's dive in, shall we?

With 'Sweet Painted Lady' we return to the restless dock life of 'Sails', only now through the eyes of a worn sex worker rather than through those of adventuring siblings playing pirate games on the pier. Bernie's lyrics portray someone who has grown used to her inescapable existence. Far from the usual rock 'n roll sex ballad, 'Sweet Painted Lady' presents us with sex as a mechanical act paid for by a string of anonymous men. Elton picks up on the vibe of indifferent coitus and replicates it in his vocals, which are deadpan and weary, and in the drowsy saloon piano work that drifts in and out, while Newman has the particular inspiration of bringing in a singular brass instrument to play a lonesome melodic line in the background, only to hand that role off to a desultory sounding accordion, which perfectly reinforces the atmosphere of lone individuals, coming and going, wrapped up in their own private miseries. The whole piece pulls out to the sounds of the ocean and seagulls, as we leave behind the docks and all the people there going through their grim daily routines. It is a pitch-perfect musical portrait that smartly dials back on instrumental virtuosity to key into the plodding despair of the subject.

And speaking of pocket masterpieces, it is now time to discuss 'The Ballad of Danny Bailey (1909–1934)', which is on every Elton fan's shortlist of songs that should have been singles. The story of Bernie's 'composite gangster' begins with a simple Dragnet-style blast from the piano, appropriate to the theme at hand, and for the first lines of the song, all we have is Elton's voice emanating from the void with a few piano chords here and there, the blast of a gun that the team fired and recorded at 4.00 am, and one drum hit from Olsson, as we begin Bailey's story at its end, the moment of his early death. Murray and Newman shine on this track, providing strings and bass that provide density and volume around Elton's classic stutter-stepping piano style that pushes the piece forward in heavy strides. While the vocals are great, delivered in a low register, my favourite part is the longer instrumental closeout that sees all the instruments in their own way joining the increasingly off-kilter funeral procession in honour of Kentucky's favourite son.

All right. 'Dirty Little Girl'. Here we go. From time to time, Elton and the band were possessed of the desire to imitate The Rolling Stones. Usually, however, they restrained themselves to either paying homage to aspects of their instrumental style or to incorporating parts of Mick Jagger's (b.1943) vocal presentation, while leaving to the side the misogynistic lyrical elements characteristic of songs like 'Mother's Little Helper' or 'Under My Thumb'. That had served them well for five years, when Bernie wrote 'Dirty Little Girl', which seems to want to outdo The Rolling Stones in terms of the violent objectification of women. There are some fun things happening here musically and vocally, but they are impossible to really appreciate with these brutish lyrics.

I can't believe Bernie is being this stupid so I tend to take this song as being of a piece with 'Texan Love Song', 'Elderberry Wine' and the later 'Angeline' as a piece of satire, wherein the blatant ignorance and shoddy point of view of the narrator is being pilloried, not lionised. I take 'Dirty Little Girl' to be Bernie's sly swipe at The Rolling Stones' lyric-writing 'craft' and Elton's exaggerated vocal style on the song to be his way of accentuating that theme. I have no evidence for this other than how inexplicable the track is if it is meant in earnest, but if it lets us get through the five minutes of this song, feel free to believe it with me for a while.

Back to the good stuff. 'All the Girls Love Alice' is a dark song centring around the mysterious murder of a young lesbian who could never find her place in the world. I want to appreciate the strange and unique soundscape crafted by the band here. For most of the song, we are living in two worlds, that of the verses, dominated by the driving thrust of Johnstone's punching guitar and Ray Cooper's hissing, frantically metronomic tambourine, which is perfectly calibrated to let us experience the relentlessness of the hardships that formed the backbone of her life, and that of the chorus, a darkly seductive place dominated by Elton's beckoning voice and the warning crunch of David Hentschel's ARP synthesizer, inviting Alice in out of the chaos, only to throw her back again just as quickly. The instrumental concluding section strikes with all the fury of a murder scene, with the synths adding siren-like wails to Johnstone's flashes of guitar work that stab out from the bedlam like slices of a knife.

The final side of *Goodbye Yellow Brick Road* starts off without too much of a clue as to what the theme for our concluding stretch might be. 'Your Sister Can't Twist (But She Can Rock 'n Roll)' is an homage to early rock in the style of 'Crocodile Rock', with Elton spiralling out oddball carousel-like melodies on the Farfisa organ while Murray, Olsson and Johnstone treat us to a combination of Beach Boys harmonies and classic strings of nonsense syllables in the best doo-wop tradition. The song lacks the whimsical age past never to return aspect that made 'Crocodile Rock' such a bittersweet classic, but as an exercise in having fun without concurrently being reminded about the impermanence of existence, it's a simple good time.

Usually, by this point in an album expectations are low. This is where historically all the dross gets shoved, to fill up the remaining time on the record. Not so with *Goodbye Yellow Brick Road*, where the second song on the last disc is one of Elton's most popular songs, 'Saturday Night's Alright for Fighting', the straight up brawler detailing the violent days of Bernie's Lincolnshire youth and also, as it happened, those of Elton's time as a teenage piano player in a pub, where he'd occasionally have to escape through a nearby window when fights broke out among the inebriated patrons. Johnstone is firing on all pistons, laying down guitar track after guitar track to produce this thick sense of unpredictable forward motion, of blows being landed left and right while the piano man in the corner is pounding away on the keys. Elton's in full butch voice for the track and amazingly it works.

The last punch having been thrown and the combatants settled down to a good round of mutual drink-buying to celebrate their loose tooth brotherhood, the ground is now clear for one of the most delightful moments on *Goodbye*, 'Roy Rogers'. There's nothing quite so charming as an artist paying tribute to the icons of their youth, and Bernie's lyrics tell of a man, hemmed in by a not particularly meaningful life, who finds some peace and succour at the end of the day by tuning in to Roy Rogers (1911–1998) re-runs on TV or just sitting back in his armchair and remembering what it was like to be excited about something. Like 'Crocodile Rock' its lyrics are about joys passed, but unlike that song, which expresses a time never to return, there's a sense in 'Roy Rogers' that some things are so meaningful at a stage when we absorb them with all our hearts, that we will never cease to find refreshment in them. Just close your eyes and for a while everything will be okay again. Elton, who was also a great admirer of Roy Rogers growing up, is perfectly in sync with Bernie here, and writes the song in the full 'heroes never die' spirit that Bernie intended, with the culminating line 'Roy Rogers is riding tonight' ending on a high note that suggests, whenever we need them, our childhood heroes can rise up from memory and ride one more time.

Everything goes right in 'Roy Rogers' – Johnstone's slide guitar seems to be emanating from the prairie itself, Newman's string arrangement creates a carpet of sound that wraps the vocals in a warm haze of nostalgia, and my favourite detail of all, comes with Dudgeon's decision to end the song with the sound of hoof-beats heading away into the horizon. It's a detail that could have ruined the whole thing but Elton and Bernie's creation is so perfectly evocative of its theme that when those sounds arrive it's hard not to get caught up in the thrill of it.

With the end in sight, Elton and the boys decide to have a bit of purely ridiculous fun, telling the story of a filthy, aging, cynical individual who proudly labels himself a 'Social Disease'. He is an inveterate scoundrel but goes about it with such bad cheer that you can't help but love him and certainly the band have taken a shine to his tale, embellishing it with every bit of quirk they have at their disposal, from Elton's honky tonk riffs, to Johnstone's strutting banjo, to Dudgeon's decision to insert sounds of yard dogs as the song's intro, to the star run that Leroy Gómez takes laying down a just this side of intoxicated sax solo, everyone is doing their part to breathe life into this lovably dead weight to society, and it's hard not to get caught up in the fun everyone seems to be having.

Fittingly, the album that, after its unpromising start in Jamaica, would come to represent a golden era of musical camaraderie and mutually inspired creativity ends on the song 'Harmony'. In musical terms harmony is the art of finding the perfect notes to support not only where the melody is now but where it is going. Murray, Olsson and Johnstone took this message to heart, putting in hours of work to create the perfect supporting vocals for Elton's shifting chord structures. It is, in fact, not Elton's voice or piano that ends this monumental album, but the voices of the trio, supported by Newman's strings, a fact which is almost too perfect. Though there would be storm clouds in the future, here at least, Elton and the band are doing their best to support each other, without egos, experiencing a joint drive to make the best music they could together and for those magical couple of weeks in May 1973, that is what they did.

The Stats

Album/Single	US	UK	Australia	Canada
Goodbye Yellow Brick Road	1	1	1	1
'Saturday Night's Alright for Fighting'/'Jack Rabbit'/ 'Whenever You're Ready (We'll Go Steady Again)'	12	7		
'Goodbye Yellow Brick Road'/'Screw You (Young Man's Blues)'	2	6	4	1
'Bennie and the Jets'/'Harmony'	1	37	5	1
'Candle in the Wind'/'Bennie and the Jets'		11	5	

The Players

Elton John: vocals, acoustic piano (1 to 6, 8 to 10 and 12 to 17), Fender Rhodes (5 and 6), Farfisa organ (3, 5, 7 and 13) and Mellotron (5, 6 and 11)

Davey Johnstone: acoustic guitar, electric guitar, Leslie guitar, slide guitar, steel guitar, banjo and backing vocals (1, 2, 4, 10, 13 and 17)

Dee Murray: bass guitar and backing vocals (1, 2, 4, 10, 13 and 17)

Nigel Olsson: drums, congas, tambourine and backing vocals (1, 2, 4, 10, 13 and 17)

Ray Cooper: tambourine (12)

David Hentschel: ARP synthesizer (1 and 12)

Del Newman: orchestral arrangements (4, 8 to 10, 15 and 17)

David Katz: orchestra contractor (4, 8 to 10, 15 and 17)

Leroy Gómez: saxophone solo (16)

Kiki Dee: backing vocals (12)

The Tracks

Disc one, side one:
1. 'Funeral for a Friend/Love Lies Bleeding' (John, Taupin) (11.09)
2. 'Candle in the Wind' (John, Taupin) (3.50)
3. 'Bennie and the Jets' (John, Taupin) (5.23)

Disc one, side two:
4. 'Goodbye Yellow Brick Road' (John, Taupin) (3.13)
5. 'This Song Has No Title' (John, Taupin) (2.23)
6. 'Grey Seal' (John, Taupin) (4.00)
7. 'Jamaica Jerk-Off' (John, Taupin) (3.39)
8. 'I've Seen That Movie Too' (John, Taupin) (5.59)

Disc two, side one:
   9. 'Sweet Painted Lady' (John, Taupin) (3.54)
 10. 'The Ballad of Danny Bailey (1909–1934)' (John, Taupin) (4.23)
 11. 'Dirty Little Girl' (John, Taupin) (5.00)
 12. 'All the Girls Love Alice' (John, Taupin) (5.09)

Disc two, side two:
 13. 'Your Sister Can't Twist (But She Can Rock 'n Roll)' (John, Taupin) (2.42)
 14. 'Saturday Night's Alright for Fighting' (John, Taupin) (4.57)
 15. 'Roy Rogers' (John, Taupin) (4.07)
 16. 'Social Disease' (John, Taupin) (3.42)
 17. 'Harmony' (John, Taupin) (2.46)

Musician's Corner: 'All the Girls Love Alice'

With 'All the Girls Love Alice', Bernie handed Elton a dark tale of an underage lesbian found dead in a subway and left it to him to craft the lyrics into a popular song. It's a challenge of musical storytelling, and especially of tone selection and as we might expect by now Elton reaches for an out of the way key, in this case B flat minor with its five flats in the key signature.

There are a few things musically fascinating about this song in terms of how it is able to wrap such dark subject matter within the confines of a seemingly normal mid-tempo rocker. One of the ways he accomplishes this is by employing some pieces of musical language familiar from Chopin pieces he experienced during his classical training, which is the Polish master's ability to move melodies through blocks of chords that share notes. Here is an example from Chopin's *17th Prelude*, where we can see him using the top note of each chord to play a melody, while the two notes underneath slide around, but always with one point of contact with the chord that came before it (the shade bars here highlight those holdover notes):

The overall effect is this intoxicating mixture of a thick musical setting, which has equal parts motion and stasis and we see a similar structure at work in 'All the Girls Love Alice':

Here, that melody is trapped within these chords that are not entirely free to move, but are tied to each other and there's hardly a better way to encompass musically an individual trying and failing to rise above the web of decisions that will ultimately lead to their untimely end.

Meanwhile, one of the truly creepy parts of the song comes with the chorus. In terms of chords and progressions, nothing terribly weird happens in the verses, but then the chorus hits and introduces itself by way of a G diminished chord. Pop music tends to avoid these but Elton's a master not only of employing them, but having them resolve into places that are untraditional even by classical standards.

This is an unwholesome way to start a decidedly suggestive chorus. The dilemma here is that G minor, the chord that G diminished usually resolves into, isn't really part of the world of B flat minor, so Elton has it resolve instead to G flat major, which is an unusual place for G diminished to go, so once again your ears are left suspended between satisfaction and confusion, exactly the space we need to be in for Alice's story.

Elton's still not done pulling the sonic rug from under us, as later in this same chorus he does this to us, with the last mention of Alice's name hitting on the supremely alien chord of A major, two thirds of which is made up of keys not even in the signature of the piece, only to move into C flat major, which is equally disturbing in the musical atmosphere of B flat minor, before finally letting us mercifully come back to the B flat minor concluding chord:

Paying attention with half an ear, the average listener will get a sense of 'there's something wrong here' through the music alone, but listening with your full concentration, you come to discover it's a whole world of perfectly wrought wrongness, in the lyrics and the music, and with it we have one of the most entrancing journeys that Elton has yet crafted for us.

Chapter 10

Caribou

Recorded: January 1974
Released: 28 June 1974
Producer: Gus Dudgeon

The Story

Elton had a recording contract with Dick James Music that stipulated the production of two albums per year to 1975, a pace that would have broken a performer less prodigiously gifted. You might think that the double LP *Goodbye Yellow Brick Road* would have filled the quota by itself but Dick James thought otherwise, declaring that it represented only a single album and therefore Elton had to find time to produce another album in between the band's packed touring schedule.

The only free spot of any substance was ten days in early January, which might have been fine had the band returned to the familiarity of the château but Elton, after examining the facilities while on tour in the US, was taken with a new recording studio called Caribou Ranch, opened in 1972, and located high up in the Colorado Rocky Mountains. Elton's next three albums would be recorded here, as well as a string of records by Chicago and Amy Grant (*b*.1960), until the facilities were destroyed by a fire in 1985. As beloved as the studio would become to the band, however, it was nonetheless a new environment, which it took time to get acclimated to. Meanwhile, Bernie showed up late, putting a greater squeeze on Elton to write as fast as possible and giving him less variety of material to choose from.

Physically, the location of the studio at a high altitude would bring both benefits and challenges to the musicians. Dry, thin air is usually murder on singers. In the case of *Caribou*, the wear on Elton's voice compelled him to have to rerecord many vocals, a frustrating process for someone used to knocking out songs in one take. For the backup singers, conversely, the high altitude worked like a sort of magic elixir, allowing them to sing notes usually out of their range, which was great for recording, but paradoxically a problem for touring, as the band found that they physically couldn't replicate the harmonies they produced at Caribou when performing at sea level.

Cramming all the song composition into two days and all the recording into the remaining four, a schedule that would have been all but impossible for any other recording artist, *Caribou* did get made, with the result receiving different evaluations from all those concerned. Dudgeon for one couldn't stand it. Elton famously flew into a fit during the recording of 'Don't Let the Sun Go Down on Me', alternately screaming and mumbling the words and threatening to kill Dudgeon with his bare hands if he included it on the final record.

Half a century later, we have a bit more room for perspective on the album. Everyone points eagerly to the two big singles, 'The Bitch is Back' and 'Don't Let the Sun Go Down on Me' but the album also is home to the dark epic 'Ticking', which was unlike anything Elton and Bernie had tackled before and represents one of their greatest unsung achievements. Where the conception of the album as unbalanced comes from is in the relatively high percentage of novelty songs on it – tracks that are fun the first few times around, but that don't admit repeated deep listening. 'Grimsby', Elton's mock ballad to one of England's least interesting cities, 'Solar Prestige a Gammon', which is composed entirely of a meaningless mix of nonsense syllables and names of fish, and 'Stinker', which is literally a song about a fox who revels in his earthiness.

All this, however, affected sales not in the slightest. As had its predecessors, *Caribou* entered the American charts at #1, where it ultimately went double platinum and stayed in the Top 100 for a year, and both singles were in the Top 5 in the US, and Top 20 in the UK. Ultimately, the biggest impact of the album was on Elton himself, who knew full well that *Caribou* represented a slip in quality and heightened his determination to make the next album a resounding representation of his abilities as a musician, composer and storyteller.

The Songs

Caribou comes flying out of the gate with 'The Bitch is Back', a song that famously owed its title to Maxine Taupin's exclamation upon seeing Elton stomp into a room, his face bearing the tell-tale signs of another eruption brewing. Johnstone provides a unique sound courtesy of Fleetwood Mac co-founder Peter Green (1946–2020). A normal electric guitar has two 'pickups' that translate string vibrations into electrical signals. Usually, the magnets underlying those pickups are 'in phase' with each other, producing the standard coordinated electric guitar reaction to string vibrations. What Green and other guitar experimentalists did was to undo the first pickup, pull out the underlying magnet, and flip it 180° relative to the second pickup. The result is a distinctly hollow type sound that gives Johnstone's opening oscillating notes their iconic raspy punch, which pair perfectly with the machine gun bass Murray lays out under it. Bernie's lyrics are another in his series of portraits of lovable reprobates, aimed squarely at Elton and his moods which Elton, to his everlasting credit, found hilarious and worthy of the most rollicking musical effort on *Caribou*. A rollicking group effort, it even saw the return of Dusty Springfield (1939–1999) into the studio for the express purpose of joyously singing the background vocals. Fifty years on, the song is still among Elton's most popular, because it perfectly fills that need we all have now and then to get high on outrageous self-confidence.

A popular assessment of 'Pinky' is that it's basically 'Mellow', except in Colorado. For me, it's deeper than that, the clue coming with the switching between the second and third person. The narrator begins, gently waking up a 'you' who had been slumbering, and then goes on to talk in the third person about an individual called 'Pinky' who is perfect, wrapped up in quilts, irresistible in all things, whose silence keeps 'us' guessing. Those are all terms that perfectly describe a baby, in which case this song isn't about staying in and having sex because it's cold outside but is rather a thoroughly charming portrait of a young father and mother looking at their little Pinky, perfectly happy and warm, and silent in her dreams, with the ultimate message being that the best laid plans are as nothing next to a simple morning spent with the people you love most.

There's a small but beloved sub-genre of song out there, the ode to the mediocre thing, which is the delight of its small group of dedicated adherents and the confoundment of everyone else. Songs like Tom Lehrer's 'She's My Girl' (1959) or Glenn Erath's 'Oh Little Town of El Cajon' about one of Southern California's most underwhelming cities, all spend a song talking not about the beauty of the sun, or the perfect lips of your significant other, but rather about how the most conspicuous thing about your hometown is the bowling hall which is, you know, fine. We are united by shared underwhelming daily experiences far more than by shared monumental life moments to a substantial degree. 'Grimsby', which was the track that, left to his own devices, Dudgeon would probably have thrown into the nearest river, captures that sense of fun that we all have in talking about how boring the places we came from are. Grimsby wasn't, as Elton sometimes says, the town where Bernie was born – that was an hour away, near Sleaford, but it was the most significant seaport near Owmby-by-Spital, where Bernie's family moved when he was 9 years old. We know from the opening moments of the track that the song is a joke, as Johnstone's guitar riff features an archetypal 'musical shorthand for laughter' motif that signals all too well that we aren't to take any of what follows seriously, as Elton and Bernie do their best to make the miserable city of Grimsby sound like the most mystically thrilling of places on the planet.

'Dixie Lily' is pure countrified Dixieland fun, evoking a view of the great age of the Mississippi showboats. Elton's piano work is as Dixie as it comes, while Murray busts out with a classic country moseying bassline, and Ray Cooper and Johnstone add extra whisps of colour with their tambourine and mandolin. It's a perfect postcard of a song for sitting on the porch and enjoying a cold beverage on a hot day, the sort of track that would represent a welcome chance to catch your breath on any other Elton album, but that I think suffers from being on side one of *Caribou*, among so many other light numbers.

Speaking of lighter numbers, the next track, 'Solar Prestige a Gammon', is a bit of meaningless joy, composed at Elton's request by Bernie to be impenetrable to analysis, with lines like, 'Kool kar kyrie kay salmon/Herring molassis abounding' and the only reliable constant being Bernie's interjection of various fish names here and there as the spirit took him. Elton affects an absurd Italian accent, rolling his R's beyond all reason, while a cheesy attempt at an accordion effect is played in the background. At a time when the world was everywhere threatening to come apart at the seams, a little bit of brilliantly stupid can be the most comforting thing of all, and for 1974 'Solar Prestige a Gammon' was the brilliantly stupid it both needed and received.

We've hardly had time to recover from the weird onslaught of 'Solar Prestige a Gammon' when the arrival of the next track brings us Elton playing a piano tango riff, concluding with a click of the castanets courtesy of Cooper, and we hold our breath, realising that the weird is far from over. 'You're So Static', our closer for the first side of *Caribou*, doubles down on everything that has characterised the record so far, both its good aspects – its sense of humour and willingness to let the music augment that humour, and its weaker ones – a declining sense of substance. This is Bernie's least interesting lyrics from the album, dealing with the tired rock theme of, 'city women are often treacherous', which you sense Elton desperately trying to soup up by the unconventional tango setting, backed by the full force of the Tower of Power brass and Cooper's small army of percussive instruments. Dudgeon's production here achieves wonders, and taken purely instrumentally it's a fun trip, but that's about it.

We might well expect a song with the title of 'I've Seen the Saucers' to be yet another of *Caribou*'s joke tracks, poking fun at people who claim to have been alien abductees the same way that 'Grimsby' jabs at the town's less than romantic sluices. In actuality, it is one of the most straightly performed songs on the album, eschewing the facile opportunity to punch down at people with variously credible tales of abduction, and instead treating us to a delightful film in miniature in which the local UFO crank gets picked up by aliens, only to grow quickly tired of alien contact, as his mind wanders to thoughts of dinner and the hope that he'll be returned by morning. It's a brilliant song about how quickly we get tired of even our most fervently held dreams once we achieve them, and that even the most miraculous experience eventually grows tedious, leaving us wanting nothing so much as the basic comfort of our familiar armchair.

For me, the song would have been better without the repeat of the chorus, because returning to the chorus doesn't dramatically make much sense after the 'back before the morning light' line, but perhaps ending on such an anti-climax was deemed too risky. In all events, the band is in full 1950s sci-fi film mode, though thankfully Dudgeon stopped short of dragging a theremin into the studio. The main 'UFO passing overhead' effect is produced by Ray Cooper's water gong, which is a gong with a pulley that allows you to control how much of it is submerged in water, so as you strike it and then raise and lower it in the water, you get these broad uniform metallic rising and falling tones that perfectly capture the sense of something massive and metal moving through the sky.

'Stinker' is, first and foremost, a song about foxes. It is the animal kingdom version of 'Social Disease', where instead of an utterly irredeemable human glorying in his own irredeemability, we have an entirely unapologetic animal gallivanting through nature, stinky and selfish, loving every minute of it, and through Elton's joyous strut of a composition, as backed by the funk of Tower of Power's brass, Cooper's hissing tambourine, and Murray and Johnstone's swaggering beats, we can walk along beside him for a while, and feel vicariously the thrill of drifting along, not owing anything to anyone, at perfect peace in our manifold imperfections.

There's a bit of tone whiplash that kicks in as we transition from the down and dirty stomp of 'Stinker' to the tormented ballad that is 'Don't Let the Sun Go Down on Me'. Much in the tradition of 'High Flying Bird', this song deals with an individual at the end of their ability to keep their partner emotionally stable and who is at a crisis point himself. Personally frozen, with no more warmth to spare for those who might need it, he watches life slowly drain of meaning and is caught in the horrifying realisation that to keep going he needs the person whom he has recently pulled his emotional resources away from. What will happen? Will that person retreat into herself to not get hurt again or will she overcome that and reach out? The song doesn't answer that question, but instead leaves us deep in the narrator's well of uncertainty.

Though Elton expressed nothing but scorn for the song he'd barely been coaxed into completing a decent take on the vocals, Dudgeon and the band believed in the song and did everything they could to make it an epic ballad, returning to the musical architecture that had been a feature of Elton's greatest music since 'Your Song', allowing the layers to build over time, beginning with piano, solo voice and simple percussion, with the bass and guitar not entering until the second verse, which also features the tranquillity piercing lashes of Ray Cooper's tambourine shots, which act like slaps of reality bringing the urgency of the situation into a sharper relief. What gives the song its distinctive feel, however, is saved until the second part of the second verse, when the vocal background arrangements created and performed by Carl Wilson (1946–1998) and Bruce Johnston (b.1942) of The Beach Boys enter, lifting the whole production onto another plane, producing backing countermelodies that Del Newman can then hang his brass arrangements on as the band reaches its maximum expansiveness just as the chorus comes to its highest moment. Though Elton had entered Caribou with the intention of writing only pared down songs, his brain refused to get the memo and went on producing songs of epic scope that everyone around him believed in and treated accordingly, even if he himself didn't.

'Ticking' brings *Caribou* to the darkest close of any Elton album, then or since. Though they weren't the virtual weekly occurrence they have since become here in the US, mass shootings were part of the public consciousness in the early 1970s. The worst was the University of Texas Tower Shooting in 1966, which killed seventeen people and injured thirty-one. Some theorise that the ticking in 'Ticking' is a reference to the clock tower that Charles Whitman (1941–1966) used as the stage for his murderous spree. This was a delicate topic, which lay solidly within Bernie's talent for crawling into the heads of those who live on the fringes of society and communicating their hopes and failed dreams to the rest of us. His lyrics are poignant, seeking only ever to show and never explain. Elton's nuanced musical response to Bernie's words crafted a moving and disturbing vision of an individual lost in the forward race of society, one all the more powerful for coming at the end of an album whose defining characteristics up to the final two songs were sass, brass and strut.

The Stats

Album/Single	US	UK	Australia	Canada
Caribou	1	1	1	1
	2P	G	2P	
'Don't Let the Sun Go Down on Me'/'Sick City'	2	16	13	1
'The Bitch is Back'/'Cold Highway'	4	15	53	1

The Players

Elton John: lead vocals, acoustic piano and Hammond organ (9)
David Hentschel: ARP synthesizer (2, 5 and 10) and Mellotron (9)
Chester D. Thompson: Hammond organ (8)
Davey Johnstone: acoustic guitar, electric guitar, mandolin and backing vocals
Dee Murray: bass guitar and backing vocals
Nigel Olsson: drums and backing vocals
Ray Cooper: tambourine, congas, whistle, vibraphone, snare, castanets, tubular bells, maracas and water gong
Lenny Pickett: tenor saxophone solo (1), soprano saxophone solo (4 and 5) and clarinet (5)
Tower of Power: horn section (1, 6, 8 and 9)
Del Newman: horn arrangements (9)
Clydie King: backing vocals (1 and 6)
Sherlie Matthews: backing vocals (1)
Jessie Mae Smith: backing vocals (1)
Dusty Springfield: backing vocals (1)
Billy Hinsche: backing vocals (9)
Bruce Johnston: backing vocals (9)
Toni Tennille: backing vocals (9)
Carl Wilson: backing vocals (9) and vocal arrangements (9)
Daryl Dragon: vocal arrangements (9)

The Tracks

Side one:
1. 'The Bitch is Back' (John, Taupin) (3.44)
2. 'Pinky' (John, Taupin) (3.54)
3. 'Grimsby' (John, Taupin) (3.46)
4. 'Dixie Lily' (John, Taupin) (2.55)
5. 'Solar Prestige a Gammon' (John, Taupin) (2.52)
6. 'You're So Static' (John, Taupin) (4.53)

Side two:
7. 'I've Seen the Saucers' (John, Taupin) (4.48)
8. 'Stinker' (John, Taupin) (5.20)
9. 'Don't Let the Sun Go Down on Me' (John, Taupin) (5.36)
10. 'Ticking' (John, Taupin) (7.34)

Musician's Corner: 'Ticking'

Part of me was tempted to do 'Solar Prestige a Gammon' for the musician's corner, so people won't accuse me of just picking the dark songs every time. But 'Ticking' is one of my favourite pieces to play and sing when nobody is around, and its lyrics become more poignant with each year that my own country sinks into mass shootings as the everyday pulse of our political lives. So, 'Ticking' it is…

Like many of my favourite Elton pieces, the instrumentation here is incredibly pared down – essentially Elton's voice and his piano, with David Hentschel's understated presence on the ARP synthesizer making itself increasingly known as the song hurtles to its tragic end, creating that instant atmosphere of intimacy that makes the emotions in this song feel more real than if they were couched in elaborate orchestrations. The lack of other instruments gives Elton room to fill this space with all his piano artistry. I've always heard a good amount of Igor Stravinsky (one of Elton's favourite classical composers) and particularly the *Rite of Spring*'s irregular accents in Elton's flourishes here, along with a fair amount of those lessons in off-beat piano technique that are the essence of the lessons young piano students learn from Béla Bartók's *Mikrokosmos* series of books. Taken purely instrumentally, 'Ticking' is like a piano concerto without the orchestra, displaying the instrument's astonishing breadth of expression.

Of course, the song isn't just an extended piano tone poem, but tells a story, and as ever Elton communicates the essence of that story by cues within the structure of the music. The intro sets out a steady progression of chords, all underlain by a repeating rhythmic figure that will form the beating pulse of the song. Each verse consists of two sections, the first of which contains that pulsing steady pattern underneath, corresponding to lyrics that describe the past, mental states and other people's perceptions of the youth in question, while the second section loses that pulse, and the action moves into violent and unhinged places, which is where Elton employs the more fractured piano techniques of the modern classical tradition. Again, whether the correspondence between the loss of that grounding pulse and the snapping of the character into their most violent moments was intentional or instinctual on Elton's part, it is a masterful way of using a musical element to cue us into the coming of something bad. When that pulse goes, so does whatever was keeping the central character's mental stability barely together, and what must ensue is a tragedy, as much for the young man at the centre of this story as for those whose lives he takes.

Chapter 11

Captain Fantastic and the Brown Dirt Cowboy

Recorded: August 1974
Released: 19 May 1975
Producer: Gus Dudgeon

The Story

The progression from *Madman Across the Water* through *Caribou* can be thought of as a series of scientific experiments to see how much pressure the Elton-Bernie machine could be put under before it snapped. Giving themselves less and less time to create and record, while attempting to work in unfamiliar environments, Elton and the band were courting disaster. Fortunately, all concerned realised that things couldn't go on this way and decisions were made to rethink how the records were made, all which benefitted the next album, *Captain Fantastic and the Brown Dirt Cowboy.*

Elton and Bernie decided that their new album would be a concept record along the lines of The Who's *Tommy* (1969) and this notion would be nothing less than telling their own joint story, as it ran from their adolescence to their early songwriting attempts and culminating with the release of *Empty Sky*. Bernie decided that he was going to take time to work over the *Captain Fantastic and the Brown Dirt Cowboy* lyrics before giving them to Elton, returning to them from time to time, and editing to get everything right, perhaps out of reverence for what they had accomplished together but also likely out of a desire to combat the criticism that had been levelled at his *Caribou* lyrics for being under-baked.

Instead of composing a full album of lyrics in a matter of days, Bernie lingered over them for months. He presented the completed set to Elton on the cruise ship SS *France* that the band was taking together (though missing Murray) to America. There, Elton grabbed snatches of time on the ship's grand piano to start writing the music, often in the company of Johnstone and his acoustic guitar. He made the decision to write the songs in the order they'd appear on the album, so that he could control the mood and tempo from song to song. By the time the ship docked in America, half the material was composed.

The team returned to Caribou to record *Captain Fantastic and the Brown Dirt Cowboy*, perhaps a surprising decision considering the issues that had made *Caribou* such a frantic experience but this time steps were taken to compensate for the limitations experienced before. Most significantly, Elton booked the studio for a month, meaning that the process could be less rushed, and all concerned had more time to acclimate themselves to the thinner air. Further, Colorado in August is a less daunting affair than in January. On the technical side, Dudgeon made the decision to record the album without any live effects being attempted, thereby eliminating the production headaches that plagued *Caribou*.

Everyone learned from their mistakes and now stood on what they realised was the precipice of renewed greatness. Bernie's lyrics were better than ever, Elton was fired up by his affection for the album, the band was pared down to the essential core, most of whom had been with Elton since his early days, there was time enough to write and record, Dudgeon learned how best to utilise the resources available to him and from the first acoustic lick of Johnstone's guitar, the stage was set for a musical journey, the likes of which had never been attempted in the history of pop music.

The Songs

Captain Fantastic and the Brown Dirt Cowboy begins in innocence and fights its way through darkness. 'Captain Fantastic and the Brown Dirt Cowboy', the first song Elton wrote for the album, acts as the overture. Bernie's lyrics lay out a superhero origin story wherein Elton's city mouse escapes his regimented childhood and Bernie's country mouse edges closer to his dreams of leaving the forest for the exciting world beyond and they miraculously find each other, with music and rhyme walking hand in hand as the pair move across the world in their newfound fame.

The song starts not with a piano or Elton's vocals but rather with an acoustic guitar, setting the scene of a simpler childhood, before he and his piano had taken over the world. Even when Elton enters, it's in the form of some unobtrusive backing gestures on the electric piano, as if the scene is more important than the players. That notion is reinforced by the fact that we have three full verses before coming to bridge-like material. As the song kicks into a rock gear, Johnstone plays a scale up and then back down again, which will come to be a leitmotif throughout the record. Here, it is almost defiant in its optimism but as we move through the record, it will go through some transformations that reflect the evolution of Elton and Bernie. There's also a bit of musical storytelling in the keys Elton wanders through throughout the album. 'Captain Fantastic and the Brown Dirt Cowboy' is set in G major but the concluding track is set in a G minor that morphs into its relative key of B flat major for its second half, a deeply ambiguous statement about what all the success achieved and adversity overcome really mean.

Bernie's lyrics for 'Tower of Babel' tell a relatively straightforward story of the immorality and decadence of the music industry, which Elton backs by some of his most challenging chord progressions yet, mirroring the complicated nest of back-stabbing and career advancement through his evolving chord choices that persistently deny the listener a sense of grounding. Biblically, the 'Tower of Babel' was a gesture of humanity's power and defiance of the gods, and musically Johnstone echoes this in the instrumental section with menacing ascension gestures. Perhaps it's an overly literal gesture, but if you missed the meaning of the reference, the tone painted by the guitarwork is a definite signal that here there's pride aplenty, awaiting its fall.

'Bitter Fingers' is perhaps the catchiest song on *Captain Fantastic and the Brown Dirt Cowboy*, which is both ironic in that it covers one of the most miserable periods of Elton's early years and fitting in that it's about being compelled to create an endless stream of snappy songs for the music industry's unceasing parade of sound-alike performers. Elton's introductory descending motif, made vaguely dystopic through Dudgeon's decision to pass the piano through his new favourite toy, the Eventide Harmonizer, is a catchy circular pattern that doesn't go anywhere in particular, itself a commentary on the pop music industry. 'It's hard to write a song with bitter fingers' is a perfect encapsulation of the period in the Elton-Bernie partnership when they were trying and failing to create pop hits for other artists, while putting off writing music that meant something to them.

Instrumentally, 'Tell Me When the Whistle Blows' is the most complex track on *Captain Fantastic and the Brown Dirt Cowboy*, featuring slippery strings arranged by Gene Page (1939–1998) that lend the song a funk/proto-disco feel. Bernie's lyrics centre around the pull he felt as a young man between the comfort of home and the exciting allure of the city. The verses are largely set in the city, with Johnstone's guitar wailing out blurts on top of a seductive wall of strings sliding between notes in a tonal scramble that sums up everything compelling and repelling about the urban experience. The chorus, meanwhile, reverts to square rhythms and chord changes, as the narrator at last puts his foot on the train that will take him back to a life that makes some semblance of sense to him.

Captain Fantastic and the Brown Dirt Cowboy had only one single, 'Someone Saved My Life Tonight', Bernie's account of Elton's doomed engagement to Linda Woodrow, his early struggles with his homosexuality and his first attempt at suicide. The piece begins with that ascending and descending leitmotif from 'Captain Fantastic and the Brown Dirt Cowboy', only now it has a distinct air of resignation about it. I want to note how skilfully Elton, Dudgeon and the band maintained interest in a song of such length. In the past, they had done this by layering in more and more instruments, allowing the thickening of the sound to keep the ears engaged but here they largely keep to the same core instruments and general soundscape throughout, with the listener being kept interested not only by the deeply personal lyrics but by the song's subtle deviations from the patterns it established early on – sometimes the iconic 'oo-OO-oo' is there after the 'Bye bye', sometimes it isn't, sometimes the there and back leitmotif leads us into the verse, sometimes it doesn't. At the end, we are treated to a wall of intersecting vocals as Elton finds himself pulled from the impossible situation he'd placed himself in, finally free to figure himself out. It was a gruelling song for Elton to record, so raw in its personal history. When Dudgeon played the finished product to Elton some months later, its power was of such magnitude that Elton had to leave the room, overcome with emotion.

Side one ends on the emotionally draining journey of 'Someone Saved My Life Tonight', a venture into Elton's darkest moments that Bernie wisely decided that listeners would need some time to recover from, so the first two songs on side two are of a less traumatic nature. '(Gotta Get a) Meal Ticket' begins with the simple ascending scale type movement that was also featured in the chorus of 'Bitter Fingers' where it had associations with the music industry's cookie cutter approach to song production and here it serves that purpose again in a track that is all about the venomous jealousy that Elton and Bernie felt for the bands that were succeeding while their more genuine efforts were continually stalling. The intro presents us with the sort of rock that sold millions of copies while *Regimental Sgt Zippo* languished unreleased – an electric guitar thudding upwards on a basic scale using exactly the same pattern five times in a row. You can just picture Elton seething in a corner with his piles of carefully wrought elegant chord transitions bringing Bernie's poetic lyrics to life, all of which are accounted as nothing next to undifferentiated scales in D. More brilliantly still, at one minute and eight seconds that simple ascending figure transforms into a there and back type figure. The theme thereby takes on a dimension of mockery, as if the music industry is observing all the promise of Elton and Bernie's early life, and all the pain they had experienced since, and deriding it all as so much uncommercial dross. This grotesque transformation is rendered doubly intriguing because we as listeners can't be sure if this is meant to be the industry laughing at the downtrodden Elton and Bernie or if this is simply a representation of their perception of that industry, their view being poisoned by their own bitterness at their relative lack of success. Either way, it is a great example of how Elton and the band were able to find non-verbal means of reinforcing Bernie's main themes on *Captain Fantastic and the Brown Dirt Cowboy*.

When asked what one's favourite song is on *Captain Fantastic and the Brown Dirt Cowboy*, the thing one is supposed to say is 'Someone Saved My Life Tonight' in deference to its raw emotion and expansive genuineness. For me, however, my favourite will always be 'Better Off Dead', one of the weirdest songs Elton has ever composed. Written in the style of a Gilbert (1836–1911) and Sullivan (1842–1900) song, it's an account of pimps, sex workers, drunks and police officers in pursuit as observed by Elton and Bernie while they ate late night meals at a diner near the site of their early recording sessions. Elton's galloping chords are accentuated by the militarised thumps of Olsson's drum kit, augmented by a passage through the Eventide Harmonizer. It's the kind of musical idiom that only Elton would think to write in, completely ignoring Bernie's suggestion that the piece should be a John Prine (1946–2020) style folk piece.

By the time we get to 'Writing', we have been through six songs detailing the depths of Elton and Bernie's bitterness, failure and self-doubt, and are ready for the light of day to shine at last, and for our intrepid pair to receive the reward that they're due. 'Writing' keys us into a thematic parting of the clouds by its relaxing instrumentation choices. There's another there and back movement from Johnstone but the timbre of the instrument is entirely different from '(Gotta Get a) Meal Ticket' and now suggests something of the soft idyl of 'Captain Fantastic and the Brown Dirt Cowboy', while Ray Cooper's bops on the bongos and gentle swishing on the shaker tell us to relax a while in the tropical sun beginning to break out overhead. This is the point in the story when Elton and Bernie have found their groove, producing music that meant something to them. Our heroes are now in sync, instigating a treasure trove of new songs, and finding some light in life again. While the lyrics open into happy remembrances of their closest time together, Murray, Olsson and Johnstone employ spritely musical figures that have escaped the foreboding shapes representative of the monolithic music industry and are instead roaming freely in the prospect of better things to come.

The album concludes with the ten-minute dual opus 'We All Fall in Love Sometimes'/'Curtains', which is in many ways the photo negative of 'Funeral for a Friend'/'Love Lies Bleeding'. However, while 'Funeral for a Friend' is a journey through a multitude of tempos, 'We All Fall in Love Sometimes' keeps itself pretty much within the same basic speed and musical idiom. 'Funeral for a Friend' was a standalone instrumental exercise onto which a song that happened to be in the same key was appended. 'We All Fall in Love Sometimes' is a vocal journey meant to seamlessly flow into its companion song. The two pieces couldn't be more different but that doesn't stop people from comparing them. Sure, 'We All We All Fall in Love Sometimes' isn't as varied, and no it doesn't give us the big bangs and adventure rock jolts but that's not its purpose. What it represents is an ascent out of the inferno of composers for hire into the relative paradise of controlling their own creative futures. We see the pair finding genuine love and brotherhood in each other, writing songs that, in hindsight, seem unbelievably naïve to the mature pair but are unspeakably tender all the same. The song is filled with references to their early work, with Bernie mentioning an 'Empty Sky filled with laughter' and a 'Dandelion that said the time had come' while Elton and the band sneak in synthesised flute sounds and congas that recall the instrumentation of *Empty Sky*.

There's one musical decision that is almost too clever for its own good here, which comes with the key change between the songs. We start in G minor, which is the dark companion to the bright and hopeful G major that the album began with, and which is perhaps a reflection of the darkness that our dynamic duo were mired in before they started finding their way to each other. That is a great example of musical storytelling, and as we come to the 'Curtains' part of the song, what we expect is a new key to first, give our ears a break and second, give us a clue as to the next part of the journey. Elton chooses to move to the relative major of G minor, which is B flat major, which has all the same notes, but just with different meanings. This is interesting as it suggests that even though things are getting brighter, the problems from before haven't so much gone away as taken on new clothing, a very important message that is hidden away from all but the most curious ears. 'Curtains' aims to resolve the story into a cloud of stationary fantasy, keeping within a set tempo, leading to a three minute long wall of vocals. If you go into the piece expecting 'Funeral for a Friend'/'Love Lies Bleeding', you're probably going to be disappointed, but if you sit down with the expectation of ascending higher from the busy and complicated mess of reality into the ethereal world of dreams come true, you'll be treated to a unique experience.

The Stats

Album/Single	US	UK	Australia	Canada
Captain Fantastic and the Brown Dirt Cowboy	1	2	1	1
	3P	G	2P	P
'Someone Saved My Life Tonight'/'House of Cards'	4	22	54	2

The Players

Elton John: lead vocals, acoustic piano (1, 2, 3, 5, 6, 7, 9 and 10), Fender Rhodes (1, 4, 5 and 8), clavinet (4 and 6), ARP String Ensemble (5), harmony vocals (7 and 8), harpsichord (9 and 10) and Mellotron (9 and 10)

David Hentschel: ARP synthesizer (9 and 10)

Davey Johnstone: acoustic guitar (1 and 5 to 10), electric guitar (1 to 4, 6, 9 and 10), mandolin (1), backing vocals (3 and 5 to 10), Leslie guitar (5) and acoustic piano (8)

Dee Murray: bass guitar and backing vocals (3 and 5 to 10)

Nigel Olsson: drums and backing vocals (3 and 5 to 10)

Ray Cooper: shaker (1, 5 and 8), congas (1, 3, 4, 9 and 10), gong (1), jawbone (1), tambourine (1 to 6, 9 and 10), bells (3, 9 and 10), cymbals (5), triangle (7 and 8) and bongos (8)

Gene Page: orchestral arrangements (4)

The Tracks

Side one:
1. 'Captain Fantastic and the Brown Dirt Cowboy' (John, Taupin) (5.46)
2. 'Tower of Babel' (John, Taupin) (4.28)
3. 'Bitter Fingers' (John, Taupin) (4.35)
4. 'Tell Me When the Whistle Blows' (John, Taupin) (4.20)
5. 'Someone Saved My Life Tonight' (John, Taupin) (6.45)

Side two:
6. '(Gotta Get a) Meal Ticket' (John, Taupin) (4.01)
7. 'Better Off Dead' (John, Taupin) (2.37)
8. 'Writing' (John, Taupin) (3.40)
9. 'We All Fall in Love Sometimes' (John, Taupin) (4.15)
10. 'Curtains' (John, Taupin) (6.15)

Musician's Corner: 'Someone Saved My Life Tonight'

In a major scale, the next to last note is referred to as the leading tone, and whenever you hear it standing around by itself, what your brain desperately wants to have happen next is for that leading tone to be followed by the main note of the scale. If, for example, you're in the key of G (like this song is), these are the notes of your scale: G-A-B-C-D-E-F#-G.

When you play an F#, or an E leading into an F#, then a part of you feels distinctly uncomfortable if a G doesn't show up in close order. Composers steeped in classical traditions know this and can play with our emotional responses to a song using it, and this chorus is a miniature master class in how to maximise the effect of a run up to a leading tone. Let us take the section beginning 'Altar bound' as our textbook.

There are two things going on here. First, in the vocal line, we get 'Altar bound', which is an E leading into an F#, and which should go up again and resolve nicely to a G but instead Elton drags us back down and does another E to F# ascension on 'hypnotised' but makes it even more tension-filled by supporting it underneath with an A7 chord with C# in the bass. That C# doesn't directly belong in the key of G, so we've effectively got two teases going on at once, an F# leading tone that we want to head to a G, and a C# in the bass that we want to head anywhere but C#, preferably D because that's the direction the bass is going.

Our brain wants the satisfaction of a high G and a low D, and Elton gives us this, kinda. That high G arrives, but stuffed into the last bit of its bar, popping its head above the surface for a peek before Elton scurries back down into descending patterns in the melody while the bass note does, indeed, rise to the D and stays there. In the next measure, the bass has climbed to E and the melody is doing the E-F# bit again and we feel confident that surely Elton will hit us with the high G's we crave. We get these in spades in the next three measures, while the bass pattern starts anew from the note we began upon, C, and is working its way up, through C# to D. The climax is there on 'high away' with a long top G, supported underneath by a G chord and on the bottom by the D that we have been trained at this point to expect will rise in turn to an E like it did before.

Then Elton flips the switch, the trap door springs and with the first 'bye' of 'bye bye' we are hit with this descending triplet based around a B chord that has come out of nowhere, which ushers us into an ambiguous C on the last 'bye' after which everything descends back to the melancholic opening material, the chorus having achieved its objective of keeping us yearning for something that it will only ever give in mismatched fits and starts.

Chapter 12

Rock of the Westies

Recorded: June to July 1975
Released: 24 October 1975
Producer: Gus Dudgeon

The Story

By the mid-1970s, Elton was a creature of deep contradictions. Undisputedly the top pop music performer in the world, Elton was nonetheless prone to dark periods of depression. The cycle between the highs of performing before tens of thousands of screaming fans and the lows of fundamental self-doubt wasn't helped by substance abuse, and an entourage that found their best interest in feeding Elton's worst habits. Emotionally at cross purposes with himself, he felt that to advance to the next level musically, tectonic changes were needed. Out of the blue, he decided to fire Murray and Olsson, who were not only critical instrumentalists but two-thirds of his signature backup vocal presence as well. Johnstone, Dudgeon and Ray Cooper remained, while Elton went on the hunt for musicians who'd give him a rockier sound, tapping Quaye to add a second guitar to his arsenal and James Newton Howard (*b*.1951) as a permanent presence on the synthesizer, while Roger Pope took up Olsson's empty seat and Kenny Passarelli (*b*.1949) filled Murray's place in the band.

The new band brought a heavier drive to Elton's music but would all this change be for the better? Recording for the album that would eventually be called *Rock of the Westies* largely took place in July 1975 at the Caribou studio with Dudgeon once again at the helm. Though Elton kept to his routine of rising early to compose songs that the band could work on throughout the day, the level of substance abuse indulged in by the band during the recording process was of an unprecedented scale, with at least one song, 'Medley', stemming from a sudden blast of cocaine fuelled euphoria.

Released in October 1975, *Rock of the Westies*, riding the wave of good will from *Captain Fantastic and the Brown Dirt Cowboy*, had such heavy preordering that, like its predecessor, it entered the charts at #1, and its first single, 'Island Girl', likewise hit #1 in the US. Commercially a success, the album, however, split Elton fans, with some applauding his step into a harder rock sound, while others expressed concern that *Rock of the Westies* seemed a step down in terms of the cohesion, consequence and storytelling that they had grown to expect.

The Songs

'Medley (Yell Help/Wednesday Night/Ugly)' was written while Elton and Johnstone were high on drugs and alcohol, a fact at least a bit suspected by anybody who has ever heard it. Cobbled together from scraps of lyrics Bernie had lying in a heap in the corner, the three main sections of the piece don't share much except the general feeling of defeat that permeates most of the lyrics on this album, a product of Bernie's own failing marriage and substance abuse at the time. 'Yell Help' is a portrait of annoyance and bad luck, 'Wednesday Night' is a thin four lines simply about someone who doesn't want to be where they are and 'Ugly' is about a man rhapsodising over how ugly his girlfriend is, and if that sounds like a disconnected mess to try and construct a unified song while out of your mind on cocaine, it's because it is. That's not to say it's not fun – the sheer ridiculousness of how these pieces are patched together is never unentertaining. I'll never know why Dudgeon, whose instincts on song order were usually so spot on decided to take the massive risk of placing 'Medley' first on an album that he knew was going to be scrutinised by fans disappointed with the loss of Murray and Olsson. It's a glorious mess, which is the sort of thing you can get away with on side two, but as a side one, track one it was a dangerous venture, effectively giving ammunition straightaway to everyone who thought that Elton had gambled away cohesion in the pursuit of rock posturing.

Along the same lines, 'Dan Dare (Pilot of the Future)' seems an odd choice for the follow up track to 'Medley'. Lyrically, 'Dan Dare (Pilot of the Future)' is the dark companion to 'Roy Rogers' from *Goodbye Yellow Brick Road*. While 'Roy Rogers' was a bittersweet song about the evergreen nature of our childhood heroes and their inexhaustible ability to continue to inspire us even into old age, 'Dan Dare (Pilot of the Future)' is a sober look at the flip side of fictional hero worship, about how having heroes of galactic scale like Dan Dare (a regular feature in the pages of *Eagle* comics from 1950 to 1967 and a particular favourite of a young Bernie) can breed a sense of discontent as year after year of life passes, and one has persistently done nothing to measure up to what one's heroes stood for. Lacking the energy to do great things, we drift further away from those childhood figures, and eventually have to say goodbye to them to sustain any sense of ourselves as worthwhile. Its complicated lyrics mix the wide eyed wonder of a child's sense of the universe with the imploding sense of the possible that marks adulthood, most of the deep pathos of which is passed entirely by in the band's odd choices for how musically to set it. Johnstone kicks it off by running his guitar through an apparatus called a voice bag that makes it sound like a robot talking, which sets the tone for what is to follow. Elton's honky tonk setting of the lyrics could work as a modern recasting of what science fiction adventure might sound like, but every time it starts to hit a stride, Johnstone's voice-bag comes careening back in, shoving the piece back into the novelty category, and Elton's comically gruff and Muppet-like reading of 'He doesn't know it, doesn't know it, doesn't know it' serves to keep it there. Once again, it's a fun song, but as Bernie's psychologically astute lyrics had the potential to be something much more, it's always a bittersweet listen.

'Island Girl' was the album's first single, and is a fascinating example of a song that wouldn't even be recorded today. The band give everything to conjuring a tropical setting, with Johnstone's now iconic guitar slide opening the piece, and Ray Cooper giving as much island flavour as he can through his congas and marimbas. If you didn't understand English, listening to the music you'd assume the piece was an upbeat account of island life. The words, however, centre around the despair that a Jamaican man feels knowing that his beloved has been reduced to the life of a sex worker in New York. The subject was one that was coming to the fore in the mid-1970s as magazines like *Ms.* made the world aware of the realities of domestic abuse, rape and involuntary sex work. The theme then was timely, but Bernie's attempts at 'ethnic' writing seem to put the song more in the category of 'Jamaica Jerk-Off.' Elton might have picked up on the dark content at the song's heart and directed the band to tone down the stereotypical island paradise instrumentation, but for whatever reason, didn't. For the third time, then, we have a song that is fun but in a way that seems totally disconnected from its source lyrical material.

With 'Grow Some Funk of Your Own' we come to the nadir of *Rock of the Westies*, the last in a series of downward steps before the album finally starts coming into its own. It's a song stuffed with questionable choices. Taken literally, the lyrics are a recounting of a dream the narrator had but there are ways to make dream narratives interesting, the first of which is to lean into the ridiculous logic and imagery that lie in dreams, as in 'Bob Dylan's 115th Dream' (1965). Bernie opts not to take this route, and instead presents a relatively straightforward story about a man who notices an attractive woman in a Mexican bar and is told by her boyfriend to go away via the 'We no like to with the Gringo fight' line that gets a little worse every year. Not much of a story, but again, it's salvageable – one could go the 'Come a Little Bit Closer' (1964) route and have each repetition of the chorus given new meaning by the changes in the situation introduced by each new verse. Elton opted not to take this route and instead just repeats the entire substance of the dream sequence, word for word, twice, so that we as listeners don't have much choice but to listen to the story all over again, and without any new developments in the verse, when the chorus shows up again, it means the exact same thing it did the first time. In short, the structure is all wrong to retain interest narratively, which means that if there's to be redemption, it must come from the instruments but when they aren't being absurdly literal (Ray Cooper's castanets every time Elton says 'senorita') they are just sort of chugging forward on a series of repetitive fuzzy rock-funk riffs, with the only real excitement coming with the duel between Elton's manic piano work and Cooper's vibraphones at the very end of the song, by which time it's too late to save the patient, as valiantly as they try.

By the time we come to 'I Feel Like a Bullet (in the Gun of Robert Ford)', the last song on side one, we have been treated to disconnected chaos, a wasted opportunity, an odd disconnect between music and lyrics, and an uncharacteristically ill-conceived song architecture. Then 'I Feel Like a Bullet' comes on, and we are reminded in an instant of what Elton and Bernie are capable of. Bernie's lyrics are one of his best – a painfully honest recounting of a man living with the guilt of having destroyed his marriage through his own deep-seated character flaws. Most consider this song to be Bernie's attempt to work through the damage that he'd caused to his own marriage to Maxine, which would soon end in divorce, and it's hard to deny the parallels. Elton, perhaps realising how deeply personal these lyrics were to Bernie, put the brakes on his hard rock persona, delivering a haunting vocal that floats on top of some unsettling chord progressions that do their own heavy lifting in telling the listener how unlikely of resolution this situation is.

Ray Cooper's vibraphone provides the perfect backdrop to Elton's vocals and piano-work, and while some fans complain that Passarelli's bass is too forward in the mix, I've always rather liked it for the sheer throbbing menace that it serves up. We'll never know if Dudgeon intended it as such (he died in a car accident in 2002) but it's always felt that way to me, the demon beneath assuring us that all this introspection will ultimately come to nothing.

Having recovered its footing somewhat at the end of side one, side two has always been where the real magic happens, where Elton's new harder rock sound is put in contexts that serve to drive the lyrics to a higher level. 'Street Kids', the side's opener, is a perfect example of that. Starting on a sizzling single guitar note, it bursts into a searing guitar riff on top of which Elton layers a taunting descending motif in the piano. With all the guitar wailing and diving, we get a true sense of forward momentum. Elton's properly rocking here, and what's better, the subject to which all this is being devoted is a thoroughly appropriate one – a 'Saturday Night's Alright for Fighting' style account of an East End juvenile street gang, living a life of violence and poverty. The song struts with the cockiness of a young man bragging to his pals about the overwhelming odds he faced in the latest scuffle with a rival gang, and that spirit is infectious. For my money, 'Street Kids' is an even better paean to urban brawling than 'Saturday Night's Alright for Fighting' – the characters are better sketched, the guitar work is better integrated with the other instruments, the chorus and verses have more intricate melodies that still maintain their sense of dangerous drive, Elton's vocals are fuller and more varied, and Quaye's extended guitar solo is the personification of an adolescent, high on his own sense of daring, tearing through the streets. Most importantly, it re-established what Elton can do in the realm of a harder rock style that is in sync with its source lyric material.

'Hard Luck Story' keeps the momentum going, with Bernie's pitch perfect account of a working man who comes home and subjects his wife to an endless cavalcade of self-pitying stories about how hard his work is and about his thoughts of leaving for a job, city and wife who respect him at the level he thinks he deserves, all while being completely blind to the hardships suffered by the wife who has to deal with his verbal abuse and demands for praise from the moment he walks through the door every day. Elton and Bernie had originally written the song for Kiki Dee (*b*.1947), whose recording of it makes more sense than this one, with the song from the perspective of the woman who is dying of boredom, staring at the same four walls all day long, waiting for her abusive husband to come home. One improvement over the Dee version comes from Dudgeon's inspired decision to have the song emerge into existence on a fade in, and descend into nothingness on a fade out, which gives the story being told a perfect sense of eternal recurrence, that this cycle is going to happen over and over again, fading in with the new day, and out with the blissful coming of sleep, a steady throb of anxiety.

The traditional interpretation of 'Feed Me' is that it's a song about addiction, with the central figure's paranoia an extension of their substance abuse, and the repeated calls of 'feed me' to be taken as the primal calls of an addict's need for his drug of choice. Certainly, drugs were on the minds of Bernie, Elton and everyone in the band in the mid-1970s. So, yes, it would make sense for 'Feed Me' to be about drug addiction, and I have nothing against those who interpret it that way – they're probably right. But I've always taken the song to be a darker extension of the themes visited in 'Madman Across the Water'. The patient of 'Feed Me' has been institutionalised and wants nothing more than to return to home. He's clearly in an unstable place but believes that all he needs is whatever chemical miracle treatment is being peddled to be shot into his system to make him stable enough to leave the hospital. For me, 'Feed Me' is the tragic cry of someone who desperately wants all his demons to be solved in one chemical blow.

Musically, the song is driven forward by this neat rhythmic see-saw between the guitars, the backing vocals, and Howard's electric piano, particularly in the chorus, which create this sinister sonic carpet of mockery, taunting the song's subject.

We end the album with a bang on 'Billy Bones and the White Bird', which is essentially a fan fiction-like mashup of the story of the pirate from *Treasure Island* who carried the famous treasure map, and who died from a stroke upon being handed the Black Spot, and the tale of the White Bird, a French biplane that went missing in 1927 in an attempt to sail from Paris to New York City. The lyrics gleefully mix air and sea jargon in a jumble of classic historical and literary mysteries that are so dizzying, and that Elton makes even more disorienting through his madcap musical choices, that we are left with no real choice but to hang on and enjoy the ride.

The Stats

Album/Single	US	UK	Australia	Canada
Rock of the Westies	1	5	4	1
	P	G	P	P
'Island Girl'/'Sugar on the Floor'	1	14	12	4
'Grow Some Funk of Your Own'/'I Feel Like a Bullet (in the Gun of Robert Ford)'	14	56		8

The Players

Elton John: lead vocals and acoustic piano (all except 8)
James Newton Howard: harpsichord (1), Elka Rhapsody string synthesizer (1), ARP synthesizer (1 and 3), Hohner clavinet (1 and 2), Mellotron (3), electric piano (4, 5, 7, 8 and 9) and synthesizers (4, 5 and 9)
Davey Johnstone: electric guitar (1, 3, 4, 5, 7, 8 and 9), backing vocals (2, 3, 4, 6 and 8), rhythm guitar (2 and 6), voice bag (2), Ovation guitar (3), banjo (3), slide guitar (3 and 6), acoustic guitar (4 and 5) and guitar solo (5)
Caleb Quaye: electric guitar (1, 2, 4, 5, 7, 8 and 9), backing vocals (2, 3, 4, 6, 7 and 8), acoustic guitar (3, 4 and 5), rhythm guitar (6) and lead guitar solo (6)
Kenny Passarelli: bass guitar and backing vocals (2, 3, 4, 6 and 7)
Roger Pope: drums (1 to 5 and 7 to 9)
Ray Cooper: tambourine (1, 3, 5, 6 and 9), cowbell (1 and 9), congas (1, 3, 6, 7 and 8), jawbone (1), marimba (3), castanets (4), bell tree (4), vibraphone (4, 5 and 8), shaker (8), wind chimes (8), maracas (9) and kettle drums (9)
Labelle: backing vocals (1)
Ann Orson: backing vocals (1, 2, 3, 6, 8 and 9)
Kiki Dee: backing vocals (2, 3, 4 and 6 to 9)
Clive Franks: backing vocals (8)

The Tracks

Side one:
  1. 'Medley (Yell Help, Wednesday Night, Ugly)' (John, Taupin) (6.13)
  2. 'Dan Dare (Pilot of the Future)' (John, Taupin) (3.30)
  3. 'Island Girl' (John, Taupin) (3.42)
  4. 'Grow Some Funk of Your Own' (John, Taupin) (4.43)
  5. 'I Feel Like a Bullet (in the Gun of Robert Ford)' (John, Taupin) (5.28)

Side two:
  6. 'Street Kids (John, Taupin)' (6.23)
  7. 'Hard Luck Story (John, Taupin)' (5.10)
  8. 'Me' (John, Taupin) (4.00)
  9. 'Billy Bones and the White Bird' (John, Taupin) (4.24)

Musician's Corner: 'Billy Bones and the White Bird'

'Billy Bones? Out of all those tracks, you chose 'Billy Bones and the White Bird' to do a musical corner about? It's got four chords and 72 per cent of the lyrics are the words 'Check it out!' 'Billy Bones?'

I hear you, but here's my reasoning: first, I've always loved Billy Bones. Second, it highlights a part of Elton's catalogue that we haven't talked about in much detail yet because we've been too busy sniffing out the uses of secondary dominants, which is Elton's ability to write songs that are ridiculous fun.

Sometimes, he wants to give us a good time, without putting us through the dramatic twists and turns that his craft is capable of constructing, something we can turn on, move to and enjoy in that space of expression that music provides and this is the musical country that boasts Billy Bones as one of its citizens.

What got me hooked on this song as a kid was how unusual it was for putting a percussive idea front and centre. That 'Bam… bam… bam… BAM BAM' groove with the extra percussion artillery on the last two hits was such a different thing that I played the track over and over just to experience it and move to it. It wasn't until later that I realised that this is a juiced-up variation on a classic groove that drummers call 'The Bo Diddley' in honour of its appearance on Bo Diddley's track 'Hey, Bo Diddley' (1957). What makes it so effective is that it's this rhythmic notion from the golden years of rock 'n roll but transplanted within the confines of a miniature nautical rock epic, so your brain picks up on this danceable groove from the past but is also translating it into a representation for the violent crashing motion of a ship battering its way through the waves.

If the song was just maritime lyrics with Bo Diddley rhythms, it would get old pretty fast, which is why Elton takes us on a neck-snapping musical detour. Through the beginning of the song, we're on this cool nautical rock adventure, and then, suddenly, with the lines, 'Oh your majesty' we get knocked into another realm entirely, with sounds of canned applause running beneath lyrics that on the page look grim about the appearance of Billy's body on a shore.

Maybe Billy washed ashore, got up and walked to the nearest bar, and is okay but it sure sounds like he's dead and all that's left is a sea-ravaged corpse. But between the canned applause, the bopping instruments and the blooping organ, it's hard to know exactly what to think about the fate of Billy Bones. Elton's pulling us in two different directions, with the result that we are left with no choice but to embrace it all and do a frenzied dance upon the bones of lost mariners because, after all, life is terribly short and mostly silly, if you stop to check it out.

Chapter 13

Blue Moves

Recorded: March 1976
Released: 22 October 1976
Producer: Gus Dudgeon

The Story

By 1976, Elton stood at the top of the pop and rock pantheon, selling more records than any other act in the world, with a string of six straight number one albums. There was tremendous pressure for his new album (to be recorded in Toronto for tax reasons, and his first not under the auspices of Dick James) to show to the world that Elton still had room to evolve.

The well-oiled machine that had produced two defining albums per year for over half a decade, however, wasn't what it once was. Elton was coming out of the breakup of his relationship with manager John Reid (*b.*1949) and was still deep in the world of rampant drug use. The pressure took a toll on his consummate professionalism in the studio. Bernie was a wreck, his marriage over, mostly his own fault, but also because his best friend in the band, Kenny Passarelli, had an affair with his wife Maxine that began during the *Rock of the Westies* recording sessions. Abusing alcohol to unprecedented levels, as well as cocaine and heroin, Bernie produced some of his darkest lyrics yet and sent them to Elton via post instead of working together on site. The bitter lyrics created tension with Elton, who sensed that dance music was the new hot thing but Bernie couldn't crawl out of his mood and wrote only a handful of upbeat lyrics.

Meanwhile, Dudgeon, usually the hand of reason, had to face down a mutiny from the band, who demanded to do their recording live, without any later over dubbing, which was one of Dudgeon's primary tools for assuring the exquisite balance of their past records but which represented extra work for the musicians. It was a struggle the band ended up winning.

There was still magic aplenty on this record – Elton even at his most exhausted couldn't help being Elton and songs like 'Sorry Seems to Be the Hardest Word' and 'One Horse Town' continue to be staple favourites among Elton fans. It also bears the status as the end of several roads: the last Elton album of the 1970s with Dudgeon in the control room and Bernie as the primary lyricist, Elton's last double album, the last time the Quaye-Passarelli-Pope combination would be heard on an Elton record and the first Elton album in five years to fail to reach #1 either in the US or the UK. For most Elton fans, *Blue Moves* represents the end of the classic Elton era, and for a small but vocal minority of fans, it represents the last album featuring the 'real' Elton. But the story is far from that simple – within two years, Elton would be back, with a new sound and approach that perfectly echoed the anxious world unfolding in the late 1970s and early 1980s. The story is far from over.

The Songs

There are an unprecedented three instrumental tracks on *Blue Moves*, known unofficially (by me) as the fun one, the long one and the other one. 'Your Starter For...' is the other one. It originated from a pre-concert warm-up exercise that Quaye had written and that Elton liked enough to serve as the lead-off instrumental for the album. It's fine. It fills its allotted one minute and twenty-three seconds adequately. As an album starter, however, and particularly as a lead-in to the high drama of 'Tonight', it doesn't seem to fit the bill. This is an album full of high energy dance numbers and psychologically fraught ballads and 'Your Starter For...' doesn't really prepare us for either of those emotions. Nor does it lead naturally into the symphonic world of 'Tonight', so why is it here? My guess is that, with all the dark lyrics pouring in from Bernie, Elton felt that the album needed some lift that jam-like instrumentals might provide, and so we get a shot of pep here regardless of if it has anything to do with what follows.

What follows is one of Elton's masterpieces, a song he recorded after the Toronto sessions had wrapped up, laying the opus down at Abbey Road with the London Symphony Orchestra as led by Howard, who also worked out the symphonic arrangements for the piece, admirably stepping into Buckmaster's shoes and providing orchestral textures that had enough edge to belong on a rock album. Bernie's lyrics of one partner in a relationship caught between the desire to put an end to the night's argument via the release of sleep and to see the smile, just one more time, on the face of the person he still loves, is crushing in its defeated hopelessness, and Elton's weary vocals, emerging from a dark three minute piano concerto intro, not only communicates but makes us feel the prevailing despair.

Realising we probably need a break to cleanse ourselves of the weighty emotions evoked by 'Tonight', Dudgeon treats us next to 'One Horse Town', which features lyrics about a town in which nothing has ever happened and which one might assume would have resulted in a slow, countrified drawler with maybe Johnstone on a banjo with some inserted rooster noises in the background. That is, decidedly, not what we get. One of the criticisms you hear about *Blue Moves* is that it's filled with six minute up-tempo numbers that overstay their welcome due to back-end vamping material. But 'One Horse' is so over the top, featuring such a glorious mismatch between the scale of the instrumental weaponry wielded in its name and the modest subject matter at its core, that in the end you have no choice but to lay down your analysis brain and go with it. Does any of it make sense? Not even a little! Is it a great ride through wacky dream synths, mammoth guitar licks, Buckmaster rock orchestra shenanigans (that's right, he's back!), adventure film grooves, Elton yelling 'Gonzales!' to prod his band to higher realms of recklessness in the spirit of cartoon mouse Speedy Gonzales, blasts of brass, sci-fi flying saucer synth drops, disco flourishes, head banging electric guitar triplets, Quaye's guitar solo taking us on an intergalactic trucker journey, and Pope's frenetic drums, all culminating in a completely non-sensical orchestral rise that fully earned every second of its five minutes and fifty-seven seconds run time? It is.

'Chameleon' is infamous in Elton circles as 'the song The Beach Boys turned down'. Elton, who usually busted out new songs in under half an hour, reportedly spent months agonising over 'Chameleon' with the intention of making the best Beach Boys song ever; to then offer it to them for their next album as a tribute for their groundbreaking sound, which meant so much to him as an adolescent. When he was finally satisfied with it, he presented it to the band, whose reaction was essentially 'Thanks, but it isn't a good fit.' Thereupon Elton decided to record it himself, with longtime Beach Boy Bruce Johnston placed in charge of arranging the backing vocals that are among the song's highlights. The first half of the chorus represents one of Elton and Bernie's most infectious pairings of word sound and melodic line, a complicated sentiment about a person whose ability to be all things to all people is both her most intoxicating and confounding attribute.

The first side of *Blue Moves'* first disc, discounting the slight question mark at the opening track, represented a promising journey that seemed to display Elton back in top form, able to throw down deeply personal ballads, one after the other with the assured mastery he'd been displaying for half a decade and more.

Then we get to 'Boogie Pilgrim'. I must make a confession here – in 30 years of listening to *Blue Moves*, which represent probably 150 walks through the album, I haven't once, until this day, made it to the end of 'Boogie Pilgrim'. There's something there in the idea of a boogie pilgrim – a streetwise modern individual who also has something of the old-time justice streak about them – but Elton's idea of structuring the piece around the products of a late-night jam session drags a two-minute novelty idea on for six agonising minutes. The mind-numbing repetitions of the main brass motif, the innumerable cries of 'Boo-gie pil-grim!' both represent a mountain of self-indulgence that by all rights Dudgeon should have curbed but after the band mutiny, perhaps he felt he was no longer able to advise the band that whatever meaning the song once had left the building two minutes ago.

Growing up, the CD that I had of *Blue Moves* left out four tracks to fit the whole album onto one disc. Interestingly, those tracks were different from the ones left out for the first CD release in 1988. In 1988, the orchestral 'Out of the Blue' was pulled, along with 'Shoulder Holster' and 'The Wide Eyed and Laughing'. My disc, however, mystifyingly restored the ponderous six minutes and eleven seconds 'Out of the Blue' and got rid of 'Cage the Songbird' and 'Where's the Shoorah?' instead. For many years I wondered why suddenly 'Cage the Songbird' got the axe after making the initial digital cut. Part of the explanation lies in the fact that Dudgeon had not initially intended *Blue Moves* to be a double album but was rather pushed into making it one when he let it slip to a group of MCA executives how much material the band had recorded in Toronto. The record company jumped on the idea that they might release a double album, and suddenly Dudgeon found himself in the unenviable position of not being able to dump the songs that he felt weren't up to scratch, including 'Where's the Shoorah?', 'Shoulder Holster', 'Boogie Pilgrim', 'The Wide-Eyed and Laughing' and what he held to be the interminably over-long 'Bite Your Lip (Get Up and Dance!)'. Those who worked on the album were fully aware of the hierarchy of tracks that were originally scheduled for inclusion and which were on the chopping block, and when it came time to make cuts for the CD, Dudgeon's list was a template for what to leave out.

'Cage the Songbird's surprisingly literal lyrics are in the tradition of 'Candle in the Wind', this time centring on the death of French chanteuse Édith Piaf (1915–1963), in which we linger over the scene of her dead body. The words suggest that Piaf died by suicide, which wasn't the case, but makes for a more affecting scene. This is a unique song in Elton's canon – Elton's phrasing and vocal shape are wispier than we've ever heard them, and the underlying texture formed by Howard's oscillating Mellotron, Johnstone's dulcimer and the backing vocals of David Crosby (1941–2023) and Graham Nash (*b*.1942), all set Elton's voice in a context of fragile sounds that Elton arguably hadn't employed in a sustained way since *Friends*. At the end of the day, 'Cage the Songbird' will always suffer the inevitable comparison people make with 'Candle in the Wind', which took a poignant point of view on the classic subject of the price of fame, but on its own, it provides a different, more fleeting, sort of Elton experience.

'Crazy Water', by contrast, is a bit of inspired lunacy on par with 'One Horse Town'. The subject matter is a grim one: the tragedy of the FV *Gaul*, a fish processing ship that disappeared on 8 February 1974. The ship itself wasn't found until 1997, and all thirty-six crew members are presumed to have died. Bernie was taken by the tragedy of the story, with its links to the ancient and familiar worries experienced between wives and their mariner husbands each time the latter take to sea, perhaps never to return. More generally, it's about the stress placed on a relationship by a husband who puts himself in danger in the name of work, a theme that Bernie knew well. Considering the darkness of both the specific subject matter and larger theme, this could well have turned into yet another 'Tonight' like lament but Elton seems to have latched onto the 'Crazy' of the title and ran with it, kicking every aspect of the song into a frenzied high gear, spurred on by the twitchy freneticism of Howard's clavinet playing, and by the most artfully absurd backing vocals laid down since the high water mark of doo wop, conceived by Daryl Dragon (1942–2019) and consisting of strings of nonsense syllables climaxing on the iconic 'Dup-dup-dup watta-watta-watta' which all but entirely compensates for the fact that, once again, the last third of the song is an extended jam vamp.

Rounding out the first disc we have 'Shoulder Holster', which brings us the first woman in Bernie lyrics who actively determines her own destiny in a meaningful way. The story revolves around Dolly Summers, whose husband runs out on her to take up with another woman. Dolly, vengeance in her heart, puts a pistol in her shoulder holster and pursues the villain until she finally catches up with him only to realise that he's not worth the trouble of shooting and she heads back home. Elton is restrained on this track, settling himself into an unobtrusive narrator role in a country tradition to focus attention on Bernie's evolving story, with a little bit of sizzle added by David Sanborn's (1945–2024) saxophone.

If 'Tonight', 'I Feel Like a Bullet' and 'Someone's Final Song' represent Bernie at his most raw, 'Sorry Seems to Be the Hardest Word' brings us Elton in his full vulnerability through a melody that had long been haunting him and lyrics largely of his own creation. 'What've I gotta do to make you love me?' was the central refrain of his post-John Reid love life, as he fell deeply in love with man after man, only to either drive them away or pack them away when he grew bored of them. Lonely, even when surrounded by hangers-on, and often feeling essentially unlovable, the Elton of this period (and indeed for years to come) despaired that he'd never be able to change the aspects of his behaviour that frightened off his best prospects at a lasting relationship. For me, one of the most brilliant details here is the fact that the only backup vocals present are those of Elton himself, the perfect reflection of an individual so utterly alone that the only harmony he can find is the one he produces himself. It's a little detail, but it's exactly right. The combination of accordion and vibraphone is also well calibrated towards highlighting the pathos of the situation, with the coolness of the vibes expressing the situation the singer finds himself in, and the lilting accordion expressing the ideal, so far from any hope of realisation. Together, they are devastating, and Elton's direct lyrics are breathtaking in their honesty, creating one of the few moments where we as listeners feel we are truly listening to Elton, and not just Elton as interpreted by Bernie.

'Out of the Blue' starts out promisingly, building on its opening circular theme to generate a forward-thrusting instrumental that almost sounds like the backing soundtrack to a cool heist flick, reaching its suspenseful height with the helicoptering synths and choppy guitar interjections around one minute and eighteen seconds. The problem, of course, is that it goes on for another five minutes after that, with the second section of the song being a close repetition of the first, and the third section more of the same basic material. It's another piece that would have been great fun live but on record it comes off as more jam-based noodlery.

'Between Seventeen and Twenty' is famous in Elton circles as one of the most awkward recording experiences of any of his albums. Bernie's lyrics about his suspicions that his wife was sleeping with one of his friends were legitimate, and the individual concerned was none other than the bassist who had to lay down a quality performance while hearing how his actions had ruined his friend's life. Perhaps a small price to pay for what was a monumentally poor decision on Passarelli's part but certainly a rough moment to power through. The ages in the song represent the ages that Bernie and Maxine respectively were when they first started dating, and if the lyrics are full of recriminations for Maxine's infidelity, they didn't spare Bernie's own part in the dissolution of their marriage, including an entirely frank account of showering at 3.00 am to wipe the smell off him from whatever dalliance he'd participated in earlier that night. The lyrics alternate between tight observations of mutual infidelity and verbal clunkers that are almost unfathomable by Bernie's usual high standards of imagery and word choice, and perhaps picking up on the unpolished nature of the lyrics, Elton provides a relatively by the numbers chord progression to go with it via an army of standard I and IV chords.

'The Wide-Eyed and Laughing' is one of two songs that both the 1988 and later CD releases of *Blue Moves* omitted, and again I don't think it's because anyone was ashamed of the song but more because it's one of the distinct outliers on the record, inhabiting an instrumentation universe thoroughly different from everything else happening on the album, springing from Johnstone and Quaye's late night improv sessions in which Johnstone was eventually convinced to pull out his precious sitar. Presenting their results to Elton the next day, he made the decision to layer on top Bernie's lyrics that he had to hand. Just as the use of sitar on a record was, by 1976, a nostalgic throwback to the instrumental eclecticism of the late 1960s, so were these lyrics in many respects a reflection of the vocabulary and image choices of Bernie's earliest work, with references to 'tea leaves and tarots' that could have been pulled from 'Tartan Coloured Lady'. It's the sort of song that could go wrong but I think the band succeeds in making something very much their own here, with the regular deep thrum of a bass drum and the sci-fi phasing of Howard's synths adding enough unique elements into the overall soundscape, and Elton keeping sufficiently to his own instincts, to create a piece which sounds genuine and reverent.

'Someone's Final Song' wasn't Elton and Bernie's first song about suicide – it wasn't even the only song about suicide on *Blue Moves* – but it's by far the deepest exploration of it. 'Someone's Final Song' is an exploration of the mental state of someone who has come to the decision that the ache of living can no longer be borne. Backed by his own piano, Howard's synthesizer and the mournful background vocals arranged by Bruce Johnston and Curt Becher (1944–1987), Elton crafts a small masterpiece here that does equal justice to the tragedy of an individual who sees no other end but suicide and to the personal dignity involved in squarely facing up to that decision. One of the most poignant ways he conveys this is in the repeated 'To go on living' line, which he underscores not with a descending line in the bass that you might expect, or even a relatively stationary one representing someone paralysed by the stasis of their life but rather with a predominantly ascending line. The writer at the centre of this song has decided to end his life but not with bitterness but rather a steady sureness that it's what must be done.

I really don't know what to tell you about 'Where's the Shoorah?' A fair amount of the song's ultimate meaning centres on knowing what the heck a Shoorah is and though a few theories exist on the subject, none of them really make the song's full intent shine forth. Elton's setting is straight up gospel, strengthened by his work on the harmonium and the haunting vocals from the Cornerstone Choir, which give extra weight to his powerful major-minor chord modulations.

I love 'If There's a God in Heaven (What's He Waiting For?)' to a degree that I realise most people can't understand, but I'm going to make my case. The song's origins lie in a song by the Chi-Lites, 'There Will Never Be Any Peace (Until God is Seated at the Conference Table)' a monotonous soul ballad that proposes that all those people working to define a sustainable agricultural or economic policy are really wasting their time, because men can't possibly solve the problems involved, and what's really needed is more God, whatever that means. The story goes that Elton loved the sound but found the lyrics comically misguided and asked Bernie to craft lyrics in the same vein that he could write a song around. The result, 'If There's a God in Heaven (What's He Waiting For?)', is a frank rejoinder to 'There Will Never Be Any Peace' in which Bernie seems to be responding, 'Oh you want more God in this? Let's look at his track record, shall we?' before going into a definitive cataloguing of that deity's overwhelming demonstrable indifference to the tragedy daily visited upon the most powerless of his creations. Elton pours all the fuzziest trappings of the soul-gospel tradition at his disposal onto Bernie's lyrics, creating a jewel of a parody that pays homage to the musical structures he admired while at the same time gently urging for a bit more considered reflection in the future as regards messaging.

'Idol' is a piece about the fate of many of the 1950s musical stars whose personal decisions had brought them to a pitiable state, from Jerry Lee Lewis to The King, Elvis Presley, and exists also as a sort of narrative extrapolation of one possible future for Elton and Bernie themselves, both of whom reckoned that they were likely at the top of their story arc in the 1970s, and were fully engaged in a path of self-destruction. In telling the story of the unidentified Idol, Elton knew he might well be telling that of himself, and so this song is both an honest assessment of a hero's downfall, and an appeal to the future to treat him with the same mixture of reverence and melancholic clear-sightedness when his time comes. Elton's loose nightclub jazz setting of the song with Roger Pope on brushes and the Brecker Brothers on mournful brass is a well-chosen one, painting as it does the portrait of an artist on the way out, who played at stadiums, then auditoriums, then state fairs and ended up filling the graveyard shift at a smoke-filled Las Vegas nightclub, singing for the slot addicts and dazed newlyweds, abandoned by all the people who rode his fame on the way up and pitied by the few remaining fans who make the pilgrimage to witness what remains of their hero only to shrug their shoulders and declare, 'I have to say that I like the way his music sounded before.'

'Theme From a Non-Existent TV Series' is the third and final instrumental on *Blue Moves* and combines the best elements of the other two. Tightly constrained into less than two minutes, it also has the spirit of inventive fun that characterises 'Out of the Blue' in its best moments, as it blazes forward in its note-perfect synthed-up take on classic action tropes *á la* the *Dick Barton* theme. In a just world, this would have been snapped up by an actual television program and used as the theme song for *Manimal* or *Airwolf* but that it exists here for us to visit and revisit is perhaps enough.

The fun of 'Non-Existent TV Series' is a perfect lead-in for the sprawling bacchanalian romp that is 'Bite Your Lip (Get Up and Dance!)', the album's concluding track. Famously, Dudgeon asked the band to go through the song once to allow him to finalise his production setup but after they'd finished Elton insisted that they'd nailed it perfectly and refused to do it again despite Dudgeon's pleading that it was only intended as a technical setup run, and that there were glaring glitches across several tracks that required an adjustment of the equipment and subsequent real recording run. Elton, however, was adamant, and it was up to Dudgeon to use his wizardry to save the track. In the end, he succeeded, and though 'Bite Your Lip (Get Up and Dance!)' didn't achieve the hoped for commercial success, maxing out at the #28 position in both the US and UK, it has since grown into a cult classic for the Elton community.

The Stats

Album/Single	US	UK	Australia	Canada
Blue Moves	3	3	8	4
	P	G	P	G
'Sorry Seems to Be the Hardest Word'/'Shoulder Holster'	6	11	11	25
'Bite Your Lip (Get Up and Dance!)'/'Chameleon'	28	28	72	
'Crazy Water'/'Chameleon'		27		

The Players

Elton John: acoustic piano (1 to 5, 7 to 10, 13 to 16 and 18), vocals (2 to 9, 12 to 16 and 18), vocalese (11), harmonium (14) and harpsichord (17)
Curt Becher: backing vocals (4, 10, 11 and 13) and BGV arrangements (11 and 13)
Harry Bluestone: strings leader (18)
Michael Brecker: saxophone (5, 8 and 16)
Randy Brecker: trumpet (5, 8 and 16)
Paul Buckmaster: string arrangements and conductor (3, 7 and 15) and brass arrangements (7)
Cindy Bullens: backing vocals (4, 7 and 11)

Clark Burroughs: backing vocals (13)
Joe Chemay: backing vocals (11 and 13)
Reverend James Cleveland: choir director (5, 14 and 18)
Ray Cooper: glockenspiel (1 and 17), marimba (1 and 17), gong (3), tambourine (3, 5, 7, 8, 11 and 15), vibraphone (3, 4, 9 and 10), bells (3), shaker (4, 6 and 11), triangle (6), finger cymbals (6), congas (7, 10, 11, 15 and 18) and rototom (12)
The Cornerstone Institutional Baptist Church and the Southern California Community Choir: choirs (5, 14 and 18)
David Crosby: backing vocals (6)
Daryl Dragon: BGV arrangements (7)
The Martyn Ford Orchestra: strings (3, 7 and 15) and brass (7)
Carl Fortina: accordion (8)
Ron Hicklin: backing vocals (4 and 7)
Michael Hurwitz: cello (3)
Bruce Johnston: backing vocals (4, 7, 10, 11 and 13), BGV arrangements (4, 11 and 13)
Davey Johnstone: mandolin (2, 11 and 17), electric guitar (3, 7, 10 and 15), slide guitar (5 and 18), acoustic guitar (6), dulcimer (6), sitar (12) and slide guitar (18)
Jon Joyce: backing vocals (4, 7 and 11)
The London Symphony Orchestra: strings (2 and 9)
Gene Morford: backing vocals (4 and 7)
Graham Nash: backing vocals (6)
James Newton Howard: synthesizers (1, 3, 6, 10, 12, 13, 17 and 18), Fender Rhodes (3, 9, 13 and 17), Hammond organ (5, 11 and 15), Mellotron (6) and clavinet (7)
The Gene Page Strings: strings (18)
Kenny Passarelli: bass guitar (1, 3 to 5, 7 to 11 and 14 to 18)
Roger Pope: drums (1, 3 to 5, 7, 8, 10, 11 and 15 to 18)
Caleb Quaye: acoustic guitar (1, 4, 6, 12, 17), electric guitar (3, 4, 7, 10, 11, 15 and 18), guitar solo (3, 10 and 15) and twelve-string guitar (12)
Barry Rogers: trombone (5, 8 and 16)
David Sanborn: saxophone (5, 8 and 16)
Richard Studt: strings leader (3, 7, 12 and 15) and brass leader (7)
Toni Tennille: backing vocals (4, 7, 10 and 13)

The Tracks

Disc one, side one:
1. 'Your Starter For...' (Quaye) (1.22)
2. 'Tonight' (John, Taupin) (7.51)
3. 'One Horse Town' (John, Taupin, Howard) (5.55)
4. 'Chameleon' (John, Taupin) (5.26)

Disc one, side two:
5. 'Boogie Pilgrim' (John, Taupin, Johnstone, Quaye) (6.03)
6. 'Cage the Songbird' (John, Taupin, Johnstone) (3.52)
7. 'Crazy Water' (John, Taupin) (5.41)
8. 'Shoulder Holster' (John, Taupin) (5.10)

Disc two, side one:
9. 'Sorry Seems to Be the Hardest Word' (John, Taupin) (3.47)
10. 'Out of the Blue' (John, Taupin) (6.11)
11. 'Between Seventeen and Twenty' (John, Taupin, Johnstone, Quaye) (5.12)
12. 'The Wide Eyed and Laughing' (John, Taupin, Howard, Johnstone, Quaye) (3.27)
13. 'Someone's Final Song' (John, Taupin) (4.07)

Disc Two, side two:
14. 'Where's the Shoorah?' (John, Taupin) (4.09)
15. 'If There's a God in Heaven (What's He Waiting For?)' (John, Taupin, Johnstone) (4.22)
16. 'Idol' (John, Taupin) (4.08)
17. 'Theme From a Non-Existent TV Series' (John) (1.18)
18. 'Bite Your Lip (Get Up and Dance!)' (John, Taupin) (6.41)

Musician's Corner: 'Tonight'

At nearly eight minutes in length, 'Tonight' is Elton's second longest song (if you count 'We All Fall in Love Sometimes' and 'Curtains' as separate tracks), just behind the eleven minutes plus of 'Funeral for a Friend'/'Love Lies Bleeding'. 'Tonight' is a consistent tone poem that paints the feeling of a troubled relationship through pure instrumental music before Bernie's words start telling us about the component parts of this couple's cyclic inability to find each other.

We start in D minor and there's something inherently heart-breaking about the movement between D minor and B flat major in this introduction. Theoretically, in this age of equal temperament tuning we should feel the same way about the interplay between any minor chord and its major 6 chord, but for some reason (likely located in historical differences in how different keys sounded thanks to pre-modern tuning practices which translated into certain types of songs being written in particular types of keys) C minor to A flat major just doesn't hit the same way as D minor to B flat major does.

Elton's choice of key here produces the expectation of an unhappy ending for our protagonists from virtual note one. Getting into the piece itself, we are treated to beautiful bassline arpeggiations and ostinato patterns that put us in mind of Elton's earlier works of yearning and introspection, like 'Skyline Pigeon', with the unhappy conclusion to our protagonists' struggle brought to a close on a descending run of half-steps to the first and fifth notes of the D minor scale that hearken back to the age of Mozart (1756–1791), who employed them to similarly stunning effect in his fourth violin sonata in E minor:

Mozart, *Violin Sonata No. 4*

Elton John, *Tonight*

If the elements of 'Crocodile Rock' are a kind of love letter to the golden age of rock 'n roll, then the key choice, arpeggiations, instrumentation and classic patterns sum here to a love novel to the legacies Elton inherited from the late eighteenth and nineteenth centuries, which, at least to my ears, provides a perfectly monolithic and imposing backdrop to the fragile story of two individuals that lies at the centre of this piece. Elton's voice is plaintive and pleading, one modern individual trying to make things okay, if just for one night, surrounded by these musical structures that have existed for centuries, and will continue to exist long after this couple have broken up. The counterpoint between the majesty of the classical orchestra and the singer's lone voice suggests strongly which force will win, even if we don't understand a word of what is being sung.

Chapter 14

A Single Man

Recorded: January to September 1978
Released: 27 October 1978
Producers: Elton John and Clive Franks

The Story

A fter the spectacular failure of Elton's experiment in giving creative control to another individual that was *The Thom Bell Sessions* (see next chapter), Elton realised that, though change was certainly called for, he couldn't simply reduce himself to the role of a mere vocalist. In the empty spaces after the conclusion of the *Louder than the Concorde* tour and middling success of the *Blue Moves* album, Elton lived a largely reclusive existence. Into that void stepped Gary Osborne (*b.*1949), a jingle writer and lyricist who had written the words for Kiki Dee's 'Amoureuse' and who was perfectly content to spend an evening in playing cards.

Elton presented Osborne with a melody that had been floating around his head and asked him to set some words to it, as an experiment. Osborne's lyrics, produced after two days of finetuning, were unpromisingly titled 'Smile That Smile', but pleased Elton, and after further work it was retitled 'Shine on Through', one of the tracks that Elton brought to *The Thom Bell Sessions* only to ultimately reject Bell's homogeneous setting of it, and which he'd rerecord for *A Single Man*. After *The Thom Bell Sessions* didn't work out, Elton was eager to resume the promising partnership he'd begun with Osborne, and the two set to work exploring this new way of producing songs.

For Elton, the new approach represented a game changer where he was no longer the final arbiter of a song's meaning. With Bernie, Elton's casting of the lyrics put the final stamp on how people interpreted them and created tension when the type of song he wanted to write didn't match the lyrics at hand. In the new style, Elton got to compose the type of music that caught his fancy and then left it to the lyricist to create a story to match his tone, a more Elton-centred process that was particularly to his liking. The downside was that creating lyrics to a premade melody places constraints on those lyrics, making it much harder to craft an organic narrative. It's not impossible and Osborne would go on to produce some true gems but it's harder than allowing the lyricist to create a world and the words that live in it from scratch.

A Single Man was the first step in a new direction and while the dramatic storytelling hasn't quite figured itself out, there are some positives here: first, Elton finally gets to sing songs with goofy lyrics, instead of having to transfigure Bernie's serious lyrics into novelty numbers, and it's nice to hear him having a good time doing that. Second, Elton's exploring the lower range of his register, as Bell had advised him to do, which will be important to his sound in the years to come. Third, having detached himself almost entirely from his former bands (though Cooper is still all over this album and Johnstone shows up for one track), he has also freed himself from the temptation to include sprawling jam sessions on his records, and the two instrumentals on *A Single Man* are more effective than those on *Blue Moves*, and in the absence of extended instrumental outros everything except for 'It Ain't Gonna Be Easy' on this album fully justifies its length. These were all issues that had needed addressing and *A Single Man* gave Elton the excuse he needed to find a resolution. A decade later, those solutions, when combined with the best aspects of his old working style, would trigger a renaissance in Elton's creative output.

The Songs

The first minute of *A Single Man* features just that – Elton and his piano, alone and almost spectrally small in the stillness. 'Shine on Through' was the first song written by Elton and Osborne together, and after its disappointing production at the hands of Bell, Elton elected for a fresh perspective on the track to lead off his new album. Some four minutes shorter than the Bell version, the take on *A Single Man* is more direct and less repetitive, with Buckmaster's orchestral arrangement providing an urgent but subtle under carpet of sound more effective in supporting Elton's conception of the atmospherics than the Philadelphia effects that Bell had been tasked with shoehorning in.

The aspect of 'Shine on Through' which Elton fans obsess over, however, isn't the relative merits of Bell and Buckmaster's string arrangements but whether the third verse is about Bernie and what seemed like the end of his and Elton's working relationship: 'Oh, my friend/So, at last we've reached the end.'

It would be beautiful if these words were addressed to Bernie – a bittersweet realisation that their time together might have run down, a recognition, perhaps too late, that he didn't appreciate their time together when they had it, and that the one thing that can be counted on is that through the uncertainty, love remains and always will. I have my doubts, though, as that would require the first set of lyrics that Osborne wrote for Elton to be about the person whose job he was essentially stepping into, which seems a gutsy thing to do, even if accomplished tastefully. It's possible that Elton, whose hand was in the lyrics here and there throughout the album, saw the trajectory of the song and thought the third verse a perfect place to express his feelings. It's also possible that it's simply following the downwards pattern of the verse structure. In my heart, the verse will always be about Bernie, even if my head strongly suspects otherwise.

'Return to Paradise' has an interesting idea behind it, rarely explored in pop music, namely the perpetually alternating dissatisfaction and romanticism emanating from English tourists abroad. The song is about English people who can't wait to get away to paradise but once there grouse about lacking the comforts of their homelife, only to grow incredibly sentimental when they have to leave and return to that existence. The exaggerated tropical instrumentation in the form of Ray Cooper's marimbas and shakers, and Tim Renwick's (*b.*1949) lazy vacation guitar, cue us into the fact that this is parody, and that the ideal relationship between the narrator and the land he is living is, in fact, a romantic concoction of an individual who doesn't know where they are or what they want.

What 'Bite Your Lip (Get Up and Dance!)' was to *Blue Moves*, 'I Don't Care' is to *A Single Man*, a high tempo number meant less for close textual analysis and more for getting up out of the chair and flailing one's limbs around the room like a gummy octopus on a string. The song is two minutes shorter than 'Bite Your Lip (Get Up and Dance!)', perhaps in response to the general critique of that song's sumptuously stuffed end material. Buckmaster's strings swoop while the guitars robotically flange in a thoroughly 1978 combination of classicism and science fiction. Disco's demise was just around the corner but for the moment, the spirit of over the top space orchestra funk groove was alive and well.

Coming to track four, we have 'Big Dipper', which is easily in my top three list of best songs about gay oral sex on a roller coaster. Everything about it is delightful, from Osborne's explicitly stated intention of writing the most gloriously 'poofy' song ever to the fact that Elton brought the entire Watford Football Club team in to record backing vocals, but couldn't tell them what it was about, to the wonderful awooga honk noise that ends the piece. For my American brethren, 'Big Dipper' in England is a term usually employed to talk about roller coasters but, of course, is ripe for double *entendre* usage as a stand-in for penises, a fact which the song employs to greatest effect as it tells the story of a gay man pursuing a well-endowed fellow, working through his resistances after a few rounds of alcohol and who knows what else, culminating on a roller coaster trip during which they both teach each other a few new eye-opening tricks. While many didn't pick up on the homosexual undercurrent of the song, the Soviets realised it right away and yanked it from the Russian release of *A Single Man* on reasons of morality. Thirty years ahead of its time, 'Big Dipper' ranks today as a transgressive classic and an example of the material that Elton probably couldn't have explored within the confines of his partnership with Bernie.

There's seemingly no middle ground among Elton fans about the eight minute twenty-eight second 'It Ain't Gonna Be Easy'. You either disparage it as an exercise in self-indulgence on the scale of *Blue Moves* at its worst, or you love it as a showcase of Elton's vocal menagerie at its most esoteric. The lyrics are... fine. It's about how difficult it'll be to repair a relationship after infidelity and while it doesn't break any fresh ground it doesn't do anything terribly embarrassing. What saves the song from falling into Bell like territory is the sense of emotional build, starting from the lonesome guitar riff from Renwick and growing in emotional instability as the song progresses. By the end, Elton's a howling mess. These are sounds we're not used to hearing from Elton, and while superficially one might groan and call it 'self-indulgent', I have always maintained that this is one instance where all the repetitions have narrative meaning. We know from how Elton's singing the song's conclusion that this reconciliation is well doomed before it properly began.

Side two features one of the most satisfying final three song progressions on any Elton record, perhaps the most satisfying in terms of musical form. To get there, however, we must do some slogging. 'Part-Time Love' features the welcome return of Johnstone to lead guitar and was the first single of the album. The lyrics are told from the perspective of a man trying to coerce a woman into being his lover, on the logic that everyone has a part-time love in modern marriages, so she should stop resisting and go with it. It's a dark theme to layer on top of an upbeat musical structure. Forty years ago, it was probably much easier to think of this song as a light romp but in the intervening years we've learned a few things and it's hard to forget them and enjoy this song from the perspective of its age.

There are people who love 'Georgia'. To me, it's always represented an uncomfortable attempt to return to the unquestioning Southern nostalgia on the earliest Elton records that Bernie had long since outgrown. It's nice to have B.J. Cole (*b*.1946) back in our head on pedal steel guitar (his last recording with Elton was on 'Tiny Dancer' back in 1971) but the facile comparison of Georgia as a pastoral Eden as against the chattering artificiality of Los Angeles is rough on the ears today. Marshalling the women workers of Rocket Records as a female chorus, and once again turning to the Watford Football Club for a male chorus, Elton attempts to capture a gospel feel but the whole enterprise is so kneecapped by the naïve (even for 1978) lyrics that it's difficult to feel much sympathy for the emotional connection to Georgia portrayed in the song.

'Shooting Star' represents the start of the road to greatness that characterises the end half of side two. It's a little wisp of a song about the people left behind as an artist rises in fame. In this case, it's about an ex-boyfriend or girlfriend, who used to look on supportively during those early shows in small venues but has since been discarded and wonders what their partner's life is like now that they're famous, declaring that, should they ever fall back down from the heights of fame, there'll be no resentment, only the welcoming arms of an old friend and lover. It's a sweet number sung by Elton in a small and slightly awe-struck voice, as befits the character he's playing.

Following this tender character portrait, 'Madness' is an uncompromising and exceedingly brave account of the IRA terrorist campaign that raged through the 1970s, killing dozens and injuring thousands. Though 1977 and 1978 represented a lull in the terror campaign, the memory of the 1972 to 1976 bombings was still fresh and real, and Elton and Osborne dug into an uncompromising portrayal of the indiscriminate death wrought by domestic terrorism, making no attempt to abstractly cover the theme of the music. Elton's relentless bassline underpinning harsh ostinato patterns signal not only the dark determination of the song's subjects but his own anger at violence and terror being employed as vehicles of political debate. Elton's vocals are sharp and uncompromising, as are the orchestral blasts of Buckmaster's orchestra. In every way, this is the hardest hitting song Elton ever penned, and its condemnation of the political commodification of fear and death is, forty-five years later, as powerful as ever.

'Reverie' is the bridge between the apocalyptic hellscapes of 'Madness' and the funereal fatalism of 'Song for Guy'. Navigating the space between those two vastly different atmospheres is a tall order, which seems to call for some large scale composition but Elton realised that the contrary was the case – that the space between violent tragedy and mourning is both unspeakably small and boundlessly cavernous, and that the best way to represent that is through a small composition in which a lone pair of instruments try desperately to fill the still space. The track is given extra poignancy by the fact that the two performers of the song are Elton on the piano and Buckmaster on the ARP synthesizer, a pair who had been through their own conflicts but who found their way to each other again through music.

The album concludes with 'Song for Guy', certainly Elton's greatest instrumental composition since 'Funeral for a Friend' and perhaps the greatest he has ever penned. It's written as a sort of theme and textural variations, which is made up of two primary pieces of thematic material, driven forward by Ray Cooper's rhythm box, and around which Elton layers in shifting textures of Mellotrons and synthesizers. The title was chosen the day after the song was recorded, when Elton heard about the death of Guy Burchett, a 17-year-old courier at Rocket Records. In England, after the press misreported an anxiety attack as a cardiac episode that nearly claimed his life, the song's refrain of 'Life isn't everything' took on an eerie verisimilitude with reality, and helped push the song into the Top 10. In the US, meanwhile, Universal agreed to release the single, but refused to promote it because they disagreed with Elton about its commercial viability, driving another wedge between them and Elton, pushing him one step closer to his eventual signing with Geffen Records.

The Stats

Album/Single	US	UK	Australia	Canada
A Single Man	15	8	8	12
	P	G		P
'Part-Time Love'/'I Cry at Night'	22	15	12	13
'Song for Guy'/'Lovesick'	110	4	14	
'Return to Paradise'/'Song for Guy'				

The Players

Elton John: lead vocals, backing vocals (1, 2 and 8), pianos (1, 4 and 11), acoustic piano (2, 3, 5, 6, 7, 9 and 10), clavinet (3), harmonium and church organ (7), Fender Rhodes (8); Mellotron, ARP synthesizer and Solina String Synthesizer (11)

Tim Renwick: acoustic guitar (2 and 3), electric guitar (4, 5, 6 and 9), Leslie guitar (7) and mandolin (7)

Davey Johnstone: lead guitar and backing vocals (6)

B.J. Cole: pedal steel guitar (7)

Clive Franks: bass (1 to 7, 9 and 11)

Herbie Flowers: bass (8)

Steve Holley: drums (1 to 9), motor horn (4)

Ray Cooper: tambourine (1, 3 to 7 and 9), marimba (2), shaker (2, 8 and 11), vibraphone (5), congas (6 and 9), timpani (9), wind chimes and rhythm box (11)

John Crocker: clarinet (4), tenor saxophone (8)

Jim Shepherd: trombone (4)

Henry Lowther: trumpet (2)

Patrick Halcox: trumpet (4)

Paul Buckmaster: orchestra arrangements (1, 3, 5, 6 and 9), arrangements (2) and ARP synthesizer (10)

Gary Osborne: backing vocals (1, 2, 3 and 6)

Vicki Brown: backing vocals (3 and 6)

Stevie Lange: backing vocals (3 and 6)

Joanne Stone: backing vocals (3 and 6)

Chris Thompson: backing vocals (3 and 6)

The South Audley Street Girl's Choir: backing vocals (4 and 7)

Watford Football Club: backing vocals (4 and 7)

The Tracks

Side one:
1. 'Shine on Through' (John, Osborne) (3.:45)
2. 'Return to Paradise' (John, Osborne) (4.15)
3. 'I Don't Care' (John, Osborne) (4.23)
4. 'Big Dipper' (John, Osborne) (4.04)
5. 'It Ain't Gonna Be Easy' (John, Osborne) (8.27)

Side two:
6. 'Part-Time Love' (John, Osborne) (3.16)
7. 'Georgia' (John, Osborne) (4.50)
8. 'Shooting Star' (John, Osborne) (2.44)

9. 'Madness' (John, Osborne) (5.53)
10. 'Reverie' (John) (0.53)
11. 'Song for Guy' (John) (6.35)

Musician's Corner: 'Ego'

Okay, fine, 'Ego' wasn't on the original release of this album, but it was on the 1988 rerelease, so I'm stretching that into an opportunity to talk about this, one of Elton's most complex, introspective pieces, where lyrics and musical structure are working in perfect synchrony to tell this story of unchecked vanity.

'Ego' wastes no time on shoving listeners into an uncomfortable place. Something is deeply wrong from the outset, hinted at by the manic descending grace notes, steam whistles and pounding B's in the bass, all but confirmed in the third and fourth measures when our first big chords are a B diminished and a B diminished m7. This is the point when we realise, 'Oh man, Elton's in the Locrian mode. This is going to be *a ride.*'

Most pop music is in one of two modes – the mode you get from the intervals you hear when you play all the white keys from C up to C (the 'major' scale) and that you get when you play all the white keys from A to A (the 'minor' scale). Those two modes, based on the intervals created by those two scales, make up, conservatively, 99.7 per cent of all pop music, but in ancient and medieval times songs based on different interval patterns were common.

Locrian is what you get when you start on a B and end on a B, and it's generally considered the forbidden mode, because it's the only one that lacks a perfect fifth, which is considered an essential element to making a popular song. Take away that perfect fifth, and you take away the satisfaction of the V-I transition from dominant to tonic that is the backbone of most pop music. In 'Ego', we are based on B, but the key signature tellingly lacks any sharps or flats, which is what you would expect in Locrian mode, and Elton's not shy about making us feel that palpable loss of a perfect fifth F sharp. The only time in the first page of the music that he deviates from that pounding B in the bottom is when he slips down to an F, in order to amplify the B diminished chord he is playing on top, as if to communicate, 'This is no accident, this is where we are'. And then, after he hits us with the extremely unsettling B diminished chord, he ups the ante in the fourth measure by adding another minor third on top of that, to create a four note chord that is entirely made up of minor thirds, which is exactly what they do in movies when they want you to feel anxious that Jason Vorhees is about to murder someone with an axe.

Elton could have just used this mode through the whole song, but what I really love about this piece is how he employs different song forms as a way to portray a narcissistic personality – they are many people, depending on what they want out of you, and this song likewise goes into multiple sections, each with its own distinct but untethered character. The first bit is pure destructive Locrian chaos. The second settles into recognizable chords and even some recognizable arpeggiated structures, but something is still *not quite right*, and that something is that the chords just won't settle down, everything keeps moving and shifting with a frenzy that gives the lie to the comparative stability of the section. Each measure centres on a new chord in a dizzying array: B-F-Bb-Ebm-Abm7-Bb7-A-D-G-C-F-Bb-Eb-D-sus4.

This person isn't all right, and as if realising that we have realised that, he goes into charmer mode in the third section, slowing down, telling us, 'Everything is fine – look at these patterns, totally normal. These words, so human and normal. Trust me, I'm fine. Everything is fine.' But it can't last, and the fourth section goes straight into Napoleonic mode, with this wonderful climb by fourths that does not give two damns about what key we might have once theoretically tried to be in, as C hops to F, then D to G, then E7 to Am, getting higher and higher as the delusions get thicker and thicker, until finally, and this is my favourite part, on the line 'I had to grow and prove my ego' we get a big fat F# chord in the middle, a whole chord that we haven't seen this entire song based on the one note Elton insistently refused to give us for the first page of music, and then the whole thing ends on a regular old B-minor chord, as if that's where we've been the whole time, and the problem is clearly with us, and not with him.

Structurally, it's the best and bravest thing Elton has ever written. The stages we move through and the musical devices in each of them are a perfect encapsulation of the array of deceptions employed by a narcissistic personality to keep the focus centred on them and the things they want. It's uncompromising, true to the core and utterly brilliant.

Chapter 15

The Thom Bell Sessions

Recorded: October 1977
Released: June 1979
Producer: Thom Bell

The Story

ree at last from Dick James Music, Elton elected to publish *Blue Moves* through his own company, Rocket Records. Dudgeon, who had produced every Elton album since 1970's *Elton John*, had a few fundamental concerns about the way John Reid was handling Rocket, particularly on the financial side, and wanted those concerns addressed before he agreed to continue his relationship with the company. Reid, however, whose dictatorial presence atop the label had driven out more than a few of its more conscientious members, refused to consider his grievances, leaving Dudgeon with no choice but to walk, and Elton for his part chose not to assert his influence. The loss of Dudgeon stirred Elton to re-evaluate his working arrangements. He wondered if it was time for a clean break and to that end he and Bernie agreed to part ways for the moment, to see what it might be like to work with other people, even as they remained friends.

Disenchanted with the industrial machine that touring had become, Elton all but stopped appearing in public following the *Louder than the Concorde* tour and devoted his energies instead towards the chairmanship of Watford Football Club, which offered him a means of grounding himself. He was waiting to build up the urge to tour and write again, and in the meantime struck on a bold new idea for a new album: to do nothing. What if instead of assembling a band, writing music and playing instruments, he just sat in a booth and sang the notes that someone put in front of him and then left for the day?

He presented this concept to one of his favourite producers and a founder of the Philadelphia soul sound, Thom Bell (1943–2022), whose work with The Stylistics he admired, and asked if Bell would be willing to be the controlling force on the next album. Bell, who knew something of Elton's mercurial tendencies, asked for Elton's assurance that he meant what he said, and that Bell would have complete authority during the process. Elton shook hands in solemn confirmation of their pact and *The Thom Bell Sessions* were born.

Six tracks were recorded over a day and a half during the 1977 sessions, including one older Elton-Bernie number and one collaboration with Osborne, who'd soon become Elton's go-to lyricist. Upon hearing the mixed tracks, however, Elton was dissatisfied with the result and decided to drop the project. Three of the tracks were released two years later as an EP in 1979, including the moderate hit single 'Mama Can't Buy You Love' and the full half-dozen song lot was finally released in 1989 as *The Complete Thom Bell Sessions*. Elton, for his part, learned that doing nothing perhaps wasn't the best policy for the future and decided to press forward with the new writing partnership he'd forged with Osborne.

The Songs

Restricting ourselves to the three songs on the original 12-inch EP, we start with 'Three Way Love Affair', which starts promisingly with a mid-tempo groove accompanied by funky synthesizer embellishments. 'Maybe this is going to work!' we think to ourselves. The first lyrics, however, remind us of the gaping Bernie-sized hole at the heart of the project, and the subsequent lines do little to disabuse of that impression.

When the chorus comes it's basically the same energy and style of the verses, with dumber words. The song goes on for nearly five minutes but after you've heard the first cycle of verses and choruses you've heard everything. It's a static mass both lyrically and musically and, the worst part of it is, it's not even the worst thing on this three-song album.

'Mama Can't Buy You Love', the relative standout from the album, closed out the original first side of the EP, with production and instrumentation that were characteristic of their time, with disco strings and wakka-chika guitars. All the interest is in the opening arrangement, contributing to Elton's ultimate conclusion that the new tracks lacked fundamental energy.

The eight minute and fourteen seconds long 'Are You Ready for Love?' takes up the entirety of the EP's second side. At the end of the third minute there's one of the clunkiest modulations you'll ever hear in a pop song, leading us into the second half of the song, which is just 'Are you ready for love? Yes I am' repeated over an interminable four minutes, only taking a break in the fifth minute to make way for a generic disco instrumental interlude which is so dull you'll find yourself almost missing the chorus, until it comes back and doesn't leave for another minute and a half. Perhaps not the worst song Elton has ever done but easily in the bottom five.

The Stats

Album/Single	US	UK	Australia	Canada
The Thom Bell Sessions	51			
'Are You Ready for Love?'/'Are You Ready for Love? (Part Two)'		42	63	
'Mama Can't Buy You Love'/'Three Way Love Affair'	9		82	10

The Tracks

Side one:
1. 'Three Way Love Affair' (L. Bell, James) (5.31)
2. 'Mama Can't Buy You Love' (L. Bell, James) (4.03)

Side two:
3. 'Are You Ready for Love?' (L. Bell, T. Bell, James) (8.16)

1989 release:
1. 'Nice and Slow' (John, Taupin) (4.43)
2. 'Country Love Song' (Jefferson) (5.05)
3. 'Shine on Through' (John, Osborne) (7.46)
4. 'Mama Can't Buy You Love' (L. Bell, James) (4.09)
5. 'Are You Ready for Love?' (L. Bell, T. Bell, James) (8.16)
6. 'Three Way Love Affair' (L. Bell, James) (5.00)

Musician's Corner: 'Nice and Slow'

There's an argument that runs, 'Elton John shouldn't have gone disco', which points to *The Thom Bell Sessions* and *Victim of Love* as its two primary pieces of evidence. And, sure, listening to 'Are You Ready for Love?', which stays within the confines of disco tropes that had largely lost their freshness by 1979, one might think that Elton would have been better sticking to his usual toolbox but that song wasn't written by Elton, nor were any of the songs on either album, so they aren't really good guides to show how Elton was able to elevate the disco form. But we do have a couple of tracks demonstrating that potential – 'Bite Your Lip (Get Up and Dance!)' from *Blue Moves* and 'Nice and Slow', which wasn't originally on *The Thom Bell Sessions* but was included on the 1989 issue of *The Complete Thom Bell Sessions*, so I get to talk about it here.

'Nice and Slow' has music written by Elton and lyrics by Bernie and the difference is palpable. Now, Bernie's lyrics for 'Nice and Slow' isn't his best work but it at least manages to avoid rhyming 'me' with … 'me' and gives us some moments of personal meaning: 'Time and time again we defended a right to cling to/Our love-shy goodbyes, for broken hearts could cry'.

Instead of a pastiche of middle school love letter sentiments, we get verses with a little bit of narrative punch in them, with some conflicting emotions. This piece is primarily set in B flat major, which according to Pop Song Writing 101, means that a good choice for the bridge material would be the minor sixth chord of G minor. Elton knows that's what we're expecting, and gives us G but it's G major, which crucially features B natural instead of B flat as the central note of its root chord, so already, one chord in, we're in a different frame of mind. The sentiment of, 'it would be nice to have sex slowly', which is basically what the song is about, is here shifted into a more complicated sentiment, and the use of the major six chord announces that well.

Elton also amps up the tension at the beginning of the next line, using a B flat sus2 chord on 'Close to You', which creates dissonance with the tonic note of B flat and a tension that calls for resolution of some sort, producing a moment of anxiety which is lifted at the end of the line when he gives us a normal B flat chord to end on.

'Nice and Slow' then points towards what might have been possible if Elton devoted the full measure of his talents to the production of a pure dance album, infusing disco tropes with classical sensibilities while Bernie injected new images into the acoustic ether of the club scene.

Chapter 16

Victim of Love

Recorded: August 1979
Released: 12 October 1979
Producer: Pete Bellotte

The Story

V*ictim of Love*'s reputation has remained where it was forty-four years ago when music critics all made the same observation that the album was released one year too late and was, therefore, a failure for being an exercise in a musical genre that the music critical hive mind had decided it was no longer interested in.

Yes, this is Elton's disco album.

No, it is not an unmitigated disaster.

My apologies if this necessitates the laborious search for a new barrelled fish we as a community all acknowledge it's okay to ritually shoot.

The idea for a disco record was put to Elton by musician Pete Bellotte (*b*.1943), in April 1978. Bellotte had the idea for an album to be called *Thunder in the Night* and wondered if Elton would like to come on board. Elton, a devotee of the disco scene, agreed on the condition that the experience would follow the Thom Bell model, whereby his part would be relegated to that of a walk on vocalist. Considering how dissatisfied he was with the results of *The Thom Bell Sessions*, this was perhaps a curious model to return to but at the same time, Elton clearly thought of this as a bit of fun to make a frothy contribution to a musical form he enjoyed but that was definitely on its way out, so the less effort put in, the better, allowing him to concentrate on writing the music for what would be the *21 at 33* and *The Fox* albums. A few days into the writing session at Grasse, France, that saw him back at work with Bernie, though in a reduced capacity, Elton flew to Musicland Studio in Munich, Germany where he banged out the vocals to all seven *Victim of Love* tracks in a single eight-hour session.

On the surface a quick cash grab of a project, the album collected some of the coming decade's most distinguished musicians, including bass legend Marcus Miller (*b*.1959), drum wizard Keith Forsey (*b*.1948), Toto guitarist Tim Cansfield (*b*.1951) and Tower of Power saxophonist Lenny Pickett (*b*.1954) and featured backup vocals by none other than The Doobie Brothers themselves. Taken on its own, *Victim of*

Love is a vivacious slice of dance floor boogie that makes no excuses for what it is. The downfall of the album came in the form of its timing, being released only a couple of months after Disco Demolition Night on 12 July 1979, a date referred to by a generation of commentators keen to ingratiate themselves with the reigning punk and evolving new wave trends as The Day That Disco Died. Elton, who for a decade had blazed a trail entirely his own by a fusion of dozens of musical genres, was suddenly caught knee deep in a dead trend and the opportunity was too juicy for the press whose overwrought headlines implied that Elton had run out of ideas.

The Songs

Ironically, after that impassioned defence of this much-kicked album, my first duty is to talk about 'Johnny B. Goode', which is the one track on the album that doesn't work at all. I was so excited when I got this album as a kid, not knowing what it was, imagining what it would be like to hear how Elton modified Chuck Berry's iconic guitar rocker into a piano rocker. That is not what we get here. As a cover of Berry's song it's a grim farce and even if you'd never heard the original, it still wouldn't prove a satisfying experience, everything here being just a step too lethargic to compel reluctant souls onto the dance floor.

The next two songs, 'Warm Love in a Cold World' and 'Born Bad' are on firmer ground in terms of danceability and fun but suffer from being essentially the same song. They're both driven by the same off-beat sizzle, both feature guitar driven rock elements and both possess the same chorus structure of two emphatic monosyllabic words followed by explanatory declarations:

Warm Love – in a Cold World
Born Bad – Just Can't Seem to Help It

If you must choose one, go with 'Born Bad', which introduces new rhythmic elements to the repetitions of the chorus that provide some much needed differentiation.

If side one veered between execrable and serviceable, side two is all boogie. Lyrically, there's nothing particularly worth pondering, with the words seemingly chosen entirely for how they sound and for a dance song that's fine. When an entire wedding party yells 'Tiiiiiin roof – RUSTED!' in the middle of 'Love Shack' it's not because they enjoy the part the tin roof plays in the overall narrative structure of the piece, but because it's a fun thing to say.

'Thunder in the Night' features a menacing intro, with ricocheting guitars and looming synths prepping us for the breakup stomp to come, the ultimate song for when you feel so miserable about yourself that the choice is either to drink yourself into a corner or to dance.

'Thunder in the Night' leads straightaway into 'Spotlight', which has a brighter but equally infectious intro featuring the requisite disco beat, but with a very Elton style boogie piano in the mix. Marcus Miller's popping bass continues to be an engaging focal point, as are the backing vocals by Stefanie Spruill (*b*.1949), and Julia (*b*.1943) and Maxine Waters (*b*.1945), though in this case the relatively undifferentiated nature of the choruses causes the stirrings of definite chorus fatigue.

Fortunately, coming directly down the alley is the positive strut of 'Street Boogie', the most dance floor ready piece on the album. The call 'Is that the radio? Yes, that's the radio, Let it go, let it go, let it go!' is the perfect bridge into the chorus, which isn't only catchy but also features the exquisite dance hall call out moment of 'It's all right, it's all right, it's all right with me!' Again, we probably could have done with one or two less choruses but trim those and you have in your hands a dance floor burner perhaps too potent for this world.

With 'Victim of Love', side two closes as it began, back in the thick smoke of suspicion, only this time the tables are turned and it's the singer who finds himself the betrayed instead of the betrayer, with the song morphing from the mysterious thriller setting of the intro into the epic self-pity dance catharsis of the chorus. The connecting thread through all these are the extended high synth notes that appear in the intro and weave their way through the tale. 'Victim of Love' and 'Thunder in the Night' are about dance's ability to act as a conduit for solitary rage and disillusionment, themes lying at the heart of those few disco tunes that have remained relevant, from 'Dancing Queen' to 'Staying Alive'. While *Victim of Love* doesn't quite reach those heights thanks to its less than compelling lyrical content, neither is it the dross at the bottom of the barrel, and in it there's much fun to be had, much boogying to be done and surprisingly many emotions to be traversed.

The Stats

Album/Single	US	UK	Australia	Canada
Victim of Love	35	41	20	28
			G	G
'Victim of Love'/'Strangers'	31		38	46
'Johnny B. Goode'/'Thunder in the Night' (UK) 'Georgia' (US)				

The Players

Elton John: lead and backing vocals
Thor Baldursson: keyboards and arrangements
Roy Davies: keyboards
Craig Snyder: lead guitar
Tim Cansfield: rhythm guitar
Steve Lukather: electric guitar (2 and 3)

Marcus Miller: bass guitar
Keith Forsey: drums
Paulinho da Costa: percussion
Lenny Pickett: saxophone (1)
Michael McDonald: backing vocals (7)
Patrick Simmons: backing vocals (7)
Stefanie Spruill: backing vocals
Julia Tillman Waters: backing vocals
Maxine Willard Waters: backing vocals

The Tracks

Side one:
1. 'Johnny B. Goode' (Berry) (8.06)
2. 'Warm Love in a Cold World' (Bellotte, Wisnet, Moll) (3.22)
3. 'Born Bad' (Bellotte, Bastow) (6.20)

Side two:
4. 'Thunder in the Night' (Bellotte, Hofmann) (4.40)
5. 'Spotlight' (Bellotte, Wisnet, Moll) (4.22)
6. 'Street Boogie' (Bellotte, Wisnet, Moll) (3.53)
7. 'Victim of Love' (Bellotte, Levay, Rix) (5.02)

Musician's Corner

Since Elton didn't write any of these songs, there's nothing really for me to talk about here, so we're giving this one a miss.

Chapter 17

21 at 33

Recorded: August 1979 to March 1980
Released: 23 May 1980
Producers: Elton John and Clive Franks

The Story

E lton learned many things from *A Single Man*. First and foremost, he discovered that writing songs without Bernie, even using a method totally different to that which he'd employed over the last decade, could work and result in types of music that had been unavailable to him before. While all that was true he also found that, without the strong guide of Bernie's vision, it was much harder to scale the heights of songwriting sublimity that he'd leapt over so easily in the past.

By the time Elton settled down to write the music for *21 at 33*, he'd tried a bit of everything and was ready for a new synthesis. Bernie was back, and so was Osborne, and a couple of other lyricists besides. Murray and Olsson were back (though only on a couple of tracks – newcomers Alvin Taylor (*b*.1953) and Reggie McBride (*b*.1954) filling their spots respectively), as was James Newton Howard. Steve Lukather (*b*.1957), who had impressed during the *Victim of Love* sessions, was brought on board, while Elton and Franks remained in the producers' chair in the continued absence of Dudgeon. Oddly, neither Ray Cooper, who had survived Elton's purges and gone on tour with him, nor Johnstone were present on this album, which came thereby to represent a fusion of Elton's oldest and newest styles, without much input from the connecting middle era.

Commercially, the album represented a return if not to the heyday of 1974 then at least to the significant if lesser summits of 1976. Critically, the heterogeneity of the material caused by the presence of so many disparate elements did raise a cry of 'uneven' from music reviewers, but everyone was so relieved to see Elton and Bernie working together again, even if none of their collaborations were chosen as singles, that the patchwork nature of the record was largely forgiven.

The Songs

Our opening song asserts the return of Elton, featuring a synthesis of rock drive and danceable rhythm called 'Chasing the Crown' that is both crunchy and funky, and given undeniable substance by Bernie's history-spanning lyrics, putting us in the shoes not so much of a single individual but in those of the abstract construct of man's lust for power. It's a rocking downer that was far too complex to make a good single but that was perfectly calibrated to lead off an album intended to show that Elton remembered how to rock, and that Bernie was back and could still write about themes not centred on failed marriage, suicide and infidelity.

'Little Jeannie' was Elton's biggest charting single in three years, a ballad written with Osborne, which features the long delayed return of Olsson to the drums and Murray both to the bass and his old warm presence in the backing vocals. For many, that return of Olsson's drums and Murray's distinct voice, was enough by itself to fall in love with the track. Leaving out the points the track wins for pure nostalgia, what we are left with is a mellow piece that ends at the same level of intensity as where it began, giving it a somewhat flat topography next to the ballads Elton had written before and would write later.

'Sartorial Eloquence' was, by every metric of songwriting, a more interesting piece of music than 'Little Jeannie' but on its release only achieved a fraction of the latter's success. Like other classic Elton ballads, it features an effective build up towards a perplexed chorus cry that fully utilises the powerful backing vocals of Venette Gloud, Stefanie Spruill and Carmen Twillie (*b*.1950). The chord progressions here are masterful but it's a good time to focus on the other main story of this song, which is the presence of Tom Robinson (*b*.1950) as the lyricist. Robinson had formed The Tom Robinson Band in 1976 as a musical expression of the rising gay liberation movement and, in 1978, his song 'Glad to be Gay' was banned by the BBC. As Elton's first lyricist who was gay himself, he brought to Elton's music a refined sensitivity to the complexities of homosexual love that Bernie and Osborne could only guess at. Both 'Sartorial Eloquence' and 'Elton's Song' express that sensitivity, here in an investigation of a relationship tried by jealousy and in 'Elton's Song' as a heartfelt rendering of the first flowerings of schoolboy love and the elation and self-torment arising therefrom. Between its musical quality and lyrical openness, even if 'Sartorial Eloquence' wasn't one of Elton's most financially successful singles, it was certainly one of his most important.

'Two Rooms at the End of the World' closes out the first side of *21 at 33* and it's nothing less than Elton and Bernie's celebration of working together again, and their explanation that nothing had ever personally separated them beyond geography and scheduling. Filled with some of Bernie's most memorable lines and some of Elton's most exuberant writing in commemoration of their renewed partnership and newly found positive outlook, the first three and a half minutes of this song are an undiluted and deeply welcome joy.

Side two presents us with four different lyricists through its five songs, and it's here where *21 at 33* potentially earns its 'uneven' status. We begin with a Bernie piece, 'White Powder, White Lady', which is about exactly what you think it's about. Arriving in France to work on *21 at 33*, Bernie was in the thick of his ongoing problems with alcohol and cocaine (a habit he'd not break until the late 1980s), which were increasingly interfering with his ability to form connections with people. Elton, of course, was still addicted to alcohol and cocaine himself, and so the song presents us with not so much a kiss-off or love ballad to cocaine but a complicated triangle with Bernie, Elton and drugs as its three vertices. Elton's vocals and the instrumentation are so exuberant that it's hard to consider the song as a deep self-criticism, which is what makes it so eternally compelling – the unresolved push and pull between the lyricist, who clearly recognises the dangers brewing but still wants to give in, and the musician, who mainly wants to keep using drugs but kind of wants to get clean. Though we know what forces would ultimately prevail, that was anything but clear in 1980.

It's tempting to consider 'Dear God' to be what it appears on the surface – an uncomplicated bit of gospel or Christian pop expressing piety before the divinity, complete with church organ and choir backing vocals. Elton touches on religion multiple times throughout his career, and rarely with blithe credulity. 'If There's a God in Heaven (What's He Waiting For?)' (1976) is an unambiguous criticism of God as a benevolent being and of Christianity's approach to social problems. 'Religion' (1983) is a straight satire on conversion moments and televangelism. 'God Never Came Here' (2001) updates us on the litany of suffering inflicted on the innocent, which God still hasn't done anything to ameliorate in all his goodness. With that track record, we need to be careful before condemning 'Dear God' to the category of naïve Christian balladry, and all the evidence is there in the words. Like 'If There's a God in Heaven (What's He Waiting For?)', 'Dear God' is another account of an absent deity, one who hears the earnest prayers of those who believe in him, who lift up their voices in chorus, who take all the blame on themselves for failing his plan instead of blaming him for having crafted such a poor plan to begin with, and who are rewarded for all this devotion with total indifference. C-Pop it decidedly isn't, but Elton's musical casting of Osborne's lyrics is so letter perfect that he is able to slip them by as such.

As personal and revelatory as Tom Robinson's lyrics for 'Sartorial Eloquence' and 'Elton's Song' were, his words for 'Never Gonna Fall in Love Again' range from adequate to unfortunate. The middling lyrics are given a middling musical treatment, and the overall vibe is one of sedation.

'Take Me Back' opens as a love song to the country music of the 1950s and the first two verses feature a simple melodic idea and repeated chord structure that could have come from an old Hank Williams (1923–1953) song, and Osborne for his part picks up on Elton's musical cue and crafts lyrics of that era. In the B section material Elton allows the country form to meld with his own musical sensibilities, and we get an interesting tension between the old time country yearning ballad and the destabilising force of Elton's modernly chorded reading (though you can make an argument that the harmonies here are The Louvin Brothers adjacent, thereby tapping another classic country sound). While closely constructed call-backs to musical forms long past would become a sub-genre of their own in the 1980s (Billy Joel's 'The Longest Time' and Taco's 'Puttin on the Ritz'), few of them featured such a subtle dissolution of the featured form at the centre.

'Give Me the Love' is a disco seduction ballad for which Elton only performed the vocals on the recording, leaving piano duties to Howard whose echoey interjections are one of the sonic highlights of the song. Lyrically, the song was mainly assembled by giving the melody to Judie Tzuke (*b*.1956), whom Elton had signed to Rocket Records in 1977 and had had a significant hit with 'Stay With Me Till Dawn' in 1979, who came up with a whole sheaf full of lines that fit and told Elton to pick whichever ones took his fancy. It's a nearly five and a half minute smoulder with a powerful musical casting of the song's central demand and some truly unexpected engaging choices for how the background vocalists echo that demand.

The Stats

Album/Single	US	UK	Australia	Canada
21 at 33	13	12	7	10
'Little Jeannie'/'Conquer the Sun'	3	33	9	1
'Sartorial Eloquence (Don't You Wanna Play this Game No More?)'/ 'White Man Danger'/'Cartier'	39	44	91	57
'Dear God'/'Tactics'/'Steal Away Child'/'Love So Cold'			82	

The Players

Elton John: lead vocals, backing vocals, acoustic piano (1, 3, 5 and 6), overdubbed piano (1, 3, 5, 6 and 8), Yamaha electric piano (4) and Wurlitzer electric piano (8)
James Newton Howard: Fender Rhodes (2, 6 and 7), Yamaha CS-80 (2), electronic keyboards (3 and 7) and acoustic piano (9)
David Paich: organ (6)
Steve Lukather: electric guitar (1, 3, 4, 6, 7 and 9)
Richie Zito: acoustic guitar (2 and 7) and electric guitar (5 and 8)
Steve Wrather: electric guitar (7)
Reggie McBride: bass (1 to 4 and 6 to 9)
Dee Murray: backing vocals (2) and bass (5)
Alvin Taylor: drums (1, 3, 4 and 6 to 9)
Nigel Olsson: drums (2 and 5)
Victor Feldman: tambourine (1, 3, 5 and 9)
Clive Franks: tambourine (4 and 6) and cowbell (4)
Lenny Castro: congas (5 and 9)
Jim Horn: brass arrangements (2 and 4), piccolo flute (2), alto saxophone (2) and tenor saxophone (4)

Richie Cannata: alto saxophone (7)
Larry Williams: tenor saxophone (9)
Chuck Findley: trombone (2 and 4) and trumpet (2 and 4)
Bill Reichenbach Jr: trombone (9)
Jerry Hey: flugelhorn (2 and 9), trumpet (4 and 9) and brass arrangements (9)
Larry Hall: trumpet (9) and flugelhorn (9)
Byron Berline: fiddle (8)
David Foster: string arrangements (9)
Venette Gloud: backing vocals (1, 3, 6 and 9)
Stefanie Spruill: backing vocals (1, 3, 6 and 9)
Carmen Twillie: backing vocals (1, 3, 6 and 9)
Bill Champlin: backing vocals (2 and 9)
Max Gronenthal: backing vocals (2)
Glenn Frey: backing vocals (5)
Don Henley: backing vocals (5)
Timothy B. Schmit: backing vocals (5)
Curt Becher: choir vocals (6)
Joe Chemay: choir vocals (6)
Bruce Johnston: choir arrangements (6) and choir vocals (6)
Jon Joyce: choir vocals (6)
Peter Noone: choir vocals (6)
Toni Tennille: choir vocals (6)

The Tracks

Side one:
1. 'Chasing the Crown' (John, Taupin) (5.36)
2. 'Little Jeannie' (John, Osborne) (5.14)
3. 'Sartorial Eloquence' (John, Robinson) (4.45)
4. 'Two Rooms at the End of the World' (John, Taupin) (5.40)

Side two:
5. 'White Lady, White Powder' (John, Taupin) (4.34)
6. 'Dear God' (John, Osborne) (3.47)
7. 'Never Gonna Fall in Love Again' (John, Robinson) (4.09)
8. 'Take Me Back' (John, Osborne) (3.52)
9. 'Give Me the Love' (John, Tzuke) (5.30)

Musician's Corner: 'Sartorial Eloquence'

'Sartorial Eloquence' is another one of Elton's songs in a remote key, in this case that of D flat major, which features five flats and was a regular go-to key for Stevie Wonder (*b*.1950) and Ray Charles (1930–2004).

This song has one of the best non-Bernie lyrics Elton had to work with in the early 1980s, and when I was a kid, I simply assumed that these lyrics were by Bernie, because it was so good when compared to, say, 'Are You Ready for Love?' Elton tends to have interesting things happen when he finds interesting things in the words, and Bernie usually provides these in abundance, with his idiosyncratic sense of word choice. Here Robinson provides a few of those moments himself. 'You've got a self-sufficient swept-back hairdo' is a lovely line, and Elton sets it off with a descending line of chords featuring a cool thing you can do whenever you're trying to write your own Elton-style song. Look at the chord progression here:

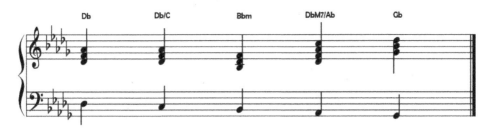

Those notes in the base are heading steadily downward, from D flat to C to B flat to A flat to G flat, but since D flat, C, and A flat are all part of a D flat major 7 chord, he uses their appearance to bounce back to D flat in between his other chords, so you keep returning to this D flat chord in your ear, but each time, it's grounded in a lower position bass note, which provides this generally sinking feeling that is perfect for the generally melancholic tone of this song.

My favourite transition happens on 'Your lifestyle shows in the clothes you chose':

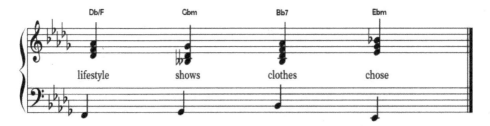

The internal rhymes perhaps provides some inspiration here to compose the musical equivalent, which is a mirrored jump up by a minor fourth (from D flat to G flat for the first half of the lyrics, and then from B flat to E flat for the next), which would have been cool enough on its own, but to make the structure perfectly parallel, with each section featuring a jump from a major to a minor chord, Elton makes the first chord of the second part major, a chord not in our key that provides this wonderful bit of foreignness amidst what is theoretically a perfectly smooth mirroring.

I have never been a fan of choruses that repeat the same line but at least here Elton's working to make each repetition musically distinct, and to conclude I want to share my favourite quick transition, a little musical escalator with D flats and A flats slipping past each other on their way to the top:

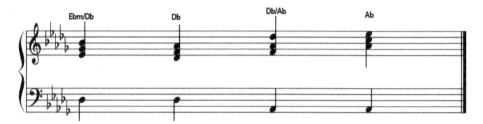

Chapter 18

The Fox

Recorded: 1979 to 1981
Released: 20 May 1981
Producers: Elton John, Clive Franks and Chris Thomas

The Story

T*he Fox* is an interesting amalgam of five songs that were left over from the *21 at 33* sessions, and six new ones composed at Geffen Records' request nearly a year later to fill out the album. That is usually not a recipe for a unified album but the result was one of Elton's most creative and audacious albums, if not his most commercially successful. Personally, I regard it as one of his greatest achievements, representing the pinnacle of his oeuvre in terms of raw reality, and a disturbing mixture of electronic starkness and lyrical grit that had never been heard on an Elton album before.

Elton had originally intended *21 at 33* as a double album and wrote a plethora of songs in that expectation until compelled to relinquish the double concept. Many of the songs that didn't make the cut for *21 at 33* ended up as B sides but five were rescued from that fate for inclusion on *The Fox*, including 'Elton's Song', 'Carla/Etude', 'Chloe', 'Fanfare' and 'Heart in the Right Place', all of which but the last tending towards the melancholic. To counterbalance that trend, the new songs written for *The Fox* mostly boasted darker lyrics, including 'Fascist Faces' and 'Nobody Wins'.

This was Elton's last album until the twenty-first century to feature instrumental tracks, and his first to employ new electric drum (or 'rhythm box') technology. It featured his first unambiguously gay love ballad and the arrival of Chris Thomas (*b.*1947) as a track producer. Though featuring the Bernie, Osborne and Robinson trio of lyricists that were featured on *21 at 33*, here their work is more uniform, each lyricist digging into the depths of their personal experiences and the grim world of global politics to produce a series of lyrics expressing a unilateral pessimism about both humanity's prospects for a bright future and the potential of its individual members to experience long term happiness.

The Songs

Interestingly, though *The Fox*'s core is composed almost entirely of a complex mixture of bitterness and disappointment, the album is bookended by pieces expressing optimism about the individual's ability to survive and even thrive in harsh environments. Starting with the sound of Olsson's drums and Elton's powerful ascending G major arpeggios, 'Breaking Down the Barriers' is almost aggressively positive in its outlook, with Osborne's lyrics embracing the theme of overcoming personal reticence. Until the very last moments, it's a mid-tempo rock romp of self-affirmation. Then, in my favourite section of the song, Elton sets the tone for what is to come by having the last repetitions of 'I'm breaking down barriers of time' cast in a minor key, the only minor chords of the song, our first hints that all this optimism might be self-deception rather than self-evolution and that reality is about to hit, and hard.

'Heart in the Right Place' takes us into the perspective of a spiteful journalist, practiced in offering the defence that he is only doing his job and that his heart is in the right place, all while knowing perfectly well that he revels in the use of misrepresentation to wreck the lives of those he has selected for destruction. Beginning as a heavy blues stomp, the piece devolves over time into a duel between Steve Lukather's raging acid guitar wails and the steady roboticisation of the vocals via Howard's vocoder as the journalist reveals more of his actual intent, the fiery vengefulness of his intentions (the guitar) being only matched in intensity by the cool efficiency with which he goes about his assassination (the vocals).

Like many of Bernie's best lyrics, it's hard to say for sure what 'Just Like Belgium' is about, and Elton's habitual counter-programmed musical treatment doesn't make the task any easier. From the music, with its alto sax, bouncy bass, major chord strummings, and intermittent whispered French, you would think that the song is perhaps from a montage in a romantic comedy but the lyrics are ambiguous, describing two people reflecting on their time as poor student tourists in Belgium, getting blind drunk, having their money stolen, sleeping it all off on the steps of a church, and otherwise generally having the time of their lives with the implication that everything in the present is but a pale imitation of those halcyon days.

'Nobody Wins' is the only song on *The Fox* not written by Elton. The story goes that Elton heard Janic Prévost's *'J'veux d'la Tendresse'* on a car radio and was taken by its haunting melody – written by Jean-Paul Dréau (*b.*1953) – and synthesized sound and approached Osborne with the task of crafting English lyrics to the piece. The result was possibly the best Osborne lyrics on any Elton album, a story of a young man standing helplessly by as he watches his parents' marriage fall apart, a tale that Elton knew only too well. It's a devastating account of the waves of discontent that radiate out from a struggling couple, consuming themselves and their children, a war that nobody wins. The musical material is entirely synthetic, appropriate to the story being told, with a rhythm box filling in for the drums creating an unforgiving beat, while Howard's synths, following Dréau's original lead, weave a cavernous aura of cold emptiness that amplify the distress of the youth at the piece's centre.

'Fascist Faces' is built on a dystopic foundation consisting of an entirely unique presentation of Elton's voice, booming Olsson bass drum, deconstructed piano licks, distorted spoken lyrics courtesy of the Reverend James Cleveland (1931–1991), disconcerting background clicks and reverse-sounding lashes from the guitar, resulting in an arresting statement of concern about the rise of fascism masquerading as patriotism, and the return of the paranoia of the late 1950s.

Side one of *The Fox* represents probably the single darkest sequence of songs on any Elton album, while side two ultimately achieves something of a balance between the light and gloom. 'Carla/Etude', composed in honour of the relationship between Franks and his wife, Carla, is an instrumental number featuring Elton at the piano and Howard at the podium of the London Symphony Orchestra. Howard's arrangements for the orchestra are masterful, utilising the full orchestral palette with an instinct for instrumentation that sees the right moments given to the woodwinds, the strings and the brass to keep Elton's piano theme evolving in classical style until a synthesizer announces the arrival of the electronic 'Fanfare', driven on by the synthed heartbeat underlying the simple dialogue between a descending synth line and wind effects that give us hints of the musical material of the song to come, 'Chloe'. It's a slip of a song that comes in just under a minute and a half, but it gives us a tantalising glimpse of the mix of classical piano concerto writing and electronic music that Elton might have produced if he'd had the inclination to continue the instrumental album he wanted to record as the follow-up to *The Fox*.

'Chloe' takes all the pieces of thematic material we heard in 'Carla/Etude' and 'Fanfare' and brings them together to tell the relatively conventional story of a man who doesn't' deserve the woman he's with, who lies to her and is likely unfaithful, who brings her pain, and who doesn't seem to do much to relieve the problems she has to deal with, but who'd like her to stay with him anyway, because he needs her, and to top it off, puts the onus of the decision on her shoulders: 'Chloe, what you gonna do 'bout me?' The lyrics are centred around such an unlikable character, so alternately deceitful and callow, that the beautiful instrumentation in support of Elton's graceful descending melody serves brilliantly to catch us in a quandary of how we feel about it all.

'Heels of the Wind' centres around much of the same thematic material as 'Chloe' but in Bernie's hands, the theme gets a more worldwise treatment. The narrator has a balanced sense of what his lifestyle has meant for those around him, both its positive and negative aspects. He admits to being unkind, and that his partner is better off without him but rather than simpering on about how she should take him back and try to fix him, he takes a philosophical view, admits to their basic incompatibility, and resigns himself to a life on the heels of the wind. In 'Heels of the Wind', we see Bernie finding his way to starting over again, and his old friend Elton's in full celebration mode, crafting the catchiest song of the album around that thought.

With 'Elton's Song', Robinson gifted Elton one of the most personal and profound lyrics of his career, focusing on his own experiences as a school boy, when he fell in love at the age of 13 with another boy, and was so tormented by confusion that he attempted to take his own life at the age of 16. Robinson put into Elton's hands an opportunity to sing openly about the unique pains and exhilarations of gay love and Elton, never one to back down from saying something that needed saying, recorded it without a second thought to any repercussions it might have for his career. To give the song the full feel of an individual sitting alone in their room, thinking about the person they love without hope, the song features only Elton on voice (utilising the higher register he'd been steering away from) and piano, and Howard on the synthesizer (not entering until after the first minute). It's a perfect, charming reflection of boyhood love. As to why it's called 'Elton's Song', the reason is rather more prosaic than the material, with Robinson believing that he wrote those words on the top not as the designation of a title or dedication but merely as a written note to himself that, of all the songs he'd written, this was the one he was writing for Elton, and that Elton simply kept it, thinking it to be Robinson's intended title.

Elton and Bernie finish the album together, and after two sides of war, divorce and fascism, one might wonder whether the pair had any sliver of hope for the future left in them. Bernie's answer, beautiful and direct, is that he has faith in his friend: Elton John, The Fox. Though hunted and harried, and often his own worst enemy through his cleverness and susceptibility to temptation, he will always be two steps ahead of whoever tries to snare him, tougher than he seems, and with reserves of energy and a will to live unfathomable to others. He won't slow down and won't be stopped, and in a world where everything is falling apart, having someone like that can be all you need to feel a twinge of optimism for a better world ahead.

The Stats

Album/Single	US	UK	Australia	Canada
The Fox	31	12	4	43
		S		
'Nobody Wins'/'Fools in Fashion'	21	42	46	23
'Just Like Belgium'/'Can't Get Over Losing You'				
'Chloe'/'Tortured'	34			34

The Players

Elton John: lead vocals, vocal solo (1), backing vocals (1, 2, 4, 5 and 9), pianos (1, 3 and 5) and acoustic piano (2 and 6 to 11)

James Newton Howard: synthesizers (1 to 4, 7, 9 and 10), vocoder (2), synthesizer programming (4 and 10), string arrangements and conductor (6, 7 and 8), Fender Rhodes (8) and Hammond organ (11)

Steve Porcaro: synthesizers (5)
Richie Zito: guitars (1, 3, 5, 9 and 11)
Steve Lukather: guitar solo (9)
Dee Murray: bass (1, 3, 5, 9 and 11) and backing vocals (8)
Reggie McBride: bass (2 and 8)
Nigel Olsson: drums (1, 3, 5, 9 and 11)
Alvin Taylor: drums (2 and 8)
Roger Linn: drum synthesizer programming (4)
Jeff Porcaro: drum programming (5)
Stefanie Spruill: tambourine (1 and 9) and backing vocals (9)
Victor Feldman: percussion (7 and 8)
Jim Horn: alto saxophone (3)
Mickey Raphael: harmonica (11)
Marty Paich: string arrangements (8)
London Symphony Orchestra: strings (6, 7 and 8)
Bill Champlin: backing vocals (1, 8 and 9)
Venette Gloud: backing vocals (1 and 9)
Tamara Matoesian: backing vocals (1 and 9)
Colette Bertrand: French girl (3)
James Cleveland: spoken voice and choir director (5)
Cornerstone Baptist Church Choir: choir (5)

The Tracks

Side one:
1. 'Breaking Down Barriers' (John, Osborne) (4.42)
2. 'Heart in the Right Place' (John, Osborne) (5.15)
3. 'Just Like Belgium' (John, Taupin) (4.10)
4. 'Nobody Wins' (Dréau, Osborne) (3.40)
5. 'Fascist Faces' (John, Taupin) (5.12)

Side two:
6. 'Carla/Etude' (John) (4.46)
7. 'Fanfare' (John, Howard) (1.26)
8. 'Chloe' (John, Osborne) (4.40)
9. 'Heels of the Wind' (John, Taupin) (3.35)
10. 'Elton's Song' (John, Robinson) (3.02)
11. 'The Fox' (John, Taupin) (5.20)

Musician's Corner: 'Fascist Faces'

The Fox is in my top five favourite Elton albums. The sound palette, lyrical themes and production are all bleak to a degree that Elton will approach in subsequent records, but never equal. 'Nobody Wins' is probably the most hopeless song on the album but as the music wasn't written by Elton, I'll forego the pleasure of talking about its remarkable musical structure, and head for the next bleakest song, 'Fascist Faces'.

Bernie's lyrics hit a few different theme clusters but generally centre around the grim hypocrisies masquerading as self-assured patriotism that were the hallmark of the Cold War in the late 1970s and early 1980s. Elton's voice throughout the song is produced in a way that makes it seem strained, distant and vaguely metallic, like we're hearing it over an old radio. It's a presentation of his vocals that we haven't seen before, and won't see again, and it puts us a bit instantly ill at ease, like he's broadcasting to us from somewhere far away and not too pleasant. Meanwhile, the song itself is one of his most brutally mechanical, as befits a song that treats of the resurgence of fascist archetypes in the public sphere. All the cleverness of Elton's usual songs is deliberately bulldozed to give us a flavour of a world without nuance, a grey soundscape to match the theme at hand and the direction of global politics. His chords trudge back and forth between Bb/F and C with a relentless resistance to new tonal colours, creating a sonic architecture that could be the soundtrack to *1984*.

'Okay, this is dark', we say to ourselves, 'but the chorus is just around the corner, surely there will be a break in the clouds then.' Guess again. When the chorus hits, it starts with the chord of B flat, which is one of the two chords we've been hammered with for the last minute. Where 'Ego' employed a structure that was all frenetic change and instability to depict the lived experience of narcissist personalities, 'Fascist Faces' sees Elton portraying totalitarianism perfectly in big, drab motions that crush utterly all attempts at invention. It's a chilling musical moment, depicting a world as cold and bereft of light as Elton could imagine, and while it's bracingly illuminating to live in that stark world for a while, it's also good to know that there's no direction to move from here except up.

Chapter 19

Jump Up!

Recorded: September to October 1981
Released: 9 April 1982
Producer: Chris Thomas

The Story

After the success of the instrumental tracks on *The Fox*, Elton was keen on the idea of an all instrumental album and he was uniquely poised to achieve something great in the form, with his unfailing melodic sense and ability to compose comfortably in interesting fusions of multiple genres but Geffen Records were understandably wary of the project – they wanted something that would revive Elton's struggling, though still popular appeal, not drive him further into the state of a rarefied niche artist.

Characteristically, Elton paid no attention to the label's pleas and pressed forward with composing instrumental music until old habits kicked in and he found that one of the tonally shifting melodies he'd written would pair nicely with lyrics sent to him by Tim Rice, whose last stage success had been *Evita*, in 1976, and who was in the process of writing a treatment of George Orwell's *1984* with Rick Wakeman (who had been involved with a few tracks on *Madman Across the Water*). The song was 'Legal Boys', one of Elton's truly under sung masterpieces, and between its success and Elton's natural impatience, it turned him back towards the idea of putting out another traditional album.

The result, *Jump Up!*, recorded at AIR Studios in the British Lesser Antilles, represents an almost violent lurch back to pop normalcy after the wide exploration of dark themes that marked *The Fox*. Gone are the interconnected instrumentals and the pervasive note of global dread, and in their place we have a more classic Elton mix of rockers, ballads and novelties, with lyrical duties evenly split between Bernie and Osborne (with the one contribution from Rice), whose words were fit onto melodies Elton had already written, with surprisingly fluid results.

The one exception to this new method was 'Empty Garden (Hey Hey Johnny)', the lyrics to which Bernie wrote almost immediately upon hearing of John Lennon's assassination on 8 December 1980, as his personal way of working through his feelings of the violent passing of his friend. Elton was composing an instrumental tribute to

Lennon, 'The Man Who Never Died', on the assumption that any standard song treatment could only trivialise the tragedy but the simple power of Bernie's words changed his mind, and he slipped easily into the old routine of setting Bernie's words to new music, thereby creating the emotional anchor of the album.

Jump Up! performed comparably to *The Fox* – a bit worse in the UK, a bit better in the US – and its main single, 'Blue Eyes', outperformed all the singles on *The Fox* without reaching the heights in the US of 'Little Jeannie' from *21 at 33*, contributing to the impression that, while still a success by any definition, Elton in the early 1980s was somewhat treading water commercially, with the quality of his work somehow failing to manifest on the sales charts. What seemed necessary was either a radical step forward, or a complete return to form, and for his next album, and greatest success of the early 1980s, Elton found a way to do both.

The Songs

To make good on the implied promise of the album title, Elton opens with one of *Jump Up!*'s most high energy tracks, even if it means once again leading with one of Osbornes's more workaday lyrics. 'Dear John' is, as one might surmise, a song about Dear John notes, and doesn't delve into much more depth than the fact that they're not pleasant to receive but can represent a solution to a relationship that has run its course. It's hard to get too upset about the lack of penetrating drama, though, as Elton's musical setting is infectiously fun, replete with Jerry Lee Lewis style piano pyrotechnics and Murray's characterful bounding bass work. It won't leave you pondering humanity's place in a forbidding universe but it's an effective update of 1950s piano rock sensibilities and for an album starter that'll do.

Bernie's first song on the album, 'Spiteful Child', is about vengefulness and, well, spite. Though the title suggests a one sidedness to the bad behaviour, the lyrics are more complicated, with the narrator showing their true colours, giving the lie to their claims of emotional maturity through their glee at how the appearance of having moved on will enrage their former partner. Nobody here is the good guy, despite the narrator's patently unsuccessful attempt to cast himself as such, and the combat-like atmosphere is highlighted by Porcaro's war toms, and Elton's uncompromising descending vocal line in the chorus, and powerful if increasingly unstable calls of 'Spite-FUL' at the song's end.

By all rights, we should respond to 'Ball and Chain' with, 'Okay, Elton – we enjoyed the retro-country simplicity of "Take Me Back" a couple years ago, but this is pushing it.' Why we don't is tough to explain – nothing astonishing is happening in the lyrics but the elevation of the track by Pete Townshend's (*b.*1945) scrappy acoustic guitar, the rhythmic counterpoint of vigorous handclaps in the chorus, and the brute force of the simple bassline all provide enough for the ear to nibble on that we unconsciously forgive the fact that we've been here before.

'Legal Boys' is the secret jewel at *Jump Up!*'s heart, with one of Elton's best melodies since 'Tonight', where the sparse piano and plunging bass of the first verse are complexified in the second by a disorienting Glassian motif in the synths that pushes the song further into the realm of the Kafkaesque suggested by Rice's lyrics. In addition, the low string thrum in the bass of the chorus creates a malevolent under carpet that assures us that the only winners of this conflict will be those interminably adjudicating it.

Okay. Here we go – our next song is 'I Am Your Robot', which is one of Bernie's most gloriously insubstantial lyrics ever put to paper, and certainly the silliest since 'Solar Prestige a Gammon', the result of desperately trying to find something to fit overtop Elton's musical idea. The song has all the cheesy electronic synth effects you'd hope for, and Elton's doing everything he can to ham the piece up with his vocal performance, all of which makes the song tremendously fun but the piece still has a rocking drive to it that gives it more bite than your average sci-fi novelty number.

'Blue Eyes' presents us with Elton's most resonant accessing of his lower vocal register up to that point in his career. Each repetition of 'eyes' brings with it a plunge down to a full and rich B flat, which resonates with the power of revelation, opening a whole new dimension to what an Elton song can be. The lyrics, about one of Elton's lovers, whose picture is featured in the artwork of the album, is also unique for Elton, as it represents his first proper body part ballad.

Elton was no stranger to writing tribute songs for iconic individuals who left us too soon – 'Candle in the Wind' and 'Cage the Songbird' both managed tasteful accounts from unique perspectives on the legends they portrayed – but when it came to John Lennon, whom Elton knew personally, it seemed to him at first that no words could do any but trite justice to his friend, and he resolved on a purely instrumental treatment, but when Bernie's words, expressing his own anguish, arrived, Elton saw that they perfectly encapsulated the tragedy of the event. Lennon's story in 'Empty Gardens' is told allegorically, through the tale of a gardener, grown wise through the long years of his craft, but possessing still the sense of joy of a child.

This sets up the dual sense of loss we feel when we hear the song – not only are the fields falling fallow in the absence of their tender but we have also lost our playmate. Like children, we call for Johnny to come out and play, even as our adult eyes survey the arid garden and all that it betokens of a future that much less magical. Everything coalesces musically to capture this dual loss in the song – Elton's use of harpsichord puts us in mind of 'Skyline Pigeon' and its sense of boundless, impossible yearning, while the presence of Murray's voice in the backing vocals reminds us of a time rapidly receding. Howard's synths hop in and out of the song with small bird like interjections that carry a child-like quality, which will be brought to the fore in the song's central query, and most importantly, Elton's voice achieves a vast depth here made all the more poignant by its sense of innocent incomprehension that something so vital, a spirit so eternal, could ever come to an end.

'Princess' brings us a necessary dialling down of emotional intensity, allowing us to recover somewhat before Bernie drags us into the trenches of war at the album's end. There's not too much to this song – it's an innocuous disco ballad sway that would doubtless have done well five years earlier, but that in 1982 was simply quaint, with Osborne's lyrics remaining entirely within the realm of the expected. Some excitement comes at the end of the song, however, when Howard leaps in from the rafters and provides a delightfully deranged synth solo that doesn't fit with the atmosphere of the song, which would be a weakness in any other piece but is a positive godsend here.

One's immediate reaction to 'Where Have All the Good Times Gone?' is that it's exactly what it says it is, a 'Crocodile Rock' style lament of innocent pleasures gone by. Bernie's lyrics are subtler than that, however, and this isn't so much a song about how things were better back when but rather a piece about the sort of people who idealise both their personal and country's past, picking mundane things like weekends and jukeboxes to fixate on while conveniently dropping all the trauma of past ages, and then declare, with a straight face, 'Where Have All the Good Times Gone?'

That sounds a stretch until you realise that the next song is an exploration of the horrors of the First World War as told by its most realistic and disillusioned chronicler, Erich Maria Remarque (1898–1970). 'Good times, eh? Like when millions of young men killed each other because an Austrian archduke died?' Now, if I could chop the introductory material off any Elton song, it would probably be that of 'All Quiet On the Western Front'. It's a baffling way to set the scene of this otherwise thought-through depiction of the war, with bright oscillating synths perhaps symbolising the relative innocence of Europe before the war (if you leave out the whole global colonialism bit) but accomplished with sounds incongruously foreign to that time.

Elton's long sustained notes in the chorus, made up exclusively of the title phrase, evoke perfectly the sprawling sadness of beholding the great emptiness inhabited that morning by living men. The most intriguing element, though, is a repeated two-part instrumental section, featuring light synths and tinkling bells (most likely a reference to the Christmas Day Miracle, which represented the last flowering of brotherhood and humanity in the conflict), blasted apart by a subsequent section of Porcaro's thundering drums, and the funereal blare of a pipe organ. That combination, played several times throughout the song, conveys a relentless sense of life snuffed out, with the final word on the song and the album given not by a vocal line or angelic harp, but by that organ, as death triumphant closes the proceedings, and we look behind us to see how far we've come since 'Dear John'.

The Stats

Album/Single	US	UK	Australia	Canada
Jump Up!	17	13	3	19
	G	S	P	
'Blue Eyes'/'Hey Papa Legba'	12	8	4	5
'Empty Garden (Hey Hey Johnny)'/'Take Me Down to the Ocean'	13	51	63	8
'Princess'/'The Retreat'				
'Ball and Chain'/'Where Have All the Good Times Gone?'				
'All Quiet on the Western Front'/'Where Have All the Good Times Gone?'				

The Players

Elton John: lead vocals, backing vocals, acoustic piano, electric grand piano and harpsichord on 'Empty Garden'
James Newton Howard: Fender Rhodes, synthesizers, brass and string arrangements, and conductor
Richie Zito: guitars
Pete Townshend: acoustic guitar (3)
Dee Murray: bass and backing vocals
Jeff Porcaro: drums and percussion
Steve Holley: tambourine (3) and synth drum (5)
Martyn Ford Orchestra (as 'Mountain Fjord Orchestra'): brass and orchestra (6)
Gavyn Wright: orchestral direction (6)
Gary Osborne: backing vocals (5 and 7)

The Tracks

Side one:
1. 'Dear John' (John, Osborne) (3.31)
2. 'Spiteful Child' (John, Taupin) (4.15)
3. 'Ball and Chain' (John, Osborne) (3.27)
4. 'Legal Boys' (John, Rice) (3.05)
5. 'I Am Your Robot' (John, Taupin) (4.43)
6. 'Blue Eyes' (John, Osborne) (3.25)

Side two:
7. 'Empty Garden (Hey Hey Johnny)' (John, Taupin) (5.09)
8. 'Princess' (John, Osborne) (4.56)
9. 'Where Have All the Good Times Gone?' (John, Taupin) (4.00)
10. 'All Quiet on the Western Front' (John, Taupin) (6.03)

Musician's Corner: 'Legal Boys'

Here we have a lyric so depressing that I always assume it's another Gary Osborne or Bernie Taupin composition and am always surprised when I remember that it's Tim Rice, who'd go on to be Elton's writing partner for *The Lion King*. It feels so much like 'heart in the right place, but this time it's about lawyers' that I have to stop myself every single time.

To me, 'Legal Boys' is the culmination of dystopian Elton's songwriting craft, as honed across the late 1970s and early 1980s, featuring the best elements from all the songs about misery, dysfunction, charlatanry, and egotism that preceded it. Like in 'Nobody Wins' we get verses that conclude in half or whole step descending pulses, the most pronounced one (after 'lies unopened on the tray') feeling much like a slamming door motif.

As in 'Sartorial Eloquence' we get a neat movement between bass notes and chords as A flat gives way to an Fm6 chord with an A flat in the bass, and in turn a regular G7 chord gives way to a C minor chord with a G in the bass, which carries with it some implications (to my ears at least) of high expectations brought low. What it also lets Elton do is hang out on the same bass note for extended periods of time, giving A flat and G each a full four measures of sitting statically at the bottom, this insistent thrum that's made bearable by the change of chords on top, but that produces this impression of waiting, of things taking abnormally long, which is exactly appropriate for evoking the Kafkaesque world of divorce attorneys.

Finally, as we saw in the second section of 'Ego' there's a psychologically telling restlessness in the chord structure of the verses that suggests perfectly someone pacing, unable to stay in one place for more than a few seconds because his fate is in the hands of forces outside his control. In the three opening measures we move from G minor (the key of 'Nobody Wins') to E flat major, to F major, to C minor, to B flat major with an extra sixth, to A flat, and when the first line finally ends on an expected G minor, it's a G minor with a D in the bass instead of a G. Now, in music theory, if you want to end strong, what you do is start on the version of a chord that has the fifth in the bass, go through some other chords, and then end on the version that has the tonic in the bass. This section goes the other way, starting on the stable version of the chord and ending on the least certain version of it, which, again, is a clever way of telling a story using music.

Chapter 20

Too Low for Zero

Recorded: September 1982 to January 1983
Released: 31 May 1983
Producer: Chris Thomas

The Story

J*ump Up!* represented a return to marketable pop-rock sensibilities, which was welcomed by studio executives but, while successful, failed to represent the hoped for return to sales dominance Elton had enjoyed as a matter of course in the early 1970s. Something about the music first, words later format wasn't gelling. Elton's solution to the problem was simple but daring: a return to the methods that had resulted in his most monumental records but cast within the soundscape of the early 1980s electronic turn.

The old crew was reassembled – for the first time since 1975 – Murray on bass, Johnstone on guitar, Olsson on drums and Bernie in charge of the lyrics. Kiki Dee returned on backing vocals and the talented Skaila Kanga (*b.*1946) was present to play the harp for the first time since *Tumbleweed Connection*. Falling into the old rhythms they had perfected back at the château, the original Elton John Band composed and recorded the dourly titled but generally ebullient *Too Low for Zero* album over the course of two weeks – a blazing pace for most bands but a leisurely stroll by the team's previous standards.

This was the album where Elton definitively found comfort with the synthesizer, opting for electric keyboard sounds throughout the record, all played by himself, with trusty Howard relegated to arranging the album's elegiac closing track. The new formula provided the jolt needed to establish Elton firmly in the 1980s pantheon, with the album reaching #7 in the UK (though 'only' #25 in the US) and most importantly with both 'I'm Still Standing' and 'I Guess That's Why They Call it the Blues' penetrating the Top 5 in the UK, and the latter reaching #4 in the US. The stage was set for an Elton renaissance, with old friends and a fresh outlook combining to produce a potent one-two punch of nostalgia and relevance, with the only person possibly standing in the way of a new string of triumphant albums being Elton himself.

The Songs

Too Low for Zero ends Elton's early 1980s trend of leading off an album with up-tempo pieces and instead sticks us directly in the middle of one of Bernie's most devastating lyrics, 'Cold as Christmas', about an older married couple who go on a tropical holiday in a last ditch effort to reconnect, only to find that they no longer can. More mature lyrics than either 'Spiteful Child' or 'Dear John', here Bernie is focusing not on the flames of a dissolving couple determined on a course of mutually assured destruction but rather a couple who tried and simply found nothing in each other anymore.

Originally conceived as a survivor song *á la* 'I Will Survive', when the lyrics of 'I'm Still Standing' fell into the hands of Elton and the band, they morphed into something far grander – an anthem asserting their new vitality, an arrow into the heart of grousing Geffen Records' executives, and a personal testament to Elton's utter musical indestructibility. Taken at a blazing speed, 'I'm Still Standing' sees each member of the band pushing themselves to prove in their individual musical persons the truth of the song's message. Olsson pounds away, Murray drives, Johnstone delivers one of rock's most iconic instrumentals, all three produce ecstatic backing vocals, and Elton pushes himself to new levels of vocal defiance to create a song fuller of life and dash than those being put out by musicians half Elton's age. Blazing to #4 in the UK and #12 in the US, the song put Elton solidly back on the musical map and gave the rest of us a song to crank up whenever we emerge triumphant through adversity.

'Too Low for Zero' is set in an almost entirely synthetic atmosphere, perfectly matched to its subject of a man unable to rouse himself to any sort of action, purpose or genuine relationship. He is an individual too low for zero, incapable of reaching even the razed ground reset point from which progress might begin anew. The drum machine hammers home this idea of a person with no other human passion in their life, and the gorgeous backing vocals of Murray, Olsson and Johnstone add an almost unreal quality to the incantation of the title line.

'Religion' gives us a gleefully irreverent glimpse at conversion and what it amounts to in the civilised and modern world. The song is a series of portraits of down on their luck individuals who feel the hand of the Lord suddenly upon them, and who then go right back to sinning, comfortable in their ultimate salvation. As a commentary on the voluble but paper-thin religiosity of President Ronald Reagan's (1911–2004) America, it's note perfect, and Elton and the gang, rather than setting it in an obvious gospel idiom, opt instead for a down home country yarn, where the earthly pull of a good ole time easily wins the day. In more recent times, after a conversion to Presbyterianism brought about by his relationship with Heather Kidd, Bernie has explained this song as having a generally 'positive' take on religion, which has a whiff of revisionism about it, and which if true flattens most of what makes the song compelling, so for my part I'm just going to go ahead and keep believing it to be a work of keen and observant satire.

'I Guess That's Why They Call it the Blues' brought Elton back to the top of the charts, scoring a #5 position in the UK and #4 in the US. As a tribute to the 1950s sock hop slow dance ballad, it's flawless in its combination of doo-wop background vocals, swaying guitar arpeggios and tragi-romantic lyricism. Written by Bernie as the expression of his feelings of being apart from his girlfriend, and elevated by its association with the GI songs of the 1940s expressing yearning for loved ones back home, the song taps both into the universal theme of separation and the nostalgia for the sacrifices of the greatest generation that began to rise in the 1980s as the children of that generation headed into their thirties and rediscovered their curiosity about their stoic parents.

Musically, there's a cornucopia of delights to choose from on the track, each layer offering something compelling to contemplate, from the plunging figures of Murray's bass to the nostalgic backing vocals of the DND trio to Elton's resonant piano playing to the warm melancholy of the vocal line. This song gave a whole new generation the chance to fall in love with Elton, propelling his legacy securely for another decade to come.

There are many elements at work in 'Crystal' and while they don't always seem to pull in the same direction, there's often an underlying method to all these superficially diverse ends. We begin with Gothic wind-swept-effects soon joined by the crunching tread of the drum machine, a combination of the modern and ethereal. Bernie's lyrics are about a love triangle and the worry that a long standing friendship might not withstand Crystal's decision about which friend she prefers. The lyrics on their own carry emotional weight as our narrator contemplates the potential dissolution of his friendship while wishing Crystal well. While a good proportion of Bernie's protagonists are irredeemably broken men, our narrator here seems a thoroughly decent sort who wants the best for everyone but who is afraid of losing the people most important to him.

Elton takes us to entirely new realms in the song, balanced between the minor key ruminations of the verses and the bright major setting of the undeniably catchy chorus. Narratively, this decision reflects the dichotomy between how our subject feels internally and the more cheerful exterior he presents to the world. Psychologically, this is a clever piece of writing by Elton, and explains the unease of the intro as a preview of the protagonist's stormy internal contradictions that threaten to tear him apart.

If there's a song you cannot accuse of subtle psychological construction it's 'Kiss the Bride', which Elton casts as an upper-mid tempo rocker, telling the story of a man who shows up at his ex-girlfriend's wedding, contemplates asking to kiss the bride as a prelude to absconding with her but ultimately thinks better of it. There's not a great deal of nuance to uncover here and as a rocker it doesn't hold up next to the heady combinations of lyrics and drive of 'I'm Still Standing' and 'Whipping Boy', leaving it solidly at the bottom of this album's rock offerings, though still with enough bounce and brass to have made #20 in the UK and #25 in the US.

'Whipping Boy' is another story altogether. It's a wonderfully conceived parody of rock sensibilities in which each verse gets a little less comfortable as we learn more about our protagonist's approach to the world. I've never understood why it's called 'Whipping Boy' as the reference to a medieval child whose job it was to receive whippings whenever their princely friend misbehaved doesn't quite fit the story at hand, at least as I understand it.

But what a story that is, in which, driven on by Johnstone's fiery guitar work and Elton's infectious enthusiasm, we are treated to the tale of a man who is depicting the torments inflicted on him by his energetic romantic partner, starting with their tendency to flirt with people, proceeding to their boundless sexual appetite, which has aged our narrator twenty years physically and thirty-three years emotionally, and concluding with the fact that they are, minor detail, underage and that therefore this relationship might end in prison time.

'Saint' was a late addition to the album and a welcome one as it gives us one of our most clearly described women characters in any Bernie lyric – a self-determined and entrancing figure whose basic toughness and personal drive have allowed her to survive in new surroundings. She's the first woman in a Bernie song since 'Shoulder Holster' we feel like we not only know but would like to meet. Ironically, the standout moment is the place where the lyrics are at their weakest: the chorus. Elton pushes his voice into its upper regions in a soaring melody in service of lyrics that are, compared to the verse material, on the vague side. It's not made clear in what way the woman in question is a 'saint' and if anything the verses suggested she was something far more interesting and dynamic than that.

'One More Arrow' closes the album on a note of loss. Most see Bernie's lyrics as an appreciation for a passed father but they have always struck me as a song about an older brother or best friend, rough on the outside but capable of empathy within, a youth who wants to grow up to look like Robert Mitchum (1917–1997) but who never got the chance, and now rests, forever young. That is poignant enough but a part of me has also always heard the song as a product of its time, which was during the AIDS crisis after it arrived in the US in 1981. By 1983, many young men had lost their partners to the disease, which the government resolutely did nothing about. With that in mind it's not difficult to hear 'One More Arrow' as a eulogy a man wanted to give to his late partner but was unable to as their relationship was never accepted.

The Stats

Album/Single	US	UK	Australia	Canada
Too Low for Zero	25	7	2	17
	P	P	5P	P
'I Guess That's Why They Call it the Blues'/'Choc-Ice Goes Mental' (UK) 'The Retreat' (US)	4	5	4	9

'I'm Still Standing'/'Love So Cold' (US) 'Earn While You Learn' (UK)	12	4	3	1
'Kiss the Bride'/'Dreamboat' (UK) 'Choc-Ice Goes Mental' (US)	25	20	25	37
'Cold as Christmas (in the Middle of the Year)'/ 'Crystal'	33		12	
'Too Low for Zero'/'Lonely Boy'			52	

The Players

Elton John: lead vocals, backing vocals, acoustic piano (1 to 5, 8 and 10), Fender Rhodes: (1), synthesizers (1 to 7 and 9) and clavinet (9)

Davey Johnstone: acoustic guitar (1, 4, 5, 6 and 9), electric guitar (2 to 10) and backing vocals

Dee Murray: bass guitar and backing vocals

Nigel Olsson: drums, tambourine (8) and backing vocals

Ray Cooper: percussion (1)

Skaila Kanga: harp (1)

Kiki Dee: backing vocals (1)

Stevie Wonder: harmonica (5)

James Newton Howard: string arrangements (10)

The Tracks

Side one:
1. 'Cold as Christmas (in the Middle of the Year)' (John, Taupin) (4.19)
2. 'I'm Still Standing' (John, Taupin) (3.02)
3. 'Too Low for Zero' (John, Taupin) (5.46)
4. 'Religion' (John, Taupin) (4.05)
5. 'I Guess That's Why They Call it the Blues' (John, Johnstone, Taupin) (4.41)

Side two:
6. 'Crystal' (John, Taupin) (5.05)
7. 'Kiss the Bride' (John, Taupin) (4.22)
8. 'Whipping Boy' (John, Taupin) (3.43)
9. 'Saint' (John, Taupin) (5.17)
10. 'One More Arrow' (John, Taupin) (3.34)

Musician's Corner: 'One More Arrow'

One of the last times Elton employed the highest register of his voice on a major album was on 'One More Arrow'. He sets essentially the entire song in that high register and not only that but features vocally punishing leaps between his regular and falsetto voice ('Where the days and nights blend into one').

It's a fragile song about a gentle soul who died too soon, made even more poignant by the knowledge that at this time, Elton was only four years away from a vocal meltdown that would all but ensure he could never perform this song live again as he originally wrote it.

Elton's high register wasn't gone forever with this song – it returns in the haunting 'Burning Bridges' from *Breaking Hearts* (1984) and in 'Stones Throw From Hurtin'' from *Sleeping With the Past* (1989) but essentially 'One More Arrow' represents a final grand gathering of his old vocal forces before his transition to the lower-based singer he'd become in the late 1980s and beyond.

Chapter 21

Breaking Hearts

Recorded: December 1983 to April 1984
Released: 18 June 1984
Producer: Chris Thomas

The Story

T*oo Low For Zero*'s mix of modern atmospherics with classic musical elements proved the runaway hit Elton needed to re-establish his rightful position at the top the pop charts, which immediately led to the question of how to follow it. Elton's solution was to return to the habits of the 1970s, when texturally complex albums like *Madman* and *Elton John* regularly alternated with more outwardly directed rockers like *Tumbleweed Connection* or *Rock of the Westies*. That formula continues with *Breaking Hearts*, if to a less extreme degree than in the past. Of the ten songs here, six are up-tempo numbers, centred on Johnstone's guitar heroics.

Breaking Hearts featured largely the same team as *Too Low for Zero*, with Murray, Olsson and Johnstone working their miracles for the last time together on an Elton album, Thomas in the booth, and Elton and Bernie working essentially as they did at the château. *Breaking Hearts* contains more pieces that engage with happenings in the world than *Too Low for Zero*, though overwhelmingly the album is given over to relationships in various stages of dissolution, with pop and rock idioms reigning, pushing *Breaking Hearts* to #2 in the UK and #20 in the US, though its singles struggled to gain traction.

For us today, *Breaking Hearts* is a bittersweet final opportunity to hear the classic Elton John Band playing together (neither Olsson nor Murray returned for *Ice on Fire*), a potentially masterful concept album in disguise, and an oasis of undistilled Elton sensibilities.

The Songs

Both 'Restless' and 'Passengers' represent the horrors of the real world intruding on the otherwise traditional pop themes that make up the core of *Breaking Hearts*. 'Restless' is a rhythm and blues stomp driven by the dialogue between Johnstone's pounding guitar and Murray's pulsing bass, to which Elton adds one of his gravelliest rock vocals to date. Released in the same year that George Orwell's (1903–1950) Nineteen Eighty-Four (1948) novel was set, it's not a coincidence that themes of Big Brother predominate, with issues of Cold War tensions, the psychological impact of financial hardship and the growth of authoritarianism all in the dark mix.

After placing us on a global-scale level of angst, Elton and Bernie throttle back for a while, returning to the familiar waters of relationship-based stomp themes. One interesting thing about *Breaking Hearts* is the sequence of the relationship type tracks on the album, which viewed from afar form a downward spiralling thread that, if not intentional, is a tremendous narratively rich coincidence. 'Slow Down Georgie (She's Poison)' can be thought of as starting this arc, with an individual entering a relationship against the advice of his friends. In the spirit of 'Don't Trust That Woman' from *Leather Jackets*, its lyrics are centred on a stereotypical gold digging woman, who has no features save vicious greed. Lyrically, there's little here to amaze, its saving grace is its catchy chorus with distinctive background vocals, totalling to a song that is more delightful to hear than to listen to.

'Who Wears These Shoes?' presents the potential next stage of the relationship in 'Slow Down Georgie (She's Poison)', where we find our hero, having ignored his friends' advice, placed precisely in the situation they had warned him of, agonising over his new girlfriend's infidelity. 'Shoes' is an examination of the mental trauma created by jealousy, and a story of obsession. The hero is being cheated on and he must decide whether to move on, as his friends advise, or push forward in a myopic need to uncover his replacement's identity even at the cost of his sanity.

The mid-pace stomp of the musical material has a repetitive insistence well-matched to the topic of a man treading the same ground over and over in search of his rival. Elton's arrangement of the lyrics to lean into the character's obsessive rehashing of his mania for the truth is among his most skilful, helping the song to reach #16 in the US in October 1984.

'Breaking Hearts' takes a hiatus from the story of our hapless hero and brings us one of the album's most compelling marriages of emotionally complex lyrics and melancholic musical setting. The piece is one sustained introspection of a man wondering what has happened within himself that his old approach to love now leaves him so unfulfilled. Recognising his former status as a lothario, intent on taking as much as possible while giving as little of himself as he could, he seems baffled by the diminution of his will to cruelty. How did that happen? He knows he is no more enlightened than he was before, leaving him with the sobering conclusion that, rather than feeling more with the passage of time, he has simply grown even more dead inside.

This is a crushing tale of an individual who has lost all sense of identity and has realised that loneliness is his lot for the rest of his days. Elton perfectly conveys that sense of total self-loathing with his halting verses and almost prayerful chorus that skilfully mixes his highest and lower registers to convey a sense of fleeting hope, buffeted to destruction by the subject's sense of self-awareness.

And so, to 'Li'l 'Frigerator'. I know I shouldn't love you as I do. You have horribly dated misogynistic lyrics and in your scrambling for a sense of over-the-top bawdiness never reach the heights of 'Whipping Boy'. I should hate you. But you are so enthusiastic about how bad of a song you are, that you have become endearing. I'm convinced everyone on this recording knew full well what's going on with you, and resolved to make you one of the most unforgettable musical car crashes in recording history. As high kitsch performance art, you are, quite simply, a masterpiece.

Westerners adopting native African musical forms is as often a recipe for disaster. 'Passengers' comes out somewhere in the middle, with good political intentions hindered by awkward production sensibilities. The song takes Phineas Mkhize's recording of the South African folk song 'Isonto Lezayone' (1963) as its musical starting point, with the notes of the 'Deny the Passenger, who want to get on' melody being a direct quote from Mkhize's recording. The original lyrics, about Zion Church, were over-written with an anti-apartheid theme stemming from Elton's regret about performing in South Africa. Bernie's lyrics, about segregation on public transportation specifically and more broadly about a nation whose infrastructure was built on the suffering of those denied its use, has powerful moments but they're all but buried in the incongruous fusion of the song's new melodic material with the original folk tune, making it difficult to pay attention to the words. Elton tries to pick up on the rhythm of Mkhize's song and carry it through but the resulting lightness of gait doesn't make a solid foundation for Bernie's words, and the message gets lost along the way.

'In Neon' lies in a lineage with 'Honky Cat' and 'Goodbye Yellow Brick Road' as a tale of rural innocence broken by the big city. A decade after those iconic tracks, Bernie's thoughts on the subject of making it big in the city have grown distinctly darker. 'In Neon' portrays an irreversible downward spiral of an innocent soul hoping for stardom who ends up commodifying herself and free-falling into a state of self-loathing with no apparent road to recovery. She has been hurt too deeply by the city for any change of location to ever truly heal her, and has seemingly given up all hope of trying, an expression of self-destruction on par with that of 'Breaking Hearts' and miles away from 'Tell Me When the Whistle Blows'.

I see 'Burning Buildings' as the resumption of the hero's story we left at 'Who Wears These Shoes?' The song features some of Bernie's most striking imagery, with the contrast between some lovers leaping off a burning building while others cling desperately 'on the edge of a house on fire' viscerally portraying the two paths of a partnership started in the throes of passion, and terminating in one of two forms of self-annihilation. The chorus is a gem, with ascending instrumental lines and descending back vocals crossing each other beneath Elton's anguished vocal flights. This is dissolution as the natural end of an initially profound union, placing our hero, already tormented by his lover's infidelity, in the position of having to choose which of two self-destructive ways to end the relationship.

Before arriving at the album's final song, we must pass through the gates of the album's second question song, 'Did He Shoot Her?', which is a glorious chaos composed of wildly discordant parts that patch together into one of Elton's most puzzling musical chimeras. Bernie's lyrics are difficult to untangle – on a hyper-literal level, they're about wanting to get to the bottom of an ex's murder but more generally it's about the compulsion to know how the partners of one's former lovers are treating them.

So, we have ambiguous lyrics, now what do Elton and the boys do with them? The answer is everything. Johnstone is playing the sitar for some reason. Olsson is going full animal mode on the toms. Elton's sticking to big blocky chords and synth blasts, and every so often the background vocals get flanged for about as much reason as that underlying the presence of Johnstone's sitar. Nothing fits anything, and that absolute incoherence is poetry of the highest order, giving us the full flavour of the mental state of our poor central figure.

By his own account, Elton composed 'Sad Songs (Say So Much)' in one sweeping go through. The effortlessness of its conception is echoed in the pop elegance of the lyrics and music. It's a song about songs, and music's power to heal us at our lowest moments, and Elton's call to action to 'Turn Em On!' has lost none of its power to direct us to our album collections to let our favourite singers do their divine work allowing us to embrace our sorrow through their artistic embodiment of it. When everything goes wrong, there's something in a sad song that lets us bridge all the hurt and find in the commonality of world sorrow something of community, and a way forward.

The Stats

Album/Single	US	UK	Australia	Canada
Breaking Hearts	20	2	1	10
	P	G		
'Sad Songs (Say So Much)'/'A Simple Man'	5	7	4	4
'Passengers'/'Lonely Boy'		5	9	
'Who Wears These Shoes?'/'Tortured' (UK) 'Lonely Boy' (US)	16	50	76	36
'In Neon'/'Tactics'	38			92
'Breaking Hearts (Ain't What It Used to Be)'/ 'In Neon'		59		

The Players

Elton John: lead and backing vocals, synthesizers (1, 2, 3, 5, 6, 7, 9 and 10), pianos (3, 4, 5, 7, 8, 9 and 10), Hammond organ (5), harmonium (6), Fender Rhodes (7), harpsichord (7) and clavinet (10)

Davey Johnstone: backing vocals (1 to 4 and 6 to 10), electric guitar (1 to 3, 5, 7, 8 and 9), acoustic guitar (2, 6, 7, 8 and 10) and sitar (9)
Dee Murray: bass guitar (1 to 3 and 5 to 10) and backing vocals (1 to 4 and 6 to 10)
Nigel Olsson: drums (1 to 3 and 5 to 10) and backing vocals (1 to 4 and 6 to 10)
Andrew Thompson: saxophone (5)

The Tracks

Side one:
1. 'Restless' (John, Taupin) (5.17)
2. 'Slow Down Georgie (She's Poison)' (John, Taupin) (4.10)
3. 'Who Wears These Shoes?' (John, Taupin) (4.04)
4. 'Breaking Hearts (Ain't What It Used to Be)' (John, Taupin) (3.34)
5. 'Li'l 'Frigerator' (John, Taupin) (3.37)

Side two:
6. 'Passengers' (John, Taupin, Johnstone, Mkhize) (3.24)
7. 'In Neon' (John, Taupin) (4.19)
8. 'Burning Buildings' (John, Taupin) (4.02)
9. 'Did He Shoot Her?' (John, Taupin) (3.21)
10. 'Sad Songs (Say So Much)' (John, Taupin) (4.55)

Musician's Corner: 'In Neon'

My take as an adolescent on 'In Neon' used to be, 'I love the song but hate the intro'. For a song with so much dark imagery, the introductory material of straight descending notes seemed far too simple and disconnected with what follows. Fast forward a decade or so, when I sat down with the piece more intently to get to the bottom of what Elton's doing with the intro, only to have the whole subtle brilliance of it slap me full across the jowls, because something really cool is happening here.

All my young brain was noticing was that the intro is basically just a descending scale in a flat, regular rhythm. What it wasn't noticing was the trickery Elton's playing with the chord structure under that melody, and what that structure might have to say about why that intro is so simple. Considered together, the intro goes from being pedantic to narratively powerful in a way that only Elton would have thought up.

The chords of the intro are incredibly simple: Db-Ab-Eb-Ab-Ab7 with a repeat of the first four chords again to end the intro. Our ear is set up with the idea that we are in D flat, and that idea is hammered home by the fact that we next hear A flat, the V chord. Things then get a little strange when the next chord is E flat but we rationalise that away instinctively as another one of Elton's classic uses of the secondary dominant.

But here's the thing, the piece isn't in D flat at all! That interloper chord, that E flat, that's the key of the piece! The piece is centred in the chord that wasn't supposed to be there in the first place, in a song about someone who uproots themselves, moves to Hollywood and comes to find that they don't belong. The intro is deceptively simple with a little bit of country flavour and a little bit of tension in the chords, because the dreams of a hopeful starlet moving out West are simple, with a little bit of fear at the centre but still overall painted with the broad strokes of American optimism. And so, once again, we have a strong sense of what the story will be, before we hear a single one of Bernie's words.

Chapter 22

Ice on Fire

Recorded: January to June 1985
Released: 4 November 1985
Producer: Gus Dudgeon

The Story

Though popularly known as 'The Soviet Album' due to the presence of 'Nikita' and 'Cry To Heaven', and the stark cover design, *Ice on Fire* is a continuation of the thematic mix of *Breaking Hearts*. We do get two unique additions to the mix in the form of the first of what will be a series of Dylan-esque Bernie lyrics surveying the ills of the world ('Tell Me What the Papers Say', the precursor to 'Goodbye Marlon Brando' and 'Sweat It Out'), and a song Elton had been hoping would be the theme to the next James Bond film ('Shoot Down the Moon') and which, failing that goal, he tossed onto the album as its melodramatic final track.

The question then becomes, if the album wasn't all that different to the previous two albums, why did it perform less well than they, topping out at a mere #48 in the US? One of the easy solutions to the riddle is the issue of consistency – while *Too Low for Zero* and *Breaking Hearts* were creations of the old Elton John Band from start to finish, *Ice on Fire* featured a cavalcade of visiting musicians, masterfully produced by a returning Dudgeon but lacking a connecting approach or sound. Certainly, Elton's albums of the 1970s featured a robust mix of song types but the impression on those was always a unique fusion of styles born from Elton's omnivorous mind and the band's consistent approach, whereas on *Ice on Fire* there's more of a sense of chasing musical trends at the expense of personal innovation, which Elton fans weren't slow in noticing.

At its best, however, *Ice on Fire* is the equal of anything Elton made in the 1980s, with many tracks expertly mixing classic Elton-Bernie sensibilities with the evolving sound of the now half-complete decade, taking advantage of the talents of emerging artists without being subsumed by them, even as Elton struggled with demons that would bring his recording career to its lowest ebb in one brief year.

The Songs

Ice on Fire begins on a piece of scorching political commentary, 'This Town', significant in the Elton canon for being Elton's last successful donning of a 'Saturday Night's Alright for Fighting'/'Street Kids' style working class narrator persona until he began composition of 'Billy Elliot' some two decades later. Elton makes some bold choices here in setting Bernie's lyrics of coal town inertia and hopelessness, perhaps spurred on by a desire to expand into new sonic territories. When you have access to Rick Taylor's trombone and Raul D'Oliveira's trumpet for the day, you tend to use them, regardless of how far their sounds take the song from its lyrical roots. Still, the song's avoidance of maudlin sentiment through a left field musical approach stands out in its audacity and renders the song a very Elton-Bernie affair.

The pair tune back into the same wavelength for 'Cry to Heaven', which hearkens back to *The Fox* in its icy atmospherics portraying the cost of war as borne by the children whose towns are destroyed and parents slain in an unspecified conflict, perhaps the one to come if the Cold War fails to find a peaceful resolution. Bernie's words highlight the sadism of war's instigators as against the helplessness of its victims, and Elton portrays this in the musical texture as a tug of war between acoustic and synthetic instruments, with Elton's piano and Johnstone's guitar attempting to establish some notes of humanity among the artificial sounds, a dichotomy he employed in 'All Quiet on the Western Front', but has perfected here, where once again the sounds of war are given the chilling last note.

The early 1980s saw an explosion of White Soul music from the likes of Wham! and Phil Collins (*b.*1951), which it was inevitable that Elton, with his long admiration for the original soul greats and friendship with George Michael (1963–2016), would contribute to. That sounds good on paper – unfortunately 'Soul Glove' isn't only out of place amidst the Cold War ethos of 'Cry to Heaven' and 'Nikita' but isn't that interesting considered entirely by itself. Bernie's lyrics don't have much to say, and the composition stays at a uniform intensity throughout with a repetitive chorus our reward for making it through the platitudinous verses.

'Nikita', however, promptly reminds us what Elton can do when given compelling lyrics, free of any rigidly determined stylistic form. The lyrics of a love story made impossible by the Berlin Wall is inherently compelling, and Elton brings his best to its realisation, setting the warmth of his lower register against the higher cries of George Michael's backing vocals while Dudgeon ensures that, unlike on the monochromatic 'Soul Glove', the ear always has some new element to hone in on, with the subtly funkified guitar working well with Elton's more classic melody to produce a sense of the West and what it has to offer – emotional warmth but also a sense of freedom, while the carpets of backing vocals create an ever shifting sound suggestive of omnipresent snow in which the figure of Nikita roams in the form of Elton's high synth line. The only fault is the percussive element which I think is a wood block, that Dudgeon put high in the right channel mix and which drives me batty whenever I listen to 'Nikita' on headphones because it's intermittent enough that your brain won't let it fade into the background. Otherwise, this is a true mid-1980s masterpiece, joining the roll call of Elton's perfectly realised musical miniatures of the era.

'Too Young', meanwhile, brings us our third Bernie lyrics in as many years treating of the problems of being an older man pursuing a much younger partner. The problem is that, while in 'Whipping Boy' that theme was farcically explored, and in 'Li'l 'Frigerator' it was ridiculously explored, in 'Too Young' there's an attempt to portray it as a sort of doomed but beautiful Shakespearean ideal. Certainly, that mid-life-crisis sentiment was common currency in its time some four decades ago but it hasn't aged well in the interim. Elton's voice is marked by the expressive raw hoarseness that would make *Live in Australia* so poignant and devastating some two years later, and he is giving it all to sell these lyrics to their full potential but there's not sufficient density of musical material to keep us going through the song's five minute run-time.

Speaking of sprawling run-times, let's talk about 'Wrap Her Up', the George Michael duet beloved today for the high camp factor of two of music's most fantastically homosexual individuals singing a song about all the women they definitely lust after. The song is centred around the compelling combination of Elton and Michael's differently ranged voices, and while starting as a down and dirty synth grind, as it develops it morphs more into a *Blue Moves* style disco stomp, replete with swirling strings and generally boisterous messing around that fills out the last minute and a half of the song. It's not a song for every day but for those times when only the campiest of camp will do, it ever emerges, the hero of the hour.

When *Ice on Fire* was remastered, the decision was made on 'Satellite' to extend the intro with a heavy electronic beat to amp up the galactic atmospherics of the song, which represented the most extreme modification to any track on the album, likely in an attempt to give the song a more distinctive flavour than it initially possessed. This is another one of Bernie's more middle of the road lyrics that over stretches its central idea, and Elton didn't seem to know much what to do with it except make it a vaguely funky disco style ballad in the vein of 'Little Jeannie'. It's this retro quality that saves the song in the end. Perhaps not of its time, 'Satellite' was yet a song for its time, and that surely deserves a few extra bleeps and bloops, four decades later.

'Tell Me What the Papers Say' is a combination of a broader criticism of the media's limited range of scurrilous interests, and a spotlight on some of the serious and outrageous concerns of the time, a form that would be continued in 'Goodbye Marlon Brando' on *Reg Strikes Back*. Elton's music is utterly madcap, dominated by a bopping bassline from David Baton, a manic cowbell in the bridge, Lawrence Welk (1903–1992) style backing vocals in the chorus, and an instrumental section swamped with synthetic brass and classic piano licks. It's a bag of joyous stuff celebrating the utter inanity of the British and American press, mocking their self-seriousness and pretence to profound integrity.

I have never been sure what to make of 'Candy by the Pound'. Bernie's unusually happy-go-lucky lyrics and Elton's 'I Gotta Golden Ticket' music, are distinctly out of place among everything else Elton did in the 1980s. Partially, I think this is again an instance of Elton chasing the trend of pop in the mid-1980s that included 'Wake Me Up Before You Go-Go' (1984), 'Take On Me' (1984) and 'You Spin Me' (1984). It's an example of Elton attempting to port the innocence of 1960s pop balladry over to an audience primed for light fluff, which ended up largely turning off devotees of both forms.

'Shoot Down the Moon' would have been the Bond franchise's most introspective intro theme had it been accepted. Lyrically, it does exactly what a Bond song is supposed to do, providing us with a parade of striking phrases to be considered individually rather than as a narrative whole. Elton's music features a gorgeous melody built on top of a series of chord transitions that take us on a journey through interesting tonal territories. It's a great Elton song but had far too little of the big bang build that audiences expected from their Bond themes and so the producers opted instead for Duran Duran's peppier, action track. Bond's loss is our gain, however, as this contemplative mix of spy and broken romance imagery, set within a musical structure that denies us a feeling of a stable tonic, is a wonderful closer for *Ice on Fire*, and to the first half of Elton's 1980s catalogue, which had brought us anthems of high flown global anxiety and deeply intimate dives into the psychology of shattered relationships, all of which won't be seen again in an Elton album for three long years.

The Stats

Album/Single	US	UK	Australia	Canada
Ice on Fire	48	3	2	11
	G	P		
'Nikita'/'The Man Who Never Died'/'Restless'/'I'm Still Standing'/'Don't Let the Sun Go Down on Me'	7	3	3	2
'Wrap Her Up'/'The Man Who Never Died' (US) 'Restless' (UK)	20	12	22	26
'Cry to Heaven'/'Candy By the Pound'		47	86	

The Players

Elton John: lead vocals, acoustic piano (1 to 3, 5, 8, 10 and 11), Yamaha GS1 piano (4 and 5), synthesizer (4, 7, 9 and 11) and backing vocals (4)

Fred Mandel: synthesizers (1, 4, 5, 10 and 11) and keyboards (2, 3 and 6 to 9) and sequencer (6), electric guitar (7 and 11), finger snaps (7) and arrangements (10)

Davey Johnstone: electric guitar (1, 3, 5, 6, 8, 9 and 11), Spanish guitar (2), synth guitar (2 and 7) and backing vocals (3, 5 and 6 to 9)

Nik Kershaw: electric guitar (4, 7 and 11) and backing vocals (4)

Paul Westwood: bass (1, 2 and 6)

Deon Estus: bass (3, 7 and 11)

David Paton: bass (4, 8 and 9)

John Deacon: bass (5)

Pino Palladino: bass (10)

Charlie Morgan: drums (1, 2 and 6)

Mel Gaynor: drums (3, 7 and 11)

Dave Mattacks: drums (4, 8 and 9) and military snare (5)

Roger Taylor: drums (5)

Frank Ricotti: percussion (3 and 5) and vibraphone (9)

James Newton Howard: string arrangements (3 and 6)

Gus Dudgeon: horn arrangements (3 and 6), Simmons drums (5 and 11) and arrangements (10)

David Bitelli: horn arrangements (1, 3, 6 and 9), baritone saxophone (1, 6 and 9) and tenor saxophone (3 and 6)

Bob Sydor: tenor saxophone (3)

Phil Todd: alto saxophone (6)

Nick Pentelow: tenor saxophone (9)

Pete Thomas: tenor saxophone (9)

Rick Taylor: trombone (1, 3, 6 and 9) and horn arrangements (9)

Chris Pyne: trombone (9)

Raul D'Oliveira: trumpet (1, 3, 6 and 9)

Paul Spong: trumpet (1, 3, 6 and 9)

Sister Sledge: backing vocals (1)

Alan Carvell: backing vocals (3, 5 and 7 to 9)

Kiki Dee: backing vocals (3, 5, 6, 8 and 9)

Katie Kissoon: backing vocals (3, 5, 6, 8 and 9)

Pete Wingfield: backing vocals (3, 5 and 6 to 9)

George Michael: backing vocals (4) and lead vocals (6)

Millie Jackson: lead and backing vocals (11)

The Tracks

Side one:
1. 'This Town' (John, Taupin) (3.56)
2. 'Cry To Heaven' (John, Taupin) (4.16)
3. 'Soul Glove' (John, Taupin) (3.31)
4. 'Nikita' (John, Taupin) (5.43)
5. 'Too Young' (John, Taupin) (5.12)

Side two:
6. 'Wrap Her Up' (John, Taupin, Johnstone, Mandel, Morgan, Westwood) (6.21)
7. 'Satellite' (John, Taupin) (3.57)
8. 'Tell Me What the Papers Say' (John, Taupin) (3.40)
9. 'Candy By the Pound' (John, Taupin) (3.56)
10. 'Shoot Down the Moon' (John, Taupin) (5.09)
11. 'Act of War' (John, Taupin) (4.41) (CD release only)

Musician's Corner: 'Synthesizers and This Town'

I haven't talked much about the instrumentation on Elton's records thus far, firstly because it's information that other Elton authors cover in detail, secondly because I'm more interested in how Elton sculpts a song at the keyboard, before producers and arrangers start their work, and thirdly because it's something you can largely hear for yourself. That being said, Elton's inclusion of increasingly synthetic sounds from the 1970s into the early 1980s is a shift worth noting.

To some degree, these had been with Elton from the beginning, as he was playing a Vox Continental organ at pubs to make some extra record-buying cash as a teenager. However, when you think of Elton in the 1970s what you think of is him on piano, harpsichord or organ, Olsson on drums, Johnstone on guitar, Murray on bass and Ray Cooper playing a variety of percussive instruments, with some orchestral instruments making an appearance here and there at the behest of Buckmaster.

Most of the sounds you hear emerging from these early Elton records are those you might have heard from albums released a decade, or even two decades, earlier, with occasional walk-on star turns for the synths ('First Episode at Hienton', 'Rocket Man (I Think It's Going to Be a Long, Long Time)', 'I've Seen the Saucers' and 'Funeral for a Friend') until you get the first glimmer of the fully synthetic future in the form of 'Theme From a Non-Existent TV Show' (1976). In the early 1980s synthetic sounds were more regularly woven into the front of Elton's instrumental soundscape, existing as structural elements in their own right rather than sounds enhancing the structures set out by other instruments. By 1983 in *Too Low for Zero*, we see Elton regularly using highly synthetic sounds for something other than novelty or support purposes, with the title track in particular employing synthesized effects to create an echoey and stark backdrop for Bernie's tale of inertia.

Which brings us to 'This Town', which baffled me for a long time. Bernie's lyrics are a dark reflection on being trapped in a town where the destruction of the union has brought job insecurity, creating a state of stifling restlessness as the unemployed haunt the pubs and streets with no purpose or direction. The music, however, is a synth and sax fuelled up tempo bop, ready for the dance floor.

This is clearly satire, a juxtaposition of dark source material with bouncy presentation that highlights how even suffering gets commodified for popular consumption and shares more than a little family resemblance with 'I Think I'm Going to Kill Myself'. The mechanical synth line, which begins the piece and enters and leaves at will but never changes, is so synthetic, so jarring, so present, that surely it must be a reflection on how pop music generally engages with working class subject matter, a theme amplified by the lengthy flashes of groovy sax soloing. It's a clever use of instrumental choice to accentuate the satirical direction of Elton's take on Bernie's earnest lyrics, and thereby brings us two messages for the price of one: that the despair is real and our attempts to understand it through dramatisation are often little more than self-indulgent and synthetic exercises in absurd romanticisation.

Chapter 23

Leather Jackets

Recorded: January 1985, January to February and May to September 1986
Released: 27 October 1986
Producer: Gus Dudgeon

The Story

L ook up any ranking of Elton albums online and you'll find *Leather Jackets* either last or next to last, depending on the compiler's feelings about *Victim of Love*. It's 'the album that cocaine made', 'Elton's least favourite album', 'Dudgeon's secret shame' and any of a dozen other nicknames affectionately bestowed on it by Elton fans who love to hate it but don't quite hate to love it, and so settle for affectionate derision.

Elton was out of his mind on cocaine while making this album, resulting in tracks that even Dudgeon's famed post-production heroics couldn't save. So it's towards the bottom of the pile as an Elton album but place it against the other output of the pop industry in 1986 ('Party All the Time' anyone?) and suddenly it doesn't look so bad.

And yet, though Elton at his worst is still better than 100 music industry look alikes at their best, *Leather Jackets* didn't represent the breath of fresh air or return to form that fans who had been let down by the unevenness of *Ice on Fire* needed to refuel their Elton mania, and the album stalled out at an abysmal #91 in the US and an almost incomprehensibly respectable #24 in the UK. His voice shot, his addictions running rampant and his recording career at a place it hadn't been since 1969, something major needed to change, and for the first time in a decade, a year would pass without a new studio album from Elton.

The Songs

We start with 'Leather Jackets', which brings with it whiffs of chrome and leather that place it in the tradition of 1950s nostalgia. Bernie mentions Buddy Holly and Elvis, who have passed on into eternity, and generally treads the same ground as 'Crocodile Rock' with a particular focus on the greaser sub-culture. It's not mind-blowing lyrics but it has its moments, which Elton puts the absolute minimum of effort into supporting, coming out of the gates with a three chord G-F-C progression

Little Richard's explosive performance style and theatrical appearance in the late 1950s served as important references for Elton's later approach to the piano. (*Wikimedia Commons, photo by TCG-Topps*)

Leon Russell's distinctive slippery, beats akimbo playing style worked its way into Elton's own technique, as did his fusion of eclectic musical genres. (*Wikimedia Commons*)

Elton in 1971, at the start of his fame. The addition of Gus Dudgeon and Paul Buckmaster to his production team had given *Elton John* a unity of sound and density of experience that would define Elton's work of the early 1970s. (*Wikimedia Commons, photo by Bert Verhoeff*)

Elton and Bernie in 1971. At this point, the pair were working at a legendary rate, Bernie crafting lyrics in an hour that Elton was able to set to legendary tunes in even less time. (*Wikimedia Commons*)

Elton's original band of Dee Murray on bass and Nigel Olsson on drums would eventually find their way into his studio recordings, lending expert backup not only with their instruments, but, in combination with Davey Johnstone, creating the iconic backing vocals to his tracks of the early 1970s. (*Wikimedia Commons*).

Dee Murray was one of the most accomplished album bassists of his age, and one of the most universally beloved musicians of his era. (*Wikimedia Commons, photo by Dick James Music*).

Davey Johnstone's guitar has been a towering presence on Elton John's albums and tours since 1971. In 2019, he played his 3000th live show with Elton. (*Wikimedia Commons, photo by Raph_PH*)

By the mid-1970s Elton had reached the pinnacle of his first wave of success, performing on television in a series of increasingly outlandish outfits while his albums went regularly to the top of the charts. (*Wikimedia Commons*)

By the late 1970s Elton decided a change to his usual working style with Bernie and the band was needed, experimenting with albums on which he wrote none of the music, and working with new lyricists and musicians. (*Wikimedia Commons, photo by Eddie Mallin*)

Tom Robinson was a musical icon of gay culture whose lyrics pushed Elton to write songs in the early 1980s giving voice to the experiences and emotions of gay men. (*Wikimedia Commons, photo by Bryan Ledgard*)

Broadway lyricist Tim Rice first worked with Elton writing the words to 'Legal Boys' (1982). The pair would reunite later on both *The Lion King* and *AIDA*. (*Wikimedia Commons, photo by Thecharmschool*)

Percussion wizard Ray Cooper has been not only a steady presence on Elton's albums, bringing his fleet of water gongs, congas and the tambourine he plays like no man ever has or will again, but an intoxicating energy to Elton's road shows. (*Wikimedia Commons, photo by Lori Lum*)

By the 1990s Elton was clear of his worst addictions, and producing some of the most powerful albums of his career, constructing complex songs that also had massive popular appeal, as in the song 'Live Like Horses', which he performed with Luciano Pavarotti. (*Wikimedia Commons*)

The *Farewell Yellow Brick Road* tour, Elton's forty-ninth world tour, began in 2018, and concluded (with a break for Covid) in 2023, bringing in nearly $1 billion from fans eager to say goodbye to their favorite musician. Elton was joined by the musicians who had worked with him on albums over the previous half century including Cooper, Johnstone and Olsson (Murray died in 1992). (*Wikimedia Commons, photos by slgckgc*)

that couldn't be less Elton, and that outlines the tonal constraints of the whole song. It's a good time song and the instrumental interlude represents a fun conversation between synth bass and guitar but those elements are not enough to rescue the song for most Elton fans, though I'll say I've never skipped it when it comes on as it's enjoyable to move to all the manic synth gestures and sing along with.

'Hoop of Fire' also takes a conservative approach to its chord structure, remaining rigidly within its key signature; it has at its core a woman who, while not as intriguing as the one in 'Saint', has something of a defining character trait, a desire for the standard romantic tropes of beaches and candlelight, while aching for something adventurous and slightly dangerous. 'Hoop of Fire' trudges forward at a glacial pace aiming for the seductive but the flat backing vocals, inexplicable presence of timpani and perfunctory piano solo all work against it. There's definitely a good song in here, at a different pace or with different orchestration – the melody is sound and the expansiveness of the chorus is catchy, but the supporting material works largely against its own best aspects.

There isn't much of much to be found at the heart of 'Don't Trust That Woman', the song Elton co-wrote with Cher (b.1946) and which he was so embarrassed by that he fobbed it off on his alter-ego, Lady Choc Ice. The lyrics, about a lazy, blood-thirsty, sado-masochist woman who, under no circumstances, is to be untied or believed, is so over the top that it could have been written as a parody. I don't think the song is doing that , however, and that it's an earnest warning against vampiric women of the world, my reasoning being that there isn't much musically to suggest otherwise. There are no exaggerated musical elements to make us feel in the midst of a parody. The lyrics don't build outwards to absurdity revealing an overarching joke structure, so we take the lyrics literally and conclude that in striving for edgy sexuality it accomplished little more than adolescent tittering.

'Go it Alone' gives us one of Elton's rare two-chord songs which bounces back and forth between the tonic (I) and subdominant (IV). That isn't necessarily a bad thing and it works well for a song that is all about an individual, deep in the myopic rage of a failed relationship. Like with 'Spiteful Child', the vehemence of the narrator against his ex tells us far more about him than it does about her, and this song is fundamentally about the flagrant lies we tell when we are hurt, attempting to rebound. The brutal synths, the shrieking guitar, the primal simplicity of the chord structure, all speak to a person reduced to an animal-like state, incapable of any adult sentiments, stomping about his empty house deceiving himself because the truth hurts too much. While most hearing this will think of it as another angry kiss-off song, I think the vehemence of the man's statements bend towards the idea that this is another Bernie character study of a self-destructive individual.

A holdover from *Ice on Fire*, 'Gypsy Heart' is a song about not being quite enough to convince a free spirit to settle into a long-term relationship with you. The individual with the roving Gypsy heart in the song comes back from time to time but is always off again in search of greener pastures, but she (or he – the gender is unclear) is so captivating that our singer finds himself committed to a lifetime of either being with them or waiting for their return, and doesn't seem overly bothered by the fact, seemingly sure that in the end his depth of ardour will win the day. Bernie's portrayal of both the hero and the object of his affection is well drawn, with the hero's sense of alternate resignation and confidence particularly compelling. The background vocals are on the flat side but Elton's build into the chorus has a sweeping desperation to it, a defiant confidence against everything to the contrary, perfectly attuned to the heartache felt by anyone waiting for their dream partner to come to their senses and claim the loyal friend right next to them instead of reaching for that which will hurt them.

By the time of *Leather Jackets*, British rock icon Cliff Richard (*b*.1940) – whose 'Move It' (1958) was credited by John Lennon as being the first British Rock record – had clawed his way back from the relative obscurity in which he languished in the late 1960s and early 1970s, and was remaking himself as a pop rocker, with four early 1980s albums charting in the Top 10 in the UK charts. Elton was thrilled with the renaissance being experienced by one of his idols and expressed interest in recording a duet, which became 'Slow Rivers'. Lyrically, the song bears some similarities to 'Gypsy Heart' with the singers lingering over memories of a past lover who is expected to return one day 'in a flood of tears' due to her own inability to truly give her heart to anyone. The prospect of performing with his hero seems to have roused Elton to a higher effort on this track, with chords full of the old poignant inversions from days past, strong handoffs of the verse material and a well-constructed build in the bridge that falls away to the sombre ruminations of the chorus material. There isn't much diversity of vocal style but thematically that tracks, demonstrating two individuals who have been frozen in the depths of a relationship who have come out the other side bearing similar scars.

'Heartache All Over the World' is widely known as a piece that Elton has nothing good to say about, and most follow his lead, but I'm not so sure. It's not the deepest song in the world – it's basically about how it sucks not to have a date for the weekend, which is on the superficial side by Bernie's standards but was perfectly in line with most pop songs of the mid-1980s. There's a fun modulation in the middle and the switch to the parallel minor for 'Heart's on fire' with its little synth riff is a good time too. It's a song to perk up the spirits of the lovable losers out there, if only for a few minutes, and sometimes that's all a song needs to be.

'Angeline' is a portrait of a reprehensible individual which we might be tempted to write off as a piece of unadulterated misogyny but I think that what Elton and Bernie are doing here is patently not about holding up the song's narrator as an example to be followed but rather as a case study in the most brutish of individuals. The lyrics represent such next-level misogyny, in which the male figure is demanding sex, hard manual labour, and money from the poor, eternally put-upon figure of Angeline that it's impossible to view him as anything but a scoundrel. Elton reinforces that message with the draught horse like rhythm of the chorus in which Angeline is reduced in the final analysis to the status of a beast of burden. The problem is that, while all that might be true, it doesn't make the song particularly enjoyable to listen to. The central figure isn't a lovable rogue, he's a horrible person, who doesn't learn anything or get his comeuppance, which doesn't precisely inspire repeat listening.

Though it can be a hard listen, at least 'Angeline' is an interesting one, which is less easily said of 'Memory of Love', which perhaps represents the nadir of Elton and Bernie's 1980s efforts. Bernie's words are almost aggressively simplistic, and Elton's music drifts through them at a uniform level of middling intensity marked by the thudding blast of the percussion that feels like drifting off under the influence of general anaesthesia.

'Paris' is a piece of surprising depth in terms of musical narrative, with Elton's employment of different tonal centres laying out demarcated realms of idealism and routine reality that make this song one of the most thoughtfully constructed on the album, a response to Bernie's interesting lyrics not so much about what Paris is but what it represents to the people waiting to go there. Even in his fantasies of what Paris will do for him, the anxieties that the narrator is trying to use Paris to escape start creeping through, infecting his ideal image of the city he's still waiting in the airport to visit.

One of Elton's favourite type of songs is the cry of loneliness ballad, the sort of song that 'Sad Songs (Say So Much)' is all about and which Elton would listen to compulsively as each of his relationships lurched towards its inevitable hurtful close. The last time he tried his hand at the genre, the result was the haunting 'Sorry Seems to Be the Hardest Word' with lyrics written partially by him. Ten years later, Bernie's lyrics for 'I Fall Apart' instantly connected with Elton. It has complicated lyrics, the meaning of which does not become clear until the last verse line, which rewrites what the whole song is about. We think it's another standard song about a man grieving the end of his relationship to a woman he loved but it's actually about a man whose lost his male partner to another woman, leaving the singer alone, wishing that 'she was me'. It's a poignant slice of heartache from a time when social pressures were so intense that living as a gay man meant constantly losing one's loves for no other reason than that maintaining an openly gay relationship was to invite omnipresent frustration.

Elton's musical setting is among his most inspired on *Leather Jackets* and wouldn't be out of place on *Too Low for Zero* or *The Fox*, with a melody replete with melancholy, and a chorus saturated with an aura of yearning after the impossible. Elton's singing is powerful and the sparse accompaniment of limited drums and celestial synths give the echoey feeling of an empty house being wandered through, while in the realm of chord progressions, Elton's in full form, employing borrowed tonalities to their full effect in producing a sense of rootlessness that amplifies the searching despair of Bernie's lyrics. The song is one of Elton's best from the 1980s, doomed unfairly to obscurity by being buried at the end of an album that nobody bought.

The Stats

Album/Single	US	UK	Australia	Canada
Leather Jackets	91	24	4	38
		G		
'Heartache All Over the World'/'Highlander'	55	45	7	58
'Slow Rivers'/'Billy and the Kids'/'Lord of the Flies'		44	82	

The Players

Elton John: lead vocals, Yamaha GS1 (1 and 8), grand piano (2, 4 to 6 and 10), Roland JX-8P (2 and 11), MIDI piano (3) and Yamaha CP-80 (11)

Fred Mandel: synthesizer programming and sequencing (1, 4 and 7), Yamaha DX7 (2, 6 and 9), Korg DW-8000 (3 and 10), Roland JX-8P (4 and 11), Roland Jupiter 8 (5, 6, 10 and 11), Roland P60 (7 and 9), Prophet 2000 (7), Yamaha TX816 Rhodes (10) and grand piano (11)

Davey Johnstone: acoustic guitar (1 to 5, 7 and 9), electric guitar (2 to 11) and backing vocals (2, 4, 5 and 7 to 10)

David Paton: bass (2, 3, 5 and 9 to 11)

Paul Westwood: bass (6)

John Deacon: bass (8)

Gus Dudgeon: drum programming (1) and electronic percussion (1, 4 and 7)

Dave Mattacks: drums (2 and 5)

Charlie Morgan: drums (3, 4, 6, 7 and 9 to 11) and electronic percussion (4)

Roger Taylor: drums (8)

Graham Dickson: electronic percussion (1, 3, 4 and 7)

Frank Ricotti: percussion (2)

Jody Linscott: percussion (3) and tambourine (7)

James Newton Howard: string arrangements and conductor (6)

Martyn Ford: orchestra contractor (6)

Gavyn Wright: orchestra leader (6)

Alan Carvell: backing vocals (2, 4, 5 and 7 to 10)

Katie Kissoon: backing vocals (2)

Pete Wingfield: backing vocals (2)

Shirley Lewis: backing vocals (4, 5 and 8 to 10)

Gordon Neville: backing vocals (4, 5 and 7 to 10)

Kiki Dee: backing vocals (6)

Cliff Richard: lead vocals (6)

Vicki Brown: backing vocals (7)

Albert Boekholt: Emulator vocals and samples (9)

The Tracks

Side one:
1. 'Leather Jackets' (John, Taupin) (4.10)
2. 'Hoop of Fire' (John, Taupin) (4.14)
3. 'Don't Trust that Woman' (Cher, Lady Choc Ice (John)) (4.58)
4. 'Go it Alone' (John, Taupin) (4.26)
5. 'Gypsy Heart' (John, Taupin) (4.46)

Side two:
6. 'Slow Rivers' (John, Taupin) (3.06)
7. 'Heartache All Over the World' (John, Taupin) (3.52)
8. 'Angeline' (John, Taupin) (3.24)
9. 'Memory of Love' (John, Taupin) (4.08)
10. 'Paris' (John, Taupin) (3.58)
11. 'I Fall Apart' (John, Taupin) (4.00)

Musician's Corner: 'Paris'

'Paris' is the song on *Leather Jackets* that Elton points to as one of the only things on the album that he doesn't consider cocaine-fuelled rubbish, so let's look more closely at it. The opening is instantly strange, starting on chimes then fading into what seems like the middle of a looping piece of calming atmospheric music. All this is in the strange and remote key of G flat major, with its six flats, that we haven't had occasion to visit since 'Indian Sunset', which makes the whole episode even more surreal still.

It's an odd place to be sonically and then Elton does the strangest thing when the verse comes in; he starts it in C major, which is a plunge from the least familiar key to our ears to the most familiar key, from a chord that contains a G flat, B flat and D flat, to a scale that contains literally none of those. This makes sense within the context of the song, where the strange G flat is the world of the dreamed of destination, the place that'll fix everything that's wrong just by being there, but the place we happen to be now is an airport lounge, the most common, unromantic thing in the world.

The song is about making your way to Paris. The verse up to the chorus represents musically that struggle to make the journey from C major to the sonic world furthest removed from it, G flat. And that's what we're doing, climbing that mountain, going through chords associated with more and more exotic locations, from C (no flats) to F (one flat) to E flat (three flats) to A flat (four flats) with some stops at D flat (five flats) to end up at G flat (six flats) on the words 'When I get to Paris', thereby pulling off the amazing trick of making a journey to the most distant place sound like a comforting return home.

Chapter 24

Reg Strikes Back

Recorded: October 1987 and March 1988
Released: 20 June 1988
Producer: Chris Thomas

The Story

People who bought Elton's *Live in Australia* album experienced something of a jolt as the voice singing 'The Greatest Discovery' and 'Take Me to the Pilot' was a harsh rasp just barely detectable as the voice from their favourite 1970s albums. That rasp and Elton's heroic efforts to sing through it made the album among the greatest of his career, testament to the true performer that Elton was but behind it lay the disturbing truth that Elton wasn't well. Nodes had developed on his vocal chords, the same sort that ended Julie Andrews's (*b.*1935) career and the only treatment for which lay in a surgery that might mean he could never sing again.

'Will we ever hear Elton again?' was the natural question people asked as they heard their musical hero fight his way through *Live in Australia*; just a year later, they had their answer in the form of *Reg Strikes Back*, a triumphant return in which Elton, humbled by the reception of *Leather Jackets*, frightened out of complacency (though not yet out of his various addictions) and facing the possibility of the end of his career, gave everything to put out an album that ranked alongside his best from the 1970s.

Reg Strikes Back was, like *Too Low for Zero*, a perfectly crafted mix of the new and old, with Johnstone and Cooper returning to their traditional roles, Thomas back in the production booth, Olsson and Murray returning for backing vocals, and the relative newcomers to the band, Charlie Morgan and Fred Mandel (*b.*1953), took their posts once again at drums and synthesizers respectively. Having swayed heavily towards the synthetic on his albums of the early 1980s, here Elton has found the mix of electronic and organic that would define his sound for the next decade, while Bernie for his part has emerged from his own trials, which had pushed him towards a focus on deep analysis of failed relationships as his primary writing topic, and is back wandering further afield, with lyrics treating of topics as widely diverse as domestic drudgery, *Rocky V*, America's failed social safety net and his evolving relationship with New York City. With every member of the band working together and with the backing of MCA Records ready and eager to promote its new megastar, *Reg Strikes Back* launched Elton back into the Top 20 on both sides of the Atlantic, reaching #18 in the UK and #16 in the US, a startling result for an artist's twenty-first studio album.

The Songs

Reg Strikes Back comes out of the gate with one of the best first four tracks on any of his albums since *Goodbye Yellow Brick Road*. There's a diversity of lyrical and musical types here, yet all within the same general acoustic universe; we feel a crucial sense of difference within overall coherence that gives an album its particular flavour. 'Town of Plenty' is one of Bernie's more resistant lyrics to easy summation, presenting us with what appears to be an open and shut case of his favourite theme of what happens to people entering the maelstrom of urban America, only here, unlike in 'In Neon' or 'Honky Cat', we are presented with an individual who isn't a wide-eyed innocent buffeted by the cynical city but rather someone who is seemingly seeking out that cynicism to profit from it, who identifies with the thieves of this new land, seeking to leave behind the challenging and authentic world of his home town and instead break into media, where his particular sense of amorality will do well. So far, so clear but then we come across these interesting lines, 'And laid across the airstrip/Were the passports and the luggage/All that once remained/Of a rugged individual'. This shunts us to seemingly another story altogether, of someone vaporised either on entrance to, or attempting to flee, the town of plenty, as observed by our antihero – a warning of what will become of him once the city has its way with him, or an encouraging sign that individualism isn't what will win here but rather his own trademark deviousness?

No matter which way you interpret it, it makes for compelling lyrics in the tradition of 'Chasing the Crown', 'Stinker', or all the great Disney villain songs, where someone is so content in their putrescence, and seems to be having such fun with it, that you almost pull for them in spite of yourself, an instinct helped along by the self-assured strut of Elton's musical setting, with its digital piano rolls evoking our antihero strolling down the block, surveying with a wicked eye all that he is about to control through his own unquenchable pursuit of position.

Leaving behind the city and its dark glories, we turn to one of Elton's best love ballads of the decade, 'A Word in Spanish', which rises and falls irresistibly on the rhythm of Johnstone's nylon guitar motif of a rising arpeggio followed by a little step down that sets a pulsing sway over which Elton places his gorgeous melody in support of Bernie's lyrics about love attempting to cross cultural and linguistic barriers. What makes the song so delightful is the mix of Johnstone's guitar line, Elton's vocal line, and the old Murray-Olsson-Johnstone backing vocal lines, which are all moving in slightly different directions with different timings, producing a sense of wave-like motion that keeps catching you up and bringing you forward as the story unfolds: a love that simply cannot be and is all the more beautiful for it.

The chain of great songwriting continues into 'Mona Lisas and Mad Hatters (Part Two)', the sequel to his song of some sixteen years earlier, in which, to the busy urban stomp of Elton's music and lively brass work of Freddie Hubbard (1938–2008), Bernie reflects on his original idealistic condemnation of New York City. No longer an 'innocent abroad' whose youthful instinct is ever to 'wage a war for the underdog', Bernie in middle age is now able to come to a more balanced consideration of what he describes in his memoirs as his favourite city in the world, still recognising its ability to crush dreams through grinding poverty but now more open to the flourishing cultures to be found there. Elton's music and vocals wrap these words up in a busy urban clutter of noises and styles that effortlessly render the liveliness of the New York streets without ever descending into flat mimicry. While the instrumentals give us that sense of the city's diversity, Elton's nuanced vocals walk the line between celebration and personal mourning, rendering Bernie's ambivalent feelings towards this world capital on an almost visceral level.

I can't be objective about 'I Don't Wanna Go On With You Like That'. The image of Elton bobbing and weaving behind his Roland electric piano, in his wide brimmed black hat and long coat essentially hard-wired itself into my adolescent brain as the ultimate in cool. Today, some thirty-five years later, I still get goosebumps every time I hear those iconic drum hits and find myself suddenly 11 years old with a whole life ahead of me. So, keep in mind that I'm not to be trusted when talking about this song.

'I Don't Want to Go On With You Like That' is the greatest song ever made by a human being. The echoey hollowness of its acoustic space, dominated by the relentless electric drum sounds and Elton's Roland digital piano, expresses the single-tracked pounding obsession within the mind of someone lingering over their partner's serial unfaithfulness – the complete inability to think about anything else as the whole world becomes reduced to an endless cycle of ruminations about the unjustness of someone else's behaviour. The song plunges forward with brute strength born of anger and frustration, which grow to a point that words can't even encompass them anymore. Elton's keyboard playing gets more unhinged as the song proceeds, until the last thing we hear from him is a frustrated dismissive gliss while the music fades out, the mark of a person fed up with all the artful discussion, desperate to flee the building and move on with life.

Reg Strikes Back's streak of creative triumph comes to a thudding stop with 'Japanese Hands', the album's second, and far less artful, song about romance across cultural lines. The music is beautiful but the whole thing falls apart on Bernie's now horribly dated lyrics, which at the time perhaps didn't raise eyebrows but which now activate our sense of cultural fetishism. The aggressive reduction of the traditions of a foreign culture into sexually exotic elements to be consumed by a Westerner doesn't work anymore and makes it virtually impossible today to appreciate the beauty of Elton's music.

The album soon gets back on track with 'Goodbye Marlon Brando', which is essentially a laundry list of things about the world in 1988 that Bernie finds tiresome, amusing or dangerous, in his role as poetic observer of the human condition. As such it was always a song that was going to grow dated in a way that 'Your Song' or 'Goodbye Yellow Brick Road' never will. Even if someone born after 1995 won't get most of the references, Bernie's overall message comes through clearly, namely that our media-bred appetite for scandal is moving us further away from the things that give our life meaning, and Elton – with Johnstone taking the lead – crafts that message into a pedal to the medal rocker bursting at the seams with aggravation for all the layers of substanceless stuff that are foisted upon us by media outlets trying to compel us to spend our time consuming their wares.

'The Camera Never Lies' is a look into the mind of a paparazzi photographer, a profession that was steadily working its toll on the celebrities of the late 1980s and into the 1990s, culminating in the death of Princess Diana (1961–1997). This portrayal is less acidic that 'Heart in the Right Place' and instead describes a sort of tug of war between the photographer and the subject of their devotion, with the celebrity using disguises to try and get away with little bursts of freedom and bad behaviour, and the photographer adapting to them, using the camera lens to cut through to the truth of the situation. To some degree, the celebrity knows that he needs people like the photographer and recognises how the contest works. Though Bernie's lyrics have a bit more bite than what is conveyed by the end product, Elton sets the song in a relatively light manner, with game recognising game, and no particular hard feelings.

Bernie continues at the top of his craft with 'Heavy Traffic' portraying a motley cast of characters treading water at the bottom of the societal food chain. We are introduced to pimps, coyotes, basement drug manufacturers, fry cooks, drug addicts and sex workers who all get along as best they can while skirting the law and living a life that seems to have its moments as they all pile in the car having adventures together out in the thick California traffic with no particular sense of where they're going or why. Elton brings flavours of the Florida music scene to his musical conception of the song, with a rhythm that suggests the Miami sound machine, and a persistent backing vocal motif that is interesting and fun in a madcap 'Crazy Water' fashion.

After stumbling into bad habits of objectification with 'Japanese Hands', Bernie uses his better instincts portraying women of depth and character with 'Poor Cow', about a woman stuck in a relationship with an unfaithful, violent man, experiencing chronic poverty and serial pregnancy, with no apparent way out of her hopeless situation, her only company her mother who comes by once a week to complain about the latest episode of *Dallas*. As a portrayal of the grinding desperation of poor American women, it's a grim masterpiece, which Elton brings to life with a stomping synth motif and dark vocals that give voice to the frustration of being a woman who gets all the misery of her situation while those around her reap the benefits of her work and resignation. Certainly, Bernie's best portrait of a woman central character since 'Saint', it might well be one of his best ever, ranking up there with 'Emily' and 'Shoulder Holster' in the fulness of its objectivity.

Closing out *Reg Strikes Back*, we have The Beach Boys inspired 'Since God Invented Girls' which, like 'Japanese Hands', has not aged well in the lyrics department. The lyrics, which are supposed to be an account of God assembling the first women and the effect that they have had on the world since, reads eerily like an account of Buffalo Bill constructing his woman suit in *The Silence of the Lambs*. Even outside of that what we get is another song that is entirely focused on the physical attributes that God brought to his creation, with not a word about the character, or intellect that he also put into them. While that might have been sufficient for a Beach Boys song from the 1960s, by the late 1980s something more was needed. Another song to hear rather than listen to, and a bummer ending for an album of such consistency in conception and execution.

The Stats

Album/Single	US	UK	Australia	Canada
Reg Strikes Back	16	18	13	6
	G	S	G	2P
'I Don't Wanna Go On With You Like That'/ 'Rope Around a Fool'	2	30	24	1
'Town of Plenty'/'Whipping Boy' (UK)		74		
'A Word in Spanish'/'Heavy Traffic'	19	91		10
'Mona Lisas and Mad Hatters (Part Two)'/ 'A Word in Spanish' (US)				

The Players

Elton John: lead vocals, backing vocals, Roland RD-1000 digital piano (1, 3, 4 and 10), synthesizers (2, 5, 6 and 9), organ (2) and acoustic piano (5, 7 and 8)
Fred Mandel: synthesizers
Fred McFarlane: programming
Davey Johnstone: electric guitar (1, 2, 3 and 5 to 9), acoustic guitar (2, 4, 5, 6, 8 and 10) and backing vocals
Pete Townshend: acoustic guitar (1)
David Paton: bass
Charlie Morgan: drums
Ray Cooper: maracas (6, 7, 8 and 9), tambourine (6, 7, 8 and 9) and timbales (6, 7, 8 and 9)

Freddie Hubbard: trumpet (3) and flugelhorn (3)
Dee Murray: backing vocals
Nigel Olsson: backing vocals
Adrian Baker: additional backing vocals (10)
Bruce Johnston: additional backing vocals (10)
Carl Wilson: additional backing vocals (10)

The Tracks

1. 'Town of Plenty' (John, Taupin) (3.40)
2. 'A Word in Spanish' (John, Taupin) (4.39)
3. 'Mona Lisas and Mad Hatters (Part Two)' (John, Taupin) (4.12)
4. 'I Don't Wanna Go On With You Like That' (John, Taupin) (4.33)
5. 'Japanese Hands' (John, Taupin) (4.40)
6. 'Goodbye Marlon Brando' (John, Taupin) (3.30)
7. 'The Camera Never Lies' (John, Taupin) (4.36)
8. 'Heavy Traffic' (John, Taupin, Johnstone) (3.30)
9. 'Poor Cow' (John, Taupin) (3.50)
10. 'Since God Invented Girls' (John, Taupin) (4.54)

Musician's Corner: 'Mona Lisas and Mad Hatters (Part Two)'

This is the first Elton song that's a direct continuation of something that he'd previously written, with some sixteen years separating the two compositions, so it's natural to look at what's the same and what's different between the original song from *Honky Château* and this one, and what those continuities and changes say about how Elton had changed within the course of that decade and a half.

Elton gives us a clue on that straight away. 'Part one' was in the key of C major, a fitting key for a piece that is about finding gratitude in the people around you even as your life isn't quite going the way you planned. It's a dark song set in a positive key, communicating the central issue: the light to be found amongst a sea of darkness. 'Mona Lisas and Mad Hatters (Part Two)' starts in G minor, which we remember as the intro chord to some of Elton's darkest-themed songs ('Nobody Wins' and 'Legal Boys'), and is a direct hint about what this story is going to be about, with the story swapped from being one about appreciating the light in the midst of dark to being open to the light and culture all around, while also being aware of the dark still at its core. To entirely pound that conflict home, the whole intro section is a war between G minor and C.

In a further example of brilliant musical storytelling somewhat at odds with Bernie's lyrics, Elton uses the music to demonstrate how the passage of time has eroded the possibilities of life itself. While 'part one' roams freely, exploring different chords with all kinds of underpinning notes, 'Mona Lisas and Mad Hatters (Part Two)' is a blocky battle that sees the verses continually dragged back to that dark G minor area, and the harsher instrumentation and faster beat only highlight that sense of a brutal force railroading forward what used to be a delicate exploratory sense of possibility even amongst tragedy.

This bleak conclusion is slammed home in the outro where, as the music fades away, Elton does this really neat thing with his voice, producing a menacing vibrato-laden climb from the lower register up to that 'kid in me' shout. The juxtaposition between the severe musical elements at play, and Bernie's lyrics, which are more laudatory than critical, keeps the song interesting on repeated listening, as each time through we adjust our mental conception of what this portrait of New York is ultimately presenting.

Chapter 25

Sleeping With the Past

Recorded: November 1988 to March 1989
Released: 4 September 1989
Producer: Chris Thomas

The Story

With *Reg Strikes Back* a success, his misstep of a marriage to Renate Blauel (*b*.1953) cleared up, his voice stronger than ever, his libel suit with *The Sun* settled, and a label that seemed to support what he was doing (though this illusion was to be shattered soon enough), Elton had enough solid ground under him to try a new direction with his next album, *Sleeping With the Past*. Instead of giving Bernie *carte blanche* to write whatever he wanted, Elton set his old partner a challenge – to write a series of lyrics, each inspired by a particular song from the golden days of Chess, Motown and Stax. Bernie wrote the lyrics, indicating at the bottom which song he'd used as inspiration and Elton used that as his starting point for composing the songs.

As was their long-worn habit, Bernie wrote at night, with Elton looking at the songs in the morning, now operating out of the Puk Recording Studios, which, like the château before it, gave Elton space away from his usual anxieties to concentrate on his craft. Instead of working the new composition through with the band, Elton largely delegated that task to Johnstone, who stepped into the role of musical director, taking Elton's raw song and leading the band through it, creating the background textures, allowing Elton to walk into the studio, hear what they had come up with, and start laying down his own parts, a remarkable act of faith in the musical instincts of the loyal guitarist who had been with him through so many evolutions of sound and working methods.

The resulting album was Elton's best seller of the decade, surging to #1 in the UK charts, and remaining in the US charts for fifty-three weeks (though only reaching #23 there). Though some critics like the *Los Angeles Times*' Mike Boehm (1955–2019) carped that the album didn't sound rhythm and blues enough to achieve its stated purpose, the song crafting connected with audiences, with both 'Healing Hands' and 'Sacrifice' hitting #1 in the UK. Both *Reg Strikes Back* and *Sleeping With the Past* proved to Elton that he still had the power within him to craft great music, but there was still one major obstacle to overcome before he realised his full potential, one that would take the better part of three years to triumph against, leading to one of the greatest albums of his career, *The One*.

The Songs

Sleeping With the Past leads off with 'Durban Deep', Bernie's take on Lee Dorsey's (1924–1986) 'Working in the Coal Mine' (1966), which takes us to South Africa, the site of the massive Durban Roodepoort Deep Gold Mine. Like in many African mining concerns, the labourers at Durban were primarily males who moved miles from their family to have a steady wage and would only see their loved ones a few times a year as a result, a condition that Bernie places at the centre of his lyrics, alongside the psychological trauma created by long shifts working away from view of the sun. The song is about monotonous work and so Elton uses perhaps too literal heavy rhythmic elements and descending lines to convey the themes at hand, which end up getting scattered themselves among the looping repetitions of the title that make up the song's last minute.

With 'Healing Hands' Elton achieved a perfect elevation of the source inspiration material, taking the gospel starting point suggested by Bernie and lifting it up to a powerful non-divinity-based statement about our ability to heal each other through our capacity for empathy. The chorus is among Elton's most powerful, with unique vocal phrasing you don't find elsewhere in his oeuvre, while Bernie is going in new directions from the breakup material he'd been writing during the 1980s, most of which focused on the inevitability of dissolution. In 'Healing Hands' we begin with the usual post-breakup mess of an individual that we have grown accustomed to in 'Elderberry Wine' and 'Legal Boys', and a half dozen other besides but instead of wallowing in recriminations, what we have here is a command to find the light again in the love of another human being. The world is too lonely a place to go through alone, and rather than seek the stoic but cold comforts of isolation, why not reach out and find healing in another person?

From gospel we move with 'Whispers' back to the world of soul, with Elton and Bernie's version of Jackie Wilson's (1934–1984) 'Whispers (Gettin' Louder)' (1966), a piece about a man who is haunted by the memory of a woman, the whisper of her departed voice growing louder the longer that they are apart. Bernie sticks to that basic idea but complexifies it with a focus on whispers as the carriers of lies that intoxicate and linger long after their basis in deception is uncovered. In this song, promises are made and a heated rendezvous accomplished but at the end the person is gone, while their whispered words are left to echo in the suddenly empty space. Elton and the band excel at painting the barrenness of that space, filled by delicate digital piano figures here and there but never anything solid enough to wash away the phantom presence of the departed lover.

'Club at the End of the Street' is a piece of nostalgic joy, with one eye on capturing the spirit of the Drifters, and another on conveying what it was like to be young and intoxicated by the sounds of new Marvin Gaye (1939–1984) and Otis Redding (1941–1967) records hitting the stores, in a city exploding with a love of music. It's an ode to all those people who form communities around their shared passion for music, and to the particular heady mixture of excitement and anticipation that comes with gathering in a local club to hear live musicians do their stuff. By 1989, Elton fans hadn't had the chance to hear Elton in full on joy mode for at least thirteen years, and for those the mere existence of this track served as a welcome sign that maybe things were finally going to get better for Elton after so many years in the harsh winter of his own addictions and problems. Though the single underperformed on the charts (#28 in the US and #47 in the UK), it's cheery organ riff, boisterous sax solo and energetic vocals make this an inexhaustible source of happiness for people who love music, love Elton and love the music that made Elton the artist he is.

With 'Sleeping With the Past' Bernie seems to be making up for the stereotypically misogynist flavour of 'Slow Down Georgie (She's Poison)' by presenting the reverse side of the coin, that of offering a woman sound advice about not returning to a toxic relationship. This guy is no good, he's not going to change, and you're addicted to the feeling of being in love rather than to the actual character of the person you were in love with. It's as if the protagonist from 'Poor Cow' managed to extricate herself from her situation, and is now, by cherry-picking her memories of her marriage, convincing herself that she ought to go back while all her friends are attempting to talk some sense into her, reminding her of why she left and what a reduced person she'd become. It's something of a qualifying addendum to 'Healing Hands' – yes, throw yourself for healing into the hands of love and other people, but be smart about it. That might sound dour but Elton sets the song in a friendly, 'dust yourself off and move on, girlfriend!' idiom, with a jaunty bassline, warm organ interjections, powerful guitar licks and direct from Motown backing vocals, which all add up to a sense of confidence that life is entirely liveable and even has the potential for magic if you summon the belief in yourself to turn your back on something that is hurtful and broken.

'Stones Throw From Hurtin'' brings us one of Bernie's best flawed relationship lyrics, in which the problems a couple is experiencing aren't of the aggressively destructive variety of 'Spiteful Child' but rather those of a steady diminution of mutual interest. This is death by inertia, a slow suffocation of the flame that nobody can rouse themselves to rekindle because things aren't quite bad enough yet to justify the effort. Things are coasting along well enough, so why risk complete dissolution of the relationship by bringing up real systemic problems? Easier to keep grinding out the years and hope that age brings change. Elton's conception here is masterful, he's singing in this haunting upper register that sounds like a man stepping on eggshells, trying to keep quiet so that no big problems get brought up, while Natalie Jackson's more strident vocals in the background and Johnstone's probing guitar threaten to overturn the delicate if ultimately untenable peace.

I haven't done a scientific study but my sense from forums and discussions with fellow Elton fans is that, if you ask the community what Elton's best song from the late 1980s is, the overwhelming response will likely be 'Sacrifice'. And it's hard to argue with that. 'Sacrifice' is as near a perfect Elton song as you're likely to find. Bernie's lyrics walk the line expertly between approachability and complexity, such that you know the broad outlines of the situation (a relationship tainted by jealousy, with an origin in Bernie's complicated feelings surrounding his infidelity to his second wife) but have enough flashes of only partially revealed meaning that you keep listening to the song to try and get at the fullness of what is happening. Elton's melody and chord choices are immaculate, while the gentleness of his performance showed definitively that he'd lost nothing of his purity of tone after his throat surgery. The interplay between the digital piano and his vocals is poetry itself, with the piano line lingering a little after each verse. There's a slow build in the textures over the course of the song, as synth vocals and understated electric guitar components make their way into the mix. Importantly, there are no actual human backing vocals for the song, which only amplifies the sense of an individual, in pain and alone, isolated from the one person who makes his life meaningful by his own actions and the brute power of circumstance. Elton famously didn't think all that much of the song on finishing it but the single rose to #1 in the UK, #18 in the US Hot 100, and #3 in the US Adult Contemporary chart, while also achieving a #1 on the Eurochart Hot 100.

With 'I Never Knew Her Name' Bernie provides us with a quaint life story about a man who is hanging out in a church when he witnesses a wedding and falls in love with the bride on sight without ever having learned her name. She exits his life as abruptly as she entered it, never giving him the chance to say all the things that welled up in his heart upon his first glance at her. It's a sweet story about a love born in an instant and never realised, and is a considerable improvement upon 'Kiss the Bride', with which it shares some narrative elements. Elton's music is likewise a more complex take on the situation, with traditional choir elements interjecting to give us the context of the scene, and Elton's strutting chorus giving a raw sense of the powerful impact the bride's presence is having on this one obscure onlooker. It's a pocket-sized tale of the sort that used to decorate Elton albums all the time and the return of its type betokened promising things for the albums to come.

'Amazes Me' is pure Ray Charles. Bernie's lyrics are a mixture of one of his favourite old themes, the particular sense of wonder he experiences when surrounded by the climate and people of the American South, and one of his more recent ones, a tendency towards ethnic fetishism, now directed towards Caribbean magic woman stereotypes.

One's immediate thought upon hearing the first line of 'Blue Avenue' is that this will be the song where Elton and Bernie confront the demon that has been stalking them for years: their issues with addiction. It's a topic they'd not directly addressed since 'White Powder, White Lady' at the decade's opening, and so an update on where they are in their progress would have made sense as the last track on the last Elton album of the 1980s. It would be another year, however, when Ryan White's (1971–1990) death brought Elton face to face with the utter insanity of how he was treating his own body and the people around him, before he was ready to face up to that topic. So, no, despite the first verse being replete with talk of drugs and obsession, it's not really about those except as metaphors for the things that keep people in relationships long after they have run their natural course. 'Blue Avenue' within the context of this song is the road you travel when disillusionment sets in and the person you idealised becomes a burden that you bear but can't summon the will to detach from, resulting in a no win situation. The digital and synthetic layers of this song do well in crafting an atmosphere of general hopelessness, with sounds rising mournfully out of the primal dark only to submerge themselves again from whence they came, like coyotes howling in the far distance. Meanwhile, iconic moments like Elton's sustaining of the last syllable of 'Avenue' give voice to the struggling humanity doing the best it can to traverse that road, even in the knowledge that nothing joyous will come from taking the next step.

The Stats

Album/Single	US	UK	Australia	Canada
Sleeping With the Past	23	1	2	23
	P	3P	4P	2P
'Healing Hands'/'Dancing in the End Zone'	13	45	14	6
'Healing Hands' 'Sacrifice'/'Dancing in the End Zone' (UK)		1		
'Sacrifice' / 'Love is a Cannibal'	18	55	7	15
'Club at the End of the Street'/'Give Peace a Chance'	28	47	19	12
'Blue Avenue'/'Stones Throw From Hurtin''				

The Players

Elton John: Roland RD-1000 digital piano, lead and harmony vocals, backing vocals (1)
Guy Babylon: keyboards
Fred Mandel: keyboards (1, 2, 3, 5, 7, 9 and 10), organ (4), guitars (1, 4 and 8) and guitar solo (6)
Peter Iversen: Fairlight and Audiofile programming
Davey Johnstone: guitars, backing vocals (1, 2, 4, 5, 6, 8, 9 and 10)
Romeo Williams: bass
Jonathan Moffett: drums

Vince Denham: saxophone (4)
Natalie Jackson: backing vocals (2, 5, 6, 8 and 9)
Mortonette Jenkins: backing vocals (2, 5, 6, 8 and 9)
Marlena Jeter: backing vocals (2, 5, 6, 8 and 9)

The Tracks

1. 'Durban Deep' (John, Taupin) (5.32)
2. 'Healing Hands' (John, Taupin) (4.23)
3. 'Whispers' (John, Taupin) (5.29)
4. 'Club at the End of the Street' (John, Taupin) (4.49)
5. 'Sleeping With the Past' (John, Taupin) (4.58)
6. 'Stones Throw From Hurtin'' (John, Taupin) (4.55)
7. 'Sacrifice' (John, Taupin) (5.07)
8. 'I Never Knew Her Name' (John, Taupin) (3.31)
9. 'Amazes Me' (John, Taupin) (4.39)
10. 'Blue Avenue' (John, Taupin) (4.21)

Musician's Corner: 'Healing Hands'

'Healing Hands' is my favourite Elton song, for a multitude of reasons. I loved the video when I was growing up. I love that Elton voice where he's experimenting with sharper ways of approaching and hitting notes, as in the 'night time' and 'there's a light' of this song, or the metallic shape of the 'is' on the outro 'love is…' repetition in 'Love is a Cannibal' or, as noted before, the eerie upwards climb on 'you took away, you took away' from the end of 'Mona Lisas and Mad Hatters (Part Two)'. Once *The One* comes along, he's pretty much completed the transition into the broader phrases pushed through the deep register where his voice tends to live now, and experiments like these become markedly fewer.

I love the arpeggiated chords at the top of the mix in the instrumental section, and the powerful but simple scale build-up leading into the final chorus. Thematically, I love it as the turning of a corner, which Elton announces through chords. G minor has traditionally stood firmly in Elton songs as a dire harbinger of tragedy, and indeed it shows up here, but now it's tackled to the ground every time it shows its face, and in general all those electric moments ruled by minor chords throughout the song are all handily vanquished by large-scale affirmations that light will conquer, and that your life can change. It's a return to the faith in the healing power of other people that lay at the heart of the original 'Mona Lisas and Mad Hatters' and even as far back as 'Friends', all set within the joyful exclamations of the gospel tradition that Elton had experienced since his earliest record buying days.

Chapter 26

The One

Recorded: November 1991 to March 1992
Released: 22 June 1992
Producer: Chris Thomas

The Story

On 8 April 1990, Ryan White died at the age of 18 after a six-year battle with AIDS. Elton had befriended the young man shortly after his diagnosis was made public, and he'd grown to be almost a member of the family himself, particularly in the difficult months before his death. That process, of watching a young man fight for every extra moment of life he could on this planet, was a humbling one for Elton, who was shamed by his own disregard for the value of his own life. That year Elton resolved to conquer his addictions, placing his recording career on hold to sort himself out.

As a result, apart from a song here and there, we didn't hear much from Elton for three years, until the release of *The One* in 1992, which brought with it the question of what we might expect from a clean and sober Elton. The result exceeded all our expectations, as the creative renaissance begun with *Reg Strikes Back* and *Sleeping With the Past* burst suddenly into its full fruition, with both Elton and Bernie putting their best feet forward, crafting songs varied in style and theme but unified by an overarching and renewed interest in life in all its forms, from tales of rebirth to stories of lives lived at the rough edge of society to accounts of individuals bravely facing the end of their allotted time. In his health, Elton seemed less concerned with chasing trends or the commercial viability of his output and concentrated instead on making quality music that brought Bernie's revitalised lyrical output to the fore.

Not aiming for commerciality was precisely what Elton needed to forge his greatest commercial success yet, with *The One* hitting #8 in the US and #2 in the UK, and three of its singles penetrating the US Top 40. After a decade and a half of investigating types of music that were structured differently to the 'pocket symphonies' of his earlier work, Elton had ultimately found his way back to the scale, drama and complexity of those compositions but cast within a simpler and deeper soundscape that only heightened their power to communicate loss, recovery and gratitude. With *The One*, the stage was set for a decade of broadly imagined compositions that stormed records, stage and screen with a rate and persistence of quality that demonstrated not only was Elton back but he was perhaps better than he'd ever been.

The Songs

The One begins with an anthem of rebirth that couldn't have been more perfectly constructed to announce to the world the arrival of a revitalised Elton. It employs instruments emerging from a sea of sound to herald a triumphant arrival of life where before was darkness. The synth harmonica appears above the web of sound like a clarion of life renewed, a role that it will fill throughout the piece. Bernie's lyrics are a joyful expression of health, strength and innocence regained, and bring to a close a circle two decades in the making. After twenty years of songs about the personal corruption wrought by city living and fame, and expressing doubt about the possibility of any thorough-going restoration to a rooted life of meaning, 'Simple Life' brings the joyous news that a return to roots is, in fact, possible, and Elton is positively radiant singing about sailing away to innocence, and getting back to the simple life again, a theme reiterated in 100 interviews since in which he has expressed his appreciation for all the little things in life that he has been able to take in and enjoy with a clear head.

Switching from the theme of life to that of love, we see Bernie again entering unfamiliarly uplifting territory with the titular track 'The One'. After a decade of unremittingly introspective and pessimistic songs about infidelity, suspicion, spite and not entirely legal lusting, Bernie gives us here a simple story of restoration through love. Elton pulls out all the musical stops to realise the scale implicit in Bernie's words, with Johnstone's guitar rising above the scene in a role inherited from the synth harmonica of 'Simple Life', while the concluding material is a sweeping web of piano arpeggios leading into the song's characteristic descending triplet figures suggestive of advancing and receding waves, and the life's love that emerged from them to bring in its wake a new shot at happiness.

With life and love locked down and solved, Elton and Bernie have some room to address other issues, and 'Sweat It Out' serves as a clearing house for all the things that were bothering Bernie about the world as it stood in 1992, from small things like an apparent distaste for the band Tears for Fears, to middling issues like the bigger picture inefficacy of celebrity efforts like Band Aid, to larger issues of global conflict, Thatcherism and environmental destruction. Like 'Simple Life', the piece is dominated by the rhythmic structure constructed by Olle Romö, here producing a pressing almost industrial beat that serves as the backdrop to Bernie's Dylan-esque observations. Those have aged generally better than the topics covered in 'Goodbye Marlon Brando' but for most listening to the song today, the highlight of the piece likely comes with Elton's closing piano solo.

'Runaway Train' didn't need to be about anything. The chance to hear the world's greatest rock guitarist, Eric Clapton (*b.*1945), trading fire with the world's greatest rock pianist is exciting all by itself, and indeed listening to the back and forth between Clapton's howling guitar and Elton's swerving rock organ is enough to earn this track its bit of immortality. Bernie, however, made the daring decision to construct lyrics that meant something potentially distressing to the two mega-stars involved: the subject of personal destruction and slow recovery. Clapton's struggle with heroin had paralleled Elton's addiction to cocaine, and by 1991 both had taken their first hard steps into sobriety. Bernie's words dig hard into the god complex of rock stars, their tendency for self-destruction, and the long, hard work of undoing the damage that their lifestyles had caused. With gospel backing vocals from Beckie Bell, Carol Fredericks (1952–2001) and Joniece Jamison (*b*.1956) reinforcing the theme of personal redemption after years of life misspent, 'Runaway Train' is a powerful anthem in which two voices of experience combine and lift the power of their instruments to exorcise the lingering spectres of their pasts.

'Whitewash County' sees Bernie returning to a theme he'd revisited many times over the past two decades: his evolving relationship with the American South. While tracks from *Tumbleweed Connection* had tended towards the romantic and idealised, by the mid-1970s he'd experienced the prejudice and hatred that lay at the heart of the modern, only recently de-segregated South, and poured that disillusionment into lyrics like 'Texan Love Song' and 'One Horse Town' only to veer back to a renewed, Ray Charles mediated, appreciation in 'Amazes Me'. That tension will never truly resolve in the albums to come but 'Whitewash County' is among the best expressions of Bernie's ambivalent feelings, the romance of the 'high hot buttered moon' of the South contrasting with the racism and the intellectual intransigence of the people beneath it, as particularly concentrated in the figure of Ku Klux Klan leader David Duke (*b*.1950), who was also a state legislator in Louisiana from 1988 to 1992 and presidential candidate. As he often does, Elton leans into a joyous setting of these complicated lyrics, the energetic square dance ethos of the piece, with its synth fiddle motif, making the lines about the rise of the South and the white boys howling in the evening feeling doubly ominous for being delivered so boisterously.

While Elton and Bernie have crafted dozens of songs about New York City and the American South, they had, prior to 1992, spoken little of their home country of Great Britain. 'The North' is a first entry in examining their shared place of origin which will expand into a fuller treatment on the duo's next studio album, *Made in England*. On its most narrow level, the song can be taken as a reflection by Bernie about his Lincolnshire youth, which was crucial in shaping him until he moved southwards to London, and his destiny with Elton began. More broadly, it's about Elton and Bernie's shared youth growing up in England, a cold place peopled by some rigid individuals, made bearable through the music coming from the warm southern climes of the US. More broadly still, it's about 'the North in us all', the hard place within us formed by our youthful experiences that form the base of who we are but that we must ultimately grow beyond. Musically, there are people who don't like the omnipresence of the snare drum, which I understand but it's appropriate for the creation of the oppressive atmosphere described in the song. Listen beyond the snare and you'll hear some lovely figuring, particularly the keyboard work in 'The North was my mother' sections of the song that complicate the soundscape at precisely the moment when the lyrics become more nuanced, recognising the debt one has to one's past even as one seeks to live a life beyond those confines.

I know there are people who like to give 'When a Woman Doesn't Want You' lots of credit for being a song that expresses the idea that, hey guys, don't force yourselves on women who continue to show no interest in you, but it does it in such an infantilising way, as if our job as men is to be the bigger party and humour women's childish whims gallantly instead of, you know, treating them like normal people who sometimes aren't interested in you, not because of youthful traumas and wilfulness but because of other valid and adult reasons. The musical setting is also on the blocky and genre side, and generally speaking 'When a Woman Doesn't Want You' represents one of *The One*'s rare missteps in theme and conception.

Fortunately, on the other side of 'When A Woman Doesn't Want You' we have one of Bernie's best ever lyrics about a woman. 'Emily' is a thorough delight, with great lyrics married to an immaculately conceived melody and structure. Emily is an elderly woman whose husband died in the war whose voice she attempts to conjure in her memory, as her little canary, who has kept her company through the long, lonely years, stands by, the sole witness to her death. This woman has lived such a full life that even though shadows come and go, and with them fears of the unknown valley ahead, the strength of her memories will always recentre her. Elton's structure here, with strolling verses that follow Emily through her day, opening into the full and wide chorus urging her away from fear and towards her own strength, does something all too rare in the realm of rock music, giving voice to the persistent heroism of old age, and the almost mythical status of those who walk that road, too often unremarked by those around them.

'On Dark Street' is essentially a continuation of the themes of 'Blue Avenue' and of a string of Bernie lyrics before it about marriages that are falling apart. Now, instead of bluely waiting at the morose crossroads of an avenue, our narrator is fully in the dark, fighting the last struggle against the total breakup of his family, as his partner is about to walk away, and he is racking his mind for what he can do to make them stay. He has suffered some hard times, getting laid off work, and watching his salary steadily dwindle, all his illusions about being able to provide a steady life for his family slipping through his fingers (dreams of an island turning to a bucket of sand) while his partner walks ahead of him, refusing to look back as she tries to find her own exit from the situation. They're effective lyrics, in which the protagonist isn't simply a cad in the vein of 'Elderberry Wine' or 'Hard Luck Story' but a person who has experienced a series of reversals of fortune and can't seem to hold on to anything that gives his life meaning, until he is either literally living on the streets or is more metaphorically 'sleeping on the concrete' of his family's declining regard for him. I tend toward the latter interpretation, both because Elton's chorus setting is a bit too sprightly to be about actual homelessness, and because Bernie clarifies the line later with the phrase 'You can't see it with your eyes/you can't find it with your feet', which makes it clear this isn't an actual street they're living on, any more than Blue Avenue was an actual avenue or the Yellow Brick Road an actual road.

Instrumentally and vocally, the next track, 'Understanding Women', is pure fire. Between the grinding guitar work of Pink Floyd's David Gilmour (*b*.1946), and the crunching synth work straight out of *Ice on Fire*, all at work beneath Elton's haunting vocal work, everything here is an ear feast where the word of the day is momentum. Lyrically, things start out promising, as the title holds a dual potential – will it be about women who are understanding, or the act of trying to understand women? To its credit, the lyrics never make it entirely clear which is the case but the evidence tends to lean towards the latter, and if so, it seems the sort of sentiment that we'd expect more from someone much younger than the 42 that Bernie was at the time.

There's no hint of the juvenile about 'The Last Song', one of Elton and Bernie's finest efforts of any decade. The song about a father coming to the bedside of his son who is dying of AIDS expressed the pent-up yearning of an entire generation of young men who hoped for reconciliation with their families while watching their lives ebb persistently away, many of whom breathed their last breath without a father or mother next to them. I have heard this song easily 100 times in my life, and it's never ceased to be emotional. The proud father who chooses his love for his son over the call of his prejudice, the young man, baffled by what is happening to him, and overwhelmed by the realisation that the man who seemed to reject him and his lifestyle does love him, and always will. It's a beautiful dynamic around which Elton builds one of his finest melodies, with the chords moving between a relative major and minor, settling at last on the major, the small miracle of these two people finding each other again overcoming the tragedy all around them. This story won't end well, but for the moment, there's reconciliation, and in that moment, it means everything.

The Stats

Album/Single	US	UK	Australia	Canada
The One	8	2	2	7
	2P	G	2P	3P
'The One'/'Suit of Wolves' 'Fat Boys and Ugly Girls'	9	10	15	1
'Runaway Train'/'Understanding Women (Extended Mix)'		31	53	
'The Last Song'/'The Man Who Never Died (remix)'	23	21	32	7
'Simple Life'/'The Last Song' (UK) 'The North' (US)	30	44		3

The Players

Elton John: vocals, acoustic piano (1 to 3, 5 to 8 and 11), organ (4 and 5) and electric piano (9 and 10)

Mark Taylor: keyboards (1 to 3, 6 and 7)

Guy Babylon: keyboards (2 to 5 and 7 to 11), programming (2 to 5, 7 and 11)

Adam Seymour: guitar (1, 2, 6 and 7)

Davey Johnstone: guitar (2 to 5 and 7 to 9) and backing vocals (7 and 9)

Eric Clapton: guitar (4) and vocals (4)

David Gilmour: guitar (10)

Pino Palladino: bass (1 to 8 and 10)

Olle Romö: drums (1 to 10), percussion (1 to 10) and drum programming (1 to 10)

Beckie Bell: backing vocals (4)

Carole Fredericks: backing vocals (4)

Jonice Jamison: backing vocals (4)

Kiki Dee: backing vocals (7, 9 and 10)

Nigel Olsson: backing vocals (7 and 9)

The Tracks

1. 'Simple Life' (John, Taupin) (6.25)
2. 'The One' (John, Taupin) (5.53)
3. 'Sweat It Out' (John, Taupin) (6.38)
4. 'Runaway Train' (duet with Eric Clapton) (John, Taupin) (5.23)
5. 'Whitewash County' (John, Taupin) (5.30)
6. 'The North' (John, Taupin) (5.15)
7. 'When a Woman Doesn't Want You' (John, Taupin) (4.56)
8. 'Emily' (John, Taupin) (4.58)
9. 'On Dark Street' (John, Taupin) (4.43)
10. 'Understanding Women' (John, Taupin) (5.03)
11. 'The Last Song' (John, Taupin) (3.21)

Musician's Corner: 'The One'

In 1995, the compilation *Elton John: Love Songs* was released, and what it threw into stark relief was the relative scarcity of the genre in Elton's catalogue. In the US, to get the album up to fifteen songs, the producers had to throw tracks like 'Circle of Life' and 'Daniel' into the mix, which are wonderful songs, but not classic love songs. Bernie's lyrics, when it comes to relationships, tend to be more analytic, pensive, and often plain grim, and so it's a rare thing to get a relatively straightforward love song out of Elton and Bernie, and to my mind 'The One' is their best since 'Your Song'.

Part of what makes the song so effective is Elton's management of space, keeping things abnormally tight in order that the later expansion can be that much more powerful. The starting lines keep things about as constrained as you possibly can, with that classic and distinct D chord with a C note in the bass that resolves down to a C major. There are few better ways to instantly conjure a musical sense of yearning than this transition, and it's therefore a perfect companion to lyrics about watching a free spirit from a distance while you yourself are anything but. All the motions beneath the main melody are similarly constrained, with our first notes there being C, C, C, B and B flat, all within a major second of each other. We have an inspired movement to a new centre at 'and water' but this is a deceptive break-out, extending the tension, as we now stay around our new base of E flat for a while, only venturing out to F until the real expansions come appropriately at, 'In the instant that you love someone'.

Love has arrived at this point, in a constructive and healing form and now we're moving not by half and whole steps, but by big fourths and fifths as the universe opens before us with possibilities to be explored with 'The One'. And because we're with Elton, these new spaces contain exciting bits of exotic new worlds, the chorus particularly going out of its way to feature F sharp, which is nowhere in the key signature of B flat major that this section of the music is grounded in, and which features as the bass note for a transition to D major, and as part of an F sharp major chord (the dramatic 'When stars collide' moment) that slides beautifully back into B flat major again. This introduces tension but instead of the anxious tension that we had with all the diminished chords in 'Ego', what we have here is a soaring tension, a raised fifth that is waiting for its chance to come down to ground.

Chapter 27

Duets

Recorded: March 1991 and July to October 1993
Released: 23 November 1993
Producers: Elton John, Barry Beckett, Louis Biancaniello, P.M. Dawn, Stuart Epps, Don Henley, Steve Lindsey, Greg Penny, Nik Kershaw, George Michael, Giorgio Moroder, Chris Rea, Chris Thomas, Narada Walden, Don Was and Stevie Wonder

The Story

November 1993 was the month of the megastar duet album, beginning with Frank Sinatra's (1915–1998) *Duets*, his first album in nearly a decade and a triple platinum smash hit, and ending with Elton's *Duets*, which, while not quite as successful, did manage to go platinum in the US and UK and spawn one #1 single in the form of 'Don't Let the Sun Go Down on Me'. The project arose from an idea for a compilation album of past collaborations which, in turn, morphed into an idea for an album of duets with artists Elton had always wanted to work with, along with some inspiring emerging voices, much the same idea as that behind his later album, *The Lockdown Sessions* (2022).

Produced at a breakneck pace, the album lacks the complexities that people had come to expect from an Elton album but as a glimpse into the magpie mind of Elton's musical interests it possessed charms entirely of its own, with not much theming connecting one track to the next other than the entirely sufficient reason that Elton thought it would be fun to play that song with that person at that time. Over time, the album has got somewhat lost in people's estimation, as tends to be the fate of duet albums generally. Fortunately, Elton was such a dynamo of creativity that those fans let down by *Duets* didn't have long to wait and would be treated not only to a full-length album featuring a dazzling array of challenging tracks but a film soundtrack that would bring to a decisive end Elton's troubled relationship with writing songs for the film industry.

The Songs

Nobody goes into a duets album expecting a profound and revelatory artistic experience – the idea is to titillate the ears with the sound of voices usually not heard together doing their level best at having a go at an old classic, and if a bit of magic, of something new, manages to somehow happen despite all the careful and tightly scheduled and arranged production, all the better, but nobody is really expecting it. To make it easier for those who just want to know which songs to download and which to back slowly away from, we're going to divide this album into four slices.

Slice One: The Must Haves

'Don't Let the Sun Go Down on Me', with George Michael

A younger artist paying tribute to one of the great songs by his friend and mentor, with that friend joining him midway through, to the rapturous applause of the audience? This is what a great duet is all about: a dialogue between generations, with two legends giving everything, egged on by a rapturous crowd. This song was recorded in March 1991, some two years before the *Duets* album headed into its marathon recording session, and at the end of a tour in which Michael had regularly included the song during his concerts, so the performance has a level of intensity and polish that we don't often get on the other tracks on the album.

Duets for One, Elton John

This is Elton singing on his own about no longer having to sing 'duets for one' now that he is back on track and his 'life has just begun'. As a song of rebirth and recovery, it's not as good as 'Simple Life' or 'Runaway Train' but it has more meaning to it than most of the other tracks on this album; it shows us Elton, a year later, still content in his new path, which is nice to hear.

'Old Friend', with Nik Kershaw (*b*.1958)

One of the few tracks on the album that isn't a love song, and features touching and insightful lyrics about the durability of long-term friendships. Elton and Kershaw's voices play off each other well, and if nothing else the track reminds us of what a good song-writer Kershaw is, and if that makes a couple of people go out and find a copy of *Human Racing*, well, all the better.

'Love Letters', with Bonnie Raitt (*b*.1949)

There's something so soul cleansing about Raitt's voice and delivery, that simultaneously brings up hurt you'd long forgotten and removes part of its sting, and to hear Elton slotting into that groove next to her with his own powerful reading of the song is magical. This material has been elevated into something entirely higher by the presence of these two artists, and that is exactly what one wants out of a duet.

Slice Two: The Perfectly Fine and Adequate Songs

'Born to Lose', with Leonard Cohen

This is such a weird song that I was tempted to bump it up to the above category. Cohen's speaker-rattling bass sounds like it belongs to a cartoon bulldog at the local pound bemoaning his fate, while Elton sounds like he is performing from a Hollywood musical set *c.*1954, and that total incongruity is one of the best things about the song.

'The Power', with Little Richard

This is probably not the song you were hoping for when you saw that Elton and Little Richard, two titans of rock piano, were on the same track together but once you get over that, it's a powerful song about marching forward, centred on your own inner strength.

'True Love', with Kiki Dee

'True Love' is a great song in itself, and Elton and Dee take it straight with a little break out at the end. If you've never heard this Cole Porter (1891–1964) classic, or just want to hear Elton and Dee's voices back together again, it's an enjoyable if not revolutionary track.

'Don't Go Breaking My Heart', with RuPaul (*b.*1960)

One of the things you don't feel on *Duets* is the fun the people had making the songs. That's not the case on 'Don't Go Breaking My Heart', Elton's update with drag superstar RuPaul of his classic Kiki Dee duet. Set to a distinctly early 1990s club beat, the song goes all over the place, and if it isn't high art, it's a good time, and the music video is so distinctly ridiculous that you can't not love it.

Slice Three: The Safe to Pass

'Teardrops', with k.d. lang (*b.*1961)

As a pastiche of 1970s musical elements, 'Teardrops' is an enjoyable song but k.d. lang isn't really used to full effect here and is instead employed as something of a modern equivalent of Kiki Dee, a role she performs fine but it's a disappointment when you think what could have been accomplished had she been given a more poignant song to perform with Elton.

'Shakey Ground', with Don Henley (*b.*1947)

It's got a good rock groove but repeats its couple of central musical ideas to death.

'If You Were Me', with Chris Rea (*b.*1951)

If you were walking into this song expecting the Chris Rea of 'The Road to Hell' (1989) you would be disappointed. Both Elton and Rea are playing and singing like they have been hit with a tranquiliser dart, and the cheesy synth strings don't compensate for the lack of drive and gravitas.

'I'm Your Puppet', with Paul Young (*b*.1956)

'I'm Your Puppet' isn't an ideal vehicle for Elton or Young's style. It's not terrible, it's just not something you need to go out of your way to listen to.

Slice Four: The Unfortunates

'When I Think About Love (I Think About You)', with P.M. Dawn

P.M. Dawn were on the last legs of the fame they had gained from 'Set Adrift on Memory Bliss' (1991) and 'Looking Through Patient Eyes' (1992) when they recorded this duet with Elton. If you like the strained grunting style of singing that was popular in the early 1990s, this might be your thing. Otherwise, best to move on.

'Go On and On', with Gladys Knight (*b*.1944)

This song is aptly named.

'A Woman's Needs', with Tammy Wynette (1942–1998)

The weird thing is that Elton and Bernie wrote this song especially for Wynette and her distinctive voice, but Bernie, in trying to write a song in the country idiom for a woman singer, descends into a mass of clichés and dumbed-down verses that result in a parody of the form instead of a heightening of it, representing a frustrating missed opportunity.

'Ain't Nothing Like the Real Thing', with Marcella Detroit (*b*.1952)

No one really knows how, with so much talent behind it (including Stevie Wonder as a producer), this song ended up so flat and lifeless but boy it did.

The Stats

Album/Single	US	UK	Australia	Canada
Duets	25	5	12	14
	P	P	G	P
'Don't Let the Sun Go Down on Me'/'I Believe (When I Fall in Love It Will Be Forever)'	1	1	3	1
'True Love'/'The Show Must Go On' (UK) 'Runaway Train' (US)	56	2	34	12
'Don't Go Breaking My Heart'/'Donner Pour Donner' 'A Woman's Needs'	92	7	45	
'Ain't Nothing Like the Real Thing'/'Break the Chain'		24		

The Tracks

1. 'Teardrops' (with k.d. lang) (Zekkariyas) (4.52)
2. 'When I Think About Love (I Think About You)' (with P.M. Dawn) (Cordes) (4.34)
3. 'The Power' (with Little Richard) (John, Taupin) (6.24)
4. 'Shakey Ground' (with Don Henley) (Bowen, Hazel, Boyd) (3.50)
5. 'True Love' (with Kiki Dee) (Porter) (3.52)
6. 'If You Were Me' (with Chris Rea) (Rea) (4.23)
7. 'A Woman's Needs' (with Tammy Wynette) (John, Taupin) (5.16)
8. 'Old Friend' (with Nik Kershaw) (Kershaw) (4.15)
9. 'Go On and On' (with Gladys Knight) (Wonder) (5.49)
10. 'Don't Go Breaking My Heart' (with RuPaul) (Orson, Blanche) (4.58)
11. 'Ain't Nothing Like the Real Thing' (with Marcella Detroit) (Ashford, Simpson) (3.34)
12. 'I'm Your Puppet' (with Paul Young) (Oldham, Penn) (3.34)
13. 'Love Letters' (with Bonnie Raitt) (Young, Heyman) (4.00)
14. 'Born to Lose' (with Leonard Cohen) (Daffan) (4.31)
15. 'Don't Let the Sun Go Down on Me' (with George Michael) (John, Taupin) (5.46)
16. 'Duets for One' (John, Difford) (4.51)

Musician's Corner: 'The Power'

There are only two times I've felt real disappointment listening to a new Elton album. The first was 'Johnny B. Goode' on *Vision of Love*. As soon as I saw the track listing for that album, I fantasied about how cool it was going to be to hear how Elton translated Chuck Berry's iconic guitar track to the piano. Within five seconds of pressing play, my heart sank.

The second time was with *Duets*. As soon as I saw that there was a duet with Little Richard, one of Elton's great piano assassin heroes, that is all I wanted to hear. I skipped straight to the third track, expecting this to be a frenetic piano battle, with each piano titan leaving it all on the keys. That is, to put it mildly, not what 'The Power' is about. I wasn't aware at the time of Little Richard's early career abandonment of wild rock 'n roll, his commercially unsuccessful turn towards gospel, his years attempting to reconcile his sexuality and love of rock performance with his religiosity, and his shame about slipping further into drug abuse. The Little Richard of 1993, then, had decidedly ambivalent views towards the sort of rock showdown I had been hoping for. He performed his wild classics on tours because that was his only way of generating revenue, and when on stage he gave everything but with a deep sense of conflict.

Elton and Bernie were aware of this, of course, and had the challenge of creating a duet that tapped into themes and musical genres that Little Richard would feel comfortable performing, and their solution was to reach into that affirming gospel tradition that Richard had repeatedly tried to get off the ground from the 1960s onwards, to little remunerative avail. 'The Power' is as direct and regular as 'Good Golly Miss Molly' was chaotic and unhinged. Bernie's lyrics are awash in gospel tropes and Elton restrains himself to an almost unparalleled degree, living almost entirely in the world of the I, IV and V chords, with a few modal interchanges. The simplicity of the musical structure reinforces the simplicity of the lyrics, resulting in a song that is less cerebrally engaging than a typical Elton number, and less fiery than the Little Richard of 1957 but that gains a sense of integrity as a result.

Chapter 28

The Lion King

Original Motion Picture Soundtrack

Recorded: 1992 to 1994
Released: 31 May 1994
Producers: Mark Mancina, Jay Rifkin, Chris Thomas and Hans Zimmer

The Story

By 1994, Elton's experience with film soundtracks wasn't a triumphant one. *Friends* had been something of a fiasco, while the inclusion of Elton songs on the critically panned films *Ghostbusters II* (1989), *Rocky V* (1990) and *Days of Thunder* (1990) did little to enhance Elton in Hollywood circles. Almost ready to give up on the industry altogether, there came one final offer that Elton found he couldn't refuse.

Disney was by 1993 in the middle of its renaissance period, thanks in no small part to the musical team of Alan Menken (*b.*1949) and Howard Ashman (1950–1991), who wrote the iconic music to such breakaway hits as *The Little Mermaid* (1989), *Beauty and the Beast* (1991) and *Aladdin* (1992), which saved Disney animation from the downward spiral it had experienced throughout the early to mid-1980s. With Ashman's tragic death from AIDS in March 1991, a new lyricist was needed to finish the projects he'd struggled valiantly to complete, and the man Disney eventually turned to was Tim Rice, who since working on 'Legal Boys' with Elton in 1981 had provided the theme to *Octopussy* in 1983, the lyrics for *Chess* in 1984 and the musical *Cricket*, which was performed once for Queen Elizabeth II's sixtieth birthday.

Meanwhile, debate was raging inside of Disney about whether the initially ill-starred film *The Lion King* ought to be a musical or not, and if so, who should be approached to do it. As Rice was at hand working on finishing Ashman's work for *Aladdin*, it seemed natural to offer him *The Lion King* job, and he proposed something of a radical idea: to split from tradition and bring in a famous pop composer to do the soundtrack, and not just any pop composer, but Elton. He knew the quality of Disney's recent work and accepted the task, figuring that if he couldn't make a success of a Disney film, that would be a good sign to give up and go back to what he knew best.

As he settled down to write songs about farting warthogs and the endless chain of death and rebirth that runs our planet, the quality and scope of his work calmed nervous Disney executives, and paved the way for the studio's greatest triumph yet, while for Elton the soundtrack achieved an unheard of diamond sales status in the US, and brought his music to an entire new generation, who listened to *The Lion King* CD over and over, as Elton's musical craftsmanship worked itself deep into their bones.

The Songs

Biographically, 'Circle of Life' holds an important place in the story of Elton. The magnificent setting of that song at the beginning of *The Lion King* showed Elton what he could accomplish as a composer, when he had world-class visual storytellers working with him. The road to *Aida*, *Billy Elliot* and *Lestat* began with this song. It shares a great deal structurally with one of Elton's other masterpieces of architecture, 'The One'. The slow build from living creatures first setting foot on the planet to the crowning glory of the complicated web of life as it exists in those corners of the globe not yet entirely devastated by the handiwork of man is masterfully accomplished, applying everything Elton had learned about musical storytelling from his very first 'pocket symphonies' to the instrumental works of the early 1980s to the steadily larger scale songs featured on the albums associated with the Elton renaissance.

'I Just Can't Wait to be King' puts Elton in the position of having to portray childish exuberance in musical form, a thematic region he definitely touched on but little during the dour 1980s, when Bernie and Osborne were feeding him a steady diet of lyrics about failed marriages, substance abuse and global crisis, but Elton was certainly no stranger to songs capturing one's own cocky approach to life, where the over the top nature of the singer's exuberance makes us inclined to forgive and even find charming character traits we might otherwise disapprove of, and 'I Just Can't Wait to be King' borrows from that tradition, a sort of G-rated version of 'The Bitch is Back' or 'I'm Still Standing'.

It's no secret that the best song of every Disney musical tends to be the Villain song – 'Poor Unfortunate Souls' and 'Mother Knows Best' – all show that there's nothing quite so fun as a good villain singing in a minor key, having the time of their life being unrepentantly horrible, and 'Be Prepared' is quite possibly the best of that august tradition. Performed with perfect feline malevolence by Jeremy Irons (*b*.1948) and visualised as a hyena Nuremberg rally of vengeance, the song and its delightfully wicked inversion of the Boy Scouts' motto proved a perfect vehicle for Elton's sense of cheeky irony.

One of the stories that Elton likes to tell about writing *The Lion King* and the difficulty he found himself in, after years of putting Bernie's thoughtful and provocative lyrics to music, is of suddenly having to turn his mind to producing a song about a farting warthog that kids would enjoy. That song, 'Hakuna Matata', has since become one of the all-time classics of the Disney canon. It's a perfect musical comedy, as we might expect from someone whose love of novelty songs was never far from the surface. The road to 'Hakuna Matata' is sprinkled with comedic gems like 'Big Dipper', 'Jack Rabbit' and 'Grimsby', all the products of a *Goon Squad* soaked mind that was never able to rest content in self-serious mode for too long.

Another bar used to measure the various Disney musicals is the quality of their love song, with endless debates around whether 'Kiss the Girl' is more romantic than 'I See the Light' or how 'A Whole New World' stacks up against 'Once Upon A Dream'. 'Can You Feel the Love Tonight?' is difficult to evaluate because in the film version it's less of an outright love song and more a song about three individuals with anxieties: Timon is worried about the breakup of their carefree trio; Nala is worried about Simba's inability to realise his full potential; and Simba is worried about showing too much of himself to Nala for fear of being judged. Instead of a straight forward love song, what we get is a set of ruminations centred on themes of doubt and fear, with love artfully weaving its way through. The eventual single, sung by Elton, would come with new, far less romantically ambiguous, lyrics, and while that's the version most of us remember, it's worth listening to the original, as a small masterpiece of theatrical writing.

The Stats

Album/Single	US	UK	Australia	Canada
The Lion King: Original Motion Picture Soundtrack	1		3	1
	D	P	4P	D
'Can You Feel the Love Tonight'/'Hakuna Matata'/ 'Under the Stars'	4	14	9	1
'Circle of Life'/'I Just Can't Wait to be King'/ 'This Land'	18	11	60	3

The Players

Elton John: composer (1 to 5, 10, 11 and 12), piano and vocals (10, 11 and 12)
Davey Johnstone: guitar (10, 11 and 12) and backing vocals, (10 and 11)
Chuck Sabo: drums (10, 11 and 12), backing vocals (10 and 11) and strings (12)
Phil Spalding: bass (10, 11 and 12) and backing vocals (10 and 11)
Guy Babylon: keyboards (10, 11 and 12)
The London Community Gospel Choir: choir (10, 11 and 12)
Lebo M: vocal arranger (1, 2 and 3), background vocals (1, 2 and 3), co-lead vocals (1) and African chant (1)
Mark Mancina: arrangements (2, 4 and 5)
Hans Zimmer: arrangements (1 and 3) and music supervision (1 to 5)

Nathan Lane, Ernie Sabella: lead vocals (4 and 5)
Jacqueline Barron, Charles Biddle Jr, Mary Carewe and Louis Price: background
   vocals (2 and 3)
Richard Harvey: ethnic pipes (2 and 3)
Joseph Williams: co-lead vocals (4 and 5)
Rodney Saulsberry: background vocals (1 and 4)
Carmen Twillie: lead vocals (1)
Jason Weaver: lead vocals (2) and co-lead vocals (4)
Jeremy Irons: spoken word and lead vocals (3)
Whoopi Goldberg and Cheech Marin: spoken words (3)
Jim Cummings: co-lead vocals (3)
Rowan Atkinson and Laura Williams: co-lead vocals (4)
Kristle Edwards: co-lead vocals (5)
Sally Dworski: co-lead vocals (5)
Rick Astley, Gary Barlow and Kiki Dee: background vocals (12)
Nick Glennie-Smith, Mbongeni Ngema and Andraé Crouch: vocal arrangements (1)
Jay Rifkin: arrangements (4)

The Tracks

1. 'Circle of Life' (John, Rice) (3.59)
2. 'I Just Can't Wait to Be King' (John, Rice) (2.50)
3. 'Be Prepared' (John, Rice) (3.40)
4. 'Hakuna Matata' (John, Rice) (3.33)
5. 'Can You Feel the Love Tonight' (John, Rice) (2.57)
6. 'This Land' (Zimmer) (2.55)
7. '...To Die For' (Zimmer) (4.17)
8. 'Under the Stars' (Zimmer) (3.45)
9. 'King of Pride Rock' (Zimmer) (5.59)
10. 'Circle of Life' (John, Rice) (performance: Elton John) (4.51)
11. 'I Just Can't Wait To Be King' (John, Rice) (performance: Elton John) (3.37)
12. 'Can You Feel the Love Tonight?' (John, Rice) (performance: Elton John) (4.02)

Musician's Corner: 'Circle of Life'

Similar puzzles suggest similar solutions, and with both 'The One' and 'Circle of Life' Elton found himself with lyrics that move from the small scale and intimate to the global and cosmic and had to find ways to mirror that movement within the music itself. 'Circle of Life' accomplishes this with a few of the structures that Elton employed in 'The One'.

Rice's 'From the day we arrive on the planet' has much the same feel as Bernie's 'I saw you dancing out the ocean' in the sense of a primal emergence from a great unknown into the light of life and existence, and Elton casts the lines similarly, but reversed. Whereas 'The One' started with that D major chord and a C underneath, and resolved it to a C, 'Circle of Life' starts with a B flat major chord and then keeps that B flat in the bass while shifting to a C minor chord above it.

The expansions, where we open ourselves to the possibilities of love in the one case, and the global web of life in the other, move similarly to each other. 'In the instant that you love someone' and 'It's the circle of life' both soar up to a B flat chord before resting back onto an E flat major. 'When stars collide like you and I' is so memorable because of the transition from the exotic F sharp major to B flat major, and the big dramatic moment between 'on the path unwinding' and 'It's the circle, the circle of life' comes from an instrumental infusion of F sharp major that resolves to B flat major. Another of the delightfully effective moments in 'The One', the presence of a chord in a major form that should, according to the key signature, be minor (the D chord on 'was the one') has its parallel here in a G chord that should be a G minor chord but isn't, providing that beautiful lift and drama after 'path unwinding'.

Of course, there are differences between the two pieces, in the timing of where the first minor shadings enter, and 'The One' also features some alternating chords over the same bass note on 'No shadows' that are the perfect musical prison to dramatically break out of on that leap to 'the sun', which is a structure you don't see as much in 'Circle of Life', which is more regular with its changes and note values, befitting the vast landscape it's calling forth. Those differences are how Elton fine tunes the architecture to the demands of the theme at hand, giving us the aura of individuals colliding like stars in one moment, and that of endless birth and renewal across space and time in the other.

Chapter 29

Made in England

Recorded: February to April 1994
Released: 20 March 1995
Producers: Elton John and Greg Penny

The Story

'Return to form' is a phrase used so often by Elton writers that it has almost lost its meaning; each of the dozen or so albums it has been applied to represents what the critics consider to be a return to purely 'Elton' musical elements after some years of straying from those core principles. For me, while each of those Return albums does represent a re-establishment of practices after a few years of experimentation, the first big arc of Elton's story comes to an end with *Made in England*. The early 1990s had built up Elton's confidence in his ability to craft meaningful musical compositions across different media forms. Since his first jobs as a studio musician and songwriter for hire in London and his first two released records, Elton centred his attention in the music and lifestyles of those in the US, with hardly a thought for his home country.

That was all to change with *Made in England*, an album recorded in England, in the studio of ex-Beatles producer George Martin, with songs referencing Elton and Bernie's British past, as well as British music history and the nation's troubled present. The album featured the return of Paul Buckmaster, the visionary whose string arrangements on *Elton John* produced the 'pocket symphony' scale and sound that Elton spent years trying to escape as he sought to establish himself as a rocker first, and introspective painter of historical and personal narratives a distant second. By 1995, Elton had gained enough emotional insight to know that it wasn't a case of either/or, that a rocker could compose a heartfelt epic while still remaining a rocker, and that letting a string orchestra back into the recording space wasn't tantamount to burning his license to shred.

The album was another success on par with *The One*, climbing into the Top 20 in the US, and into the Top 10 in the UK, Canada and Australia, and its first single, 'Believe', charted in the Top 20 on both sides of the Atlantic. *Made in England* is centred not on the themes of rebirth that dominated *The One* but rather on ideas of our origins and the long shadows they cast as we spend a lifetime trying to define ourselves in opposition to where we came from, and ultimately end up where we started, though wiser for the grand detours we took along the way.

The Songs

Decidedly *Made in England*'s flagship track, 'Believe' plunges us back into the shadowed textures of *Elton John*, with Buckmaster's plummeting strings paired with Johnstone's towering arpeggiated guitar figures instantly evoking both the oppressive mega-structures that love as a force on the world stage must contend with, the 'churches and dictators', as well as the persistent personal tragedies that seem to blot out all hope of happiness (such as the cancer referenced in the song that was 'curled up in' Bernie's father at the time). The explosive combination of Buckmaster and Johnstone is as fresh as it was in the early 1970s. Elton's delivery, meanwhile, of the line 'I believe in Love' is powerful yet menacing in its downwards progression; it evokes a complicated response that is difficult to express in words but it comes down to the cold slice of pragmatism. If there's anything to believe in it is love but few heading into later life can retain the illusion that love will triumph in the face of the universe's long-term plans to end us, and our own short-term attempts to end each other, leaving us to belt into the sky our reverence for love, even as we know that we as a species will likely fail in the end.

The end of 'Believe' features descending instrumental figures that remind us of a grand machine running down, perhaps that of human civilization itself, but from that somewhat terrifying suggestion we are rescued by mechanical-industrial hammerings, which serve as the lead-in to 'Made in England' which as an adolescent I always imagined as the sounds of Elton himself being constructed (or 'made') in between the tracks to save the day. I still partly believe that, mainly because of the image of a large assembly line putting together an Elton is irresistible to me but more likely this is in reference to The Monkees/The Beatles/Paul McCartney (*b.*1942) tendency to include various studio noses, shuffling and exclamations as intros or outros to their tracks as either *avant garde* exercises, making the listener aware of the fabricated nature of what they habitually ingested, or just for laughs. That dig into the world of British rock is further highlighted by the iconic guitar clang that began 'Hard Day's Night' and that here leads into Johnstone's energetic late 1960s electric riff. Unlike 'The North', which presented Elton and Bernie's shared heritage as a cold and unforgiving past to be appreciated but shed, 'Made in England' offers a balance between Bernie's stark words and Elton's up-tempo presentation of them, creating the impression that, as hard as things were, with gloomy childhoods only made bearable by the records of Little Richard and Elvis, in the end all that hardship formed two sturdy individuals, capable of surviving the struggles ahead of them, even if the scars still linger (my favourite moment is the devastating line 'I've had forty years of pain and nothing to cling to' which then launches, without missing a beat, into the poppy 'whoa-oah-oahhh-oh, I was made in England!' verse, which expresses in an instant how much all the rock star bravado is a mask for a mass of deep pain).

For years, 'House' was the song on *Made in England* that I routinely skipped over. The lyrics were so simple and the resulting melody so basic, that they offended my ideas of what an Elton song was about, and so I understand the Elton fans today who continue in that vein but let me offer some words in defence: the key lies in the pulsing, discordant outro to 'Made in England', which every Elton fan instantly associates with the iconic intro to 'Sixty Years On' that Buckmaster crafted while messing around with his orchestra some quarter of a century previously. This interlude was also crafted by Buckmaster, and he is such a sharp musical thinker there must be meaning in it, and I believe it to be our guide to understanding 'House', not so much as a song about Elton's wandering around his massive house alone (though that's a perfectly good interpretation) but as a song about the rapidly shrinking horizons one experiences as life moves towards its close. This might well be the tale of the last moments of the 'Sixty Years On' character, who has gone on living well past sixty years, and whose life is now reduced to a few certainties that his brain ritually returns to as the only things he is sure of anymore – 'This is my bed, this is where I sleep', 'This is my house, this is where I live'– all while steadily losing his sense of self – 'These are not my eyes – Where is my soul?' – and longingly looking out the window at nature moving on without him, hoping desperately for a return to youthful abandon that will never come again. From a song I couldn't skip fast enough, it's now one that devastates with its no punches pulled account of what it's like to feel your life collapse in on itself.

'House' represented the end of the interconnected trilogy of songs at the beginning of the album, that took us from world despair to the hurt of youth and into the depths of the brain's slow self-annihilation. Elton and Bernie are now free to roam whatever topics they please, and revisit old friends. 'Cold' is, for Elton, a return to the structure of 'It Ain't Gonna Be Easy' from *A Single Man*, in which lyrics about the difficulties and tensions involved in returning to a relationship after trust was broken provides Elton with the ability to play with minor and major shadings in the verses, while singling out the title phrase as the basis for extended vocal explorations in the last third of the song, which allow the instruments to crunch onwards while Elton improvises increasingly tortured versions of that phrase. As a vocal showcase, it's a powerhouse, that unfortunately lies directly after some of Elton and Bernie's most meaningful creations, which it isn't trying to emulate but positionally can't really avoid unfavourable comparison with.

All the up-tempo numbers on *Made in England* are centred around dark themes, with the hard knock youth of 'Made in England' handing the baton off to 'Pain', which in turn passes it along to 'Lies'. If 'Cold' was an update of 'It Ain't Gonna Be Easy', then 'Pain' is an update of 'Chasing the Crown' with, again, comparable theming and structure. With 'Chasing the Crown' Bernie gave us a look at world history through the eye of power and those who are willing to inflict global-scale suffering in the pursuit thereof. 'Pain' gives us a similar panorama onto the long story of human affairs but now glimpsed through the point of view of pain rather than that of power. As with 'House', Bernie's writing style here is stripped down to the minimum, keeping to a basic pattern of questions and answers that, at first, seem almost painfully juvenile. By this point, Bernie has earned more than our first hearing intuitions, and we should know that he is at his most complex when outwardly appearing at his most simple, and 'Pain' is a good example of this. Yes, this is a rigid pattern Bernie has uncharacteristically locked himself into (and will again, in 'Lies') but that is because pain has nothing of subtlety to it. Bernie's lyrics capture the blocky rawness of that uncompromising brute existence in the rigidity of his poetic structure, and Elton and the band amplify it in their amped up rendition of it, with Johnstone's guitar leading the way.

'Believe' might well be the flagship song of *Made in England* but 'Belfast' is its crown jewel. Buckmaster's extended orchestral introduction has all the fulness of 'Tonight', beginning with descending string figures that continue the motive from the outro of 'Believe' mixed with elements of Irish figures that are present enough to add texture but not so present as to shade towards *Riverdance*. It's, by itself, a beautiful piece of music, that gives way to Elton's piano, before the haunting vocal melody begins. The last time Elton talked directly about Ireland in a song was 'Madness' back in 1979, which was a fiery and complete condemnation of terror as a means of political discourse. Sixteen years later, Elton and Bernie are 'try[ing] to see through Irish eyes', and more generally to encompass the desperation that strikes people everywhere caught in the crossfire of conflict. Bernie's magisterial survey, Elton's serene melody, and Buckmaster's undulating strings all combine to create a sort of symphony of the oppressed, relevant beyond the strict confines of Belfast, with quiet pastoral themes seeking growth and light in and amongst cannonades of symphonic might. The only question mark Elton fans tend to have for the song is the concluding section, with its traditional Irish elements, which some feel take away from the universality of the piece, some wince at as a caricature of the Irish people in their complexity, and others find a poignant voice from the traditional past, lamenting the current state of the Emerald Island.

The next two songs, 'Latitude' and 'Please', swing into country idioms, which was in line with the general growth in popularity that country music experienced in the late 1980s and early 1990s as it expanded its appeal into the broader mass market with strong debut albums from emerging artists like Garth Brooks (1989), The Dixie Chicks (1989) and Shania Twain (1993). Rock 'n roll had its start in the fusion of rhythm and blues with country represented in the likes of Jerry Lee Lewis, Buddy Holly and Elvis, and as such country had always been an idiom that Elton was drawn to (and Bernie, for his part, had always connected most personally with country forms, The Louvin Brothers in particular striking him like lightning in his adolescence) with albums like *Tumbleweed Connection* and a multitude of songs tapping into the elements of classic country music. With 'Please' and 'Latitude',

Elton seems to be looking towards newer pop-leaning trends in country music. Lyrically, there are some sweet things going on: 'Latitude' being one of Bernie's lyrics about how time hangs on one's hands when one is physically separated from one's partner, and 'Please' either a traditional love ballad about people who have been through everything together, or a summation of everything Elton and Bernie had been up to together by this point in their careers, with a poignant request to keep the partnership going, for as long as they're able.

'Man' is one of the most interesting tracks on this album from a lyrical point of view, as it represents a kind of ultimate summation of two and a half decades of Bernie lyrics about broken men who wrought destruction among everything around them. 'Man' brings us all the glaring character faults of men as they have behaved across history and are compelled to behave in society – their credulous belief in their own natural superiority, their erection of false faces to hide the fragile child natures within, their unearned swagger. We grant all these faults, Bernie says, but points out that, nonetheless, progress is being made. 'Have a little faith in man' isn't some slogan that demands subjugation to men as they are but a plea to not give up on men because of their track record of the last several thousand years, and to believe that with education, they can become something more than the caricatures they have been. Elton sets this thesis in the realm of gospel music, complete with classic Hammond organ played by Paul Carrack (*b*.1951), as he sings Bernie's sermon of the historically disappointing yet altogether fascinating creation from whom good might yet come.

As if a continuation of the confessional nature of 'Man', 'Lies' represents an opening of the accounting books, not of men as a corporate gender but of individual men as they go about their daily business of existence. Unlike in 'House' and 'Pain', however, where the locked-in regularity of the poetic structure serve a larger narrative purpose, here I think it's more of a rhythmic and sonic device to drive the verses forward, like the 'Say goodbye to …' repetitions in 'Goodbye Marlon Brando'. The result is a list of things that people often lie about, some others that the narrator in particular has lied about (including a couple that have particular resonance with Elton's life story), and a promise that, nevertheless, in spite of all that lying, the narrator will surely never lie to the romantic object the song is being addressed towards.

We close out this album with 'Blessed', which brings us back to a theme Bernie explored on the *Elton John* album, some twenty-five years previously, that of the emotions we feel as we anticipate or become aware of a new life arriving on our planet. While 'The Greatest Discovery' told this tale charmingly from the perspective of an older sibling being introduced to their new baby brother, 'Blessed' is a story sung by a hopeful parent to their, as yet, unborn (and not even conceived) future child. It's a mature song, made all the more profound by the knowledge that, for both Elton and Bernie, each passing year would move the possibility of a child that much further from their grasp. Johnstone's gentle guitar work, and the swaths of sound conjured by Babylon on the keyboards, provide a perfect nest for Elton's intimate melody that moves from gentle verses attempting to imagine what this child will be like, to powerful choruses promising that child a world of love. It's one of Elton's greatest songs of the decade, and please don't watch the music video if you haven't already. Whereas 'Believe' has one of Elton's best visual realisations for a song ever, 'Blessed' has one of the goofiest and most painfully literal, which a lifetime won't wash from your brain.

The Stats

Album/Single	US	UK	Australia	Canada
Made in England	13	3	6	3
	P	G		2P
'Believe'/'Sorry Seems to Be the Hardest Word' (live) 'The One' (live)	13	15	23	1
'Made in England'/'Whatever Gets You Through the Night' (live) 'Lucy in the Sky With Diamonds' (live)	52	18	48	5
'Blessed'/'Latitude' (US and Canada)	34		86	3
'Please'/'Made in England' (UK)		33		27

The Players

Elton John: lead and backing vocals, acoustic piano (1 to 7 and 9 to 11), harmonium (7), keyboards (8) and string arrangements (9)
Guy Babylon: keyboards, programming, backing vocals (8) and string arrangements (9)
Teddy Borowiecki: accordion (6)
Paul Carrack: Hammond organ (9)
Davey Johnstone: guitars, mandolin, banjo and backing vocals (8)
Bob Birch: bass and backing vocals (8)
Charlie Morgan: drums
Ray Cooper: percussion
Paul Brennan: pipes and flute (6)
Dermont Crehan: violin (6)
Paul Buckmaster: orchestral arrangements and conductor (1, 3, 4 and 6)
George Martin: string and French horn arrangements (7) and conductor (7)
Gavyn Wright: orchestra leader (6) and conductor (9)
The London Session Orchestra: orchestra (1, 3, 4, 6, 7 and 9)

The Tracks

1. 'Believe' (John, Taupin) (4.55)
2. 'Made in England' (John, Taupin) (5.09)
3. 'House' (John, Taupin) (4.27)
4. 'Cold' (John, Taupin) (5.37)
5. 'Pain' (John, Taupin) (3.49)
6. 'Belfast' (John, Taupin) (6.29)
7. 'Latitude' (John, Taupin) (3.34)
8. 'Please' (John, Taupin) (3.52)
9. 'Man' (John, Taupin) (5.16)
10. 'Lies' (John, Taupin) (4.25)
11. 'Blessed' (John, Taupin) (5.01)

Musician's Corner: 'Believe'

'Believe' is a story of love as a desperate last hope among the crumbling ruins of civilization. The music video for the song is full of art deco totalitarian black and white imagery, setting off the dystopian Bernie lyrics with an impact matched by Elton's thundering music, all summing to the conclusion that there's something unbreakable in us that originates in our need for our connections to other people.

Musically, 'Believe' is a minor-key blast of virtually operatic scope set in what we are now familiar with as Elton's 'Despair' key of G minor, and is virtually unremitting in its string-born minor attacks on the poor individual, trying desperately to find something to believe in among the churches and dictators that have moved things to the state they're in. To reinforce this feeling of monolithic powers all around us, Elton again employs that method we discussed with 'All the Young Girls Love Alice' where, chord to chord, as much as possible is kept unchanging, as in the following progression from 'Without Love I wouldn't believe' onwards: Gm-Eb-Cm-Ab-Cm-Ab-Fm7.

The cycle finally ends violently with an augmented chord that leads us back to our statement of belief in love but in these transitions, we get a sense of outward change and motion masking conservative resistance that is the essence of the Kafkaesque dystopia we are inhabiting in this near perfect song.

Incidentally, this song was also included on the *Love Songs* compilation.

Chapter 30

The Big Picture

Recorded: November 1996 to May 1997
Released: 22 September 1997
Producer: Chris Thomas

The Story

Over two years separated *Made in England* from *The Big Picture*, during which time Elton expanded on his success with *The Lion King* by pushing ahead with music for a new musical, *Aida* (with Rice), and a new animated soundtrack, for the film *Road to El-Dorado* (also with Rice). When Elton returned to the studio, to record a new album at Richard Branson's (*b.*1950) London Townhouse Studios, with Anne Dudley (*b.*1956) directing orchestral additions at the AIR Studios (where *Made in England* had been laid down), it was with the notion of retaining the basic soundscape of *Made in England*, only with Chris Thomas in the production booth instead of Elton, and with a focus on introspective balladry rather than *Made in England*'s reflections on history, politics, gender and the challenges of each phase of an individual's life.

The album is famous among Elton fans as 'the one Bernie hates', after he rated it lower than even *Leather Jackets* in their joint output of the previous three decades for reasons that continue to baffle most but likely have to do with their struggles over the direction of the album, his own dissatisfaction with his lyrics, a dislike for the relative lack of 'real instruments' on the album and a general feeling that Thomas's production style was too clinical for the material at hand.

Most Elton fans, while recognising the validity of some of Bernie's issues with the album, disagree with his pessimism as to its overall merit, noting that, once you accept it as primarily a ballad album, there are a few delightful surprises waiting for you, from the sombre glumness of 'Long Way from Happiness' to the expansive 'Live Like Horses', originally slated for *Made in England* and memorably performed by Luciano Pavarotti (1935–2007) in June 1996, to the cosmic strut of 'January', to the nautical love epic that is 'I Can't Steer My Heart Clear of You'. Of course, we'll never know what people's overall reaction to the album really was. On the shelves a week after the records-shattering release of Elton's 'Candle in the Wind '97' charity single in memory of Princess Diana, *The Big Picture* stormed to the top of the charts – #3 in the UK and #9 in the US – largely on the strength of that success, and a general outpouring of gratitude that the world still had Elton to give voice to our collective grief. Since then, Bernie's evaluation of the album has loomed larger in the public perception than any more careful analysis of the album's merits, pushing *The Big Picture* further to an unmerited obscurity with each year, a trend that desperately needs reversing, so let's get to it.

The Songs

Each of Elton's studio albums from the 1990s begins with a strong indicator of what the overall landscape of the record will be. 'Simple Life' has a strong rhythm with leaping elements emerging from the sonic ground that communicate that album's celebration of life, 'Believe' is centred around Buckmaster's towering strings that give a sense of large historical structures that lone humans must navigate and 'Long Way from Happiness', the opener of *The Big Picture*, starts with a simple drop into a singular atmospheric note that never moves far from its origin, providing a sense of lone introspection that will mark much of the album. It's also an apt beginning for the song's theme of chronic depression, of that inability to experience anything beyond a restricted emotional palette no matter how your life outwardly appears. The lyrics were a source of contention between Elton and Bernie, with Elton feeling that the original lines were too complicated to fit around the melody he was producing, resulting in a request to rewrite and simplify them that Bernie reluctantly acquiesced to. Even if it's simpler the new lyrics are still affecting, particularly to anyone who has experienced what it's like living with people who are chronically depressed. Elton's music is an artful fit for this theme, focusing on repetitive motions indicating that the subject of the song is unable to break out of towards something more spontaneous, until the end when a woman's voice is given an extended solo, which feels like a break into freedom at first but which ends producing another impression entirely.

For people whose sense of Bernie as a poet was forged in the fires of 'The Scaffold' and 'Take Me to the Pilot', the album's second piece, 'Live Like Horses', represents a return to familiar and challenging ground. The song, originally intended for the *Made in England* album, and included on *The Big Picture* in response to pressure from fans of Elton's performance of the song with Pavarotti, carries with it the swelling break-out structure and spirit of both that album and *The One*, and features Bernie slipping back into constructing lyrics out of lines that have arresting images and sounds that bear a relation to the central idea expressed in the chorus, without necessarily telling a linear narrative. The verses convey a general sense of an individual who has been pushed forward mechanically in life but whose instinct for freedom has ultimately overridden his desire for security. 'Live Like Horses' starts with a tightly restricted note range, to give us a feeling of boundaries, which it will be the job of the chorus to burst apart with its sweeping melody, choral accompaniment provided by the Angel Voices Choir, and chord transitions, which make use of chord inversions to provide different types of motion, contributing to the sense of a space suddenly opening before us.

'The End Will Come' sees the album back on the track it was taking before the inclusion of 'Live Like Horses', which is to say, a return to themes of pragmatism that, year by year, gain ground on the romanticism of youth. It puts into words the wisdom that, statistically speaking, relationships die before their constituent partners do. Elton and Bernie were both happy in their relationships at this point and understandably Elton chooses the most affirming part of the lyrics as the chorus, the one where the subject asserts a belief contrary to all evidence that he's confident the end won't come to his relationship. The music highlights this dichotomy between reality and hope in the instrumentation of the verses and chorus, with the verses dominated by an empty space populated by sparse percussion and Elton's echoed voice that give the feeling of one lone individual, and the chorus, which still features the heavy echo but accompanied by so much electric guitar and synth that it feels less like the echo from the wall of a sparsely furnished apartment, and more like a defiant shout on a mountainside.

There's a tendency in Bernie's lyrics to consider anything that incorporates the word 'we' with some mention of having been together for a long time, as a song that must be about Elton and Bernie's working partnership. It's a default position with a pull so strong that sometimes it causes us to overlook the other themes Bernie might be writing about, concerning romantic relationships, the relationship between an artist and his audience, or people and the larger community. That said, 'If the River Can Bend' is decidedly another song about Elton and Bernie. There's an interesting idea at work here, which depends on whether you think of the 'I' of this song as Bernie, the person who wrote it, or Elton, the person who is singing it. The basic metaphor of the song is about an individual who stays put while the other heads out on adventures, returning when, and if, the river carrying them outwards bends back towards home, allowing them to 'build a new beginning' together, as Elton and Bernie had repeatedly done over the last three decades. The sense of a fresh start is supported by the sound of the East London Gospel Choir, gospel idioms being Elton's universal indicator that the song beneath it is about rebirth. Johnstone's distinctive back and forth with Elton in the concluding material is particularly powerful in this piece, as it's a reminder that not only has Elton and Bernie's relationship survived their life stories but so has that of Elton and Johnstone (who, during Elton's recently concluded farewell tour, performed his 3,000th show with Elton), making the song as much a celebration of his years of creative contribution as that of Elton and Bernie's.

There's a lot of poignancy to be had in 'Love's Got a Lot to Answer For', particularly in Bernie's contemplation about where the boundary between freedom and loneliness lies, and his exploration of the desire to grow cold and ultimately feel nothing, rather than knowing warmth long enough only to feel doubly pained by its sudden removal. They're touching lyrics but amidst so many other lyrics about emotional loss that Elton set at various pitches of intensity, it seems like there was nowhere to go but down with this piece, into a kind of unchanging space, reflecting the cold slowly taking over the narrator's heart.

On the strength of being connected on a CD-single with 'Candle in the Wind '97', 'Something About the Way You Look Tonight' has the distinction of being the best-selling single, not only from any Elton album but from any album released since sales first started being rigorously charted in the 1950s, with some 33 million copies sold to date. The song, therefore, keeps company not only with 'White Christmas' (50 million) but Bill Haley and His Comets' genre defining 'Rock Around the Clock' (25 million), Elvis's 'It's Now or Never' (20 million) and Whitney Houston's (1963–2012) 'I Will Always Love You' (20 million). The difference, of course, being that, while the melody of each of those songs pops instantly into the head of just about anybody who reads those song titles, 'Something About the Way You Look Tonight' only lives on in the hearts and minds of the Elton faithful.

That's a shame, because it's a great song, and, even more rare than that, an Elton-Bernie song that is unambiguously a love ballad, with no attempts to make a larger point about the undependability of the human heart and mind. Is it as good as 'The One'? Not really, but as that was essentially a perfect song, with a brilliant musical structure built on haunting lyrics, that's not a fair ask. What we have here are perfectly fine lyrics representing Bernie's later trend towards more direct verses, which is elevated as far as it can go by the power of Elton's big gear shift from the rhythm and blues balladry of the verses to the symphonic pop-rock sensibilities of the chorus, giving the song its sonic diversity.

I think the best way to view 'The Big Picture' is as the good angel counterpart to 'I've Seen That Movie Too', the *Goodbye Yellow Brick Road* track about an infidelity that has become cinematic in its predictable clichés and deceptions. The hero of 'The Big Picture' is likewise viewing themselves as a player in a film, except this time, the film is a light-hearted romcom instead of a shadowy noir flick. Bernie doesn't attempt to stretch this metaphor to cover the whole length of the song and in the second verse shifts the 'star' of the previous sections from a film context to a celestial one, which breathes new life into the lyrics. Elton adds punch to the chorus using the transition that we've heard before on this album: a I chord that drops to the major version of its VII chord in order to use that as a launch pad up to the IV chord, which has a double power as both the important sub-dominant of the original key and as a strong fifth leap upward. Elton's dynamic chord work keeps the sonic topography changing in compelling ways, giving a breadth to the song, which succeeds in elevating it to a higher plane than that inhabited by the lyrics considered on their own.

'Oh, good, more lyrics about someone finding the strength to carry on after a failed relationship, with imagery about coldness and extinguished fires and darkness... I was hoping for more ... of that ...' was not likely Elton's response upon receiving the lyric to 'Recover Your Soul'. He gamely tries to direct the song towards some soul/ gospel elements to bring their associated gravitas onto the scene, but doesn't seem to be able to rouse himself to the heroics that elevated the previous two tracks, as the song pings around on a classic I-iii-vi-IV-I-V-I pattern which does the job but doesn't quite fire us with enthusiasm to take another walk through this thematic material.

With 'January', Elton has some unambiguously joyful material to work with, and he presses the opportunity to maximum advantage, producing a song with scope and powerful thrust, which delights in slipping in and out of the key signature, in using the VI-VII-I swoop up into the tonic key, and in presenting unique tonal areas for each of the three primary sections of material in the song, so that the ear is constantly having new spaces to survey in this bounding rhapsody about a love that has particular delights in every season but none so tailored for the solidifying of a bond between two people as that of January, the 'month that cares'. Vocally, Elton's pulling out a *tour de force* here, adapting his vocal presentation to the needs of each section, with playfulness in the verses, sweetness in the bridges and power in the chorus. Both 'January' and 'Something About the Way You Look Tonight' gave Elton a chance to sing out the full measure of his happiness about his new relationship with David Furnish (*b*.1962), and that gives this already charmingly constructed song one extra layer of delight.

Everything comes together for 'I Can't Steer My Heart Clear of You', the penultimate track on *The Big Picture*, and a piece that mixes old and new in a bewitching ear brew. This is a love song but it's one saturated in a nautical imagery that has some dashes of the Norse to it, which bring us all the way back to lyrics like 'Val-Hala'. Elton, who never misses an opportunity to sing the word 'thunder' dramatically ('Thunder in the Night' and 'I Guess That's Why They Call it the Blues') is all in on this one, giving us verse melodies that contract and expand like waves, with bridges that have a stillness of anticipation to them, and the chorus steadily soars upwards, supported on Debussy-like orchestral figures composed and directed by Anne Dudley. Tonally, it's a masterpiece that takes us on sudden journeys far from home, enticing in their exoticism, and that make the fall back into the familiar even more satisfying when it comes.

With all the exotic structures employed so far, Elton likely felt that the album should end on a more resolutely popular note, which role 'Wicked Dreams' fills. Bernie's lyrics are a simple invitation to come and join him in the sexually free world of his dreams, and Elton gives it a brick and mortar chord structure, full of big catchy movements that don't make many demands of an audience but makes everyone feel like we ended on a stirring up note, helped immensely by Dudley's slick arrangement of the accompanying strings. Little did we know it at the time, but this would be the last song on a studio album we'd hear for four long years, though Elton would hardly be resting idle in that intervening stretch.

The Stats

Album/Single	US	UK	Australia	Canada
The Big Picture	9	3	5	14
'Live Like Horses'/'Live Like Horses (live)' (with Luciano Pavarotti)		9		
'Something About the Way You Look Tonight'/ 'I Know Why I'm in Love' 'No Valentines'			32	14
'Something About the Way You Look Tonight'/ 'Candle in the Wind '97'	1	1	1	1
'Recover Your Soul'/'I Know Why I'm in Love' and 'Big Man in a Little Suit'		16	92	39
'If the River Can Bend'/'Don't Let the Sun Go Down on Me' (live)		32		

The Players

Elton John: vocals, acoustic piano (all tracks) and organ (1, 4, 5, 7, 8 and 11)
Guy Babylon: keyboards (1 to 9 and 11) and string arrangements
Paul Carrack: organ (6)
Matthew Vaughan: keyboards (10) and percussion (10)
Davey Johnstone: guitars (all tracks)
John Jorgenson: guitars (all tracks)
Bob Birch: bass (all tracks)
Charlie Morgan: drums and percussion (all tracks)
Paul Clarvis: tabla (8)
Anne Dudley: string arrangements and conductor
Carol Kenyon: backing vocals (1, 6 and 8)
Angel Voices Choir: choir (2)
East London Gospel Choir: choir (4)
Jackie Rowe: backing vocals (6 and 8)

The Tracks

1. 'Long Way from Happiness' (John, Taupin) (4.47)
2. 'Live Like Horses' (John, Taupin) (5.02)
3. 'The End Will Come' (John, Taupin) (4.53)
4. 'If the River Can Bend' (John, Taupin) (5.23)
5. 'Love's Got a Lot to Answer For' (John, Taupin) (5.02)
6. 'Something About the Way You Look Tonight' (John, Taupin) (5.09)

7. 'The Big Picture' (John, Taupin) (3.45)
8. 'Recover Your Soul' (John, Taupin) (5.18)
9. 'January' (John, Taupin) (4.02)
10. 'I Can't Steer My Heart Clear of You' (John, Taupin) (4.10)
11. 'Wicked Dreams' (John, Taupin) (4.39)
12. 'I Know Why I'm in Love' (Japanese edition only) (John, Taupin) (4.32)

Musician's Corner: 'Long Way From Happiness'

Elton has released so many songs, that for Eltonians like me, if you name any song there's a good chance, we can give you a few others that are largely similar to it. Not so with 'Long Way from Happiness', which lives in its own world. The intro is dominated by a back-and-forth motion between two notes, a cycle of repetition, of getting nowhere, that is reflective of the general theme of this song, which is one of failed connection and the looming shadow of depression. Unlike other 1990s Elton classics with their big breakout moments, 'Long Way from Happiness' stays at the same level throughout, with the chorus offering little hope out of the emotional quagmire of the song's subjects. Instead of those shocking moments like the big F sharp to B flat transitions we studied earlier, here everything is by the book, going through the motions, a perfect representation of a person trying to deal with emotional numbness.

What stands out about this song is the ending, where we have a lone female voice singing a wordless melody over Elton's piano work for the last fifty seconds of the piece. It's such a strange thing – over twenty-nine years of recording albums, the only times Elton has had a voice not his own featured prominently in a song is during a formal duet but here a full fifth of the song is taken up with another voice, singing scraps of melodic lines, none of them quite going anywhere, which is appropriate to the theme, and a sign of Elton breaking into new forms to tell Bernie's stories. Of course, Bernie wasn't a fan of how this album came out, pushing the pair to a back-to-fundamental approach on the next few albums but it won't be long until Elton's at it again, taking Bernie's words to strange new places on *The Diving Board*.

Chapter 31

Aida

Recorded: 1998 to 1999
Released: 22 March 1999
Producer: Phil Ramone

The Story

Aida might seem like a curious subject for Elton and Rice's follow up to *The Lion King*, and in many ways the choice of this story made things much more complicated for the duo than they needed to be. The story, of a love triangle involving a slave and her captor who fall in love with each other, is one that had to be treated sensitively in the nineteenth century, when Verdi (1831–1901) wrote the original operatic treatment of it, and the need for subtlety and nuance in conception has only grown since then. Disney, which acquired the rights in 1994 to the children's book version of the story written by Leontyne Price (*b*.1927), thought, for some reason, it would be a good follow up animated project to *The Lion King*. Elton wisely thought it better suited to the stage though, interestingly, the first film from the rebel animation studio Dreamworks, *Prince of Egypt* (1998), was set in much the same time period and was an early success for the company.

The combination of Elton and Rice on a musical for the stage based on a quasi-historical subject seemed ripe with promise, even if the story itself wasn't entirely suited to modern narrative tastes. Elton is a classically trained musician with a wide breadth of musical styles at his fingertips, and Rice's greatest success prior to *The Lion King* was *Jesus Christ Superstar* (1971), which virtually wrote the book on how to set an ancient story in modern song idioms. Further, the book for the musical was being written by Linda Woolverton (*b*.1952), who wrote the *Beauty and the Beast* screenplay and co-wrote that of *The Lion King*. What could go wrong?

As it turned out, quite a bit but not enough to keep *Aida* from being one of the most successful Broadway musicals of all time (currently ranked at #39 in terms of total box office) from a commercial perspective. For 4 years and over 1,800 performances, *Aida* continued to bring in audiences but something about it kept people from holding it to their hearts the same way that they did with *Hamilton* or *Les Misérables*, or even *The Lion King* and *Billy Elliot*. Most critics seem to place the reason for that in two locations: the book and the lyrics, the former for failing to fully address the complicated issues lying at the centre of the story and the lyrics for shining in the small numbers but not showing up for the big ones, which leaves Elton often devoting significant musical artillery to words that are too fragile to support them.

Ultimately, *Aida*, with its four Tony Awards and long Broadway run, was a success and proved the principle of Elton as a composer for the stage, allowing him to branch out into more experimental waters, where one more triumph and two great but noble defeats awaited him.

The Songs

Two CDs of the *Aida* music were released, the first a recording of the songs in no particular order, featuring mostly famous musicians like Sting (*b*.1951), The Spice Girls and Tina Turner (1939–2023) covering the pieces from the play, with one of the cast on hand to give a sense of what the actual musical would sound like. A year later, the original Broadway cast recording was released, where the songs were in the proper order and made contiguous sense as an unfolding story. I'm doing a quick tour through the songs in the Broadway cast order with an eye towards their compositional elements rather than the performance aspects. We start with 'Every Story is a Love Story', which moves us from the framing device for the musical into the story, as it morphs from a hushed ballad to a rhythm and blues power romp that serves as the bridge into 'Fortune Favours the Brave'. This is the musical's introductory pitch, telling us not to worry much about what all the plot means on closer historical inspection and to view what follows as a story of love flourishing amid tyranny, and Elton's melody until the big rhythm and blues switch is so beguiling it's hard not to grant him that suspension of analytic uneasiness.

With 'Fortune Favours the Brave' we are introduced to our male lead, Radames, who will fall heir to the throne upon his upcoming marriage to Princess Amneris, and who has returned from the conquest of Nubia. It features some apparent clunkers from Rice which might be actually brilliant if the idea is to portray Radames as a sort of cliché prone general, who evolves over time into someone capable of self-sacrifice. The music is catchy enough to allow us to push through some of the rougher lines and effectively conveys the idea that the Egyptians are unrepentant conquerors who haven't a thought for the lives they have destroyed.

'The Past is Another Land', in which the captured Nubian slave Aida (secretly a princess of her people) rails against the actions of the Egyptians and contemplates both the destruction of the treasured places of her childhood and the steely resolution of her people's spirit, is one of the pieces in the musical rendered nearly comical by some of Rice's goofier lyrics. 'The past is now another land, far beyond my reach/ Invaded by insidious foreign bodies' in particular brings the gravitas of the song to a screeching halt as the audience has to witness a singer doing her best to render the phrase 'insidious foreign bodies' even the least bit musical. This is then followed by

'The present is an empty space between the good and bad/A moment leading nowhere, too pointless to be sad' and I still distinctly remember my first time hearing it, and biting my knuckle in fear when the 'good and bad' line ended, thinking, 'He's not going to rhyme that with sad, is he? He can't!' And then it happened. It's a beautiful melody but the emotional impact is blunted by the words and that's a problem since this piece is supposed to be the crowning statement of Aida's love of her homeland, against which she must fight as she starts falling in love with Radames.

If Rice's style wasn't suited to 'The Past is Another Land', it's exactly the right thing needed for 'Another Pyramid', a comic villain piece in a mixture of different styles, including reggae, which revels in anticipation of the coming end of the pharaoh, an end being hurried on by the singer of the piece, Radames's father. 'Sad to say our mighty ruler isn't really in the pink/Hopes couldn't be miniscule-er that he'll come back from the brink', is a set of lines that would have occurred only to Rice, and the blend of evil glee at another's demise and increasingly ridiculous ways of describing the death of the country's leader make it a highlight of the musical, and a chance for Elton to bring in not only reggae but rhythm and blues elements, as well as some bass progressions that give a little taste of classic Elton and Russell.

'How I Know You' gives the character of Mereb, a Nubian who recognises Aida, a song to sing, the content of which is basically the communication of the fact that he knows her because his father used to work at the palace. We probably didn't need a whole song for that but it provides each main character with a solo piece in the first act, clearing the way for the progression of the story.

We heard from Princess Amneris in the opening song, where she serves as the gateway into the world of Aida, but 'My Strongest Suit' represents her formal entry into the story, and between Rice's Gilbert and Sullivan patter song style lyrics about the delights of superficiality, and Elton's Motown rendering of those words, it's a fun piece of music. In terms of the musical's architecture, it serves the purpose of giving a character an extreme starting position, allowing them space to grow over the course of the musical.

'Enchantment Passing Through' is meant to begin the process of making Radames a sympathetic character. He and Aida find themselves opening up to each other about the things that are upsetting them, the problem being the comic imbalance between what they're singing about: Radames is whining about how ruling Egypt will get in the way of his expeditions with their side line in slavery, while Aida is talking about being a slave with no freedom. That imbalance makes the song's attempt at mutual recognition and the first stirrings of romance harder to buy into, which is problematic because it's the only thing the musical is about.

Tonal whiplash is something of the name of the game with the next song, 'Dance of the Robe', which mixes poignant moments of self-doubt, with a choral refrain that is supposed to come off as menacing in its demand for Aida to assume a leadership role but is written and scored in such a Disney idiom that the menace is drained substantially, with a rock 'n roll dance number, which is supposed to carry with it aggressive undertones as the Nubian slaves encircle Aida with their demands but by that point we have experienced so many reversals of tone it's somewhat at sea.

'Not Me', the quartet in which Radames announces his intention to throw away his future for the sake of love, while Mereb, Aida and Amneris weigh in on that announcement, has a lot going for it: the melody is celebratory and could have been a grand moment of release with our male lead finding humanity at last and embracing a love that, for the sake of the play, we allow ourselves to believe is a good thing. But the 'Not Me' motif that runs through the song is so gimmicky that it's hard to feel the emotional impact of the moment.

'Elaborate Lives' gives us our first big love duet. The Broadway cast recording has Adam Pascal (*b*.1970), who is constantly reverting to his *Rent* herniated rock voice, whether the words call for it or not, and which ultimately makes the song sound like a Christian rock track. Rice has another lyrical gimmick going on here that is distracting (the blocky 'I don't wanna live like that … I don't wanna love like that' structure), but if you put that to the side and listen to the song as Elton originally recorded it, there are delights to be had, in his classic chord inversions and in the little nod to his longtime frenemy Rod Stewart (*b*.1945), 'gentler, wis-er, free' is melodically and rhythmically related to 'For-e-ver young'.

'The Gods Love Nubia', Aida's anthem of pride in her homeland, is regularly cited as one of the highlights of the musical. Rice rises to the occasion here, giving Elton exactly what he needs to craft an old style Southern spiritual number that works both within the context of the song and as a larger comment on the state of Africa, both the strength it possesses and the towering problems that it has had to contend with.

Act two begins with a catch-up on the mental state of our main players, 'A Step Too Far', which is full of little Elton musical Easter eggs, which is in E flat major, famous as the key of 'Your Song', a connection he reinforces in the 'Oh-oh-oh-ohhh's and their sliding bass note under a constant chord that recall the structure underlying 'I hope you don't mind, I hope you don't mind'.

'Easy as Life', in which Aida contemplates lying to her beloved to protect her people, is a standout moment, featuring a combination of a soaring, Bond-theme-like vocal line, mixed with Eastern European and Mediterranean rhythms and piano work. The piece is alternating fire and anguish, giving the lead the opportunity to display the breadth of her vocal talent.

While in the following piece, 'Like Father, Like Son', Radames and his father, Zoser, have a chance to do an aggression-fuelled rocker duet seemingly tailor made for Pascal, and which also serves as a reminder that this music is composed by Elton, in terms of plot it doesn't do all that much other than tell us things we already knew but it's an injection of energy before we head into the tragic last stretch of *Aida*, and that's a welcome thing.

That last stretch is filled with reprises of previous material, the musical's best song, which was ultimately cut from the production, and two pieces that served as the musical's representatives on the world stage, 'Written in the Stars' – which

Elton released as a successful single with LeAnn Rimes (*b*.1982) – and 'I Know the Truth' – which Elton sings with Janet Jackson (*b*.1966) on the soundtrack. 'Written in the Stars' is a great song, though some critics used it to criticise *Aida* for being too adult contemporary pop and not Broadway enough but we can leave them to their criticism, because this is one of Elton's most memorable choruses, and Rice's lines, rather than being subtractive as they often have been, are word perfect here. 'Is this some god's experiment/in which we have no say' is a great phrase to place in the mouths of two doomed lovers, and Elton's able to spring off those words into an unforgettable skywards lament.

'I Know the Truth' lets us check in with Amneris, who has grown into a wise figure, who realises that the one thing she'd built her entire life on, her marriage to Radames, is now gone, and in its absence the future has neither shape nor content. The song has a mid-1970s Diana Ross feel to it – a mix of vulnerability and inner strength, with the instruments pulled way back to give the singer as much space as possible to go small with her voice when she needs to. There's also some interesting writing here because it keeps returning to the same musical material, exactly as one does when one has suffered a break-up and obsessively keeps lingering over the facts instead of moving on. Elton's inclusion of chord progressions from the verses in the chorus conveys that sense expertly in a way that your brain notices even if your ears don't.

The Stats

Album/Single	US	UK	Australia	Canada
Elton John and Tim Rice's Aida		29		
	G			
'Written in the Stars'/'Written in the Stars' (alternate version)/'Various Snippets'	29	10	85	22
'A Step Too Far'/'Your Song (Live at the Ritz)'				

The Tracks

(All songs by Elton John and Tim Rice.)

1. 'Another Pyramid' (performed by Sting) (3.48)
2. 'Written in the Stars' (performed by Elton John and LeAnn Rimes) (4.17)
3. 'Easy As Life' (performed by Tina Turner) (5.12)
4. 'My Strongest Suit' (performed by Spice Girls) (4.11)
5. 'I Know the Truth' (performed by Elton John and Janet Jackson) (5.35)
6. 'Not Me' (performed by Boyz II Men) (4.52)

Musician's Corner: 'The Messenger'

Of course, my favourite song from *Aida* is the one that was cut from the final show. 'The Messenger' was meant to have been the climactic final love duet between Aida and Radames as they die together in a common tomb for having betrayed the pharaoh. For some reason (I've seen speculation that the producers were uncomfortable with a new song so late in the show), in the ultimate version of the musical 'The Messenger' was replaced by a series of reprises, which are dramatically effective but I miss the satisfyingly sepulchral nature of the original ending.

'The Messenger' begins with the haunting pairing of an oboe and pipe organ, the latter of which features prominently throughout the verses, and which is a different bit of timbre in the mix of an Elton song. The verses are chock full of transitions that you don't expect and in a song that's all about defying the enormity of death itself, that defying of traditional chord progressions seems on message. The chorus is the resounding cry of death's powerlessness in the face of love, and Elton uses everything he's got – parallel minors, relative minors, a shifting tonal centre that carries into the next verse, and my personal favourite, the iii-vi-IV-V progression (centred around 'Sullen and predictable, love is versatile'), which takes your usual pop standard I-vi–IV-V progression and substitutes in the iii chord at the start, which works since iii and I share two of the same notes, but also throws your ears off enough that when the I eventually does come it feels twice as satisfying.

It's a song that mixes in more defiance, power and peace than a single five-minute number ought to be able to encompass but by the end we are well convinced that death, when faced with someone you love, loses much of its sting, and that there's triumph to be had in staring together into the coming void.

Chapter 32

The Muse

Recorded: 1999
Released: 24 August 1999
Producers: Guy Babylon and Michael T. Ryan

The Story

On 27 August 1999, Albert Brooks's (*b*.1947) sixth film, *The Muse*, opened in cinemas. Featuring Brooks, Sharon Stone (*b*.1958), Andie MacDowell (*b*.1958), Jeff Bridges (*b*.1949), and a host of cameos from the day's leading directors, the Hollywood satire didn't make back its production costs. The question here is, why, out of all the films that Elton could have done, was this his entry into Hollywood soundtrack composition?

The answer to that lies with the establishment of Rocket Pictures, which Elton and Furnish established in 1996, and which by 1999 had essentially only one film under its belt, *Elton John: Tantrums and Tiaras* (1997), with another in production, the Helena Bonham Carter (*b*.1966) film *Women Talking Dirty*, which would be released in 2001. In press statements about Elton writing the soundtrack to *The Muse*, you would sometimes hear how it was hoped that the project would bring Rocket Pictures and *The Muse*'s production company, October Films (which lasted from 1991 to 2002, when it merged with Good Machine to become Focus Features), into a closer relationship, thereby putting Rocket Pictures into a relationship with Universal Pictures, which had bought a majority share of October Films in 1997, and production legend Barry Diller (*b*.1942), who had bought that majority share in 1999. Universal Pictures would ultimately partner with Rocket Pictures in producing *Women Talking Dirty*.

In short, Elton and Furnish liked the script, and the people involved with that script had experience with production and connections to people with even more experience, which a new film production company could use. Artistically, the soundtrack also presented Elton with a chance to write purely instrumentally, as he'd wanted to back in the early 1980s, and to pursue more deeply a new musical form.

The Songs

The orchestral soundtrack of a late 1990s comedy isn't meant to take centre stage. The idea of turning out the lights, putting on your headphones and really digging into, say, George Fenton's (*b.*1949) score for *You've Got Mail* sounds like the height of absurdity. Elton's score for *The Muse*, however, is a consistent delight. Deeply mining his classical roots, Elton presents us with a sweeping tour through the last 400 years of compositional styles, including hints of Telemann ('Driving Home'), Vivaldi ('Driving to Universal', 'Better Have a Gift' and 'Back to Paramount'), Haydn ('The Cookie Factory'), Brahms ('Driving to Jack's'), Tchaikovsky ('Are We Laughing'), Dvořák ('The Wrong Gift'), Johann Strauss Jr ('Steven Redecorates'), Prokofiev ('Multiple Personality'), and, yes, even a hint of Elton ('Sarah Escapes').

The Stats

Album/Single	US	UK	Australia	Canada
The Muse Original Motion Picture Soundtrack				

The Tracks

(All tracks by Elton John except 'The Muse' by Elton John and Bernie Taupin.)

1. 'Driving Home' (1.50)
2. 'Driving to Universal' (0.18)
3. 'Driving to Jack's' (1.06)
4. 'Walk of Shame' (1.34)
5. 'Better Have a Gift' (2.07)
6. 'The Wrong Gift' (3.01)
7. 'The Aquarium' (2.11)
8. 'Are We Laughing' (1.07)
9. 'Take a Walk with Me' (1.30)
10. 'What Should I Do?' (1.11)
11. 'Back to the Aquarium' (0.54)
12. 'Steven Redecorates' (2.43)
13. 'To the Guesthouse' (0.50)
14. 'The Cookie Factory' (0.54)
15. 'Multiple Personality' (2.23)
16. 'Sarah Escapes' (1.44)
17. 'Back to Paramount' (0.44)
18. 'Meet Christine' (1.33)
19. 'The Muse' (4.23)
20. 'The Muse' (remixed by Jermaine Dupri (4.21)

Musician's Corner: 'The Muse'

Some people have declared that 'The Muse' is their favourite Elton song, and while the last thing I want to do is talk someone out of loving something that they hold dear, I can't help but see this song as a fun but cautionary example of an approach to writing that had run its course, begging for an overhaul. The Spanish acoustic guitar work that we saw in 'A Word in Spanish' (1988), which felt fresh in the wake of Madonna's (*b*.1958) 'La Isla Bonita' (1987) was already starting to drift into parody by Mariah Carey's (*b*.1969) 'I Don't Wanna Cry' (1991), comes off more like genre easy listening music in 1999, and that also goes for the 1990s adult contemporary ballad percussion track that lingers right at the front of the music. Bernie clearly isn't comfortable trying to write a song cut to Hollywood's dimensions, resulting in paired lines like 'She appears like lightning in a bottle/Like two hands on a throttle'. It's a weird image of how muses work , it's not really how throttles work, and all in all everything's a bit off. Elton's doing extra work vocally to try and right the ship, but even the fullness of his voice can't cut through the unfortunate production.

A change was clearly called for, which begins in 2000 with *The Road to El Dorado*, and comes into its full fruition with the return to basics approach that Elton and Bernie developed for *Songs From the West Coast* (2001), *Peachtree Road* (2004) and *The Captain and the Kid* (2006), a relaying of the foundation of their joint creative process, which served as a springboard for the experimentations of *The Union* (2010) and *The Diving Board* (2013), and if it took 'The Muse' to get those five albums in our hands, then maybe it's the best thing that happened in Elton's musical career.

Chapter 33

The Road to El Dorado

Recorded: 1997 to 1999
Released: 14 March 2000
Producers: Gavin Greenaway, Patrick Leonard and Hans Zimmer

The Story

In 1994, DreamWorks SKG was founded by Steven Spielberg (*b*.1946), Jeffrey Katzenberg (*b*.1950) and David Geffen (*b*.1943), three titans of the film, animation and music worlds respectively. Katzenberg had spent a decade at Disney, a time that saw not only the Disney Renaissance but also a drive to produce edgier content, made quickly and that relied on big name voice talent to bring in audiences, a strategy begun with the relative flop *Oliver & Company*, and which would become the hallmark of Dreamworks Animation in the years to come (*Shrek*, *Madagascar* and *Kung Fu Panda*). One of the early ideas Katzenberg wanted to pursue was an animated epic set in the age of discovery, meant to appeal to older audiences, with an explicitly sexualised female lead character.

The studio's first film, *The Prince of Egypt*, was so serious in tone, however, that Katzenberg reconsidered his original conception for *The Road to El Dorado*, and decided to have it rewritten as essentially a Bing Crosby (1903–1977) and Bob Hope (1903–2003) style Road film (there's even a version of their trademark patty cake), where two petty swindlers bumble their way through an adventure in an exotic setting with one of them winning a Dorothy Lamour (1914–1996) like leading lady. Katzenberg, who had incensed Disney by his constant poaching of their best animators, decided it would be a good idea to also go after their most successful song writing team, and in 1995 asked Elton and Rice to compose songs for *The Road to El Dorado*. These were to be a departure from the Disney musicals of the past two decades and were to be more like those found in *Robin Hood* (1973), in which the songs are mostly performed by a narrator figure, rather than sung by the characters themselves, which meant that Elton's voice, instead of being found just on the soundtrack, would permeate the film, an approach that Rocket Pictures would take with *Gnomeo and Juliet* some eleven years later.

The film wasn't a commercial success, largely due to critics' reports that the characterisations were flat and the film itself laden with implicit sexist and racist tropes. Praise for the soundtrack, however, was universal, though the single, 'Someday Out of the Blue', didn't approach the heights scaled by 'Circle of Life' or 'Can You Feel the Love Tonight?' Today the album, with its eclectic mix of song types and rich vocals, is much treasured among Elton fans as the last flourishing of his large scale and theatrical 1990s compositional style before the big turn towards simplicity that marked Elton's return to studio work, *Songs From the West Coast* (2001).

The Songs

Among all the back and forth of recasting the tone of the film, there must also have been a great deal of musical shuffling as well, for, of the eleven songs attributed to Elton, only five of them are used in the film itself, with one more shoved into the end credits. One of those used is a love song that doesn't remotely fit with the actual action in the film and, in fact, several songs not ultimately used in the film are love ballads, suggesting that the original film was going to have a strong love element, which got scrubbed in favour of a 'romance' story that essentially is comprised of a woman using sex to leave her hometown and a male lead figure going along with it. Those who had heard about the new Elton-narrator-centred approach to the music of the film were, therefore, understandably confused by how little music there is in it, and how only some of it fits with the content of the film.

Songs Used in the Film

'El Dorado' does exactly what it's supposed to do, providing an expansive portrait of the mythical city of El Dorado in the big triumphant key of C, with the melodic fanfare Elton employs on the words 'El Dorado' in particular forming a leitmotif that Hans Zimmer (*b*.1957) employs throughout the film to musically comment on the state of El Dorado and our protagonists' relation to it. A pared down version of the song on the soundtrack is used in the film's intro segment, which removed some of the storytelling present in the original song.

'The Trail We Blaze' is the song playing over the 'following the road to El Dorado' comedy montage, and the two work well together. Elton's song sounds much like the country-pop fusion that he'd employ throughout his work of the 2000s, and there's an amusing contrast between the confidence portrayed in the song lyrics and the bumbling adventures of Tulio, Miguel and their horse in the South American jungle.

'It's Tough to Be a God' taps into the style of the duets Crosby and Hope sang in the original Road films, in this case a celebration of the duo's new-found status as gods. Rice shines when asked to provide lyrics about larger than life people behaving badly and Elton perfectly keys into the Crosby-Hope comic dynamic of songs like 'Road to Morocco' with his infusion of Latin dance rhythms atop which simple melodic lines are laid so that the jokes in the lyrics will be easier to hear. This is the only song in the film not performed by Elton, with Kenneth Branagh (*b*.1960) and Kevin Kline (*b*.1947) taking on the vocal duties, while on the soundtrack you get to hear Elton performing it with Randy Newman (*b*.1943), which is a hoot and a half.

'Without Question', which is clearly a love ballad, is the song the directors decided to insert over Miguel's scenes where he learns to appreciate the people of El Dorado. The lyrics don't make any sense against the images we are seeing and often work directly against them. It's a nice song, it just doesn't work where it's placed. I suspect it's here because, without it, there would only be three and a half Elton songs in the film, and of the compositions at hand, it was the one that fit the least badly.

'Friends Never Say Goodbye' is perhaps the best composition in the film, and works well for the montage of Miguel and Tulio's partnership breaking up under the stress of Tulio's seduction by Chel and Miguel's desire to stay with the people of El Dorado. Musically complicated, with the minor key setting highlighting the fact that, though friends might not say goodbye, they can get torn apart when new avenues of temptation open before them. This is the high point of the film in terms of character development and Elton's haunting composition provides some much-need heightening of the emotional stakes.

The Song Stuck at the End Credits

'Someday Out of the Blue' features lyrics about love at first sight, which lost its home in the film and ended up in the credits, where as an emotional summation of the film it is entirely inaccurate. The song is about a man hoping for a reunion with a former lover. Thematically there's nothing here even closely related to what ended up happening in *The Road to El Dorado*, but with the song's potential as a single to advertise the film from the still young Dreamworks, it couldn't simply be relegated to the unused material of the album, and so was pasted onto the end credits. The single, though it brought unfavourable comparison to the singles from *The Lion King*, did manage a #5 placement on the Adult Contemporary charts, though only #49 on the Hot 100.

Songs on the Soundtrack Unused in the Film

'16th Century Man' is a driving blues number about how only suckers go to the sea and chase after gold on a different continent. It's filled with out there lines from Rice like 'Just because we are Hispanic/Doesn't mean we're oceanic' and the whole thing is so bonkers, you can understand why it wasn't used in the film.

'The Panic in Me' is another love ballad that glides between gentle verses and a tango-laced chorus, which tells of a man whose towering anxieties are soothed by the presence of his beloved. It's a great song, the subtle chord shifts of the verses giving way to the strident two-chord dance atmosphere of the chorus but it had no place in *The Road to El Dorado* as it ultimately turned out and so here it sits in song purgatory.

'Trust Me' is a song unlike anything else Elton has ever recorded, part Beatles homage, part electronic stomper, with Elton's voice modified to fit with the rest of the incongruous musical elements present. The lyrics, about 'selling lovers down the river', are so far from anything *The Road to El Dorado* might even possibly have been about that this must have been something Elton and Rice had lying around and put on the album to pad it out, like Elton did with 'Can I Put You On?' on the *Friends* soundtrack some thirty years prior. It's awesome, though, so I'm not complaining.

'My Heart Dances' is a Spanish style love ballad with some shared DNA with 'A Word in Spanish', centring around lyrics of a love lost by impatience. Like the other love songs on the album, it suggests a role for Chel that was once more fleshed out but that was lost along the way.

Finally, 'Queen of Cities' gives the most tantalising glimpse of what the original film might have been like. After conventionally listing all the wonders of El Dorado, the verses of the song grow increasingly anxious, as El Dorado is conceived less as a tropical paradise and more as a golden cage from which the singer must escape. The chorus, which is simply the name 'El Dorado' repeated multiple times, gives a sense of sadness running through the heart of the superficially perfect city, which was all but washed away in the ultimate portrayal of the town as a black and white battle between the good people led by their king and the dark priest greedy for power.

The Stats

Album/Single	US	UK	Australia	Canada
The Road to El Dorado	63			
'Someday Out of the Blue'/'Cheldorado' (with Heitor Pereira)	49			
'Friends Never Say Goodbye' (with Backstreet Boys)				

The Tracks

(All songs by Elton John and Tim Rice unless otherwise noted.)

1. 'El Dorado' (4.22)
2. 'Someday Out of the Blue' (4.48)
3. 'Without Question' (4.47)
4. 'Friends Never Say Goodbye' (4.21)
5. 'The Trail We Blaze' (3.54)
6. '16th Century Man' (3.40)
7. 'The Panic in Me' (5.40)
8. 'It's Tough to Be a God' (3.50)
9. 'Trust Me' (4.46)
10. 'My Heart Dances' (4.51)
11. 'Queen of Cities' (3.55)
12. 'Cheldorado' (featuring Heitor Pereira, by Hans Zimmer) (4.26)
13. 'The Brig' (featuring Trilogy, by Hans Zimmer) (2.58)
14. 'Wonders of the New World' (John, Zimmer) (5.56)

Musician's Corner: 'Friends Never Say Goodbye'

'Oh great, you're going to be mean about the Spanish guitar in this one just like you were mean about it in "The Muse", aren't you?'

As it turns out, I am not! As much as the guitar seemed like a production affectation in 'The Muse', its presence on *The Road to El Dorado* soundtrack makes thematic sense, and the songs are written in idioms that support that presence, rather than make it seem like a tacked on bit of audio flair. The other thing I'm going to lean against expectations about is the common line that *The Road to El Dorado*'s soundtrack is a failed attempt to recapture the heights of *The Lion King*'s critical and sales juggernaut. Yes, when it comes to the box office, *The Road to El Dorado* was a bomb, but when it comes to the songs, Elton is instantiating the unique setting of the film, and lets it creatively guide his process. While you can make the case that 'Somewhere Out of the Blue' fits in the same category as 'Can You Feel the Love Tonight?' I don't think one can find a ready analogue for 'Friends Never Say Goodbye', 'Without Question' or 'The Panic in Me' in any of *The Lion King*'s songs.

'Friends Never' is an underappreciated gem in the twenty-first century Elton canon, which gets right everything that 'The Muse' stumbled on. A unique set of instruments gathers at the outset, each sliding into place to set up a rhythm and pace that carries with it suggestions of Spanish dance forms. Unlike with 'The Muse', where the rhythmic element is rigidly square and omnipresent, here there's a subtle organ pulse in the background that you hear when the other instruments fall away.

What I enjoy most about this song is its return to a tradition that most people associate with 'Goodbye Yellow Brick Road', which is the use of the deceptive chorus. In 'Goodbye Yellow Brick Road', the way it's structured, the 'on the ground' section is a fake-out, making us feel an uncertainty about where we stand that isn't cleared up until the real chorus enters. It's a mischievous trick that keeps our ears wanting more and Elton uses it beautifully here, playing with our expectations. We expect a second verse after 'tomorrow's episode' that has the same progressions as the first but instead we move to a totally different section of musical material. Then, we expect that section to modulate towards some key that will launch into the chorus and we get the modulation but then it pulls right back to the tonic on 'as one', which leads us to believe, 'Oh, maybe that whole thing was the verse structure, and we're going to do that again one more time before the chorus, like a "Tiny Dancer" sort of situation' but nope, Elton's on the move again, to yet another new musical section, which is still not the chorus, based around the relative major key of the original C minor section, and just when we are starting to think that maybe this song doesn't have a chorus after all, that's when it shows up, with lines introduced by alternating B flat major chords and G chords, which are both not where our ears expected the chorus to be when this song opened in C minor.

The subtle rhythmic forward momentum, augmented by the visiting of complicated tonal centres and musical material at precisely those times when the audience is expecting a big soundtrack breakout moment into familiar territory, creates a new architecture that combines the best of Elton's early playfulness with the robustness of his mature compositional sensibilities.

Chapter 34

Songs From the West Coast

Recorded: 18 September 2000 to 30 April 2001
Released: 1 October 2001
Producer: Patrick Leonard

The Story

By the end of the 1990s, Elton had nothing left to prove. He'd established himself as a successful composer and re-established himself as a popular performer and recording artist, scoring a string of triumphs that would have been the envy of any young star. He was happily in love, active in philanthropy and a Knight Bachelor of Queen Elizabeth II. By all external standards, he was at the pinnacle of his career but deep down there was something amiss, something that was highlighted when he listened to the work being recorded by younger artists like Ryan Adams (*b*.1974) and Rufus Wainwright (*b*.1973), who had stepped away from the heavy production of the 1990s and cultivated instead an eclectic singer-songwriter sound that reached back to the titans of the 1960s and 1970s, whose work Elton had absorbed as a young man.

Elton approached Patrick Leonard (*b*.1956) to produce his first studio album since *The Big Picture* in 1997, asking him to take a stripped down approach. Leonard agreed, punting out the newer additions to the Elton John Band who had been central to the sound of *The One*, *Made in England* and *The Big Picture*, while retaining those individuals who had been central to Elton's more organic 1970s sound: Johnstone, Buckmaster and Olsson. Bernie, meanwhile, after three years to think about what went wrong with *The Big Picture*, brought a greater diversity of theme to the new batch of lyrics he presented to Elton and he was routinely in the room while his words were being set to music.

The album was enthusiastically received by critics, who appreciated the 'back to roots' sensibilities that replaced the synthesised adult contemporary sound of earlier albums, with the warmth of analogue tape and real instruments, and by fans, who were happy to have a studio album back in their hands after a three year drought, and thrilled that the album brought back treasured memories of their first Elton records. Freed from the need to write hits, Elton was now in the business of simply writing good songs, regardless of their marketability and he has not looked back since.

The Songs

Songs From the West Coast announces its intentions from the first song, with 'The Emperor's New Clothes', which features Elton's piano and voice thrown far into the foreground, an immediate break from the walls of synthetic atmospherics of the 1990s. Bernie's lyrics centre on two down on their luck people who are scraping by the best that they can, watching their possessions get hauled away as their life options steadily reduce, but somehow finding something in each other to bluff their way through the bad times. There are definite strands of Russell to be heard in Elton's treatment as well as elements of country music narrative styles reminiscent of *Tumbleweed Connection*, summing to a definite sense that, if you'd lived through the 1990s impatiently waiting for 1970s Elton to return, this record was for you.

'The Emperor's New Clothes' was all about pushing Elton onto centre stage, re-establishing him as the person at the heart of the new album's concept. That having been accomplished, 'Dark Diamond' lets the other musical elements take the limelight, particularly the harmonica work provided by Stevie Wonder, the classic Johnstone-Olsson backing vocals and the distinct rhythmic patterning of drummer Matt Chamberlain (*b*.1967). One neat detail is Elton's chord choice here, which leans heavily into the use of all five flats on the keyboard, a tip of the cap to one of Wonder's favourite keys. Lyric-wise, there's not much that we haven't heard Bernie say before but the point of this song lies in an appreciation for the musicianship and instrumentalism on display.

We are put back in the world of early Elton albums once again with 'Look Ma, No Hands', which has the hallmark of classic Dudgeon production sensibilities. Starting with Elton and his piano for the first verse, the drums and bass are allowed to enter at the second, and before the chorus we get the Johnstone-Olsson backing vocals and a flash of electric guitar, which carry into the chorus. The resumption of the verse, then, brings acoustic guitar into the mix as well so that the ear always has something new to savour as with 'Rocket Man (I Think It's Going to Be a Long, Long Time)' or 'Goodbye Yellow Brick Road'. Bernie's lyrics are a collection of vivid images of someone recounting their doubtlessly fictitious adventures to their mother in the hope of getting some long sought for praise. As an exaggerated case of the tendency we all have to try and make our relatively humdrum adult existences slightly grander when recounting them to the people whose approval we have sought our whole lives, it's perfect, as is Elton's spritely melody, evoking that rushing sense of pride one feels when showing off a new skill to one's parents. This is the sort of flawlessly conceived insight into a previously neglected corner of human existence that made 'The Greatest Discovery' and 'Rotten Peaches' such compelling compositions, and this song stands right in the ranks of those classics.

The tone turns distinctly darker for 'American Triangle', Elton and Bernie's account of the murder of Matthew Shepard (1976–1998). It's one of the most powerful songs the pair have ever composed, one where anger is expressed but also a sense of the larger tragedy at play. Wainwright's vocals act as an effective extension of Elton's, moving the events into a more ethereal realm as if the heavens themselves are bemoaning the tragedy at hand, while Leonard's organ and keyboard work provide little pulses of country warmth and electronic pressure that help to develop the song's tale of the pervasive hate that underlies the veneer of country hospitality, and the senselessness of robbing a man of his life because he's different.

The run from 'Look Ma, No Hands' to 'I Want Love' represents one of the best five consecutive songs available on any Elton album ever, each telling a different story in a different idiom, each perfectly suited to the words crafted by Bernie, and at its centre lies 'Original Sin'. Everything about this song is wonderful: Bernie's lyrics about a long-carried torch for a love from early days, the build of the song from acoustic guitar and bass, to the inclusion of little warm throbs from Leonard's keyboards, and rising to the fairytale romance arrival of Buckmaster's strings in the second verse, the grand sway of Elton's iconic chorus – it captures the exhilarating feeling of looking at the person you have loved for decades and feeling their presence.

At the risk of sounding repetitive, 'Birds' is also an unreasonably wonderful song. We start with a couple flashes of Chamberlain's infectious drum pattern before Elton enters with that good old Russell-esque slide from the minor to major third on the piano that lets us know we're about to go on a wild lyrical ride, and Bernie delivers in spades. His lyrics about growing older and yet still having so many questions about how life operates, while still having to posture one's way through life in order to appear as wise as one is expected to be at that point in life, is full of compelling images. What I love about this song is the subtle shift in how the rhythmic element is presented halfway through the song, as we move from the pure country barn dance instrumentation of the first half into this neat set of electronic beats that arrive with the second verse, which gives the song an entirely new sense, as if our hero has moved on to a new phase of life, which he understands about as little as he did the old one, but has to gamely push through all the same.

In a post-*Rocketman* world, it's almost impossible to think of 'I Want Love' as anything but the anthem of Elton's family during his youth, the cry from the soul of a father too pent up in his deportment to ever give vent to his needs. That is decidedly not what Bernie had in mind with these original lyrics, stemming from the end of his third marriage, which is far less a portrait of the psychological traumas of the greatest generation and their stoicism, and far more about being burned out on romantic love. It's one of Bernie's more villainous lyrics, on a par with 'Angeline' or 'Elderberry Wine', centring around a figure who takes what he wants physically and gives nothing in return but Elton casts it in the full aura of a high-flown love ballad, with the oscillating piano and descending bassline of the intro giving us flashes of The Beatles. It's a perfect bait and switch, and we feel a sense of pity for this individual that lasts until the chorus, when the rug is pulled from under us. The song ties you up in knots trying to figure out how you feel about it, with the music pulling in one direction and the lyrics another, and us in the middle, at sea as to what we think about it all, and that is precisely what great art is supposed to do.

'The Wasteland' is a down and dirty devil's blues piece that pays homage to Robert Johnson (1911–1938), the delta blues legend of the 1930s, who is on anyone's shortlist for founding figures of rock 'n roll, and who according to legend sold his soul to the Devil at a crossroads to gain his legendary guitar capabilities. Elton's pounding blues rhythm has more than a whiff of sulphur about it, with infernal backing vocals provided by Kudisan Kai and Tata Vega (*b*.1951), hellish trills from the legendary Billy Preston (1946–2006) on the organ, and wicked piano solo sections.

With 'Ballad of the Boy in the Red Shoes', Elton and Bernie deliver yet another triumph of musical storytelling. Bernie has said in interviews that the song is explicitly a tale of a dancer living with AIDS, facing the reality that he will never dance again. That is devastating on its own, but the lyrics have wider resonances, touching upon the more general process we'll all go through of being unable to do the things that give our lives meaning by the brute limitations of our physical selves. Returning to the more focused dancer storyline, however, what Bernie gives us is a heartbreaking contrast between our dancer, fighting to remember what it was like to dance on the stage to an audience, and the larger world, which for many years denied that AIDS was a problem worth solving, resulting in a great artist being robbed of his purpose not because the fight against the disease was impossible but rather because nobody could be bothered to take it up.

On a side note, there's much speculation about who 'Sigmund' is in this song, with people scouring the history of ballet for people named Sigmund who died of disease, others insisting, for some reason, that it refers to Sigmund Freud (1856–1939), and the majority claiming that it's another 'Alvin Tostig' situation. I'm inclined to believe the latter, that the name itself isn't so much significant as what it stands for: a stage name that brings with it all the memories of fame, art and meaning now long gone.

The last quarter of *Songs From the West Coast* is generally considered to be its weakest stretch despite the presence of the eventual single 'This Train Don't Stop There Anymore'. Here, weakest is a relative term, as what we have are songs that, on another album, would likely have been standouts. 'Love Her Like Me' is a fine song with decent, if not revolutionary, lyrics with solid instrumentation and melody lines that make for a pleasant experience that would have won the field on *Leather Jackets* but that here end up in the bottom of the heap by default. 'Mansfield', likewise, would doubtless get more credit as an intricate love ballad, with its gorgeous backing vocals in the chorus and weaving Buckmaster strings, if it didn't have 'Original Sin' standing right next to it, where everything that is good about 'Mansfield' is present but turned up one or two more notches.

'This Train Don't Stop There Anymore' brings *Songs From the West Coast* to a near perfect conclusion, with lyrics from Bernie that dig deeper into the issues explored in 'I Want Love', namely the narrowing of scope that comes with age. Miracles, love, months of fevered activity in the name of fame, all that doesn't really matter after a certain point – they are stations that one doesn't stop at anymore, either because you can't (your 'engine is breaking down') or because you've simply lost the will to invest what's left of your life in things that have proven hollow. There's a melancholy at the heart of the song – the image of the train of one's life passing by the eroding ghost towns of one's past pleasures is a haunting one for sure – but also a willingness to look at one's self cooly in the mirror without all pretence or self-delusion, that is courageous, a re-evaluating of priorities which Bernie leaves unresolved here, as old idols are broken down and the question arises, once one has ejected all that flotsam, what is left? Answering that question will be precisely the task Elton and Bernie set themselves in the albums of the 2000s and 2010s.

The Stats

Album/Single	US	UK	Australia	Canada
Songs From the West Coast	15	2	7	9
	G	2P	G	G
'I Want Love'/'The North Star' 'God Never Came There'		9	63	7
'This Train Doesn't Stop There Anymore'/ 'Did Anybody Sleep with Joan of Arc'		24		
'Original Sin'/'I'm Still Standing' (live)		39	54	

The Players

Elton John: lead vocals, acoustic piano and harmonium (6)
Patrick Leonard: Hammond B3 organ (2 and 4), organ (3), keyboards (4, 5 and 11) and Mellotron (10)
Stevie Wonder: clavinet (2) and harmonica (2)
Billy Preston: Hammond B3 organ (7, 8 and 10)
Davey Johnstone: guitars (1, 2 and 8), backing vocals (1 to 3, 7 and 9 to 12), electric guitar (3 and 7), acoustic guitar (9 and 11) and mandolin (9)
David Channing: acoustic guitar (3) and dobro (6)
Rusty Anderson: electric guitar (4 and 11), guitars (5, 6 and 10) and bouzouki (11)
Bruce Gaitsch: acoustic guitar (4 and 7)
Paul Bushnell: bass (1 to 12), backing vocals (1 to 3, 7 and 9 to 12)
Nigel Olsson: drums (1, 3 and 7 to 9) and backing vocals (1 to 3, 7 and 9 to 12)
Matt Chamberlain: drums (2, 4 to 6 and 10 to 12), percussion (6)
Jay Bellerose: percussion (1, 3, 5, 7 and 9)
Paul Buckmaster: horn arrangements and conductor (1), string arrangements and conductor (5, 9, 11 and 12)
Rufus Wainwright: harmony vocals (4)
Kudisan Kai: backing vocals (7, 8 and 12)
Tata Vega: backing vocals (8)
Gary Barlow: backing vocals (12)

The Tracks

1. 'The Emperor's New Clothes' (John, Taupin) (4.28)
2. 'Dark Diamond' (John, Taupin) (4.26)
3. 'Look Ma, No Hands' (John, Taupin) (4.22)
4. 'American Triangle' (John, Taupin) (4.49)
5. 'Original Sin' (John, Taupin) (4.49)
6. 'Birds' (John, Taupin) (3.51)
7. 'I Want Love' (John, Taupin) (4.35)
8. 'The Wasteland' (John, Taupin) (4.21)
9. 'Ballad of the Boy in the Red Shoes' (John, Taupin) (4.52)
10. 'Love Her Like Me' (John, Taupin) (3.58)
11. 'Mansfield' (John, Taupin) (4.56)
12. 'This Train Don't Stop There Anymore' (John, Taupin) (4.39)

Musician's Corner: 'American Triangle'

Not since 'Ticking' (1974) have we seen an Elton song delving into material as disturbing as the events portrayed in 'American Triangle', which takes as its subject the torturing of Matthew Shepard by Aaron McKinney and Russell Henderson on 6 October 1998. The subject is doubly charged for Elton and Bernie, as they're attempting to reconcile their lifelong fascination with rural America with the cold fact of violent homophobia that has become increasingly present there.

Bernie's solution is to follow the story not from the point of view of Shepard, but from that of McKinney and Henderson, to wrestle with the issue of how a region of such natural majesty could create such people, and ultimately result in 'two lives ruined, one life spent'. The weight of history, the fear of difference, the anger from ignorance, the bleak prospect of an aimless future, all combine to twist the minds of two young men.

While Bernie tried to understand the Shepard tragedy, Elton was left with the even more difficult task of setting the story musically. He could have taken the route of 'Ticking' and cleverly employed a classical musical device to signal his main characters' deteriorating sense of self. He could have gone in the direction of 'Ego' and set the entire song in the most unstable musical settings possible to convey the fundamental disconnect between the two killers and the reality of Shepard as a person. That, however, would have been to convey that McKinney and Henderson were unique manifestations of a particular type of evil, unhinged and morally bankrupt, when the real tragedy of Wyoming was that McKinney and Henderson were two individuals, like many others in their community, with the hate that they had been taught lingering in their hearts, waiting for an excuse to drive their actions.

The story's tragic triangle has been repeated hundreds of times to varying degrees throughout the US, and Elton's musical setting highlights this. He isn't trying to dazzle us with journeys to strange keys or unusual chord progressions. He's not tapping into medieval modes. The tragedy of this story is its pervasiveness, its normalcy, and Elton's conveying that in motions that are familiar and comfortable – chords moving by ultra-regular fifths and fourths, only the slightest of deviations from the notes given in the key signature. Even the appearance of G minor that we have come to expect at some point or another in Elton's more devastating songs is nowhere in evidence. It was, I think, the smartest thing Elton could have done with the music, compelling us to grapple with the fact that two unexceptional youths from the American heartland were capable of such a thing, and that their story is an all too common one that we allow to continue whenever we simply cast it in the guise of extraordinary evil and then walk away.

Chapter 35

Peachtree Road

Recorded: January 2004
Released: 9 November 2004
Producer: Elton John

The Story

In and around the composition of the music for his next stage project, *Billy Elliot*, Elton conceived the idea of a new studio album centred around American music, and particularly that of the South. This was to be the studio album that he'd have the most intimate hand in, acting as sole producer for the first time in thirty-five years of recording albums, a move he felt comfortable to take as, fundamentally, the stripped-down sensibilities that had made *Songs From the West Coast* such a commercial success would be carried over to what would become *Peachtree Road* (the name refers to the street where Elton's Atlanta residence is located).

While critics generally received the album well, sales were relatively poor, particularly in the UK, where the #2 posting achieved by *From the West Coast* tumbled to #21, and its double platinum status to a 'mere' gold, with some fans expressing disappointment that the album seemed more like a series of exercises in different strictly confined genre forms (gospel, blues, jazz and country) instead of the free fusion of traditions that had marked Elton's most revered output in the past. The singles underperformed compared to Elton's usual standards and his next studio album, *The Captain and the Kid*, would see his label make the decision to release no singles whatsoever.

Commercially the nadir of his twenty-first century output, this love song to the music of the US was nonetheless a personally satisfying experience, nestled in among the enjoyment he received from writing what would become his smash hit of 2005, the *Billy Elliot* musical. It has become, for a large segment of the Elton community, a favourite album that provides a direct conduit to the music that was formative for Elton, to be experienced both for the quality of its songs, and for the story it tells about how the mind that made pieces as diverse as 'Your Song', 'Tonight' and 'Big Dipper' came to be.

The Songs

'Weight of the World' announces a potential theme for the album to come: the joy and sorrow of a life slowed down and heading into its final third. We'll discuss how Elton conjures the sense of domestic contentment and gratitude but here I'll mention that this song, which purred from speakers a full decade after 'Simple Life' roared Elton's intention to live again, completes the story he began there. Here, Elton has found the simple life, of games of cards and sights of rainy days through living room windows, and that it suffuses him with a sense of peace every bit as fulfilling as he'd imagined it would be.

We begin our journey into American genres with 'Porch Swing in Tupelo', which has country and gospel elements woven into it, with each tradition enforcing the other, and fed through Elton's unique sense of musical motion to create a song that is equal parts tribute to the spirit of Elvis (who was born in Tupelo), and a general salute to the nothing-changing spirit of the American South, which for the moment Elton and Bernie are looking at as romantically as ever they did in 1970. As uncomfortable as that rosy conception might have been from the point of view of the sensibilities of 2004, it was largely overlooked in the joyous spirit of Elton's rendition of the song, with a melody that conveys the carefree joy of rocking back and forth on a porch swing on a warm day with memories of The King dense in the air. The gospel backing vocals and steely dobro guitar ping off Elton's exuberant vocals and all in all it's the easiest thing to put away one's knowledge of history and current politics for a while, and swing with Elton and Bernie in a place where they're unabashedly happy.

Some people point to *Peachtree* as Bernie's spiritual album. There's a good reason for this, namely Bernie's relationship with Heather Kidd, who became his fourth and current wife in 2004. A deeply Christian individual, Kidd was Bernie's conduit into a more active profession of Christianity, and particularly Presbyterianism, and ever since Bernie's statements on religion have tended to abandon the analytical complexity of, say, 'If There's a God in Heaven (What's He Waiting For?)' in favour of a more generally spiritual tone.

'Answer in the Sky' exudes a secular spiritualism, centred on wonder at the vastness of the universe, and faith in ourselves to remake our lives through contemplation of the larger existence we find ourselves in. The setting of the song is upbeat, recalling 'Philadelphia Freedom' in its opening strings, and leaning into soul and gospel elements for its sense of cosmic heft, while retaining a melody and scale that wouldn't have been out of place in Elton's work from the 1990s.

With 'Turn the Lights Out When You Leave' we head straight into genre alley, a run of half a dozen songs that you either love, as examples of Elton exploring different musical forms, or decry, as compositional exercises that don't have enough of Elton's sensibilities at their centre. 'Lights' is a straight up slow country ballad representing more the popular country music of the 1980s than the more popular trends of country rock that had emerged from the 1990s, and which will surface later in the album. Elton and Bernie both do immaculate work producing a song that wouldn't sound out of place in the mouths of Kenny Rogers (*b.*1938) and Dolly Parton (*b.*1946). Babylon has encapsulated that directive with a perfect backing orchestral arrangement that slides along, not in too much of a hurry to get anywhere. It's a great country song that doesn't sound much like an Elton song, and even Bernie is playing it as straight as possible, omitting the bits of idiosyncratic phrasing and theme that made *Tumbleweed Connection* so engaging.

'My Elusive Drug' brings us to the blues club, in which Elton gives a *tour-de-force* vocal performance and like previous songs that were about giving Elton moments to show what his voice can do ('It Ain't Gonna Be Easy' and 'Cold'), the lyrics here take a back seat. Bernie's lyrics, with its hyper-simplified lines are tailor made for the blues form, and Elton leans hard into that aesthetic here, to the point of nearly effacing himself as a strong compositional voice in the drive to do tribute to the tradition he loved. The words have some nice Elton-specific references, particularly reading like a love song to Furnish and Kidd, and how their love has swept away the need for any of the other things that counted as pleasures in the old days of excess. However, if you came for Bernie's esoteric word and theme choices, and Elton's genre-defying setting of those, you'll likely be among those who find this section of the album frustrating.

One of the most interesting songs on *Peachtree*, 'They Call Her the Cat' is a number that's all too easy to write off as a piece of by the numbers country rock. Listen closely and what you'll find are lyrics a good twenty years ahead of their time, centring on a trans woman heroine whose transformation from boy to woman is celebrated, as is her newfound femininity. Instead of agonising over issues of identity and politics, the song simply asserts, 'Hey, she was a man, now she's a woman, and she's awesome, let's rock!', a position of easy celebration that even the most progressive parts of the world are just catching up to now, and which Elton slides subversively into a rockabilly music form so easily that most don't even know it's happened.

'Freaks in Love' is the soul number on *Peachtree*, and between the relentlessly uninteresting rhythm, the generic lyrics and the blocky melody that clings too close to soul conventions to provide any surprises, there's not much to be said here for someone who isn't entering as a great connoisseur of the genre. Following quick on its heels is 'All That I'm Allowed (I'm Thankful)', which is the second track on the album that is ear-marked as knee-high to a Christian contemporary song. Certainly, the repetitions of 'I'm thankful' draw from that tradition of stadium Christianity, with thousands tearfully waving their hands in the air while expressing their gratitude to Jesus in a repeated, emotionally charged phrase. I think this is another case of a song about broad themes that happens to have Christian symbology in it rather than a Christian song that happens to have some wider applicability: life is long, and will be full of frustrations, but even with all that, there's something essential at the core of being alive which is remarkable and worth stopping to appreciate from time to time. It's a doubly sweet song as a moment of communication between Elton and the people who had showed up to his concerts, bought his albums and in many other ways shown their support throughout the good and bad times.

'I Stop and I Breathe' pulls from a few different areas, with stripes of blues and soul alternately making their appearance in support of Bernie's lyrics, which is the third love ballad (of four) on the album and comes out somewhere in the middle of the pile, more interesting structurally than 'Freaks in Love' but without quite the same degree of vocal intensity or character shading as 'My Elusive Drug'.

One of my favourite songs from 2000s Elton makes its way around the corner next, to the sound of piano, space-age synths and pizzing strings. 'Too Many Tears' has a wonderful circular motion in the melody that is enhanced by the strings arranged by Babylon, and poignant lyrics by Bernie that explore some of the best and worst moments of the twentieth century, centring around the figures and legacies of John F. Kennedy (1917–1963) and Martin Luther King Jr (1929–1968), urging us to push past the world sorrow that threatens to engulf us, be inspired by their example, and mindful of the beauty that is all around us, as we live and build dreams of our own on the foundations of those conceived by the people we have lost along the way. We get the classic Elton/Pachelbel progression of I-iii-vi-V-IV-I in the chorus, and the second verse has Dudgeon-esque additions to the instrumentation that up the ante in the richness of the sound textures as we progress through the song, driven forward by Elton's infectious melody. It's a perfect song for that moment when you've made it through a tragedy and are ready to start appreciating the world again.

In my head, 'It's Getting Dark in Here' continues the story that started in 'Weight of the World'. Time has moved on and that first glow of retirement has passed, bringing with it the irreversible constriction of activity that more extreme old age brings with it. There's no more running from the end, friends are fewer, eternal salvation isn't a thing that bears close scrutiny, and everywhere you look, the sun is slowly setting. Unlike on the rest of this album, where moments of tragedy are ultimately overcome by thoughts of the wider context of life, here there's no such redemption. You get old, things get darker and you're gone. Elton conveys the grim spirit of the lyrics through chord inversions that allow the bassline to descend while the chords themselves wander further from their tonal home. It's such an intensely executed song that I sometimes skip it not because I don't like it but because it's too sad to contemplate Elton experiencing the diminutions of life quality outlined in the song.

Elton couldn't have ended *Peachtree* with 'It's Getting Dark in Here', as that would have been a downer to inflict on his fans as the last words they'd hear from him potentially for another three years (though, in fact, *The Captain and the Kid* would emerge in two). So, as a concluding piece we get the album's fourth love song, 'I Can't Keep this From You', which again dives into soul to similar effect as in 'Freaks in Love' (bland verse percussion and genre-encrusted backing vocals), only with lyrics even less memorable from Bernie but a much more engaging and fuller chorus, and some fun flaming guitar elements that come from out of nowhere to add some spice to the formula. It's an appropriate ending to *Peachtree*, symbolic of its strengths and weaknesses, bringing to a close a fascinating outlier in the Elton canon, and as with many such albums throughout his career, a course correction wouldn't be long in coming.

The Stats

Album/Single	US	UK	Australia	Canada
Peachtree Road	17	21	44	
		G	G	
'All That I'm Allowed'/'Answer in the Sky' 'They Call Her the Cat'		20		
'Turn the Lights Out When You Leave'/'How's Tomorrow' 'Peter's Song'		32		
'Electricity'/'Indian Sunset'		4		

The Players

Elton John: lead vocals, acoustic piano, backing vocals (1, 3, 4, 6, 7, 8, 10 and 12) and Rhodes piano (10)

Guy Babylon: programming, orchestral arrangements (1 to 5 and 7 to 12), Hammond organ (2 to 9, 11 and 12) and Rhodes piano (6 to 9 and 11)

Davey Johnstone: electric guitar, acoustic guitar (1 to 4, 7, 8, 9, 11 and 12), dobro (1, 2, 6 and 10), backing vocals (1, 5 and 10), baritone guitar (3 and 6), slide guitar (3, 5 and 10), Leslie guitar (5), sitar (8) and mandolin (10)

John Jorgenson: pedal steel guitar (4)

Bob Birch: bass, backing vocals (1, 5 and 10)

Nigel Olsson: drums, backing vocals (1, 5, 10 and 11)

John Mahon: percussion, backing vocals (1, 5 and 10) and programming (9 and 11)

Larry Klimas: baritone saxophone (6)

Walter Parazaider: tenor saxophone (6)

James Pankow: trombone (6) and horn arrangements (6)

Lee Loughnane: trumpet (6)

Martin Tillman: electric cello (10)

The Tracks

1. 'Weight of the World' (John, Taupin) (3.58)
2. 'Porch Swing in Tupelo' (John, Taupin) (4.38)
3. 'Answer in the Sky' (John, Taupin) (4.03)
4. 'Turn the Lights Out When You Leave' (John, Taupin) (5.02)
5. 'My Elusive Drug' (John, Taupin) (4.12)
6. 'They Call Her the Cat' (John, Taupin) (4.27)
7. 'Freaks in Love' (John, Taupin) (4.32)
8. 'All That I'm Allowed' (John, Taupin) (4.52)
9. 'I Stop and I Breathe' (John, Taupin) (3.39)
10. 'Too Many Tears' (John, Taupin) (4.14)
11. 'It's Getting Dark in Here' (John, Taupin) (3.50)
12. 'I Can't Keep this From You' (John, Taupin) (4.34)

Musician's Corner: 'Weight of the World'

In 2000, Elton's record-smashing run of thirty consecutive years of Top 40 hits came to an end, and the following year saw the conclusion of his thirty-one-year run of Hot 100 hits, and while Elton's fans lamented the end of the streak, Elton described it as a relief. The compulsion to keep the record going, to keep crafting pop hits, exerted a pressure to conform to current pop standards that increasingly stood at cross purposes to his growth as a composer, and to some degree, as a human being.

By 2004, many weights had been lifted from Elton's shoulders. His relationship with Furnish had turned the decade mark, and they were one year away from their civil partnership. The spectres of drug addiction and food disorders had long since been put to rest. His Las Vegas residency, *The Red Piano*, started in February of that year, and would last for 5 more years, the original 75 shows eventually expanding to 247 due to its unprecedented success. Finally, the lack of pressure to constantly produce commercial singles allowed Elton and Bernie to follow once again the advice they had received in 1968: to make the music they wanted to make.

'Weight of the World' seems like the pair's grand expression of the gratitude they have found in a life of relative tranquillity but, of course, things are never that simple in an Elton-Bernie song. The piece begins with the sound of rain striking a roof, evoking the feeling of a rainy morning spent happily at home. Over this rainfall Elton adds a steady thrum of piano chords that are joined by strings, and the entire introduction lets us know, just in the choice of timbres introduced to our ears, that we are about to pull the curtain back on a different Elton than that we've known heretofore. We've talked about Elton's use of an unchanging bass note beneath shifting chords on several occasions, and just what that static grounding note means in each case is largely determined by what Elton's trying to do with the song. Here, it allows the song to move to new chords while still retaining that sense of the domestic bliss. Digging deeper into the verses, we can see a neat little detail – each five line verse only features a minor chord in the third line, and each time before the arrival of the chorus, that third line is the one that features a sentiment of uncertainty. After the chorus, however, which is the formal statement of the sheer relief of no longer having to be a troubled musical titan, those third lines change their flavour – still accompanied by a minor chord, but now with more complicated thoughts about what life can still offer to failing senses but still youthful minds.

That chorus is worth a look all its own. It begins in the relative minor key of E minor but intriguing transitions happen with the arrival of the most psychologically fraught lines – 'Excuse me if I take some comfort in that' has so much meaning to it – the idea of feeling guilty about slowing down, of letting others down, is a feeling familiar to anyone who has based their lives on their work and the people dependent on that work, and Elton highlights that difficult sentiment with a transition to a secondary dominant chord, and then complicates the following statement, so definitive on the page, but so resistant to easy conclusions in the music, 'Happy today, happy to play', by resisting the resolution back to the dominant chord of D and instead landing on the distant and unsettling chord of C minor. It's a moment of high tension, where for an instant we are wondering, 'Wait, is he happy with the weight of the world off his back, or is that just something he's telling himself, and this is the moment when he realises he's not so sure?'

In the end, I think that the song is supposed to be a genuine reflection of gratitude about a happier life but the addition of those moments of musical tension makes the world of difference between a run of the mill song about how nice it is to slow down for a while, and a human story about mixed emotions at the approach of one's autumn years.

Chapter 36

Billy Elliott

Original Cast Recording

Recorded: 2005
Released: 10 January 2006
Producers: Nick Gilpin and Martin Koch

The Story

I f ever an artist and a story were meant for each other, it was Elton and *Billy Elliot*. Attending a preview screening of the *Billy Eliott* film, Elton immediately saw the parallels of a young boy struggling to assert himself creatively in an atmosphere of stoic manly ideals with his own youth: growing up with a father who didn't understand his love of rock 'n roll in conservative Pinner. Unlike *Aida*, the story of which didn't have much resonance either with Elton's life or the modern world generally, *Billy Elliot* is set in the world of the mid-1980s coal miners' strike in Britain that dragged on for a year in the face of strong opposition from Prime Minister Margaret 'Maggie' Thatcher (1925–2013), which meant an entirely different set of compositional possibilities for Elton, allowing him to dig not only into his own experiences as an artist to portray Billy's personal world but into the resonant sounds and rhythms of the time to bring the struggle between labour and government to life.

Soon after viewing the film and realising its potential for the stage, Elton approached its writer, Lee Hall (*b*.1966), about producing a musical version of his screenplay, and by 2005 that musical was on the stage and in 2009 tied the Broadway production record set by *The Producers* by gaining fifteen Tony Award nominations in a single year (a record since broken by *Hamilton*), winning in the categories of best musical and best book for a musical, best performance by a leading actor, best performance by a featured actor, best choreography, best scenic design, best orchestrations and several others besides. The production was a smash hit, running on Broadway for 4 years with over 1,300 performances, proving that Elton could succeed with a contemporary theme outside of the protective radius of Disney.

Generally, Elton's music sticks close to the conventions of Broadway musical theatre and to the traditions of the music associated with organised labour in the twentieth century, with flashes of Elton's style emerging in the climatic solo 'Electricity' and in the high camp of the drag celebration 'Expressing Yourself' and gloriously unhinged irreverence of 'Merry Christmas Maggie Thatcher'. Some hypothesise that by reverently pushing his own personality to the background in order to allow the focus to rest on the drama and dance elements of the piece, Elton cost himself the Tony Award for best original score but then this has been Elton's way since the earliest days at the château, when he gave his band complete freedom to craft their parts according to their own artistic instincts. *Billy Elliot* is, first and foremost, a musical about dance, and Elton's instinct to make the music engaging but not distracting was absolutely the right one and a major part of the musical's ultimate success.

The Songs

The overriding challenge of *Billy Elliot* was striking a coherent balance between the two worlds of the performing arts and the struggles of the coal miners in 1984. The former is mostly represented in the musical through the location of the children's dance studio run by the jaded Mrs Wilkinson, where the ole razz-matazz is alive and well, and the latter through the union hall and coal pit. Between these two pillars is the figure of Billy himself, who must carve out his own world and identity wherever he can in the spaces left him: his home, the dance academy and his friend's house. Each of these locations has its own musical genres, which allows us as an audience to compartmentalise in our heads the different tonal realms competing for attention within the musical.

The Union Songs

The musical material here is treated the most reverently by Elton, through big choral numbers ('The Stars Look Down' and 'Once We Were Kings') with simple melodies characteristic of the labour music of the twentieth century, featuring just enough tantalising chord shifts to keep them from being too plodding. 'Deep in the Ground', meanwhile, is a representation of the union folk tradition, with its focus on cyclic melody elements for a lone voice with light choral accompaniment. These all stick close to their respective traditions, with the big break-out in form coming with 'Solidarity', which also represents the only time that, musically and physically, the two main spaces of the play bleed into each other. Interwoven among the goings-on of a typical group dance lesson is a confrontation between the police, gloating that they are receiving increased pay for their overtime while the workers are starving, and the workers, proud in their solidarity and moral stance. This is a tall order, musically speaking, to wend back and forth between the heretofore comic dance hall material, and the aggressive back and forth between the police and workers, which Elton pulls off by casting the former in a more regimented tone, and setting the latter in a more rock idiom, which allows rhythm to more easily link these two musical worlds. It works like a charm, and as a result, the choreographer was able to hang one of the musical's visual standout moments on top of Elton's sonic architecture, creating an interwoven texture as the movements of the police, workers and dance students start cutting across and blending into each other.

The Dance Hall Songs

Both 'Shine' and 'Born to Boogie' centre on the experience of being a dance student starting out and finding your way, with 'Shine' an essentially comic number that leans into *A Chorus Line* style tropes of giving 'em that ole style, Broadway razzle dazzle, the humour coming from the fact that this is a girl's dance school in coal miner country and, therefore, all the students are various degrees of hopeless at what they're doing, which Mrs Wilkinson must push through as best she can with her weary show must go on spirit. Elton's having a grand time recapitulating the musical elements of classic Broadway, though as the musical's first big dance number it goes on for *a while*, which is fine in person, but on CD is a tougher journey to see through to its end. 'Born to Boogie' is also a number with comic elements but delves into finding one's personal joy in dance, musically tapping into the style of early Elvis dance numbers, with the chorus utilising the phrasing and rhythm of Elvis's '(Let Me Be Your) Teddy Bear'. Through both pieces, we get a sense of the dance studio as a sanctuary where, no matter what is happening outside, some measure of joy can be had, even if just for an hour.

The Personal Numbers

The songs that are not constrained to either of the two main locations of the musical are those that focus on more strictly personal conflicts and in which Elton is free to place his own imprint on the material at hand. The first of these is 'Grandma's Song', which is the 'Why is this song in this musical?' song. Every musical has one of these, often to ensure that each main member of the cast gets the spotlight musically, and this one allows the grandmother to have a number, talking of her deceased husband, who was horrible to her except for the nights where they'd get drunk and dance. Sure, the song mentions dance, but in a musical trying to hold within its circumference the themes of personal growth, dance, union policies and 1980s politics, reminiscing about an earlier time, which is never mentioned again, however nice the song is, mostly feels in the way.

Another song that might be considered in that vein is 'Expressing Yourself', in which Billy's gay friend encourages him to cast reservations to the wind, put on some women's clothes and enjoy whatever makes him happy. Until this point, the musical hasn't been about being comfortable in one's gay or drag persona but this is such a joyfully bananas number that it's hard to resent having one more theme added onto the pile. Billy and his friend are having such a grand time trying on outfits, dancing and eventually being joined by massive anthropomorphic dancing articles of clothing, that they sweep all reservations before them. Elton introduces the piece with a large Liberace piano climb before heading into a classic jazz pastiche that spares no trick in making the camp of the music fit that of the words and action. Both this song, and 'Merry Christmas Maggie Thatcher', represent the comic high watermarks of the musical material, where the words, onstage realisation and musical setting are all working seamlessly to create an indelible theatre experience.

Emotionally, there are four centrepieces distributed throughout the play to communicate Billy's evolving sense of self: 'The Letter', which lets us know the weight of loneliness Billy has experienced up to now, 'Angry Dance', the only words of which are screams of frustration as Billy works his way through the fury of not being able to do the thing that gives him the most satisfaction in life, the imagined ballet dance with his older self, set to the music of Tchaikovsky and 'Electricity', his culminating statement of what dance means to him. 'The Letter' is a tearjerker, a sweet song in which the letter that Billy's mother, who died when she was young, left behind for him is read aloud by Billy and his dance teacher. Elton's treatment reminds me a bit of 'Goodbye' on *Madman Across the Water*, a delicate and tragic little melody that pierces right to the heart. 'Electricity', meanwhile, was the big single to come from the play, which was eventually included on the 2005 rerelease of *Peachtree Road* in an attempt to boost the album's disappointing sales by hitching it to the runaway success of *Billy Elliot*. This is definitely the most Elton-sounding piece on the soundtrack, complete with descending basslines derived from chord inversions, use of parallel minor chords, shifts into tonal regions not contained in the original key signature (this one's really cool – the key of the original verse shifts to its parallel minor for the bridge and then shifts into the relative major of that parallel minor for the chorus), providing structures and movements that are undeniably flowing from the pen of Elton. When released as a single, 'Electricity' went to #4 in the UK, Elton's first time in the Top 10 with an original song since 'I Want Love' went to #9 in 2001, and his last time until 'Cold Heart' went to #1 in 2021.

The Stats

Album/Single	US	UK	Australia	Canada
Billy Elliot: The Original Cast Recording				
'Electricity'/'Indian Sunset'		4		

The Players

Craig Armstrong: vocals
Daniel Coll: vocals
Erica Ann Deakin: vocals
Alex Delamere: vocals
Damien Delaney: vocals
Steve Elias: vocals
Susan Fay: vocals
Alan Forrester: vocals
Trevor Fox: vocals
Chris Hornby: vocals
Isaac James: vocals
Gillian Kirkpatrick: vocals

Chris Lennon: vocals
David Massey: vocals
Michelle McAvoy: vocals
Karl Morgan: vocals
Daniel Page: vocals
Steve Paget: vocals
Lee Proud: vocals
Stephanie Putson: vocals
Mike Scott: vocals
Phil Snowden: vocals
Tessa Worsley: vocals
Ralph Salmins: drums
Steve Pearce: bass
David Hartley: piano
Adam Goldsmith: guitar
Philip Bateman: keyboards
Jeremy Holland-Smith: keyboards
Stephen Henderson: percussion
Martin Koch: conductor

The Tracks

1. 'The Stars Look Down' (John, Hall) (7.32)
2. 'Shine' (John, Hall) (6.07)
3. 'Grandma's Song' (John, Hall) (4.40)
4. 'Solidarity' (John, Hall) (8.50)
5. 'Expressing Yourself' (John, Hall) (5.14)
6. 'The Letter' (John, Hall) (3.48)
7. 'Born to Boogie' (John, Hall) (4.26)
8. 'Angry Dance' (John, Hall) (3.50)
9. 'Merry Christmas Maggie Thatcher' (John, Hall) (3.27)
10. 'Deep Into the Ground' (John, Hall) (3.36)
11. 'He Could Be a Star' (John, Hall) (4.51)
12. 'Electricity' (John, Hall) (5.54)
13. 'Once We Were Kings' (John, Hall) (4.15)
14. 'The Letter – Reprise' (John, Hall) (2.53)
15. 'Finale' (John, Hall) (5.35)

Bonus CD (performed by Elton John):
1. 'The Letter' (John, Hall) (2.32)
2. 'Merry Christmas Maggie Thatcher' (John, Hall) (3.36)
3. 'Electricity' (John, Hall) (3.31)

Musician's Corner: 'Merry Christmas Maggie Thatcher'

Elton's Christmas songs split evenly down the middle, between those you play at festive parties for mixed company and those you play for your actual friends. The former include 'Step into Christmas' (1973) and 'Merry Christmas' (with Ed Sheeran (*b*.1991), 2021), the latter the off-kilter celebration of yuletide intoxication, 'Ho Ho Ho Who'd Be a Turkey at Christmas?' (1973), and this song, a working-class two fingers to the austerity measures of Thatcher's Britain that is structured musically as a straight-forward popular Christmas song.

Elton's no stranger to using energetic music forms to set off dark lyrics ('I Think I'm Going to Kill Myself' and 'And the House Fell Down') but the idea of using a Christmas song as the setting for an expression of working class frustration with Tory policies is an inspired choice, and Elton starts laying it on thick from the start, with jaunty sleigh bells followed by skipping piano chords that all suggest traditional Christmas merriment. That atmosphere is enhanced by Elton's chord choice in what follows – right away we get a shift from a major chord, C, to its relative minor, Am, which is a popular trope in post-Mariah Christmas music ('All I Want for Christmas is You' (1994) gets a lot of its distinctive sound from major-minor transitions). Everything continues to be played entirely straight, with strong traditional descent by fifths until the giveaway line 'Oh it's blood Maggie Thatcher and Michael Heseltine' at which point the gloves are off and we launch into a chorus in which we are all to give thanks for this Christmas Day because it's one day closer to when Thatcher will be dead.

Musically, the chorus is played entirely straight, with some borrowing from the parallel modality of C minor, which lends some extra musical interest but is entirely within the rules of what a modern Christmas song is expected to do. The icing on the cake, in which the facade of pop conventionality at last drops, is the closing material, which is set to the melody of the folk classic 'My Darling Clementine' and features the lyrics 'Oh my darling, oh my darling, oh my darling Heseltine/You're a tosser, you're a tosser/And you're just a Tory swine', which is, lyrically, the end of the song, the point at which all pretence to Christmas radio norms is dropped and we tumble straight into the pub, where the only thing you can do to fight against the immensity of the system aligned against you is to get drunk and lob musico-lyrical grenades at the architects of that system.

Chapter 37

Lestat

Never Released

The Story

Why, of all things, did Elton and Bernie team up to produce a musical based on the vampire novels of Anne Rice (1941–2021)? Well, the answer to that question is corporate rivalry. Warner Brothers was sick of Disney scoring massive Broadway successes adapting its intellectual properties for the stage and wanted in on the action. They figured that, with a diverse catalogue extending back decades, they should easily be able to mine it for material to generate hit musicals for years to come and settled on *Interview with a Vampire* as their first choice for adaptation, with *Batman* next if it did well. Once the material was decided on, the next question was, who will create it? The logical answer was to use as much of the team responsible for Disney's successes as possible, bringing in Elton to do the music, Linda Woolverton to write the book and Robert Jess Roth to direct it. One departure from the old team, however, was the utilisation of Bernie as lyricist instead of Tim Rice, a solid decision given the more sombre nature of the material in question.

The original announcement of the deal with Elton was made in 2003, with its pre-Broadway premiere in 2005 and its Broadway premiere following on 25 March 2006, with the show closing on 28 May 2006, after a mere thirty-nine performances and thirty-three previews (though even this disaster was better than Elton's next musical, *Tammy Faye*, which closed after just twenty-nine regular performances in 2024). A cast recording was made but never released due to the swift demise of the play, so our only clue to what this show was like is confined to Elton's demo recordings of the song's material, leaked tracks from the cast album, and a few bootleg audience recordings from the early shows.

So, what happened? In the aftermath of the show's collapse fingers were pointed but ultimately the explanation has fallen into two camps: first, that this was the third in a string of vampire based musicals to hit Broadway, coming after *Dance of the Vampires* and *Dracula* and enthusiasm for the topic was low among critics, translating to bad reviews and low attendance. Second, that the material itself had severe restrictions placed on it, in particular the requirement that it cover multiple novels' worth of material, which set up Elton and Bernie to fail. Meanwhile, the overriding directive of the production was to take its source material seriously, centring on the turmoil vampires face, meaning no vampires on stage singing rock 'n roll and no *Buffy* style campness. This limited the range of material at the duo's disposal, shifting it towards relentlessly sombre hues.

Elton has gone on to state that *Lestat* is one of the finest things he and Bernie ever did, a challenge that pushed him to the limits of his musical invention. A survey of the available recordings compels us to agree that our favourite duo laid out a sumptuous feast for us here, which ranks as high as anything they've done together but which never had the opportunity to make it to a larger public audience that might have better appreciated its sepulchral atmosphere and complicated compositional forms.

The Songs

As the cast recording was never released and the structure of the musical changed significantly as it moved from San Francisco to Broadway, it's difficult to talk about the definitive form of *Lestat* musically but some general points can be garnered from Elton's demos and leaked performances, which can be seen in the seven songs that have percolated through as underground fan favourites over the last decade and a half.

Not surprisingly, the character of Claudia, the young orphan who Lestat turns into a vampire, and who turns out to be more violent than any adult vamp, while frustratingly caught in an eternal childhood, steals the show whenever she shows up, and her two solos, 'I Want More' and 'I'll Never Have That Chance' are a large part of the general opinion that the second act, which figures her prominently, is generally the superior one. 'I Want More' is set to an almost country gallop and gives Claudia a chance to vocally blow out the rafters while singing of her unquenchable thirst for blood, to the horror of Lestat and Louis, who are effectively her parents. The flip side of her personality is presented in the haunting 'I'll Never Have That Chance', which is filled with the things she will never get to experience because she'll never be an adult, like having a child or knowing romantic love, regrets which Elton perfectly sets atop an ascending and receding melody. The song is doubly poignant with the knowledge that it's Bernie behind the words, whose lyrics have so often captured the simplicity of youth, now confronting what an eternal childhood would encompass. Being young forever is as tragic as leaving childhood behind, with the conclusion being that life is impossible to win.

Vampires and superheroes have long been a proxy through which we tell stories of people on the outskirts of acceptable society, and as such have been taken up as iconic characters by marginalised people, and particularly the LGBTQ+ community, from the trans vampire hero of *Let the Right One In* to the heroic X-Men, who will never be accepted but won't let that stop them trying to save the world that fears them. Anne Rice makes the connection between the prejudices faced by vampires, who can't help being who they are and have to form found families to stop them going mad, and the gay community, who in the 1990s were caught in a similar predicament and in a couple of songs Elton gives himself license to write the type of songs that, with a few exceptions, he shied away from on his regular studio albums. 'Nothing

Here' was I believe in the San Francisco production but not the Broadway one (do drop me a note if I have it wrong!) and is a song urging Lestat to leave the 'narrow minds' of his home village and plot a course for Paris, where people have a broader understanding and sense of what love is. Like much of the material in act one, it's heavy on piano, strings and atmospherics, which is powerful and the dual meaning speaks not only to those who have left small towns to experience something more but particularly to gay people who have headed to the city to escape the prejudice of their country neighbours. More explicit still is 'Right Before My Eyes', which I understand wasn't in the San Francisco show but was in the Broadway one, and which is just a full-on gay love ballad that happens to have vampires in it. Swap out a couple of lines about death and taking, and you've got something that could have been on *West Coast* or, more likely, *Crazy Wonderful Night*, which served the secondary purpose in the musical of giving the first act something less sepulchral for the ear to dwell on.

'To Kill Your Kind' is a great Oingo Boingo type number from the second act, with a chorus reminiscent of Danny Elfman's (*b*.1953) 'Sucker for Mystery', driven by rhythmic vocals with ear-catching instrumentation underneath. It's completely unlike anything else in *Lestat*, and if you're going to pull in a more pop-oriented ethos for a song in a musical about vampires, Oingo Boingo is definitely the place to look to for reference, a type of music that Elton hadn't composed much before but which he slides effortlessly into here. Meanwhile, 'Crimson Kiss' is a number from the first act's scene stealer, Lestat's mother, Gabrielle, whose 'Make Me As You Are', an impassioned plea to be changed into a vampire so that she won't disappear from Earth, was already great, but which is easily topped by this song. In it, she bids her son and sire farewell as she sets out to see the wider world, rather than remain with Lestat in his endless quest to get to the bottom of the origins of the vampire race. While Bernie is up to some of his more lamentable habits here, Elton's sweeping melody conveys the full rush of both Gabrielle's excitement at striking out on a new path and her anguish at having to leave her son, whom she is closer to now than she has ever been.

Some Possible Tracks

1. 'Theme from Lestat' (John)
2. 'Right Before My Eyes' (John, Taupin)
3. 'From the Dead' (John, Taupin)
4. 'Nothing Here' (John, Taupin)
5. 'In Paris' (John, Taupin)
6. 'The Thirst' (John, Taupin)
7. 'Make Me As You Are' (John, Taupin)
8. 'To Live Like This' (John, Taupin)

9. 'The Origin of the Species' (John, Taupin)
10. 'The Crimson Kiss' (John, Taupin)
11. 'Instrumental Interlude' (John, Taupin)
12. 'Welcome to the New World' (John, Taupin)
13. 'Embrace It' (John, Taupin)
14. 'I Want More' (John, Taupin)
15. 'I'll Never Have That Chance' (John, Taupin)
16. 'After All This Time' (John, Taupin)
17. 'To Kill Your Kind' (John, Taupin)
18. 'Sail Me Away' (John, Taupin)
19. 'From the Dead (Reprise)' (John, Taupin)

Musician's Corner: 'Sail Me Away'

Lestat closed before I had the chance to see it and the official cast recording remains unreleased to this day, so my only experience of it has been through the eighteen demo recordings and the few bootleg audio files that have been posted by people who attended the final shows. If you never thought much about how much vocal register matters in how we interpret a song, I'd suggest listening to the Elton demo and fan recordings of Hugh Panaro's (*b*.1964) live performance of 'Sail Me Away'. In Elton's rich baritone, the resignation of the song's lyrics and melody take on a different meaning than in Panaro's youthful tenor. One isn't necessarily better than the other, it's just a unique experience.

The song is a beautiful inverse to 'The Messenger' – whereas that closing message was about victory over death through love, 'Sail Me Away' is about resignation, failure and loss, and the irresistible yearning to crawl back to a safe space after having been battered by the world. It is about the bittersweet relief of conceding defeat. This is a difficult theme to convey, simultaneously about the warmth of anticipating a return home and about the anguish of all the tragedy that necessitated that return.

I'm going to focus on how Elton deals with these conflicting emotions in the chorus, where his solution is among the cleverest he's ever produced to a lyrical puzzle tossed his way by Bernie. The lyrics are about a grand motion outward towards the wider world, which fell apart, and which now must fall back to the place where the hero's story began. Narratively, that is analogous to the motion of a wave, roaring forward, falling apart under its own weight and then receding. The whole story, in its boldness, failure and yearning for home, is wrapped up in the motion of the sea on which Lestat seeks to sail, and Elton mirrors that motion in his progressions. Waves to us appear as big blocks of water that experience gradual shifts and extensions until they end up as totally different objects than their original forms, and that is what we see in Elton's chords: each one makes less sense in terms of the theory of V chords and secondary dominants, and more in terms of the motion of the individual notes, of keeping some stationary while little slippages break out, small in themselves but that sum to overall profound change, expressing in miniature the entire arc of the musical.

Chapter 38

The Captain & The Kid

Recorded: Spring 2006
Released: 18 September 2006
Producers: Elton John and Matt Still

The Story

After the commercial disappointment of *Peachtree Road*, it seemed a good idea to give fans what they had long been asking for, a sequel to *Captain Fantastic and the Brown Dirt Cowboy*, an idea that Elton and Bernie readily agreed to when it was first proposed by Elton's manager, Merck Mercuriadis (*b*.1963), in 2005.

Though Bernie was in top form lyrically exploring the last three decades of his and Elton's shared life, and Elton was similarly reinvigorated musically at the prospect of a sequel to *Captain Fantastic and the Brown Dirt Cowboy*, and though many of the songs have gone on to be treasured classics among Elton fans, particularly 'The Bridge' and 'And the House Fell Down', Interscope's promotion of the album wasn't up to Elton's standards, especially the decision not to release a single and then reversing that decision when the buzz from the album died down and the single had no way of charting. As a result, though the album did manage to reach #6 in the UK and snag silver status for sales of 60,000 units, worldwide the album didn't sell more than 200,000 copies, which, combined with the collapse of *Lestat* in May 2006, made this year a commercial low point for Elton, even if he was creating some of the most interesting work of his life. Rebuffed at the theatre (though *Billy Elliot* was still going strong at the Victoria Palace Theatre, its Broadway triumph was another two years away) and as a solo artist, Elton threw himself into the project that was indisputably succeeding, his Las Vegas concert residency, The Red Piano, which stretched from 2004 to 2009, and as a result we didn't get a new studio album until 2010, when he collaborated with Russell on *The Union*, and didn't get a new solo studio album until *The Diving Board* in 2013, which allowed Elton to conquer the recording world all over again, and on his terms.

The Songs

Our first track, 'Postcards from Richard Nixon', picks up right where *Captain Fantastic and the Brown Dirt Cowboy* left off, with our heroes still a relatively unknown creative team, coming to the US on Dick James's hunch that it was the land where they would make their fortunes. The song is filled with references to the events leading up to, and resulting from, the mythic Troubadour Club performance that put Elton on the map, from trips to Disneyland, to their surreal meeting with the reclusive Brian Wilson (*b*.1942), to the titular and unreal meeting with President Richard Nixon (1913–1994), who thought being associated with an up and coming but squeaky clean musical talent could help his faltering image. The piano part also has references to the rhythmic patterns and motifs from the original 'Captain Fantastic and the Brown Dirt Cowboy' song, which will be made more explicit still on the album's final track, providing a powerful book-end effect of reminiscence for the record. The presence of Johnstone and Olsson backing vocals also adds to the overall impression that we have taken a step back in time and are standing at the threshold of 1970 once again, with the future stretching out before us in all its possibilities.

'Just Like Noah's Ark' moves the story ahead to pull the curtain back on what happens when the music industry senses a new talent on the rise, as the stock characters that run the game emerge from the woodwork to ride the coattails of the promising artist in their midst, from the thuggish brutes angling after Elton to be his new manager, to groupies hoping for a taste of the band's fame, to radio hosts willing to promote any record provided they get a kickback. Musically, it's a blues scale stomper in which Elton parades this outlandish cast of characters before us in the verses, while in the chorus he and Bernie are deftly attempting to dodge all the mass of grasping humanity around them and retain their grasp of reality. This is clearly a song in The Rolling Stones takedown anthem vein, except instead of coming off as snide, Bernie's laser-like observations have the ring of sharp accuracy, honestly capturing the feeling of what it was like to suddenly have a menagerie of industry stereotypes converging upon their still naïve persons in a mangle of flesh and promises.

'Wouldn't Have You Any Other Way (NYC)' represents the most positive portrayal of the city yet, almost doubtlessly influenced by the general swell of sympathy following the attack of 11 September 2001, which Bernie references directly in the line, 'No matter what might happen/They'll never sink this ship.' Here, the instinct to write an anthem to boost the spirits of a city that had been historically important to them, and to avoid anything that might appear like kicking the city while it was down, won the day, resulting in pleasant enough lyrics that Elton turned into a pleasant enough ballad that doesn't have the same compelling indeterminate complexity as its predecessors. There's a neat musical reference to listen out for in the backing vocals, which for a moment quote those of 'We All Fall in Love Sometimes' from the original *Captain Fantastic and the Brown Dirt Cowboy* album.

The warts are all on display on 'Tinderbox', Bernie's song about the pressure put on his and Elton's creative partnership by their runaway success in the early 1970s. The song is about massive structural tensions that are threatening to buckle at any moment. Musically, Elton starts with a small acoustic signal that something isn't right with the use of E major, a key he used to employ somewhat frequently ('Candle in the Wind', 'Skyline Pigeon', 'Salvation' and 'Your Sister Can't Twist (But She Can Rock 'n Roll)') but had avoided pretty steadily in the quarter century before 'Tinderbox' ('Satellite', 'Goodbye Marlon Brando', 'Look Ma, No Hands' and 'Please' are the only examples that come readily to mind, songs which don't have a particularly strong association between them). The use of E major, a key that, unlike E flat major, A minor, G flat major or G minor doesn't have many built-in associations for Elton fans of the last three decades, accomplishes two ends: first, it make us feel a bit ill at ease and second, it acts as a swivel for two chords that Elton does tend to like, G sharp minor and C sharp minor, which produces all kinds of tensions within the song. Bernie's lyrics reflect honestly, with the understanding granted by the passage of time, on the strains in his partnership with Elton that ultimately led to their decision to explore other avenues of creativity with other people for a while in the late 1970s and early 1980s. There's no bitterness or finger pointing here, just a realisation that they were trapped in a volatile situation created by their success (a tinderbox, if you will), and which compelled them to seek different paths, and Elton seconds that feeling by setting the lyrics not as an angry rock burner but as an easily paced ballad with pop and country elements (Johnstone hauls out a virtual artillery of traditional country instruments here, including harmonica, mandolin, acoustic guitar and banjo) to give the music a bit of both Elton and Bernie's flavour, working together in the overall structure of the song, rather than pulling in separate directions, signifying that, whatever short-term disagreements there might be, in the long term there's no way of permanently separating Elton and Bernie.

There would have been no way of writing an album about Elton and Bernie in the 1970s without addressing the monumental substance abuse that both began engaging in towards the middle of that decade, and which by the 1980s had reached self-destructive levels that they were lucky to have survived. 'And the House Fell Down' is an uncompromising look at this shared aspect of their lives in which Bernie captures the reality of addiction, the wholesale junking of precious life and the horror accompanying systemic self-abuse. Elton avoids the obvious route of casting this as a dirge of self-criticism and opts for a characteristically more nuanced musical setting, tapping into the up-tempo songs of the old blues tradition in which the singer lays bare their failings, not so much in celebration of them, but as if from the point of view of the devil himself, who is having no end of fun watching humans destroy themselves for fleeting pleasure. It's horrifying, but it's also human, and the higher pace replicates nicely how we sometimes make our own destruction into a full time job.

Despite the drugs, Elton and Bernie are still with us today, while many of those who walked that same road are not, circumstances ripe for survivor's guilt, which is the subject of *The Captain and the Kid*'s emotional centrepiece, 'Blues Never Fade Away'. 'How did we get so lucky?/Targets on the rifle range' is a perfect encapsulation of the terrifying reality of how Elton and Bernie spent a decade and a half of their lives, participating in activities that put them regularly in the path of annihilation. The verses present us with a series of portraits of individuals who weren't so lucky, taken by AIDS, drugs overdose or murder before they had a chance to live a quarter of the lives, while the choruses reflect on what it means to live with the knowledge that one should be dead as a result of one's actions and that many people who behaved far less flagrantly than you are gone. Despite the title, Elton does not set this piece as a straightforward blues number but rather more as a gentle elegy, employing the related chords of E flat major (which is one of Elton's preferred keys for expressing introspection and melancholy) and C minor. His vocal gentleness in the verse, and increasingly impassioned delivery of the choruses, each repetition of which sees a heightening of the disbelief at the blunt brutishness of fate, make for a powerful listening experience, which speaks to anybody who surveys their fortune amid so much loss and wonders why me?

With 'The Bridge' Elton gives us a timeless melody, supported by his own piano, as he sings Bernie's words about the impossible choice faced by individuals who have succeeded in their life's work, particularly entertainers. There's no stopping, no time to rest but rather only the constant demand to summon up the energy to cross over the next bridge placed before one by the industry, fans, and your own need for achievement, and then the one after that, and then the one after that. Each time, you have a choice: 'Do you cross the bridge, or fade away?' Do you keep moving and try to maintain your level of fame, even as you know that this next journey might be the one that breaks you, or do you say, 'It is enough' and grow a little bit dimmer in people's memories with each passing year? For every time that Elton swore he was going to retire, or return to the simple life, he always ended up back in the thick of it, juggling touring, recording and a growing list of compositional projects, driven by the need to prove that he was still a living creative force, and to fight back with all his considerable reserves of energy against the fading of his legacy.

After the run of emotionally profound compositions running from 'And the House Fell Down' to 'Blues Never Fade Away' and into 'The Bridge', almost any song following that trio is bound to fall a little bit flat, so production logic dictates that, if that song is going to struggle anyway, you might as well put your least consequential song there, which will also achieve the goal of making the song after that one seem more profound by comparison. So, this is where we get 'I Must Have Lost it on the Wind' (a title which references a bit of rodeo talk that Bernie picked up during his years as a competitive horse cutter), in which Bernie talks about the stream of lovers that Elton and he have known over the years: some of whom are remembered, some of whom are not, some of whom imparted great wisdom during their brief residency in the duo's lives and others of whom were sort of there. These aren't particularly inspiring lyrics, and Elton sets them in a straightforward manner, with the appearance of the occasional secondary dominant being the only thing intriguing for the ear. One fun bit of Elton history here is the fact that this is the second song in which Bernie uses the wind as a metaphor for moving on from a relationship and that both 'I Must Have Lost it on the Wind' and 'Heels of the Wind' feature the same primary chords of A minor, G and C. Coincidence? Yeah, probably, but still, neat bit of trivia.

'Old 67' is a unique subject for a song: it isn't about events in the past so much as it's about having the opportunity to sit with someone from the old days and talk about past events with a glass in one hand, and an 'older version' of your friend from youth next to you. While having those conversations can be the highlight of one's week as time moves on, they also carry with them a pain, expressed by Bernie in the phrase, 'What a time of innocence/What a time we've lost', which recognises that the arrow of time trends generally downwards, that with knowledge comes fewer opportunities to experience real discovery with a friend. Elton employs a sort of Ray Charles narrative structure here, with the chords wandering further away from the song's starting point to make it feel like the verses represent stories that are organically evolving, taking us to new places as we listen. It's a bittersweet celebration of gratitude for the people you have, who make bearable what has been lost along the way.

Bernie also packs a nice little Easter egg into 'Old 67' in the form of the line, 'Sitting here side by side/You and me on a balcony/It's a little bit funny this feeling inside', which sneaks the iconic opening line of 'Your Song' into the last line of the second bridge of the song, a little reward for the fans who are listening to the songs on the album all the way through.

Our tour through the second phase of Elton and Bernie's career together comes to an end on 'The Captain and the Kid', the title of which comes from the line of the original 1975 song 'Captain Fantastic and the Brown Dirt Cowboy', which runs 'Hand in hand went music and the rhyme/The Captain and the Kid stepping in the ring/From here on sonny sonny sonny, it's a long and lonely climb'. The intro to 'The Captain and the Kid' is the same as its 1975 counterpart, only played a whole tone down, in F, instead of G, for reasons one can only begin to speculate about, including the possibility that this is a musical joke Elton's playing. In any case, Bernie's lyrics here are a sustained portrayal of Elton's development into the star he became and Bernie's into a kind of poet cowboy, as expressed in several lines of direct comparison some of which employ key phrases from their storied joint career: 'You a tumbleweed and me on the yellow brick road', 'Waiting for a plan to turn you into the brown dirt cowboy and me into a rocket man'. And some of which don't: 'But I got a brand new pair of shoes/And you're on a horse in old cowboy boots'. Just when you are about to get frustrated with the same lyrical structure getting employed repeatedly, the chorus appears around the corner, in its whimsical vocal setting from Elton and everything is forgiven: 'No lies at all, just one more tale/About the Captain and the Kid'.

The Stats

Album/Single	US	UK	Australia	Canada
The Captain and the Kid	18	6	37	12
		S		
'The Bridge'				

The Players

Elton John: lead vocals and acoustic piano
Guy Babylon: keyboards
Davey Johnstone: guitars, banjo, mandolin, harmonica and backing vocals
Bob Birch: bass and backing vocals
Nigel Olsson: drums and backing vocals
John Mahon: percussion and backing vocals
Matt Still: backing vocals

The Tracks

1. 'Postcards From Richard Nixon' (John, Taupin) (5.14)
2. 'Just Like Noah's Ark' (John, Taupin) (5.33)
3. 'Wouldn't Have You Any Other Way (NYC)' (John, Taupin) (4.39)
4. 'Tinderbox' (John, Taupin) (4.26)
5. 'And the House Fell Down' (John, Taupin) (4.49)
6. 'Blues Never Fade Away' (John, Taupin) (4.45)
7. 'The Bridge' (John, Taupin) (3.38)
8. 'I Must Have Lost it on the Wind' (John, Taupin) (3.53)
9. 'Old 67' (John, Taupin) (5.01)
10. 'The Captain and the Kid' (John, Taupin) (5.01)

Musician's Corner: 'And the House Fell Down'

I haven't done the maths on this but I feel that most of Elton's best up-tempo numbers are about dark topics. 'Saturday Night's Alright for Fighting' is about fighting. 'Act of War' is about a failed relationship. 'I Think I'm Going to Kill Myself' is a tap-dance infused look at suicide. 'I Don't Wanna Go on With You Like That' is about being serially cheated on. 'Whitewash County' is about wilful ignorance in the deep South. 'Ego' is about destructive personality types. 'Bitter Fingers' expresses frustrations at the music industry. 'Goodbye Marlon Brando' is about everything wrong with the world. 'I'm Still Standing' was originally bitter lyrics about Bernie surviving his third divorce. Even 'Crocodile Rock' is at least bittersweet, a look back to a happy era now past. There are certainly exceptions, 'Club at the End of the Street', 'Philadelphia Freedom' and 'Honky Cat', but all in all Elton has his best successes in this genre in marrying dark lyrics with driving beats.

Lyrically, 'And the House Fell Down' is a song about one of the lowest periods in Elton's life, strung out on cocaine, leading a bleary eyed existence, rising higher in fame as his addiction grew correspondingly in scale, and threatened to uproot his own life and those of all around him.

The lyrics are bleak, invoking suspension over hell as the general spirit of that time in Elton's life, but the music is catchy. Starting with a groovy little blues riff, and a syncopated strut in the verses, this song could as easily be about how great geese are, and the jarring nature of that juxtaposition between the jaunty bop of the music and the realities portrayed in the lyrics, works as a perfect encapsulation of the individual John was at the time, to all appearances, a man on top of the world when he stepped out onto the stage and behind his piano but in private a self-destructive wreck. That manic combination is incredibly hard to live and work with on a steady basis and Elton puts us in the position of those around him at the time by confronting us with these diametrically opposed messages in the lyrics and music (though a few diminished chords sneak into the musical structure, small cries for help, perhaps). All in all, this is a much more effective presentation than if he'd written a simple slow lament á la 'Sorry Seems to Be the Hardest Word' or 'Sacrifice'.

Chapter 39

The Union

Recorded: November 2009 to March 2010
Released: 19 October 2010
Producer: T-Bone Burnett

The Story

The tale of *The Union* is one Elton has told many times but it's such a beautiful one that it's worth telling again. Russell was a large presence in Elton's formative days. His work as a studio musician for Phil Spector (1939–2021), a member of Delaney & Bonnie and Friends, and as a solo recording artist was a revelation to Elton in his late teens and early twenties, particularly Russell's distinctive piano playing style and gift for fusing musical traditions, such as Tulsa rock, gospel, blues and carnival elements, into his own compositions. In late 1970, Elton and Russell performed on the same bill at the Fillmore East, but they had fallen out of contact with each other. Russell went on recording, putting out new albums every year or two, and scoring a string of Top 40 albums in the early 1970s, but by 1977 his prominence as a recording artist was on the decline and his last album to chart in the Top 200 was released in 1981. As his health deteriorated, so too did his performance schedule, and during the 1990s and 2000s he was rarely seen in concert.

By the time 2009 rolled around, even his devoted fan Elton had stopped thinking about Russell until one day 'This Masquerade' happened to come up on a playlist of songs that Elton had recommended to Furnish, and Elton felt a sudden flood of gratitude for Russell's music and grief that such a great artist was now virtually forgotten by the world. For the first time in decades, he called up Russell, and soon after hanging up the phone he knew what he wanted to do: make an album with his old piano idol and bring him back into the spotlight one more time. He called up T-Bone Burnett (a producer Bernie had been urging Elton to work with) to see if he'd be interested in producing the project, and when Burnett agreed, Elton phoned Russell right back and asked if he wanted to put out an album together. Russell was worried about his health (and the recording process was in fact put on hold when Russell had to have an operation for a brain fluid leak, and treatment for pneumonia and heart failure), and being able to give Elton the level of performance he was hoping for, but Elton would hear none of it, and found that, once back in the studio and behind a piano, Russell absolutely blossomed.

Elton and Russell were both insistent that the album be done the right way, and instead of performing a series of easy covers and duets, wrapped up in a few breezy days, they committed to writing enough new music to fill a double album, including songs written solely by Russell, songs by Bernie and Russell, songs by Elton and Bernie and songs by Elton and Russell, the diverse lyrical content unified by a production that leaned on a darker hued mix of piano, heavy percussion, bass, and prominent backing vocals, resulting in a new instrumental topology that would influence Elton to restructure his sound on his next solo album, *The Diving Board*.

The album went to #3 in the UK, #7 in Canada, and #12 in the US, was ranked as the #3 album of the year by *Rolling Stone* magazine, and launched a mini Russell renaissance, including an album executive produced by Elton, *Life Journey* (2014), which cracked the Top 200 in the UK. Unfortunately, though Russell's recognition were on the rise, his health wasn't and, in 2016, he died, at the age of 74, but not before experiencing one more time how much he was loved by musicians and fans the world over.

The Songs

Okay, straight talk time. You were probably like me when this album first came out: heart melted by the story of what Elton did for his musical mentor and thrilled at the possibility of hearing Russell again after decades, and in that heady rush of sympathy and enthusiasm, you experienced *The Union* as a rare and tremendous thing for a month or so. Then you put it back on your CD rack, only to revisit it a few years later, when Russell died, and that relistening was heightened by the knowledge that this was among his last recordings ever released. Then back on the shelf it went until a few years after that, when, for a change from your usual rotation of your top twelve or so favourite Elton albums, you pulled it down again and gave it a listen with ears rendered sober by the passage of time and started to hear things about it that you didn't notice in your early eagerness. A multitude of unfortunate things.

It doesn't give me any joy but we're going to talk about those things in what follows, so if you want to preserve the album as you originally experienced it, just skip this section. I honestly think you'll be happier if you do, but if you've already experienced some of those things, then perhaps what follows will help you appreciate the good aspects of the album, of which there are many, while recognising that the flaws take nothing away from the artistry of Elton and Russell.

Elton starts the album with 'If It Wasn't for Bad', putting Russell in the spotlight, with a song written solely by Russell, beginning with the sound of his characteristic piano emanating unaccompanied from the speakers before being joined by gospel vocal harmonies, which serve as the introduction to the sudden arrival of the iconic angular piano work and vocal twang, accentuated by heavy percussion elements, that instantly remind us of Russell's classic work. Elton keeps himself well in the background for this song, contributing just perceptible backing vocals to the chorus, while in the instrumental break Burnett throws a full ensemble of brass, Marc Ribot's (*b*.1954) electric guitar and a cluster of background vocals into the mix to broaden the scale of Russell's composition. The impression is of a group of dedicated individuals doing everything they can to make sure that Russell's standout solo track succeeds, and somewhat losing the madcap fun of Russell's original composition in the process. If you listen to a song like 'Tightrope' (1972), which has a similar sense of wordplay being set off by a strong rhythmic pulse, you hear that there are interesting instrumental additions but they're always given space to sound off in so that their distinctive voice can shine and add to the atmosphere of the piece. Here, between the piano, background vocals, electric guitar, acoustic bass, two percussionists, Hammond organ, keyboards, trombones, tuba, baritone horn, trumpet and bass trumpet, there's no space to feel how unique Russell's style really is, and all the instruments, shoved in so densely together, end up being subtractive rather than additive.

'Eight Hundred Dollar Shoes' reverses the focus, with Elton's voice featured prominently while Russell's is heard in the backup position during the vocals. This is a piece that Elton and Bernie wrote together and is in the unique-for-them waltz-associated time signature of 3/4. It would be easy to think of the song as a depiction of Elton, all success and majesty, strolling into Russell's life again after thirty years. For Bernie, poking fun at Elton's eccentricities was old hat by this point, but I have the sense that Russell would have been uncomfortable singing a song that spoke ill of the person who had done so much for him, and so we get the strange situation where Elton's seemingly singing a song about himself from the perspective of Russell, through the words of Bernie. It's a nice song of self-effacement in a different flow than we're used to hearing Elton's melodies, which works well until the arrival of the percussion that is too dramatic for the song, particularly in the chorus where the bass drum dominates the sound and shunts the song in a cavernous direction not hinted at remotely by the lyrics or the somewhat whimsical melody.

'Hey Ahab' is the song that finally gets the instrumental mix right, with a great build that lets the pianos have their due time to build up the elements of the piece's rhythm, allowing the drum to take up that baton to enhance the established pattern, while the arrival of Elton's powerful vocal does the job of making sure that that strong drum underneath doesn't totally dominate the song. As a piece that features forceful piano work playing off a big drum sound, it not only calls back to Russell's early work, but the first days of the Elton John Band, when Olsson, Murray and Elton had to hold the stage with just a drum, bass and piano. The entry of the gospel backing vocals is tactical here, adding a punch to the infectious, stomp-inducing fire of Elton's chorus, while Russell's vocals in the chorus add some higher register elements that come at the right time to relieve the ear of so much low register artillery during the verse. The last two minutes of the song give Elton and Russell space to have fun with variations on the piece's central piano riff, though these can get lost somewhat in the heavy presence of the percussion and gospel elements of the mix.

'Gone to Shiloh' is a song tailored to Burnett's production sensibilities, with a theme of devastation and war that absolutely works with the dominant percussion elements that have featured so strongly so far on the album. It leads off with a forty-second piano melody that has been mixed with a hiss and distort to suggest an old phonograph record, which then repeats without the effects to lead into the main melody, surrounding a single soldier's experience of the 1862 Battle of Shiloh. The battle saw not only the death and wounding of thousands of men but also the inevitable capitulation of a part of the country that had historically been viewed romantically by Bernie. The grim topic justifies the regular thrum of the bass drum in a way that 'Eight Hundred Dollar Shoes' decidedly didn't, and the combination of three of the most distinctive voices of the 1970s in Elton, Russell and Neil Young (*b*.1945) is a magical mix of Elton's rich depth, Young's thin wail and Russell's mournful twang. The interweaving descending and ascending piano lines cut across each other like the fall of soldier's bodies and subsequent ascent into their final reward, while the brass adds funereal accents that work with the overall theme here to augment, rather than muddy the story at hand. Easily one of the best songs Elton has written, the sense of still pathos has an impact unlike anything since 'Indian Sunset'.

Jimmie Rodgers (1897–1933) was one of the special favourite recording artists of the young Bob Dylan and a touchstone to many of the American roots rockers of the late 1960s, including Russell and Levon Helm (1940–2012) of The Band. 'Jimmie Rodgers' Dream' is a salute to Rodgers, and to his last hard years, struggling through the Great Depression to keep his career alive despite a creeping case of tuberculosis that was diagnosed in 1927, and that made it that much harder every year to keep himself afloat financially through revenue from his performances and recording. This was not Bernie's first time writing a song about a beloved figure from the almost mythical past, but unlike 'Roy Rogers' and 'Dan Dare', these lyrics aren't about what Rodgers meant to those who listened to him, but is told strictly from Rodgers's point of view, a worn out musician whose health is failing and who sees death stretching before him, a situation not dissimilar from that which Russell himself was facing at the time of recording *The Union*, creating extra poignancy in those sections where Russell is singing lines like, 'In that mirror maybe that's what's left of me/Wheezing like a freight train hauling sixteen tons of steel'.

'There's No Tomorrow' continues the story of 'Jimmie Rodgers' Dream', except now we have advanced from the position of summoning our last vestiges of energy in order to put a line under our life's work to the last day of our lives, the day when we realise we won't see the sun again. It's a grim take on death, offering no ideas of redemption or salvation or a reward beyond but just the simple fact that, someday, you will be over, and that in the face of that knowledge the only adequate response is abject dread. The song takes its power from the chorus, where Russell exerts himself to the fullest vocally in the invocation of 'There's no tomorrow/There's only today', against backing vocals that sound like the chorus of the damned. Elton takes the verses, and does a good job making them as menacing and final as possible but, it has to be said even though I hate having to do it, those lyrics aren't at the level of the rest of the album. When the album first came out, I think we were all so happy to hear Russell again that we gave little things like that a pass but with each subsequent year I can't help but notice them a bit more even if I don't want to.

'Monkey Suit' is the 'Delta Lady' of *The Union*, the rocking showstopper, utilising every bit of musical talent in the room to achieve a level of constant energy suitable for a grand finale, as Russell's 'Delta Lady' was the high point of Joe Cocker's (1944–2014) legendary *Mad Dogs and Englishmen* concerts of 1970. The lyrics are a dark version of 'Eight Hundred Dollar Shoes', where the conquering figure isn't merely eccentric but relentless in his pursuit of power, stepping on the backs of whoever will get him a rung further up the ladder, allowing him to return to his home dressed in a fine suit, his heart filled with a desire to rub his success in the faces of anyone who ever doubted him. Bernie's words continue a theme of the album, which is the battle between authentic relationships and the deceptive allure of those chasing power or glory. For most it isn't the lyrics that they'll be paying attention to but Elton's towering vocal performance and the big sound that Burnett brings to making this, if not the equal of 'Delta Lady', at least a strong update to the central idea, some four decades and an uncountable number of monkey suits later.

In 1972, Bernie wrote 'Mellow', a song about newlyweds spending their days drinking alcohol and having lots of sex. Two important years of personal growth later, he penned 'Pinky', a song about the joy of spending a lazy morning with one's spouse and newborn. Fast forward some thirty-six years, and Bernie has completed the story with 'The Best Part of the Day', a song about waking up to the dawn in the company of one's love and best friend, whose off-key singing is the perfect accompaniment to the echoes from the canyon and the rumble of a thunderstorm coming in from the east. These beautiful lyrics, in the mouths of Elton and Russell, serve as a later-life hymn of thanks to the people who have made their day to day lives rich through the steadiness of their presence.

'A Dream Come True' is a good idea on paper – a bouncing Delta stomper that radiates the feeling of a New Orleans wedding being hosted on a steamboat with a carnival band playing for the careening guests, with half the song devoted to giving Elton and Russell space to carry out some pianistic hijinks. The first half comes off according to plan – Elton and Russell are singing feel-good lyrics about their joy in playing music, and particularly in getting the chance to play it with each other. The second half, however, is ruined by that persistent bugbear of *The Union*, Burnett's over-cramming of the track so that what you hear during the part that is supposed to highlight the piano artistry of two of the greatest rock pianists ever is the repetitive, looping background vocals and percussion section, from which the sound of the piano escapes every so often if you've got good enough speakers to separate the sonic miasma into its constituent parts. It would have been a sad waste in 1990, but in 2010, with one of the last chances to showcase Russell's technique to a new generation, it's borderline tragic.

'When Love is Dying' has the same basic problem as 'Eight Hundred Dollar Shoes' – perhaps because he didn't trust Bernie's simplified lyrics and Elton's basic but effective melody to convey the gravitas of the situation, Burnett fills the chorus with drum hits that are out of all proportion to everything else in the mix, highly distracting to the vocals at hand, and bordering on the farcical in the choices of percussive timbre. I will be the first one in line when they create a mix of this that lets the piano and voice tell the story, but until then I generally have to skip it to maintain my sense of the dignity of the album.

We get a unique opportunity with 'I Should Have Sent Roses' to hear Russell composing directly to a set of lyrics by Bernie, the problem being that Bernie has de-Bernified himself here, producing a set of abnormally straightforward lines, as he did in 'When Love is Dying', which I've always wondered the reasoning behind. Most likely, he's trying to approximate Russell's lyrical idiom, which, while highly inventive in certain genres, tended to be less so in ballads centring on romance. Fortunately, Russell's singing is so full of remorse and the melody and chord choices are so interesting that for the most part we hardly notice the lost opportunity to hear what Russell would have done with fully Bernified lyrics.

'Hearts Have Turned to Stone' is a good chugging blues number with lyrics neither markedly great nor aggressively bad, featuring Russell at piano so there's no ambiguity to wade through as to whether what one is hearing is Elton's or Russell's work, and for the most part that piano work is even audible in the mix, a nice change of pace from 'A Dream Come True'. There's nothing particularly stunning here but it's a nice opportunity to spend some time with Russell's voice and piano work.

'Never Too Old' sees the return of the out of place drum blasts in the chorus that ruined 'When Love is Dying', though by this time we've grown so used to that omnipresent element of the album's soundscape that we've almost grown immune to it and so it's nowhere near as distracting as that earlier track. Once our brains have tuned the drums out, we get a lovely song not so much about raging against the dying of the light, as about refusing to accept that there comes a point when being alone is the only choice available to you. The world is full of love, and no matter how much loss has come your way, you're tougher than you think you are, and will always have it within you to find one more real human contact to see you through the next stretch of life. Languorously paced to fit the general theme that time is vast, and that within it there's always enough space to find comfort in the touch of another human, the song forces you to slow down for a moment and listen to the advice of three men who have known their share of fast living, and of loneliness, and have some advice to impart as you start down the path they have known.

There's nothing to be said against the album's final track, 'In the Hands of Angels', and even if there were, I wouldn't do it. This is the song Russell wrote specifically for Elton and Burnett to express his thanks at being given the chance not only to play music again, but to feel how much he is loved as a musician by generations of those whose lives he touched. I highly recommend watching the documentary about the making of *The Union* if for no other reason than to watch Elton's reaction when he first hears Russell's song coming over the speakers, and has to leave the room, overcome with emotion. There's a lot of cynicism in the music industry, but here, in this one song, there's nothing but love, unity through music, compassion and gratitude, and if all Elton's efforts resulted in the production of just this one song, it was all more than worth it.

The Stats

Album/Single	US	UK	Australia	Canada
The Union	3	12	28	7
		S		G
'If It Wasn't for Bad'				

The Players

Elton John: vocals (1 to 15) and piano (2 to 4 and 6 and 15)
Leon Russell: piano, vocals and background vocal arrangement (1, 5, 7, 10 and 16)
Jim Keltner: drums and percussion (1 to 9 and 11 to 15)
Jay Bellerose: drums and percussion (1 to 15)
Mike Piersante: tambourine (3 and 8) and percussion (11)
Debra Dobkin: beaded gourd (6)
Mike Ford: percussion (11)
Dennis Crouch: acoustic bass (1 to 4, 6 to 10 and 12 to 15)
Don Was: bass guitar (5 and 11)
Davey Faragher: bass guitar (5)
Drew Lambert: electric bass (16)
Marc Ribot: guitar (1 to 4, 6, 7, 9 and 10, and 13 to 15) and acoustic guitar (8)
T-Bone Burnett: electric guitar (3, 6 and 12)
Doyle Bramhall II: guitar (5 and 11)
Robert Randolph: pedal steel (7)
Russ Pahl: pedal steel (6)
Booker T. Jones: Hammond B-3 organ (1, 5, 9 and 11)
Keefus Ciancia: keyboards (1 to 15)
Marty Grebb: keyboards (7 and 16)
Jason Wormer: dulcimer (4) and percussion (11)
Darrell Leonard: trumpet (1, 4, 5, 8, 11 and 13), bass trumpet (1, 11 and 13), horn arrangements and conductor (1, 4, 5, 8, 11 and 13)
Ira Nepus: trombone (1, 4 and 11)
Maurice Spears: trombone (1, 4 and 11)
George Bohanon: trombone (1, 4 and 11) and baritone (1, 4 and 11)

William Roper: tuba (1, 4 and 11)
Thomas Peterson: saxophone (5, 8, 11 and 13)
Joseph Sublett: saxophone (5, 8, 11 and 13)
Jim Thompson: saxophone (5, 8, 11 and 13)

The Tracks

1. 'If It Wasn't for Bad' (Russell) (3.43)
2. 'Eight Hundred Dollar Shoes' (John, Taupin) (3.23)
3. 'Hey Ahab' (John, Taupin) (5.39)
4. 'Gone to Shiloh' (featuring Neil Young) (John, Taupin) (4.50)
5. 'Hearts Have Turned to Stone' (Russell) (3.47)
6. 'Jimmie Rodgers' Dream' (John, Taupin, Burnett) (3.42)
7. 'There's No Tomorrow' (John, Russell, Burnett, Shaw) (3.45)
8. 'Monkey Suit' (John, Taupin) (4.46)
9. 'The Best Part of the Day' (John, Taupin) (4.45)
10. 'A Dream Come True' (John, Russell) (5.07)
11. 'I Should Have Sent Roses' (Russell, Taupin) (5.21)
12. 'When Love is Dying' (John, Taupin) (4.51)
13. 'Never Too Old (To Hold Somebody)' (John, Taupin) (4.58)
14. 'In the Hands of Angels' (Russell) (4.43)

Musician's Corner: 'Gone to Shiloh'

Reconnecting with Russell helped Elton turn a corner into a starker musical landscape, the impact of which can be felt throughout his next studio release, *The Diving Board*, and 'Gone to Shiloh' is a perfect encapsulation of that temporary new direction. *Songs From the West Coast*, *Peachtree Road* and *The Captain and the Kid*, in line with the back to basics approach Elton and Bernie adopted in the wake of *The Big Picture*, stay squarely in the soundscape of the band as it was in the mid-1970s, and *The Captain and the Kid* in particular features an array of catchy songs with space left for instrumental showmanship that would do well in any sort of live performance.

The problem with playing with a familiar group of musicians is that it makes it all the easier to bend towards the familiar in your compositional choices as well. We all loved living in the nostalgia of *The Captain and the Kid* but by the end of it, we were also waiting for Elton to break out into new territory, and thinking about composing with Russell seems to have unlocked that drive for musical exploration. New thematic material from Bernie suited to Russell's past both as an Oklahoman and as a writer of dark war balladry called for something grittier than Elton had composed in a while, and the end product, with its mournful pianos, funereal bass drum, sparse guitar and low brass intonations, puts us in a different place than we have been with Elton for a while, and with that new mix of sounds come new possibilities. Once it was completed, Elton considered it one of the finest songs he'd ever written, and with that success in a darker, stripped-down milieu, the stage was set for the dirge-like 'My Quicksand', the wistful solo majesty of 'Oceans Away' and the melancholy dance set to low strings, brass, piano and bass drum of 'The New Fever Waltz'.

Chapter 40

Gnomeo and Juliet

Recorded: 2008 to 2011
Released: 8 February 2011
Producers: Elton John, David Furnish, Stuart Michael Thomas and Jim Weidman

The Story

It took eleven years to bring *Gnomeo and Juliet* to the big screen, a feat ultimately accomplished by Elton's persistence as executive producer (his first time in this role) to keep the project alive in face of determined opposition from Disney, where the film originated. Around the year 2000 the idea of an adaptation of William Shakespeare's *Romeo and Juliet* employing garden gnomes was formed, with the original conception being a mix of CGI and live action in a sort of twenty-first century update of *Mary Poppins*. Disney head Michael Eisner (*b.*1942) reportedly hated the whole idea, and for four years there was no motion on it. To save the film, Elton agreed that he'd allow songs from his back catalogue to be used in the film, which seemed like enough of a sure thing to Disney that the project was revived temporarily, until 2006, when Disney acquired Pixar and, as part of the process of that merger, legendary Pixar CEO John Lasseter (*b.*1957) was placed in charge of all Disney animation. Viewing all the ongoing Disney projects he'd inherited as part of their merger, Lasseter saw *Gnomeo and Juliet* and was baffled as to why this film was being made and dropped the project altogether.

Elton, however, having already put a good six years into *Gnomeo and Juliet*, wouldn't be put off that easily and worked through a deal with Disney subsidiary Miramax in 2006 to release the film. Things seemed to be going along nicely – James McAvoy (*b.*1979) and Emily Blunt (*b.*1983) were brought on board in 2008 to add some star power to the lead roles – when, in 2010, Miramax was sold off, and *Gnomeo and Juliet* ended up being one of the few films that Disney retained and then handed over to its other subsidiary, Touchstone Pictures, which meant a minimal marketing campaign and a seemingly kiss of death release date in mid-February.

Against all expectations, *Gnomeo and Juliet* was a hit upon its final release in 2011, featuring a classic lineup of Elton songs, including two new numbers, one of which was a duet with Elton's 'new best friend' Lady Gaga (*b.*1986), and bringing in just short of $100 million domestically and $200 million globally. To put that in perspective, two years earlier Disney released *The Princess and the Frog* with all its marketing muscle thrown behind the project and it pulled in $104 million domestically. This success allowed Rocket Pictures to produce a second gnome-based film, *Sherlock Gnomes*, released in 2018, featuring the original cast plus Johnny Depp (*b*.1963) in the new titular role, and a batch of Elton songs supporting it, including a new song, 'Better Together', performed by Jessie Ware (*b*.1984). The sequel wasn't as well received as the original and ended up with a global total less than half that of *Gnomeo and Juliet*, bringing in $90.5 million overall against a $59 million budget. Thus, after nearly two decades, did the Gnome saga end, and though I can't speak to *Sherlock Gnomes*, *Gnomeo and Juliet* was an entirely delightful film for which James Newton Howard did an excellent job with weaving little Elton motifs throughout the score.

The Songs

There are only two new songs to talk about, the first of which is 'Love Builds a Garden'. Within the context of the film, it's a real tear jerker. If you have ever said to yourself (and who hasn't), 'There is no way I would ever openly weep about the fate of a lawn flamingo voiced by the legendary Jim Cummings', be prepared to be proven wrong. Bernie's story is one of union and separation, represented by a garden that a young couple used to tend lovingly together, and the steady decline of which becomes emblematic of the growing distance between them. While minor storms are weathered, eventually a major frost settles in, the flowers die and both come to the realisation that 'There's only so much you can do to keep some things alive'. This is a lot of emotional ground to cover but Elton does it masterfully by a mixture of the sense of quiet intimacy he'd developed in songs like 'The Emperor's New Clothes', 'Original Sin' and 'Weight of the World', with classic Elton melancholia *á la* 'Sorry Seems to Be the Hardest Word'. In terms of progressions, a lot of this tension is built up by the opposition of C major and F minor, two chords that don't live particularly near each other in a tonal sense, and that as a result always create a striking and disturbing effect when placed next to each other in a song, and are positively haunting at the conclusion of the chorus.

The Stats

Album/Single	US	UK	Australia	Canada
Gnomeo and Juliet: Original Motion Picture Soundtrack				

The Tracks

1. 'Hello Hello' (John, Taupin) (3.45)
2. 'Crocodile Rock' (with Nelly Furtado) (John, Taupin) (3.28)
3. 'Saturday Night's Alright for Fighting' (John, Taupin) (4.54)
4. 'Don't Go Breaking My Heart' (with Kiki Dee) (John, Taupin) (4.33)
5. 'Love Builds a Garden' (John, Taupin) (3.35)
6. 'Your Song' (John, Taupin) (4.01)
7. 'Rocket Man (I Think It's Going to Be a Long, Long Time)' (John, Taupin) (4.42)
8. 'Tiny Dancer' (John, Taupin) (6.14)
9. 'Bennie and the Jets' (John, Taupin) (5.21)
10. 'Gnomeo and Juliet' (Howard, Bacon) (4.22)
11. 'Dandelions' (Howard, Bacon) (4.25)
12. 'Bennie and the Bunnies' (Howard, Bacon) (2.52)
13. 'Terrafirminator' (Howard, Bacon) (5.35)
14. 'The Tiki Tiki Tiki Room' (Burley, Ravenscroft, Boag, The Mellomen) (2.37)

Musician's Corner: 'Hello Hello'

At the beginning of this journey, I was resistant to those who label 'Regimental Sgt Zippo' as a mere Beatles pastiche based solely on the first five seconds of the song. One hears the same sort of analysis tossed at 'Hello Hello', due to a similar tendency to conflate the part with the whole. Certainly, the chorus is very Beatles, and Bernie, who was concerned about his ability to write a straight-up pop song after decades of composing some of rock's most idiosyncratic lyrics, found his North Star in the form of The Beatles' 1967 album *Magical Mystery Tour* (1967), the psychedelic follow-up to *Sgt Pepper's Lonely Hearts Club Band*. That album was famously plagued (or some would say graced) by the presence of heavy LSD use that made for recording studio chaos in the best and worst senses. In Britain, that album was released as a double EP containing six songs but in the US, it was released as an LP with extra tracks from that year's singles, including the song 'Hello Goodbye', which features the infectious call 'Hello! Hello!' in the chorus that this song is referencing.

The verses belong purely in the realm of Soundtrack/Broadway Elton, with a walking up by fifths and back down again given extra flavour by Elton's gift for choosing interesting inversions that propel us forward onto new ground. But the chorus, even if it didn't start with the iconic 'Hello! Hello!' we'd know in our bones is a Beatles tribute. Those strutting strings in the bass are good clues, as are the harmonies, but when we look to the chords, what we see is a beautiful mix of Elton and The Beatles. During 'Hello, hello! My my my what have we here?' what we get is E-A-C#m-G. C#m is the relative minor to E, and The Beatles used relative chords quite a lot at important moments in their songs. 'Yesterday' places a relative minor chord on the words 'far away' and 'I believe'. The 'Everything seems to be right' and 'Feeling you holding me tight' sections of 'A Hard Day's Night' are both kicked off with the relative minor chord. 'And I Love Her' gives us our first release from minor key chords with the line 'You'd love her too', which is the relative major chord of the tonic. 'All My Loving' messes with our heads by starting out in the world of E minor before finally letting us know that, just kidding, we're actually in its relative major of G. 'She Loves You' pings back and forth between C minor and E flat major. The first two chords of 'Penny Lane' are B flat major and its relative, G minor.

There are more examples, boy are there ever, but hopefully that sampling conveys the idea that the sonic trick of moving around between relative chords is something The Beatles solidified in our pop-listening ears. Elton knows this, which I'm guessing is why we see that little bit of flavour here in the chorus, but Elton can't let it rest there, and has to show us a clever direction out of that relative minor that neither we nor our Beatles-attuned ears would have suspected, which is where the dive into G comes in. G belongs nowhere here. It's as surprising as if someone filled in the blank in 'Hammer is to nail as screwdriver is to _____' with the word sweatshirt. What it does let you do is bop up by fifths, landing at A major from underneath by jumping G to D, and then D to A, a motion that feels as satisfying as the move from C# minor to G is surprising.

Chapter 41

The Diving Board

Recorded: January 2012 to January 2013
Released: 13 September 2013
Producer: T-Bone Burnett

The Story

B y 2012, it had been six years since Elton's last solo album, and though *The Union* had to a good degree slaked the public's thirst for new material, it had also piqued the curiosity of a public who hadn't heard Elton's voice in the new instrumental configurations conceived by T-Bone Burnett. Was Elton going to remain in that sonic realm and what might it sound like when given a full solo album to explore those possibilities? While his label wanted him to release an album of Motown covers, which he resolutely deflected, Elton instead reteamed with Burnett, who insisted on continuing the return to the original Elton John Band sound as heard on *11-17-70*, which had been begun on *The Union*. Recorded on the warm vintage equipment at LA's Village Recorder studio, Burnett pushed Elton's voice and piano into the sharp foreground for this album while relying on essentially the same world of bass, percussion, brass and backing vocals that made up the soundscape of *The Union*, even to the point of ejecting Johnstone, marking the first Elton solo album in three decades that the guitarist wouldn't be included on.

With Bernie, now free from the need to compose lyrics in a particular style, writing some of the most thought provoking lines of his career, and Elton free to compose in whatever style he felt suitable, often opting for infusions of classical elements that hadn't been seen in full force in his music for some four decades, the resulting fifteen track album was pushed back from release on four separate occasions as Elton kept wanting to write more new material to highlight the emerging themes he saw bubbling up from the album's original twelve tracks, which had been written in two days and recorded in four, a sign that, in his mid-sixties, Elton's creative vitality had not ebbed.

The public responded to this mature collection of songs, pushing it to #3 in the UK and #4 in the US and the first single, 'Home Again', scored a #14 position on the US Adult Contemporary chart, which, with the #18 scoring of 'Can't Stay Alone Tonight' extended Elton's lead over Barbara Streisand (*b*.1942) for the most songs that charted in the Adult Contemporary category (if you're curious, the count currently stands: Elton at #1 with seventy-six charting songs, Streisand at #2 with sixty-four and Neil Diamond (*b*.1941) at #3 with fifty-nine). With the critical and commercial success of *The Diving Board*, the question then became, is this mournful Elton simply the Elton we're going to get from here on out or will the old joy find a way to return?

The Songs

The Diving Board begins with the album's star attraction solidly in the spotlight. 'Oceans Away' is Bernie's salute to the vanishing generation of the Second World War veterans, of whom both his and Elton's father were examples, and is a touching extension of the story begun in 'Talking Old Soldiers', of veterans whose memories are wrapped up with those who were left behind on the battlefield, only now, instead of the sense that these individuals are forgotten, unable to live lives outside of the harrowing memories they seek to drown in a series of stiff drinks at the local pub, we get flavours of the community of white haired veterans, as they gather in decreasing numbers, finding strength from their shared bond and from the celebration from the community that 'lets them shine'. Elton explores this theme musically through arpeggiated piano work similar to 'Skyline Pigeon', which leads up to the defining moment of the song, a statement of 'Oceans Away' presented first as a lament in B flat minor over the graves of those buried on foreign soil but then restated in an F sharp major that resolves into B flat major, communicating the idea that, over time, that initial impulse towards inconsolable grief that was evident in 'Talking Old Soldiers' does evolve into a firm sense of appreciation that you can carry within you, allowing it to fortify, rather than hobble, the steps you take into a future that those comrades will never know.

'Oscar Wilde Gets Out', in which Bernie tells the long hard story of Oscar Wilde's (1854–1900) final years of imprisonment and exile for what the Victorian era considered the 'crime' of his homosexuality, is perfectly set up by Elton from the start with a repeated piano line that features circular and ascending elements, which convey before we've heard the first word that this is going to be a song about deep frustration in the place you're in, followed by a journey to a new place, where the same cycle starts again, a perfect encapsulation of the story of Wilde's roving late years. The instrumentation here is like that laid out by Burnett on *The Union*, only mixed a great deal better. The same type of percussion and bass elements are there but pushed further back into the mix so that they don't drown out Elton's piano work in the way that they did Russell's on the previous album, which is a wonderful thing, as Elton's piano ideas here are among the most interesting of any he has composed to this date, and this song overall ranks among the top of Elton and Bernie's exploration of historically based themes.

The desirability of small-town life has been a variable quantity throughout Bernie's work of the last half century. Sometimes those towns represent small minded, maddening prisons and sometimes they're a font of personal rejuvenation. 'A Town Called Jubilee' splits the difference in its portrayal of a family packing up their possessions to leave the stifling place they've lived all their lives, waved off by the colourful character of Old Cotton. In previous times, this exit might have terminated in a trek to California but here they're aiming for a city called Jubilee, which is either a literal place (of which there are three in the US), or is more of a stand-in for the general idea of a better life in another town. Elton, once again, does a remarkable job casting this idea musically using major chords that take the place of the minor ones which the song's key would normally employ, and which are borrowed from the parallel minor of that key. This produces unexpected patches of brightness, re-enforcing the theme of unchecked optimism at the core of the lyrics, that even in those places where darkness might exist, light will reign. This is storytelling through chord progressions on a level with 'Goodbye Yellow Brick Road' or 'Ego' and we're only a fifth of the way through this remarkable album.

Blind Tom Wiggins (1849–1908) was one of the most successful American pianists of the nineteenth century, a former slave whose owner, General James Bethune (1803–1895), recognised his prodigious talents and provided him with a small room equipped with a piano off the main house where he played for hours on end. Blind from birth and likely autistic, Wiggins displayed feats of hyper-memory, able to play back any composition performed for him, to recall word for word speeches he'd heard only once years before, and to play three different melodies at once, one with each hand, and one with his voice. The story of the neurodivergent blind slave turned intercontinental sensation, as detailed in Deirdre O'Connell's (*b. c.*1953/1954) *The Ballad of Blind Tom*, would prove irresistible to Bernie. Once again, the combination of bass and percussion is employed to produce an extra layer of forward momentum, and once again, the mixing is a vast improvement from *The Union*, with Elton's piano clearly audible throughout, while the drum and bass are at a high enough level to provide thrust without becoming the dominant elements of the sonic topology. One neat detail is the alternating octave notes Elton's playing with his left hand throughout the intro, which adds a mechanical element to the more elaborate right-hand work that serves as a great introduction to the song's story of a certain form of intellectual rigidity producing unparalleled musical abilities.

'Dream #1' brings us our first purely instrumental track on a solo album in some thirty-two years, with an oscillating upper motion that takes its otherworldly power from the inclusion of a B that regularly works against the F minor 7 that is established in the left hand, creating this sense of an intermittent diminished chord flavour that is no sooner resolved than it returns, creating a loop of unease and familiarity that serves as a perfect introduction to the dark dirge of 'My Quicksand'.

If you listen to Elton and Bernie's songs for long enough, you realise that for every dark song there is a later light counterpart and vice versa. In the 1980s, Bernie wrote a few songs centred around Europe as a place that could heal the aches of British monotony and American workaholic bustle, where even when you were down on your luck, you could have adventures to live for and all problems would seem to melt off your skin in the climate of art and creativity. 'My Quicksand' plays on themes of foreignness and being entrapped by something which you were convinced your basic good sense would prevent you from losing yourself in. Unlike the poet-types who come to cities like Paris or Amsterdam to live high and die young, the protagonist here had thought himself more level-headed, possessed of a good sense of where they want to go and why, until something snares them, and they find themselves waking up 'with an accent', i.e. permeated by something, be that a toxic other individual or a way of life that rests uncomfortably within your skin, that represents a point of no return, the moment when you realise the quicksand is up to your waist and help isn't on the way. This isn't really like anything we have ever heard from Elton before, with more abrupt stops to the melody and a greater willingness to rest with heavy chord transitions to make a brutal point than we've ever heard before.

At this point, we've been through themes of existential dread, slavery, homophobia and the painful realisation that one of our bravest generations is slowly fading away, and it's decidedly time for a little change of pace, which comes in the form of the loping contemporary country ballad 'Can't Stay Alone Tonight', which doesn't try anything fancy in the lyrics, chord progressions or melody, with the only bit of perplexment coming from Burnett's decision to bathe Elton's voice in heavy reverb during the bridge, which I can't see a particular reason for in the musical structure or the lyrics, and presents a marked case of whiplash from the simple sound that had been established in all that came before. When you've got an album of fifteen songs, many of which are complex ruminations on mortality, a song like this is necessary every now and then to prepare you to descend into the next chasm.

Recharged, we head into 'Voyeur', at the centre of the album, and the title of which was long considered for the name of the entire record. There's so much to like about this song but my favourite bit comes at the end with the outro instrumental, which is the best Elton has ever written. The topic of the song returns us somewhat to the world of 'The Camera Never Lies' (1988), where we were presented with a paparazzi detailing the loving cat and mouse antics that underlie the basic symbiosis between himself and his target, a conception that couldn't have been more different from the spirit of 'Heart in the Right Place' (1981). 'Voyeur' leans more towards the former than the latter, presenting an alarmingly intimate portrait of an individual taking every chance he can get to peer into the life of another, and wrapping all that gleaned information into a fable of real connection with the object of his observation. One of the brilliant things about the song is that Elton's music is among the most poignant of anything that he has ever written, and it's all in the service of a romanticised portrait of a stalker, which is either a parody of the type of ballad that has as its basis a lover gazing at the object of their affection from afar, taking that central principle to extremes, or making a broader point that we're all voyeurs in one way or another, trying to find out as much about each other as we can, and that rather than being creepy, this is really a sign of our deep need to connect with each other.

'Home Again', which was the first single off *The Diving Board*, begins with a series of descending motions on the piano that seem in search of an end they can't find. Bernie has communicated this idea before but never so resolutely. While previous songs have expressed some hope that one can be reborn to some degree with a return to a simpler life, 'Home Again' is among a handful of Bernie's later creations that look us dead in the eyes and states simply, 'You can't'. You need to leave, because if you don't, you'll never know what home really is, but the act of leaving means that you can never again experience it as you once did. Here, Burnett's injection of brass elements is perfectly considered to add a sense of dark finality to Elton's soaring statement of the essentially eternal homelessness we enter once we leave childhood.

After the hard truths of 'Home Again', it's difficult to know what to do with 'Take This Dirty Water', which is full of the sort of easy feel-good clichés that 'Home Again' had definitively swatted down. On Elton's end, we get a by-the-numbers blues and gospel mixture, which doesn't really help to push Bernie's words to a higher plane.

Set in a 3/4 time that prepares us for the coming arrival of 'The New Fever Waltz', 'Dream #2' continues exploring the airy quality of 'Dream #1' but with less insistent dissonance and a greater range of motion, suggesting that horizons are broadening and that in what is to come we shall see something of a parting of the clouds.

I can't tell you what 'The New Fever Waltz' means. Any story one might start put together from a pair of thematically similar lines will always be dashed apart by what follows. The chorus is one of the most evocative Bernie has ever written, and if there's anything uniting its images beyond a general ethos of the ending of First World War (the influenza pandemic, downfall of several continental aristocracies and the unconditional surrender of the Central Powers all potentially being referenced in the lyrics), I have yet to figure it out. As a result, I generally stuff it in the same pocket where 'Take Me to the Pilot' and 'Hymn 2000' live, as a song to be savoured line by line, and Elton seems to have a similar take on the matter, treating it a series of snapshots of misery united by a general sense of humanity waltzing on because it doesn't know what else to do, and because when you stop going through the motions and start thinking about all the pain around you, it becomes almost impossible to maintain the will to live. So, we push on, doing our daily things, summarised here in the mournful image of a sweeping waltz, as the hurt happens all around. Elton, who does not generally write in 3/4 if he can help it, more or less had to in this instance, and the sound of Elton's voice gliding through the swaying motion of that time signature is electric, while once again the brass add an element of melancholy that keeps this waltz well away from any sense of joyful Straussian abandon.

One of the problems with listening to a lot of Elton is that you can drag associations of previous songs into newer ones, preventing you from hearing the new one on its own terms. 'Mexican Vacation' in its key signature, heavy blues beat, and use of A major as the chord that launches into the ascending motion of the chorus's final line, immediately feels like a faster version of 'Stinker' from *Caribou*, a song about the gloriously nasty behaviour of foxes. Mentally, it's hard then to forget that association that has been hard-wired over the course of the last three decades of my Elton-listening life, and suddenly take those elements and associate them with the anguish of a couple whose honeymoon occurs within view of suffering and revolution all around them. Bernie's wider point, about our attempts to wilfully ignore the suffering that our pleasures are based on, and about how the realisation of that suffering then rightfully paralyses our ability to partake of those pleasures is an interesting one worth exploring, but I'm not sure that, even without the association with 'Stinker', this idiom is the way to do that.

'Dream #3' brings to the close this triptych of short form instrumentals, and this time the close confines and obsessive repetitions that drove 'Dream #1' have been thoroughly exploded, as the piano gallops through different motions from a plethora of different traditions, egged on by the suddenly present bass and drum whose sporadic interjections have a marked martial character that seems to torment Elton's piano, which grows more hectic in their presence. If there's a story to be taken from all this, it's that sudden freedom from the mechanical systems that have governed your life often brings with it a troupe of anxieties that make that freedom ultimately more trouble than it's worth.

Elton spent much of the 2010s cultivating relationships with the newer generation of musicians whose creative output delighted his omnivorous musical tastes, from rising icons like Lady Gaga and Ed Sheeran to obscure dance, hip hop and jazz fusion figures who had not yet penetrated the world's attention. He did all he could to promote their music and to develop relationships with them personally, acting as a wise uncle who had experienced everything, and could offer sound advice on what habits to cultivate and which temptations to avoid. 'The Diving Board' is ultimately an expression of his concern for this new flock of young talent he'd taken under his wing. Elton and Bernie admit to familiarity with the giddy feeling that comes from being perched on the heights, looking down at all who adore you, but caution that those who urge one on to higher rungs are often doing so because they want to see what it will be like when you fall. It's a specific message to close out an album, which has featured so many larger-scale themes, but it's also a message of personal meaning to Elton, much as was 'In the Hands of Angels', which closed out *The Union*. It's a song about fame and temptation, and what's important to keep sight of as those mount to unsustainable levels, and as both a father himself and a self-appointed steward for the next generation of musical talent, few themes could have been closer to Elton's heart.

The Stats

Album/Single	US	UK	Australia	Canada
The Diving Board	4	3	26	7
		S		
	US adult contemp.			
'Home Again'	14			
'Mexican Vacation (Kids in the Candlelight)'				
'Can't Stay Alone Tonight'	18			
'A Town Called Jubilee'				

The Players

Elton John: acoustic piano, lead vocals (1 to 4, 6 to 10, 12, 13 and 15)
Keefus Ciancia: keyboards (2, 3, 4, 6 to 10 and 12)
Larry Goldings: Hammond B3 organ (15)
Doyle Bramhall II: guitars (3 and 10)
Raphael Saadiq: bass (2, 3, 4, 6, 7, 8, 10 and 12 to 15)
David Plitch: bass (9)
Jay Bellerose: drums (2, 3, 4, 6 to 10 and 12 to 15)
Jack Ashford: tambourine (3, 4, 7, 8, 10 and 13)
George Bohanon: baritone horn (9), trombone (12 and 15) and euphonium (12 and 15)
Bruce Fowler: trombone (9)
Ira Nepus: trombone (12 and 15)
Chuck Findley: flugelhorn (9)
Darrell Leonard: flugelhorn (9, 12 and 15), horn arrangements (9, 12 and 15 and trumpet (12)
William Roper: tuba (9, 12 and 15)
Stjepan Hauser: cello (2, 4 and 12)
Luka Šulić: cello (2, 4 and 12)
Bill Maxwell: BGV arrangements (3, 4, 7, 10 and 13)
Bill Cantos: backing vocals (3, 4, 7, 10 and 13)
Alvin Chea: backing vocals (3, 4, 7 and 13)
Carmel Echols: backing vocals (3, 10 and 13)
Judith Hill: backing vocals (3, 10 and 13)
Perry Morgan: backing vocals (3, 4, 7 and 13)
Louis Price: backing vocals (3, 4, 7 and 13)
Rose Stone: backing vocals (10)

The Tracks

1. 'Oceans Away' (John, Taupin) (3.58)
2. 'Oscar Wilde Gets Out' (John, Taupin) (4.35)
3. 'A Town Called Jubilee' (John, Taupin) (4.30)
4. 'The Ballad of Blind Tom' (John, Taupin) (4.12)
5. 'Dream #1' (instrumental interlude) (John) (0.40)
6. 'My Quicksand' (John, Taupin) (4.47)
7. 'Can't Stay Alone Tonight' (John, Taupin) (4.48)
8. 'Voyeur' (John, Taupin) (4.16)
9. 'Home Again' (John, Taupin) (5.01)
10. 'Take This Dirty Water' (John, Taupin) (4.25)
11. 'Dream #2' (instrumental interlude) (John) (0.43)
12. 'The New Fever Waltz' (John, Taupin) (4.38)
13. 'Mexican Vacation (Kids in the Candlelight)' (John, Taupin) (3.34)
14. 'Dream #3' (instrumental interlude) (John) (1.37)
15. 'The Diving Board' (John, Taupin) (5.59)

Bonus tracks:
1. 'Candlelit Bedroom' (John, Taupin) (4.14)
2. 'Home Again' (live from Capitol Studios) (5.19)
3. 'Mexican Vacation (Kids in the Candlelight)' (live from Capitol (Studios) (4.28)
4. 'The New Fever Waltz' (live from Capitol Studios)

Musician's Corner: 'My Quicksand'

Perhaps the most funereal work on any of Elton's studio albums, 'My Quicksand' digs deep into all the musical tropes of the death march tradition before taking a side road to, well, I'm not entirely sure. To start with, Elton's filling our ears with things that we don't expect from his songs but do expect from the world of classical funeral marches. The rhythm is highly regular, recalling the steady bass note pulses of Chopin's 'Funeral March' and the chords stay remarkably regular as well, growing more basic and primordial as we move into the chorus, almost shocking in their lack of the distant chords we have come to expect from a mature Elton slow tempo piece. This is a dirge, where the colours of life drain away the closer we move to the chorus, leaving blocky chords delivered with a steadiness as relentless as time.

What I think stands out most to people is the rhythmic sharpness of the repetitions of 'my quicksand' in the chorus, coming as they do in the middle of a piece that is entirely regular in its rhythmic structure. Suddenly, at the end of the chorus, we get this jagged off-beat element that stands starkly out, and which is again part of the more classical funeral tradition – think of the great double blasts that tear through the serenity of 'Siegfried's Funeral March' in Wagner's *Götterdämmerung* – those sudden breaks from the primary rhythm conjure mortality itself, the suddenness of death, and whenever someone employs that structure, we have been trained through centuries of musical tradition to hear it as dire, as a signifier of the approach of the end, and so through rhythm and chords Elton's putting us precisely in the mindset to understand the story he and Bernie are telling.

And then the instrumental section comes, which quotes Edvard Grieg's (1843–1907) 'Into the Hall of the Mountain King' amid some jazzy piano work that would seem at home in a bar in Las Vegas at 2.00 am but is an odd fit amongst the seriousness of the rest of the song. My best guess is that this is picking up on the fugue and fever dream themes of the rest of the album, that something in the subject's brain has snapped and they're hallucinating or remembering bits of their life, disconnected scenes that are fleeting and that crumble away as they're reminded of the reality of their situation, and the dirge proceeds onwards.

Chapter 42

Wonderful Crazy Night

Recorded: January to April 2015
Released: 5 February 2016
Producers: Elton John and T-Bone Burnett

The Story

Sixty-eight years on, Elton wasn't only still going musically, but was happier than he'd ever been, and more in touch with the newer trends in music than people half his age. His children were born in 2010 and 2013, and he settled into family life with a sense of fulfilment. Though the dark gravitas of *The Diving Board* had positioned Elton solidly as a master craftsman still more than capable of rising to new challenges, it was all but inevitable that this joy at life would bubble to the surface eventually. *Wonderful Crazy Night*, Elton's thirtieth studio album, was conceived as a record of celebration, and Bernie was given a specific directive to create lyrics that leaned towards the positive.

Anyone who is familiar with Bernie's lyrics knows that, for every song about the beauties of life and the satisfaction of a solid partnership, there are eight about broken relationships, deception, the loss of innocence, failure to meet the expectations of one's self and others, murder, terrorism, the vacuity of modern media and being a robot. Elton could have set him the challenge of writing twelve lyrics about the sub-Saharan gold trade in the eleventh century and Bernie would have likely been more comfortable than having to generate a rough dozen songs about happiness but he found a way, finding inspiration in the pageant of things that were finally right in his life after years of wandering – his two daughters, his marriage to Heather Kidd (his fourth and current marriage, and at the time of *Wonderful Crazy Night*'s release also his longest marriage, tied at twelve years with his 1979 to 1991 marriage to Toni Russo), his victory over his addictions, and the beginning of his career as a visual artist in 2010. Bits of his newfound happiness had been seeping into Bernie's lyrics for years but this was the first time he'd ever been called upon to display all his blessings in one continuous cavalcade, with results as striking as those of *The Diving Board*, though directed to a far different end.

Meanwhile, what would a celebration be without friends? After their exile from *The Union* and *The Diving Board*, the rogues' gallery was reassembled, with

Johnstone and Olsson reassuming their traditional positions after a decade's absence, and even Cooper rejoining the mix for the first time in twenty-one years. Babylon unfortunately died in 2009, and his place at the keys had been filled since that time by Kim Bullard (*b*.1955). On bass, meanwhile, Murray's old spot, which had been filled by Bob Birch (1956–2012), fell vacant again with Birch's death in 2012 from complications stemming from a 1995 motorbike accident. Taking up the bass reins for *Wonderful Crazy Night* and the subsequent tour was Matt Bissonette (*b*.1961), a jazz and prog metal musician known primarily for his work with David Lee Roth (*b*.1954), Joe Satriani (*b*.1956) and Rick Springfield (*b*.1949). This, then is the core of the band that Elton took with him on the record-breaking Farewell Yellow Brick Road tour that has occupied so much of Elton's time in the seven years since the release of *Wonderful Crazy Night*, and which at time of writing has wrapped up with promises of a new album just on the horizon, posing the tantalising question, which Elton will we get next?

The Songs

'Crazy Wonderful Night' sets the tone for what is to come. Set in the jubilant key of C major, with the bouncing sound of rock organ serving as our leading timbre, one is informed right away that this will be a different experience from *The Diving Board*. Many believe the lyrics present a night experienced by Elton or Bernie, but there's a classic 1950s Americana feel to the words, which leads me to believe it's more Bernie's construction of an archetypal crazy night, replete with young lovers under a Calypso moon (whatever that is – I'm pretty sure it isn't a reference to Saturn's satellite), cars parked in the lot of a chicken stand with their radios turned up, and the forming of definite plans for the future that more than likely never came true but that were fun to think about at the time. Some of the problems in mixing that plagued *The Union* are in evidence here, with the bass and percussion creeping up through the layers, threatening to overwhelm Elton's vocals, but while not balanced as well as on *The Diving Board*, it's still definitely better than *The Union*, and Elton's energetic piano work is clearly featured at the front, as it should be.

'In the Name of You' is less the coherent story about a relationship that the title suggests and more a series of esoteric lyrical gestures detailing hypothetical situations in which the singer would be willing to perform variously scaled acts of sacrifice in the name of the titular 'You'. Were the 'You' a one-man band, he'd give you his last dollar. Were he on a game show, he'd find a way to claim the $1 million prize for you. And so on. They're lyrics reminiscent of the ballads of the 1950s that were essentially lists of the things that the singer was willing to do for his beloved, and the appeal to older forms that specialised in uncomplicated expressions of love gave Bernie a handy way out of the problem of producing a mass of lyrics in an idiom less comfortable to him. Elton, with the help of some sizzling licks from Johnstone, frames this not as a retro ballad in the 'I Guess That's Why They Call it the Blues' tradition, but as a stomping strut that mixes Jon Bon Jovi (*b*.1952) style country rock, classic rock and even some hints of gospel in a fusion that couldn't be more Elton.

There are a couple of ways to interpret 'Claw Hammer'. One is that it's simply a song about being faced with someone of the 'twenty-first-century kind', who might be willing to spread themselves all over social media, but who, one on one, is reserved and shut-off, having lost the capacity for genuine openness and conversation like some vestigial tail. An onion-like construct of public faces, so used to dancing the knife's edge of public opinion that guardedness is their resting state, these individuals, if they have any genuine self left, will need a claw hammer to pry off all the layers they've encased it in if they're to have an actual human relationship. More specifically, the song might be keying in to some statements of Elton's about his status as one of the only pop stars left who genuinely says what he thinks and stands by it, since he is part of a generation of performers who weren't groomed by PR specialists in the fine art of saying nothing. While this go-to constructed persona might be safe, creating a 'tight-lipped modern mind', it's also a restrictive straitjacket on not only one's self, but on the general honesty of the public space. The solution: claw hammer. Musically, you're in for a journey, as we start off with a hint of strange sitar-like flavours that give way to a relatively normal Elton mix of country and rock, until we reach the outro and things flip over to full Peter Gabriel (*b*.1950) with a dizzying mixture of instrumental sounds and that insistent bass pulse we remember from albums like *So* and *Security*. It seems like the sudden shift makes no sense, but if you think about it as an extension of the ideas in the three 'Dream' pieces of *The Diving Board*, the decision becomes a little clearer. I take this explosion of sound as a representation of the post claw-hammer world, where the tight control that characterised the verses has been at last pried loose, and the free expression of self that lay beneath is now allowed to run wild.

'Blue Wonderful' is the second track to feature 'wonderful' in the title, and the difference in content can be judged by simply listening to how differently that key word is delivered in the two songs. In 'Wonderful Crazy Night', the word 'wonderful' is rushed through at high speed, as the song sprints onwards trying to take in everything about that mythical night as possible, while in 'Blue Wonderful' Elton draws its syllables out, lingering with awe over being in the presence of so much wonder concentrated in the form of a single person. Elton delivers the ballad in almost hushed tones, as if not wanting to break the spell by singing too loudly, and the effect is hypnotic. The lyrics are all about how age melts away in the presence of this 'blue wonderful' individual, and Elton's vocal work here reflects that, eschewing all the dark lower register work that had coloured *The Diving Board* in favour of a wispy innocent presentation that puts one in mind of nothing so much as 'Your Song' or 'I Need You To Turn To'. As a love ballad (or possibly a parenthood ballad) it might not have the complexity of 'Original Sin' but it offers instead the hope that a return to the wide-eyed wonder of one's first love isn't only possible, but actively happening in the song you are listening to.

It's hard for me to be objective about 'I've Got 2 Wings'. One of the things I've always enjoyed about Bernie's lyrics is his frank realism even in the midst of fancy. This has generally been true of his songs centring around religion, such as 'If There's a God in Heaven (What's He Waiting For?)', 'God Never Came Here', 'Believe' and 'Religion'. In those songs, Bernie looks at all the fables that man has invented to construct systems of power, fear and persecution, and coldly calls them out for their manifest flaws. 'I've Got 2 Wings' reverses this trend, producing a saccharine narrative about Elder Utah Smith (who was a real person who preached the gospel while wearing paper wings and playing his Gibson guitar) with lines like 'I reside elsewhere these days/Thanks to souls I've saved', which are either an instance of Bernie play-acting a naïve religiosity in order to tell a story he found interesting, which feels a little unseemly, or it's an honest statement of the broad credulousness stemming from Bernie's newly adopted Presbyterian faith, which is a bit disappointing. Elton's down home spiritual humming and general saintly presentation doesn't offer a broader perspective to Bernie's naïve-leaning words. There are certainly moments here where Bernie tries to cast Smith in a more general light, as a figure preaching universal love and unity among men, and had he stuck to that, without the references to the literal salvation of Smith's soul by the particular god of Judaeo-Christianity, this would have been far less of a let-down.

The circular introduction to 'A Good Heart', wrapped around an oscillation between C minor and the VI chord with which it shares two of its notes, strikes the ear initially as something from *The Diving Board*, which employed such devices to give glimpses of the frustrations to be encountered in the song to come. One immediately wonders, upon hearing such a motif on *Wonderful Crazy Night*, 'What are you doing here? Has something gone wrong?' To some degree, yes, something has, and that thing is time. This song is a plea to another soul, be they a child or a prospective new partner, to look beyond the flaws (or 'between the lines' in Bernie's phrase) that come with age, and see the good heart that lies within. That opening figure is the anxiety that all older people feel when encountering the young: will they find me frightful? Will they turn away or be cruel? Nevertheless, in this instance, boldness and the desire for human connection carry the day, and the singer states their case: 'It's a good heart/To be a part of'. Here, age proudly states its worth, and the instrumentation swells to join it, producing a lush sound in horns, the sweet familiarity of Johnstone and Olsson's backing vocals, and Johnstone's layered guitars. There aren't many songs like it out there and in an age when celebration of hyper-youth and micro-second faddishness seem the norm, it's a song that needs to be heard.

The rhythm and blues rock gallop 'Looking Up' is as much about keeping one's gaze directed forward as up, in a high-energy appeal to resist the call to endless ruminations about past mistakes, and self-beratement over things that couldn't have been helped, and to instead put one's energy into viewing the road ahead in all its rich potential. By letting go of ego and the relentless drive to fill life with convoluted personal plotlines in which one must emerge the victor, you can have a life filled with more laughter, more meaningful interactions, more chances to help other people, and the ability to see the world from a broader perspective. This isn't a radically new message by any means, but rarely has Elton delivered it with so much vim and verve, rivalling 'I'm Still Standing' as an expression of positive defiance against the forces that conspire to keep one mired in the past.

'Guilty Pleasure' continues the momentum of 'Looking Up', presenting us with another rock-pop barn burner where Bernie's lyrics about sitting down with a partner and hammering out what they want from you, and how they see you in the context of their lives, which might have ended up a blues-soaked downer, is here kicked into the rocker lane, with multiple layers of Johnstone's guitar work, making the song feel less like a desperate appeal for clarity preceding a final breakup, and more like a matter of passing concern – yes it would be sad if you moved on, but ultimately, it might be for the best. It's hard to consider a situation too dire with synchronised handclaps abounding.

With 'Tambourine' Bernie aims to capture snatches of experience that register to him as adjacent to the experience of listening to a tambourine, from seeing the face of someone you love, to being taken aback by something unexpected said by a friend to a flash flood rushing through a dry creek bed. The theme is tailor made for Cooper to be featured front and centre, as the man who elevated tambourine playing as a visual art form. Elton's easy vocals, and particularly the warm blanket like legato of his rendition of 'Roll and rattle', are delicious here, and reset your experience of time somewhat. The slow but sure waves of the melody nudge you into a slightly slower personal pace for a while, like a Bruckner adagio, where the only thing you need to worry about is letting the light sound of a tambourine wash over you.

'The Open Chord' is the best song on *Wonderful Crazy Night*, a perfect use of a musical concept to bridge the worlds of music, words and emotion that represent the triforce of creativity of Elton, Bernie and the stories they have told for so many years. It's a great idea that works on multiple levels, and Elton and the band run with it, with Olsson laying down a light rhythm which serves as the perfect bed for Bullard to stretch some surging pizzicato synth strings across, which Johnstone then supplements with his characteristic guitar work, creating a notion of forever upwards and forward motion, which lets Elton's resting in resolute contentment on one repeated note for the line 'You're an open chord I'm going to play all day' stand out even more as a statement of having reached a fundamental level of personal satisfaction through the company of a beloved individual. It's a perfect last song for an album of this type, in which we see Elton creatively vibrant and radiating personal happiness and though it's my fervent-unto-maniacal hope that it isn't the last final track we shall hear on an Elton solo album, if it happened to be, if Elton decides after all not to release the material he's been recording in 2024, then it could all hardly have ended on a better and more poignant note than this.

The Stats

Album/Single	US	UK	Australia	Canada
Wonderful Crazy Night	8	6	11	18
	US adult contemp.			
'Looking Up'	12			
'Wonderful Crazy Night'				
'Blue Wonderful'				
'In the Name of You'				
'A Good Heart'	17			

The Players

Elton John: acoustic piano and lead vocals
Kim Bullard: keyboards
Davey Johnstone: guitars and harmony vocals
Matt Bissonette: bass and harmony vocals
Nigel Olsson: drums and harmony vocals
John Mahon: percussion and harmony vocals
Ray Cooper: tambourine (3, 5, 8 and 9)
Tom Peterson: baritone saxophone
Joe Sublett: tenor saxophone
Jim Thomson: tenor saxophone
John Grab: trombone
Nick Lane: trombone
William Roper: tuba
Allen Fogle: French horn
Dylan Hart: French horn
Gabe Witcher: horn arrangements and conductor
Ken Stacey: harmony vocals

The Tracks

1. 'Wonderful Crazy Night' (John, Taupin) (3.13)
2. 'In the Name of You' (John, Taupin) (4.33)
3. 'Claw Hammer' (John, Taupin) (4.22)
4. 'Blue Wonderful' (John, Taupin) (3.37)
5. 'I've Got 2 Wings' (John, Taupin) (4.35)

6. 'A Good Heart' (John, Taupin) (4.50)
7. 'Looking Up' (John, Taupin) (4.06)
8. 'Guilty Pleasure' (John, Taupin) (3.38)
9. 'Tambourine' (John, Taupin) (4.17)
10. 'The Open Chord' (John, Taupin) (4.04)
11. 'Free and Easy' (John, Taupin) (deluxe edition)
12. 'England and America' (John, Taupin) (deluxe edition)

Musician's Corner: 'The Open Chord'

When you start playing a string instrument like the guitar, most of what you start out doing is learning to play open chords, which are chords that contain strings that you strum without putting your finger down on some of the frets. Here is a typical way of playing E minor, for example:

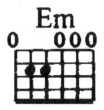

Those open circles above the first, fifth and sixth string mean that you play them as they are, let them vibrate freely at the notes they naturally want to vibrate at, without putting your finger down to shorten the string length and produce a higher pitched note. That idea of 'vibrating freely' is one you'll see at the centre of any definition of an open chord and carries with it this idea of simplicity and harmony, of music naturally happening rather than being whipped into existence by human machinations.

Open chords are much easier to play than closed chords, and as such they are the chords that our ears are used to hearing in rock songs and guitar-driven pop pieces. You get a lot of pieces in G because it has chords like E minor in it, and not a lot of pieces in F sharp minor with chords like this:

When we hear open chords, our brain goes to the songs associated with them, which tend to be catchy, simple songs. Bernie's lyrics, of a person being a fresh breeze who enters into your life like an open chord is heavily signalling Elton to tap into that sonic world, and Elton gets the memo, producing a song that is so back to basics that, looking at the chords, you would never think Elton would have written it, with lots of C's, G's, A minors and D minors, each of which has three open notes in its standard guitar fingering. The only interlopers on the scheme are F major, which usually has two open strings, and B flat major with a C in the bass, which is awkward no matter what you do and generally has no open strings at all. From the point of view of the piano and from that of music theory, those two chords are part of Song Composition 101, being the IV chord of the original key of C major and the IV/IV chord that lets you feel like something interesting is happening when it resolves back to the IV chord.

The result of all this restraint on Elton's part is an uncomplicated tonal world that we can bask in, enjoying it as we do a good spring cleaning or a nice walk in the park with a loved one – it's a song about light and creation, appreciation and optimism about what a day can bring, even the most ordinary ones.

Chapter 43

Rocketman

Music from the Motion Picture

Recorded: 2019
Released: 24 May 2019
Producers: Greg Kurstin and Giles Martin

The Story

Elton had been attempting to produce a film of his life since the early 2000s, when the project rested with Disney. Understandably, the studio was nervous about producing a picture that would have drug use and homosexuality as primary components, and Elton for his part was insistent that, if a film were going to be made of his life, it would have to encompass all aspects thereof. At an impasse with Disney, Elton shopped around for partners for years until in 2013 everything seemed to fall into place with FilmDirect and Focus Features. Lee Hall (*b*.1966), the scribe behind *Billy Elliot*, was to write the script, with Tom Hardy (*b*.1977) playing Elton and Michael Gracey (*b*.1976) directing. Elton and Focus Features, however, couldn't quite see eye to eye, and so Elton was back nearly at square one, looking for a studio to finance the film, which he finally found in 2017 through the production of New Republic and the distribution of Paramount. By then Gracey was at work on *The Greatest Showman*, and was replaced with Dexter Fletcher (*b*.1966), who had come from his success replacing Bryan Singer (*b*.1965) on *Bohemian Rhapsody*. The new producer, Matthew Vaughn (*b*.1971), brought Taron Egerton (*b*.1989) on as the new Elton, and finally, in 2018, filming began, with the film launching in May 2019, and earning an impressive (though far short of *Bohemian Rhapsody*'s $910 million global haul) $195 million against a $40 million budget.

All Elton's songs in the film are sung by Egerton, whose performance was well-nigh universally praised, both in capturing Elton's manic energy, and in staying faithful to Elton's vocal style. The soundtrack features Egerton's performances, with Elton appearing only in the last track, in the duet with Egerton which played over the film's end credits, and which went on to win the Academy and Golden Globe Awards for best original song.

The Stats

Album/Single	US	UK	Australia	Canada
Rocketman: Music from the Motion Picture	4	5	6	
		G		
	US adult contemp.			
'(I'm Gonna) Love Me Again'	12			

The Players

Taron Egerton: vocalist
Kit Connor: vocalist
Sebastian Rich: vocalist
Gemma Jones: vocalist
Bryce Dallas Howard: vocalist
Steven Mackintosh: vocalist
Richard Madden: vocalist
Celinde Schoenmaker: vocalist
Jamie Bell: vocalist
Elton John: vocalist
Billy Adamson: guitar
Jerry Barnes: bass
Joby Burgess: percussion
Ben Castle: saxophone
Jason Evans: trumpet
Barry Clements: trombone
Laurence Davies: French horn
David Fuest: clarinet
Dave Hartley: piano
Skaila Kanga: harp
Alasdair Malloy: harmonica
Eliza Marshall: flute
Kate Moore: trumpet
Mark Pusey: drums
Aaron Redfield: drums
Phil Todd: saxophone

The Tracks

(Performers noted in parentheses.)

1. 'The Bitch is Back' (Egerton, (Rich) (1.53)
2. 'I Want Love' (Connor, Jones, Howard, Mackintosh) (2.13)
3. 'Saturday Night's Alright for Fighting' (Egerton, Connor) (3.10)
4. 'Thank You for All Your Loving' (Egerton) (3.24)
5. 'Border Song' (Egerton) (3.25)
6. 'Rock and Roll Madonna' (interlude) (Egerton) (2.42)
7. 'Your Song' (Egerton) (4.01)
8. 'Amoreena' (Egerton) (4.20)
9. 'Crocodile Rock' (Egerton) (2.53)
10. 'Tiny Dancer' (Egerton) (5.25)
11. 'Take Me to the Pilot' (Egerton) (3.43)
12. 'Hercules' (Egerton) (5.26)
13. 'Don't Go Breaking My Heart' (interlude) (Egerton, Muldoon) (1.34)
14. 'Honky Cat' (Egerton, Madden) (2.34)
15. 'Pinball Wizard' (interlude) (Egerton) (2.02)
16. 'Rocket Man (I Think It's Going to Be a Long, Long Time)' (Egerton) (4.31)
17. 'Bennie and the Jets' (interlude) (Egerton) (2.28)
18. 'Don't Let the Sun Go Down on Me' (Egerton, Schoenmaker) (2.40)
19. 'Sorry Seems to Be the Hardest Word' (Egerton) (2.15)
20. 'Goodbye Yellow Brick Road' (Egerton, Bell) (4.05)
21. 'I'm Still Standing' (Egerton) (3.58)
22. '(I'm Gonna) Love Me Again' (John, Egerton) (4.11)

Musician's Corner: '(I'm Gonna) Love Me Again'

Motown as medicine. There are two genres that Elton has repeatedly mentioned when he talks about music's ability to convey pure unalloyed joy, and those are gospel and Motown, and while he allows himself to incorporate elements of gospel music with consistent frequency into his music, there isn't any song on his studio albums that has tapped into Motown with the same unrestrained reverence and gratitude as '(I'm Gonna) Love Me Again'.

The spirit of this song is certainly that of Motown, and the instrumentation (from the opening bass groove to the explosive horn section and strings to the persistent hand claps), rhythm and hooks are all entirely of that world. My favourite Motown detail comes with the arrival of the chorus. The verse was in the celebratory world of C major, and the chorus is in D flat, just a half step up. You see this quite a bit in Motown songs, where the chorus, instead of being based around the V or IV chord of the song, is set a half or whole step up from where we started, sometimes to do a V/V sort of motion, and sometimes just for fun. 'I Hear a Symphony' (1965), like '(I'm Gonna) Love Me Again', starts in C major and sets the chorus off a half step up in D flat major. 'Reach Out (I'll Be There)' (1966) starts out in G minor and hits us with that powerful A major for the chorus. 'I Can't Help Myself (Sugar Pie Honey Bunch)' (1965) starts in G and bursts out with A minor for the big 'I can't help myself' moment. You get the idea. And when the Motown greats aren't setting their choruses half or a whole step higher than the tonic, they often move there for the post-instrumental verses, 'My Girl' (1964) and 'Tears of a Clown' (1970) all have verses moved up by a whole step. All in all, it's a Motown sort of place to move, and it's never not great.

So, yes, undoubtedly this song is a love song to Motown but it's also Motown as filtered through Elton's musical sensibilities. There are certainly Motown songs that take exotic journeys through strange chord progressions, but as a rule apart from a few key artists Motown composers don't worry over-much about wowing you with tonal movement. 'Dancing in the Streets' (1964) is a five-chord song. 'You Can't Hurry Love' (1966) has more, but they are all firmly in the key signature. 'My Girl' (1964) looks like it has eight, but it really has four that are shoved up a whole step after the instrumental. 'Please Mr Postman' (1961) has four. 'Mickey's Monkey' (1965) has two.

The chords featured in '(I'm Gonna) Love Me Again', by contrast, could be used as a good start in rebuilding the dictionary: A, Bbm, C, Dm, Ebm, F, Fm, G and Gb.

For a piece supposedly set in C, that is a galaxy of unexpected places to visit and yet, so strong is Elton's grounding in so many different musical traditions, none of it sounds out of place. Taking a classic form and moving it into new territories can be disastrous in the wrong hands, but '(I'm Gonna) Love Me Again' is a perfect update of a timeless form, with enough complexities to keep modern ears engaged, but not so much to strike purists as an act of violence against a beloved form. This is Elton, happy, reborn and ready to find the good in himself with a little help from the sounds that gave him joy as a young man, and as such, it's perfect.

Chapter 44

The Lockdown Sessions

Recorded: 2020 to 2021
Released: 22 October 2021
Producers: Louis Bell, Taylor Bird, John Cunningham, Forrest Frank, Gorillaz, Remi Kabaka Jr, Samuel George Lewis, Colin Padalecki, Pet Shop Boys, Pnau, Stuart Price, Julian Raymond, Bruce Roberts, Jasper Sheff and Andrew Watt

The Story

Like many musicians, Elton used the interruption to the Farewell Yellow Brick Road tour occasioned by the Covid pandemic to pursue projects and collaborations that would otherwise likely not have seen the light of day, from composing duets to perform with old friends, to appearing as a guest vocalist on the work of younger artists, to simply adding a piano track to a record, much as he did in his earliest days as a studio musician. Over time, these excursions and collaborations summed to enough material for an album, which was duly released as *The Lockdown Sessions*. As one might imagine, and as was the case of many of the pandemic-induced albums that started hitting the shelves in 2021, the results are uneven but show a consistent ability to meet new music on its own terms that has eluded most of Elton's generation but that flows from his wide musical spirit as a matter of course.

The Songs

As a collaboration album, we're going to treat this the same way we did *Duets*, with a quick break down into three slices.

The Greats

Cold Hearts
Leave it to Pnau, whose quirky sense of mixing and matching Elton's back catalogue within a modern dance paradigm resulted in the fun 2012 remix album *Elton John vs Pnau: Good Morning to the Night*, to think to combine the seemingly utterly irreconcilable Elton classics 'Sacrifice', 'Kiss the Bride', 'Where's the Shoorah?' and

"Rocket Man (I Think It's Going to Be a Long, Long Time)'. Teaming up with Dua Lipa (*b*.1995), whose vocals add a sense of cool chic to the proceedings, this song served as a gateway to Elton's music for a whole new generation. When I saw Elton in San Jose for the Farewell Yellow Brick Road tour, sitting in front of me were four teenagers who came to Elton through 'Cold Hearts' and were cheering and whooping for 'Tiny Dancer' and 'Crocodile Rock' as if Elton were the latest thing, which was rather beautiful to behold.

The Pink Phantom
Musically the most interesting track on the album, with halting melodic and dreamlike rhythmic elements that defy pop conventions, and interweaving tripartite vocal structures amongst which Elton's powerful baritone forms the most prominent feature in the landscape, as against the searching voice of Damon Albarn (*b*.1968) and the thin mutterings of 6LACK (*b*.1992). On an album that generally trends towards the reigning conventions of the music industry, this is a great example that oddball musicality is still alive and well and has room within its corridors for the original oddball, the piano playing classically trained kid in a decade full of guitar rowdiness, Elton.

I'm Not Gonna Miss You
Over the five decades of his career, country legend Glen Campbell (1936–2017) released sixty-four albums and sold over 40 million records, with a string of hit singles spanning from 1965 to 1977. In 2010, he was diagnosed with Alzheimer's disease, and spent the next two years on the road, performing for his fans one last time before the disease claimed his mind. In January 2013, he recorded what he knew was going to be his final song, 'I'm Not Gonna Miss You', which was included in the following year's documentary of his life and won in the category of best country song. It's one of the most powerful songs ever written, in which a man who knows he is condemned to slowly disappear is vocalising his realisations of the things he soon won't be doing, even though he will still be alive, like telling his children that he loves them, or holding them the way he once did, because he won't know who they are. Campbell's family asked Elton, when Campbell died in 2017, to do his own version of 'I'm Not Gonna Miss You', which became this poignant virtual duet.

Simple Things
Brandi Carlile (*b*.1981) is a national songwriting treasure who has been a friend of Elton's for half of her life and who, like Elton, is known for her ability to cross and meld genres to tell her stories. This is a classic country duet about the lessons learned along life's long road, which bubbles over with a sense of friendship, shared memories, and plain old good advice from a pair who have experienced a thing or two.

Chosen Family

Is the melody eerily similar to the chorus of 'The Way I Was' in terms of lyrical, rhythmic, and chord structure? Sure, which is a fact that will bother all twelve of the people that saw the 2015 *Jem and the Holograms* film, and which is almost definitely a coincidence. The rest of you can appreciate the story Rina Sawayama (*b.*1990) and Elton are telling here, which would be the most touching on the disc, if 'I'm Not Gonna Miss You' weren't also on it. The artistic coupling of a gay man from a generation when homosexuality was more often than not considered a form of mental disease, and a pansexual woman from a couple generations down the line, when the LGBTQ+ community is forging ahead to extend rights to new sections of the population, is a powerful one, particularly as the theme of the song is the relationships that one forms when one's actual family lets you down, and your friends fill the role of your go to emotional support structure. Two members of the same struggle, separated in birth by decades, but claiming each other as members of their chosen family – it's a beautiful thing.

After All

There are people who hate on 'After All' but I honestly enjoy it. Charlie Puth's (*b.*1991) high, often autotuned voice pairs well with Elton's, the upward leap on the last note of the chorus is never not fun, and though the words aren't much to write home about, they don't have to be, as this song radiates the spirit of a simple modern fairy tale, like a track from *The Princess Diaries* or *Ella Enchanted*. Plus, it's positively dripping with musical elements from the early 1990s pop tradition, which are built into my DNA, so I am biologically compelled to love it.

Finish Line

We were cheated out of a Stevie Wonder-Elton duet on the *Duets* album, on which Wonder played a producer role but never added his iconic vocals to the proceedings, and we were nearly cheated of it again on this album, which was only meant to feature his piano and harmonica work, but hearing the power of the chorus Elton wrote, he ultimately couldn't resist laying down a vocal track himself. Part of me thinks this was Elton's plan all along, as this is the most blatantly Wonder-style melody yet composed by hands that weren't Wonder's, as if tailor made to tempt his old friend into a performance. Soaring and grand, with deep roots in the gospel music that, now as ever, Elton employs to express themes of optimism and rebirth, this would have been a great song even without Wonder's voice, sounding every bit the same as it did half a century earlier, but with Wonder, it surpasses the status of mere song, and assumes that of historical event.

The Goods

Nothing Else Matters
This is a great cover of Metallica's classic track from *Metallica* (1991) album. The video clip of Elton reducing James Hetfield (*b.*1963) to tears by genuinely calling it one of the greatest songs ever written is something everyone should see, and Miley Cyrus (*b.*1992) is absolutely killing it with her rich low metallic vocal intonations. The only reason it's here among the goods is that, Elton-wise, there's not much to be had – a few sprinklings of piano that are kept mostly within the song's dominant ostinato pattern, and which feature some neat Elton-ish ornamentations, but which otherwise could have been performed by pretty much anyone.

Stolen Car
The voices of both Elton and Stevie Nicks (*b.*1948) have significantly matured over the years, growing in character and expressiveness which, considering the advanced point they started from, is truly saying something. This duet doesn't offer much in terms of lyrics, and rests content with repeating its stock of a few powerful music ideas, but none of that really matters. Hearing Nicks and Elton pounding out a big vocal about stolen cars and freeways is an experience that transcends the musical material at hand, an assertion of an indomitable vagabond spirit that seventy plus years of often hard living has not succeeded in suppressing.

Orbit
This is sort of a proof of concept, that you can take an Elton song, remove the typical instrumentations associated therewith, slap on a new dance hall electronic beat, and come out with something eminently listenable. This track shows that there's nothing fundamentally wrong with placing Elton-style melodies and Elton's rich voice, in the context of more modern production sensibilities, and who knows but that this realisation will feed yet a new turn in Elton's recording career on his hopefully upcoming album. This song is entirely fine – the lyrics are adequate if not particularly memorable, the melody is catchy enough, and if you put it on during a wedding, I'd find a way to dance to it.

It's a Sin
In January 2021, Years and Years unveiled a stripped-down version of the Pet Shop Boys' classic track 'It's a Sin', which traded the cool heat of the original for a raw emotionality accompanied only by mournful piano. This version with Elton keeps that approach for the first section of the song, then launches into a rendition that maintains more of the electronic features of the original. It's an interesting idea, which allows Elton to leap into the song vocally and add some heft to the proceedings, but I don't know, there's something to the 'The time for emotionally intense vocal

inflections is always' approach from Years and Years that tends towards the wearisome because it doesn't give the track anywhere to go narratively.

E-Ticket
This is a fun if nowhere particularly surprising rocker that, if you didn't know Pearl Jam's Eddie Vedder (*b*.1964) was the other singer, you probably wouldn't guess it. E-ticket rides, for those too young to have experienced them, is a reference to the old way that Disneyland used to function, where the top attractions required fancy E-tickets to ride. The line 'You gotta figure it's an E-ticket ride/Why else stand in line?' is a surprisingly deep one, which has almost undoubtedly unintentional resonance with the entire theory of religions of salvation: you spend your life not experiencing things, assuming that by doing so you are queuing up for some grand fate in the hereafter, but what if you aren't? What if you're standing in line for no good reason, on the assumption that, because it's a big line it must be worth it but, in fact, you and everyone around you, is waiting in a line for a drinking fountain that closed thirty years ago?

The Largely Unfortunates

Beauty in the Bones
A generic song that sounds like a number played by the Good Band in a Disney afternoon special. The production is a bit all over the place, thrusting former country star Jimmie Allen (*b*.1985) – who at the time of writing was dropped from his label due to two separate allegations of sexual assault – and Elton into a haze of pop dance gestures that don't really work for either.

Learn to Fly
The first time you hear this song's melodic idea, you think, 'Oh, that's fun, a bit of throwback retro nostalgia, I'm honestly curious as to where it goes'. The fourteenth time through that melodic idea, you are about ready to throw yourself from the plane with all the other people featured in the song's music video. It just keeps going, and your only real reward for your patience through all the monotonous cycling is about twenty seconds of Elton's guest vocals.

Always Love You
Nobody can blame Elton for wanting to record a song with Nicki Minaj (*b*.1982). One of the most electrifying presences and wordsmiths of the last fifteen years, she is a phenomenon unto herself, and the idea of finding a way to fit what she does with what Elton, arguably the greatest living songwriter, does, is tantalising. Unfortunately, it doesn't quite come off here. The chorus, which is performed by Elton and placed at the beginning of the song, is absolutely gorgeous – it breaks your heart in the span of twenty seconds, with Elton richly singing about a love that will last even as he

moves into old age, and that will continue even if the man he loves should choose to let him go. The song then comes to a full crash with Young Thug's (*b*.1991) addition, which is about a woman who 'be f***ing me good and I'm hooked like crack' amongst other lyrics denigrating women as 'bitches' whose primary value lies in the fact that one can have sex with them. It's an outdated, patently dumb addition that works at total cross-purposes to Elton's opening sentiments to such a baffling degree that one begins to wonder if it's a joke. Minaj, on the other hand, seems to have read the assignment and produces lyrics that are, in fact, about relationships, picking up the idea of being let go, and jogging forward with it. You can sense that, unlike Young Thug, she is trying to produce something within the same universe of emotions as Elton, but that in the process she held back elements of her normal approach to a theme like this, and so we end up with something neither Elton nor Minaj, but that rests rather somewhere in between which is of necessity a step up from Young Thug's contribution but that doesn't live up to what people had hoped for from a collaboration between two such iconic songwriters.

One of Me
Easily the worst track on the album, and I don't think I'm exaggerating when I say it's probably the worst track on any Elton album, ever. Elton gave Lil Nas X (*b*.1999) some piano and vocal recordings, which Lil Nas X then promptly cut down to a few tiny samples of piano, tossing the vocals entirely, in order to make room for an aggressively banal chorus, and a set of tired verses that bring nothing new to the 'people are giving me a hard time about my first hit single being the result mainly of luck and I'd rather they didn't' trope.

The Stats

Album/Single	US	UK	Australia	Canada
The Lockdown Sessions	10	1	2	5
		G		
'Cold Heart' (Pnau remix)	7	1	1	
'After All'				
'Finish Line'				
'Merry Christmas' (with Ed Sheeran)	42	1	16	
'One of Me'	88			
'Always Love You'				

The Tracks

1. 'Cold Hearts' (Pnau remix) (with Dua Lipa) (3.39)
2. 'Always Love You' (with Young Thug and Nicki Minaj) (John, Wotman, Tamposi, Bell, Williams, Walsh, Minaj) (4.17)
3. 'Learn To Fly' (with Surfaces) (Frank, Padalecki) (3.31)
4. 'After All' (with Charlie Puth) (John, Puth, Hindlin) (3.28)
5. 'Chosen Family' (with Rina Sawayama) (Sawayama, Lattimer, Harte) (4.40)
6. 'The Pink Phantom' (with Gorillaz and 6LACK) (Albarn, Kabaka Jr, Valentine Jr) (4.13)
7. 'It's a Sin' (with Years and Years) (Tennant, Lowe) (4.44)
8. 'Nothing Else Matters' (with Miley Cyrus, Watt, Yo-Yo Ma, Robert Trujillo, Chad Smith) (Hetfield, Ulrich) (6.35)
9. 'Orbit' (with S.G. Lewis) (John, Lewis, Cooke) (3.28)
10. 'Simple Things' (with Brandi Carlile) (John, Wotman, Campolo) (4.11)
11. 'Beauty in the Bones' (with Jimmie Allen) (Allen, Bird, Bentley, Roberts) (3.50)
12. 'One of Me' (with Lil Nas X) (Hill, Cunningham, Sheff, Juber) (2.41)
13. 'E-Ticket' (with Eddie Vedder) (John, Vedder, Wotman) (3.18)
14. 'Finish Line' (with Stevie Wonder) (John, Wotman, Tamposi, Campolo) (4.24)
15. 'Stolen Car' (with Stevie Nicks) (John, Wotman, Tamposi) (5.37)
16. 'I'm Not Gonna Miss You' (with Glen Campbell) (Campbell, Raymond) (2.56)

2022 issue bonus tracks:
1. 'Hold Me Closer' (with Britney Spears) (3.22)
2. 'Merry Christmas' (with Ed Sheeran) (John, Sheeran, Mac) (3.28)

Musician's Corner: 'After All'

Oh, bVI-bVII-I, who doesn't love you? This is an example of what's called a modal interchange, which is when you are in one mode but are pulling in stuff from another, related mode, to add tension and excitement. We hear it all over the place in this song. 'That you're better than my dreams' and all the verse sections like it sound weird and instantly interesting because they're employing this idea of modal interchange. We are in F major, to which the chords D flat and E flat (which are the first two chords on this line) don't belong. But they do belong to F minor. They are visitors from another modality of F, and they make our ears freak out a little bit – they belong, but they don't.

It turns out, what they do is lead us perfectly back to F major in an ascending motion that can't really be done well if we stuck with the chords in the original key. Major modalities have this problem, which is that the vii chord is always going to be diminished if you stay within the key signature. So, if you want to do a cool walk upwards to the tonic from below, starting on the vi chord, you're always going to run smack into that diminished chord on your way up which isn't satisfying at all. By borrowing the VI and VII chords from your minor modality, however, you get rid of that problem. You can walk up using totally normal if vaguely exotic chords and land perfectly back on the tonic. Instead of being off-put, listeners are exhilarated, and that's why this bVI-bVII-I progression is so beloved of musicians, and a whole game can be made of spotting it in Elton's twenty-first-century work, long may it continue.

Abbreviations

2P: Double Platinum
3P: Triple Platinum
4P: Four Times Platinum
5P: Five Times Platinum
D: Diamond
G: Gold
P: Platinum
S: Silver

The Stats
Any blank fields in The Stats indicates an album or record that didn't chart.

The Players
Numbers in brackets after a player's name indicates the track that the artist appeared on. If no number appears in brackets, this indicates that the artist appeared in all tracks on the album.

Bibliography

Altschuler, Glenn C. *All Shook Up: How Rock 'n' Roll Changed America* (Oxford University Press, Oxford, 2003)

Bernardin, Claude, *Rocket Man: Elton John from A–Z* (Praeger, London, 1996)

Buckley, David, *Elton John: The Biography* (Andre Deutsch, London, 2007)

Cohen, Leonard, *Beautiful Losers* (HarperCollins, London, 1966)

DeCouto, David, *Captain Fantastic: The Definitive Biography of Elton John in the '70s* (Triple Wood Press, Chandler, Oxford, 2018)

Helm, Levon, *This Wheel's on Fire: Levon Helm and the Story of The Band* (Chicago Review Press, Chicago, 1993)

Janovitz, Bill, *Leon Russell: The Master of Space and Time's Journey Through Rock & Roll History* (Hachette Books, New York, 2023)

John, Elton, *Me* (Henry Holt and Company, New York, 2019)

Norman, Philip, *Elton John: The Definitive Biography* (Fireside, New York, 1991)

Ollivier, Romuald and Roubin, Olivier, *Elton John: All the Songs – The Story Behind Every Track* (Black Dog and Leventhal, New York, 2023)

Quaye, Caleb, *A Voice Louder than Rock & Roll* (Vision Publishing, United States, 2006)

Ribowsky, Mark, *The Big Life of Little Richard* (Diversion Books, United States, 2020)

Spitz, Bob, *The Beatles: The Biography* (Black Bay Books, New York, 2005)

Taupin, Bernie, *Scattershot: Life, Music, Elton and Me* (Monoray, United Kingdom, 2023)

Ward, Ed, *The History of Rock & Roll: Volume II: 1964–1977 – The Beatles, The Stones, And the Rise of Classic Rock* (Flatiron Books, London, 2019)

Index